ALSO BY MICHAEL MELLO

Dead Wrong: A Death Row Lawyer Speaks Out Against Capital Punishment

Against the Death Penalty: The Relentless Dissents of Justices Brennan and Marshall

THE UNITED STATES OF AMERICA

versus

THEODORE JOHN KACZYNSKI

THE UNITED STATES OF AMERICA

versus

THEODORE JOHN KACZYNSKI

Ethics, Power and the Invention of the Unabomber

Michael Mello

CONTEXT BOOKS
NEW YORK

www.contextbooks.com

Designer: Marion Delhees
Jacket design: Susan Carroll
Production: Larry Flusser
Typeface: Minion

Context Books
368 Broadway
Suite 314
New York, NY 10013

Library of Congress catalog card number: 99-72701

ISBN 1-893956-01-6

9 8 7 6 5 4 3 2 1

Manufactured in the United States of America

Dedication

For my mother and the memory of my father

Acknowledgments

I owe a special debt of gratitude to Laura Gillen, Judy Hilts and Virginia Fifield of Vermont Law School, who word processed the manuscript in all its various incarnations and to Ellen Swain, Jason Ferreira, Ingrid Busson, Richard Hentz and Brian Marsicovetere for providing invaluable research assistance. Lydia Eccles, Sanford Thatcher, James Acker, Theodore Kaczynski, Richard Bonnie, Doug Samuels, Joy Richards, Ron Arnold, Chris Waits and Lisa Stefanoni read and commented helpfully on this or earlier versions of the book. Alston Chase generously shared with me his own work on the Kaczynski case. I consulted several especially valuable books on the Unabomber case, Robert Graysmith, *Unabomber: A Desire to Kill* (1998 revised edition); Ron Arnold, *Ecoterror: the Violent Agenda to Save Nature*; Chris Waits and David Shors, *Unabomber: The Secret Life of Ted Kaczynski*; Theodore Kaczynski, *Truth versus Lies* (unpublished book manuscript); FC (the Unabomber), *Industrial Society and Its Future* (the Unabomber's manifesto); Nancy Gibbs, *et al. Mad Genius*; Mark Olshaker and John Douglas *Unabomber*; and David Gelernter, *Drawing Life*. Thinking about these different works forces one to remember "the vast untidy sea of truth." I have no doubt that each of these books contains at least the kernel of certain truths. I also have no doubt that each of these books – mine included – errs from the truth. The story of the Unabomber is large, complex and conflicting; the book that encompasses it all has not yet been written.

The excellent prosecutors and defense counsel in the Kaczynski case, Robert Cleary, J. Douglas Wilson, R. Steven Lapham, Stephen Freccero, Bernard Hubley and Paul Seave for the prosecution and Quin Denvir, Judy Clarke, Gary Sowards, Lauren Weil and John Balazs for the defense created a splendid and indispensable record of events, which will be mined by historians for many years to come.

Russell Banks's magnificent novel, *Cloudsplitter*, rekindled my lifelong interest in John Brown and helped me find the parallel between the lawyers who defended Brown and Kaczynski respectively. Edwin Cotter, recently retired as Superintendent of the John Brown House and Grave in Lake Placid, read portions of the manuscript and saved me from one gigantic pitfall and many smaller gaffes. He was also indispensable as a guide among the mountains of material on Brown. Lydia Eccles (again) helped me understand Kaczynski's antitechnology politics. William Finnegan's *New Yorker* article, which remains the best piece yet published on the wars between Kaczynski and his lawyers, was illuminating. William Booth's superb work for *The Washington Post,* Tom Nadeau's first-rate reporting for *The Sacramento Daily Record* and William Glaberson's excellent coverage for *The New York Times* shed further light on the Kaczynski non-trial.

Rick Melberth of Imagine Books in Chelsea, Vermont, tracked down many John Brown books for me. Paul Perkins gave me permission to use our collaborative work on Theodore Kaczynski's journals. I am grateful to the *Vermont Law Review* and the *Criminal Law Bulletin* where earlier versions of material from this book first appeared.

I extend my heartfelt thanks to everyone. The remaining errors in this book are solely my own.

In the interests of full disclosure, I should note that I did correspond with Kaczynski when portions of this book were written. In July 1998, after I had begun writing, Kaczynski wrote to request some newspaper commentaries I had published about his case. In my reply to Kaczynski's first letter to me, I wrote that I was happy to correspond with him, but that he needed to understand at the outset that (1) I was writing a book about his case and nothing he wrote to me would be protected by any attorney-client privilege and (2) that a man I loved as a father had been murdered by a mail-bomb, so I would probably bring to the correspondence something of a chip on my shoulder. That initial contact led to a correspondence that lasted from July 1998 to the present.

In September 1998, Kaczynski gave me written permission to quote passages from his letters to me in this book. In late December, after the manuscript had been completed and accepted for publication, Kaczynski withdrew his permission temporarily for legal reasons. Although he soon reinstated his permission, I came to realize that the letters created an unbalanced treatment (in the absence of similar correspondence from the other parties discussed in these pages), and I decided to leave things be, and not take advantage of Kaczynski's letters.

Additionally, soon after Kaczynski first contacted me, he asked if I could help him find an attorney who could file an appeal that drew into question the legality of his guilty plea. I could not represent Kaczynski myself. I had already begun writing this book, which would have been a conflict of interest. During the fall of 1998, I attempted, without success, to find a qualified lawyer who was willing to represent Kaczynski. Kaczynski then decided that, if he could not locate counsel, he would represent himself on a motion to vacate his guilty plea. Kaczynski asked me to draft a motion to attack his guilty plea. Along with the indispensable assistance of three Vermont Law School students – Ingrid Busson, Jason Ferreira and Rich Hentz – I drafted the motion. The plan was then that Kaczynski would file the motion *pro se* in the event that a lawyer could not be secured by the filing deadline. Thankfully, an attorney agreed to serve as Kaczynski's *pro bono* counsel that December, and our draft motion was never filed.

I provided Theodore Kaczynski with ample opportunity to review the book manuscript and to suggest any corrections and perceived inaccuracies, and I was pleased that he did so. I also solicited comments on this book manuscript from Theodore Kaczynski's two principal trial attorneys, Quin Denvir and Judy Clarke. For legal reasons entirely understandable to me, Kaczynski's former lawyers declined my invitation to comment on the book manuscript.

The frequent reference to newspaper articles requires some explanation. My goal in this book is to recount the manner in which the Unabomber case was represented – by the lawyers and by the press. I am interested in perception as well as reality. Thus, I do not necessarily cite newspaper accounts for their accuracy (some were wildly inaccurate) but rather to show the manner in which the Unabomber case was reported by the press.

A word about this book's intended audience: While I hope that it passes muster under the conventions of scholarship, I have not written this book for legal academics. It was written for the laity. And although it does discuss legal theory and doctrine, I have made a concerted effort to make it accessible to a general, non-expert audience.

This book and its author owe an enormous debt of thanks to Beau Friedlander, my editor and publisher, whose devoted service rose above and beyond the call of duty. I thank him for editing this text with the eye of a poet, the hand of a stonemason and the heart of a parent. Thanks also to Beau's assistant Travis Wieboldt Taylor, for his insights and diplomacy.

As always, I am grateful to my wife Deanna for graciously putting up with the trips to Harper's Ferry, the John Brown House and Grave and all the rest.

Table Of Contents

CHAPTER THREE
Considerations

CHAPTER FOUR
John Brown's Body

CHAPTER FIVE
The Politics of Insanity

CHAPTER SIX
Live Free or Die (You decide.)

CHAPTER SEVEN
The Missing Link

CHAPTER EIGHT

CHAPTER ONE

Inventing the Unabomber
(Reinventing John Brown)

                              No one can say
That the trial was not fair. The trial was fair,
Painfully fair by every rule of law,
And that it was made not the slightest difference.
The law's our yardstick, and it measures well
Or well enough when there are yards to measure.
Measure a wave with it, measure a fire,
Cut sorrow up in inches, weigh content.
You can weigh John Brown's body well enough
But how and in what balance weigh John Brown?

            Stephen Vincent Benét, *John Brown's Body* (1928)

An *Apologia*

Nine winters ago, a man I loved as a father was murdered by a mail-bomb: A few days before Christmas 1989, a racist coward with a grudge against the federal judiciary mailed a shoe-box sized bomb to federal appellate judge Robert S. Vance.[1] The bomb detonated in the kitchen of Judge Vance's home on the outskirts of Birmingham, Alabama. His assassin now lives on Alabama's death row and, although I have spent a large portion of my life as a lawyer defending death row prisoners, part of me will cheer when Judge Vance's killer is executed.

Judge Vance was the first federal appellate judge murdered in the history of the United States. He is the only person I have known to be murdered. I was Judge Vance's law clerk for about a year following graduation from law school in 1982. He was far more than a boss. Over subsequent years, I came to rely on his wisdom, guidance and experience. I loved him. By the time of his death, he had become my friend and my father in the legal profession. I was much too distraught to attend the funeral. I had the plane tickets, but couldn't force myself to use them. I mourn for him every day. I miss him every day, and pray for him every night.

I mention Judge Vance's murder because I want to be clear at the outset that I harbor a special venom in my heart for people who kill by sending bombs through the mail. That's what the Unabomber did. For nearly two decades, the Unabomber created, and mailed, increasingly deadly bombs. Judge Vance, and the mail-bomb that murdered him, are never far from my mind whenever I think or write about the Kaczynski case. Every aspect of this book was influenced, in some immeasurable way, by the fact and the means of Judge Vance's killing.

My personal belief is that Theodore Kaczynski is the Unabomber.[2] Had Kaczynski gone to trial for the UNABOM attacks, he almost certainly would have been found guilty; the prosecution's case against him – a case built largely on the Unabomber's own words in his own writings – was by most accounts overwhelming.[3] However, there was no trial. After weeks of increasingly bitter struggle with his lawyers over control of the defense, Kaczynski pleaded guilty on January 22, 1998.

When Kaczynski pleaded guilty, he confessed to being the Unabomber, who was responsible for a series of bombings between 1978 and 1995 throughout the United States.[4] He was called the Unabomber because the first bombs targeted universities and airlines. The Unabomber sent or set a total of sixteen bombs that killed three people and injured twenty-three others during his seventeen-year career. After the anonymous attacker's 35,000-word manifesto on the ills of modern industrialization and technology was published in June 1995 by the *The Washington Post*, Kaczynski's younger brother David began to suspect him and eventually turned him in to the FBI. The brother's divided soul (after turning his brother in, David Kaczynski fought to save his brother from a death sentence) is the latter-day version of a story as old as Cain and Abel.[5]

I would prefer to be writing about nearly any other case. I'd rather write about Ted Bundy again. The courts, the media and the public have closed the book on the Unabomber case. I should do the same.

But it's not that simple, not for me anyway. Our government wanted to execute Theodore Kaczynski. I oppose capital punishment with a ferocity that matches Kaczynski's hatred of technology. Over a period of four years during the mid-1980s, I was a capital public defender in Florida, and since then I have devoted much of my professional energy and time writing and speaking out against the death penalty as a legal system.[6]

Also, I must confess to recognizing something of myself in parts of Theodore Kaczynski, although certainly not in the murderous parts. Like Kaczynski, I have devoted a substantial portion of my life and passion to a cause many Americans view as doomed, if not crazy: abolition of capital punishment. Like Kaczynski, a while back I gave up big-city life and moved to a rural area (for me, it was Vermont), and I live there semi-reclusively. Like Kaczynski, I have kept a private diary for years.

To my surprise, I found myself agreeing with many of the ideas in the Unabomber's manifesto when it was published in *The Washington Post*. Like Kaczynski, I worry about technology's encroachments upon privacy and other cherished American freedoms. For me, the right to be left alone is a fundamental aspect of being an American. Somewhat like Kaczynski, I have mixed feelings about the mixed blessings of technology (I am writing these words with pen and paper in the hammock in my backyard, below a flawless, blue Vermont sky), and I am cheerfully clueless when it comes to computers. Unlike the Unabomber, my problem with technology lies with those who use it; the same science that made possible the miracles of manned space flight also made twentieth-century nightmares like the Holocaust and nuclear weapons.

There is one more thing I share with Theodore Kaczynski. I treat "experts" in forensic psychiatry (and law) with some skepticism. This skepticism comes from long experience as a capital defender, working with mental health experts on behalf of my condemned clients, trying (and often succeeding) to sculpt their professional opinions and reports in ways helpful to my purposes as an advocate for my death row clients. Like the legal profession, the mental health profession has its own rules and conventions that have little to do with the complex reality of human experience and action. Reality is too large a thing for any single profession to grasp in full, and the reductionism of both law and psychiatry explain human behavior only at the cost of oversimplifying it.

Still, these are not the reasons I had to write this book.

I felt compelled to write for a simple reason: Theodore Kaczynski was denied his day in court. This fact does not make his case particularly unique among capital cases in America. But Kaczynski was denied his day in court by his own defense lawyers, and not because these attorneys were inexperienced or underfunded or overworked – far from it.

Kaczynski's experienced and well-financed lawyers simply decided that they, the lawyers, and not Kaczynski the client, were in control of the defense and that they had a mandate to save his life. His lawyers insisted that only a mental defect defense would sufficiently sway the jury and avert a death sentence. Kaczynski refused to cooperate with this defense. The struggles between Kaczynski and his paternalistic lawyers for control in his defense, raise the most fundamental moral issues with regard to lawyers, clients, ethics and power.

The Unabomber trial received massive media coverage. Seventy-five news organizations congregated at "Club Ted," a parking lot near the Sacramento courtroom. With rare exceptions, the mainstream media bought into the defense attorneys' spin on their epic struggle with Kaczynski, during its daily coverage of Kaczynski's interaction with the criminal justice system. In particular, the daily press accepted (1) the claim that Kaczynski was a paranoid schizophrenic; (2) that his lawyers acted properly in raising a mental defect defense regardless of their client's vehement objections; and (3) that Kaczynski himself, not his lawyers, should be held responsible for the disruption of his trial. The chaos into which Kaczynski's trial plunged was blamed on the client's alleged manipulation of the judicial process, rather than on the lawyers' ultimately successful manipulation and control of the defense.

I believe the popular wisdom to be wrong on all counts. First, the claim that Theodore Kaczynski was a paranoid schizophrenic must be qualified. To be more precise, I do not believe the existing public record supports the conclusion that Kaczynski suffers from any serious or organic mental illness, much less that his supposed mental illness justified the hostile takeover of the Unabomber defense. The daily press for the most part accepted the portrait of Theodore Kaczynski as a paranoid schizophrenic whose profound mental illness prevented him from seeing that the supposition of a mental defect was his only real defense.[7] I am not criticizing the daily press; the reporters did the best possible job with the scanty facts that were available at the time. It is only because I have access to transcripts of the closed-door meetings between Kaczynski, his defense team and Judge Garland Burrell, that I am able to present a more complete picture of the drama that unfolded between Kaczynski and his lawyers. That picture convinces me that Theodore Kaczynski was unquestionably competent to stand trial. I believe that Kaczynski understood exactly what he was giving up in foregoing a mental defect defense. And for him it was worth it, even though it virtually guaranteed a death sentence. The death penalty was acceptable to him.

I do not believe that Kaczynski's lawyers had any legitimate right to force their mentally competent client to stake his life on a mental defect defense. So long as he followed their instructions, Kaczynski's attorneys never voiced doubt that he was mentally competent to stand trial, which meant that Kaczynski was competent – and constitutionally entitled – to make important decisions about his defense (*i.e.*, how to plead, whether to testify, whether to appeal and whether to raise a mental defect defense). Given Kaczynski's decision months before trial that a mental defect defense was unacceptable to him, his lawyers were ethically obligated to either honor their competent client's wishes, or step aside so that another defense team – one that was willing to follow their client's instructions – would have sufficient time to prepare for Kaczynski's defense.

It is evident that the defense lawyers, and not Kaczynski, were responsible for disrupting the trial, when they monkey-wrenched it from his control.[8] During the months leading up to the trial, Kaczynski's lawyers kept him uninformed about the defense they planned to raise. By the time Kaczynski figured out what his lawyers were planning for him, it was too late to change lawyers or, Burrell ruled, to represent himself. Cornered by his lawyers and the judge, Kaczynski had only two ways to prevent his court-appointed lawyers from portraying him as a madman: He could either kill himself, or plead guilty. On the eve of his capital trial, Theodore Kaczynski made a serious suicide attempt. Failing suicide, Kaczynski was left with only one way to prevent his lawyers from portraying him as mentally ill. He would have to plead guilty.

In short, I believe the Unabomber was poorly represented by his attorneys and, along the way, was also misrepresented by the media. That's why I needed to write this book. Virtually no one else seems inclined to make the argument that I make in this book: that Kaczynski's defense lawyers denied their client his day in court. The defense lawyers will not make that argument, for obvious reasons, and neither will the prosecutors. The Unabomber case ended, for them, when Kaczynski pleaded guilty. Few writers will be inclined to make the argument, because the Unabomber trial has long been old news, and because they by and large believe that Kaczynski was crazy and lucky to have escaped a death sentence. Kaczynski himself might want to raise the argument (and he has), but who will listen to him? [9]

What happened between Kaczynski and his lawyers raises foundational issues of law, ethics and public policy; I believe that legal scholars are obligated to write about such important issues, even when that research takes them to places that make them uneasy.[10] For reasons set out elsewhere, I have reached a point in my life where I do my own thinking and writing without regard to party lines articulated and enforced by self-appointed guardians of the "One True Faith of Capital Punishment Opposition." I was exiled from the abolition movement for my last book, and this one will not endear me to the head of that congregation or the adherents to its "Articles of Faith."[11] So be it. I will continue to write where the research takes me, even when, as here, it takes me into territory that I might rather avoid.

I certainly detest the Unabomber's crimes. I don't share the Unabomber's willingness to use violence or the view that technology's problems require such a drastic and lethal response. I do feel strongly about something that most other Americans do not worry about too much: capital punishment. I can identify with a "voice in the wilderness," more easily than I can identify with the content of that cry or its specific call to action. I also like and respect his public defenders tremendously. I have much in common with them. As an opponent of capital punishment, I'm squeamish about setting out a factual argument that could invalidate Kaczynski's guilty plea and expose him again to capital punishment. Yet none of these reasons have struck me as persuasive grounds not to write about the Unabomber trial. William Finnegan, writing in *The New Yorker*, was dead right that "Kaczynski's quietly fierce performance [during the pre-trial] raised fundamental questions about a defendant's right to participate in his own defense, the role of psychiatry in the courts and the pathologizing of radical dissent in the courts and the press."[12]

Ultimately, I wrote this book because it addresses important issues of law, ethics and psychiatry, and because I saw no intellectually legitimate reason *not* to write it. But maybe this last statement is a cop-out. The fact is, I have a deep ambivalence about this subject matter. The issues of law, ethics and public policy raised by the Unabomber case are important to me – and, they are important to me for the very same reasons I feel ambivalent about the Unabomber. The issues that concern me are discussed in the Unabomber's manifesto, with its argument about the problems associated with paternalism and modern modes of socialization.

My only sympathy for Kaczynski is informed by his status as a capital defendant who was cheated by the justice system and by his own public defenders, and *not* as a fellow traveler regarding his views about violence or technology. But I *do* share his ideas about autonomy, freedom and privacy – and that's why I'm interested in the moral, ethical and legal issues raised by his case. This story is about the interaction of two ideologies with irreconcilable differences.

My professional background and experience as a former capital public defender affords me a certain insight into the war that developed between Kaczynski and his lawyers. For a long time, my job was to read trial transcripts – and to read between the lines of those transcripts – and then develop a narrative of what was really going on during the court proceedings and behind the scenes. To distill an accurate narrative from a massive trial record, particularly in a case that didn't go to trial, one must know the language of the law and be steeped in the chess-like world of short-term trial tactics and the long-range legal strategies of the actors who made that record. Based on the extensive court files in the Kaczynski case, I think I have a fairly clear picture of what his lawyers did and why they did it. In their court filings, the lawyers explained in some detail why they assumed control of the Kaczynski defense. The existing record is more than sufficient to allow examination of those reasons.

The Unabomber case is fascinating on any number of levels: the genuinely brilliant mathematics-professor-turned-Montana-hermit-serial-bomber had a Harvard degree at age twenty and was a rising star at the University of California at Berkeley, which boasted one of the world's top mathematics departments. Next, there is the Cain-and-Abel dimension of the case which carries with it the conflicting loyalties that David Kaczynski owed to his family and his responsibility to society. Finally, there is Kaczynski's pro-freedom and anti-technology politics and the defense he wanted his court-appointed attorneys to raise against the capital murder charges. My guess is that Kaczynski wanted the defense to be based on the political ideology articulated in the 35,000-word manifesto that he forced

The Washington Post to publish in 1995. All these matters will be interwoven into the fabric of this book, but they are not its principal focus.

I want to focus on how two historically distinct groups of lawyers, confronted with the impossible task of representing would-be political martyrs, clients with political ideologies as well as alleged evidence of mental illness who were on trial for their lives, chose to proceed with their respective defenses. Kaczynski's defense team in 1997-98 and John Brown's trial lawyers in 1859 present a true study in contrasts. But they also have something in common. Both cases provide insights into what one historian of John Brown has aptly called, in a somewhat different context, the "politics of insanity – or, specifically, the politics of the mental defect defense."[13] I do not believe that Theodore Kaczynski or his cause are comparable to John Brown and the anti-slavery movement. But this is of little interest to me. What interests me are the very different ways in which Kaczynski's lawyers and Brown's lawyers dealt with their respective ideologically-motivated martyr-clients.

Of the two cases, John Brown's lawyers served him better than their counterparts served the Unabomber. The issues raised in this book are matters about which reasonable people of conscience can and will disagree, even when all parties to the conversation possess all the facts, which in this instance I certainly do not. Kaczynski's lawyers know far more about their client than any outsider ever will. I am not here to put the Unabomber defense team on trial.[14]

Capital defense lawyers work in an ethical hall of mirrors. They must attempt to reconcile, harmonize and live with a host of conflicting ethical values. Because the stakes are life and death those ethical conundrums are placed in especially bold relief. For the capital defense lawyer, issues of ethics are neither theoretical nor abstract. How he or she addresses these issues will drive virtually every aspect of how the client's case will be investigated and litigated.

I have worn the same professional masks as those donned by Kaczynski's attorneys, and I have spent a significant portion of my life as a lawyer representing people who the government wants to execute.[15] Like Kaczynski's lawyers, my experience has taught me that capital punishment as a legal system has not lived up to its promises of fair and equitable treatment for those on trial for their lives. Like Kaczynski's lawyers, I know how complicated the attorney-client relationship can be in the best of times and that, when the stakes are life itself, the times are rarely the best.

But on the most fundamental aspect of the attorney-client relationship, I part company with the Unabomber's lawyers. Kaczynski's attorneys apparently viewed their essential role as saving their client's life by any legal means necessary – to save him in spite of himself. Although they conceded again and again that Kaczynski was mentally competent to stand trial, his lawyers saw it as their decision – not their client's decision – to stake their client's life on a defense based on mental defect – a defense that he found reprehensible on many counts, not the least, one would think, being that it was in direct conflict with the Unabomber's manifesto.

I believe his lawyers' primary duty was to empower their client, not to manage him. The choice of whether to stake Kaczynski's life on a mental defect defense – or on a political defense based on the Unabomber's ideas about technology – belonged to Kaczynski and not his lawyers. I agree with Kaczynski's lawyers that, as a strategic matter, a mental defect defense was more likely than a political defense to spare Kaczynski from a death sentence (although, given the crimes and Kaczynski's coldly rational explanations for committing them, I doubt that any defense could have kept him from a death sentence).[16] I also agree that a political defense probably would have backfired, as it reportedly did with Timothy McVeigh, angering the jury and thus making a death sentence more likely.[17]

But this is not the point. Given the overwhelming evidence that Kaczynski was mentally competent to stand trial, the decision to forgo a mental defect defense was his to make, tactically wise or not. The columnist Ellen Goodman, writing about the case in early January 1998, asked rhetorically if the "Mad Hatter" should be "running the show."[18] My answer is emphatic: Hell yes, when the Hatter is on trial for his life and especially when the evidence of his madness is flimsy.

My conclusion in this regard depends, of course, on my belief, as well as that of the judge and prosecution, that Theodore Kaczynski was mentally competent to stand trial.[19] His lawyers certainly thought he was sufficiently competent to stand trial – so long as he followed their instructions regarding the mental defect defense. Only when Kaczynski refused to allow his lawyers to portray him as a madman – and the manifesto as the mere rants of a madman – did they entertain questions about his mental capacity to stand trial, and then only desultorily.

This book explores how Theodore Kaczynski was represented – by his lawyers, and by the news media. The book proceeds in eight parts. This introductory chapter sets the stage. Chapter two tells the story of the war that developed between Theodore Kaczynski and his attorneys. This narrative is based largely on court documents, some of which were sealed during the trial itself. They have provided me with sufficient information to piece together a fairly complete account of what happened between Kaczynski and his lawyers.[20] Chapter three considers the aftermath of the Unabomber non-trial and the possible repercussions. Chapter four departs from Sacramento to unravel the eerie parallels between the ethical choices faced by Kaczynski's lawyers and those of John Brown. Chapter five evaluates the very different courses of action taken by the two groups of lawyers and concludes that Brown's lawyers got it right. Using a hypothetical scenario, chapter six explores the ethical issues associated with attorney-assisted suicide.

Chapter seven discovers a point of contention that has not received much attention to date. By pleading guilty, Kaczynski waived his right to challenge the government's decision to use his private journals as a basis for a death sentence. This chapter examines the legal rights Kaczynski gave up by pleading guilty and suggests that any conviction of murder would have been extremely vulnerable to reversal by an appellate court. The diary issue first attracted me to the Unabomber trial. During the summer of 1997, I worked as an informal advisor to the Kaczynski legal team, on the diary issue (my limited involvement in this narrow aspect of the Unabomber defense is a matter of public record). Chapter eight brings the book full circle, remembering the mail-bomb murder of my friend, Judge Robert S. Vance, and concluding with some final considerations.

Equally important to me is what this book is not. This book is not an attempt to psychoanalyze the Unabomber, and it does not represent any search for the "real" Theodore Kaczynski. For that reason, I have not included the information I possess about, for example, Kaczynski's sexual life or fantasies. Dr. Sally Johnson's forty-seven-page psychiatric evaluation of Kaczynski has now become public information, and there is more than enough available on that score to satisfy the most prurient voyeur. Such information is not germane to this book, and I do not include it.

I would like to also stress that this book was not written to provide grounds for Kaczynski to invalidate his guilty plea. If that happens, then so be it.

It has not been my intent to argue that criminal defendants suffering from seriously delusional mental illness ought to be allowed to serve as their own lawyers. A defendant whose illness renders him mentally incompetent to stand trial should be found mentally incompetent to stand trial. Again, there was never any serious doubt about Theodore Kaczynski's mental competency to stand trial. The legal test for competency is low, and Kaczynski clearly met it.

When the principal "evidence" of the defendant's mental illness is a minority lifestyle, a minority political ideology and inexplicably horrible crimes committed to advance that ideology, we should be very careful about how we label that defendant.

Was Theodore Kaczynski
a Paranoid Schizophrenic?

"Mental health" programs, "intervention" techniques, psychotherapy and so forth are ostensibly designed to benefit individuals, but in practice they usually serve as methods for inducing individuals to think and behave as the system requires.

Unabomber Manifesto

The Unabomber is many things. He is a coldly methodical killer who, over a very long period of time, destroyed human lives with clinical detachment. He is an assassin. He is a terrorist. A survivor of the Unabomber's attacks argues that he is evil.[21]

Theodore Kaczynski may be all these things, but in my opinion he is not crazy. If Kaczynski is the Unabomber (as I believe he is) then he did crazy, homicidal things. He exhibited crazy behavior – but he is not insane, at least not in a way that matters to the law. Even Kaczynski's own defense lawyers acknowledged again and again as much.

There are questions that need to be addressed here: Was Theodore Kaczynski suffering from a serious or an organic mental illness? Was he a paranoid schizophrenic, as his lawyers claimed and the media reported? If so, might his mental illness have caused a reasonable jury to spare him the death penalty for his crimes? If he was mentally ill, was his illness severe enough to significantly impair his ability to make an informed decision to veto his defense team's determination to raise a mental defect defense? Specifically, was he too crazy to choose whether or not to stake his life on a mental defect defense? And what actual evidence is there to support the claims that Kaczynski was a madman?

Based on available public information, the evidence that Theodore Kaczynski suffers from paranoid schizophrenia, or any other serious mental illness, is surprisingly flimsy – unless antitechnology politics, a willingness to kill for them and a reclusive lifestyle constitute mental illness.[22] The central facts of Kaczynski's illness as it was diagnosed by the psychiatrists retained by his court-appointed defense counsel were (1) his antitechnology politics and (2) the crimes themselves.[23] In short, because Kaczynski hated technology enough to kill and chose to live reclusively in one of the most physically beautiful places in America, he must be out of his mind.

Theodore Kaczynski's defense attorneys have claimed that Kaczynski suffered from paranoid schizophrenia.[24] The media believed it. Paranoid schizophrenia is associated with delusions of grandeur and feelings of persecution. The illness is characterized by a preoccupation with one or more delusions, or with frequent hallucinations related to a single theme.[25] It might be argued that Kaczynski demonstrated some of these symptoms, but the linchpin of delusion is nowhere in evidence.

However, the line that distinguishes the political defendant and the clinically paranoid defendant can be extremely difficult to limn. In my experience, capital defense lawyers, driven by the needs of advocacy and not professionally trained in the art of psychiatric medicine, are not especially adept at drawing that line. Thus, lawyers have come to rely on mental health experts while advocating on the behalf of the client. But these mental health experts are not much better at drawing the line between paranoia and political belief — particularly when, as with the Unabomber, the political ideology espoused happens to be harshly dismissive of their "soft science" and all its diagnostic wizardry.[26]

In early January 1998, *The New York Times* ran a story that began: "Theodore J. Kaczynski, the hermit standing trial on charges that he is the Unabomber, has told his defense team that he believes satellites control people and place electrodes in their brains. He himself is controlled by an omnipotent organization which he is powerless to resist, he told his lawyers."[27] According to William Finnegan's *New Yorker* article, these lines were a "collage of fragments from various sources pasted together to produce remarks that were never made, and if they had been made, would almost certainly have been shielded by the attorney-client privilege."[28] The attorney-client privilege is certainly one of the problems here.

A more fundamental problem, Finnegan wrote, is that "there is no credible evidence that [Kaczynski] hears voices, has hallucinations or is 'out of touch with reality' — unless reality is defined as having conventional social and political views."[29] Sure, Kaczynski *may* suffer from some form of schizophrenia; "mental health *is* a continuum."[30] "But [Kaczynski] is nowhere near any clinical extreme," as his lawyers' misleadingly implied during the non-trial, and as Kaczynski's lead defense counsel continues to assert even after the trial.[31]

Although Kaczynski reportedly refused to cooperate with the forensic psychiatrists retained by his lawyers, those defense experts characterized Kaczynski as "a high-functioning paranoid schizophrenic.[32] Medically speaking, that would place him at the least-ill end of the spectrum, where obvious symptoms are often absent."[33] What really indicated such a diagnosis for Kaczynski? "Anti-technology . . . His view of technology as the vehicle by which people are destroying themselves and the world."[34]

The psychiatrists hired by the defense attorneys didn't think much of Kaczynski's lifestyle in the Montana high country where, in 1970, he bought 1.4 acres of land and built a simple cabin heated by a woodstove, with no electricity or plumbing. He planted a large garden, hunted deer, elk and snowshoe hares and gave some of his vegetables to neighbors. Kaczynski claimed that he had made a reasonable lifestyle choice in leaving the high-stress world of the Berkeley math department to pursue a simpler life. In 1970, such migrations back to the land were not uncommon.

It is not uncommon in the 1990s either.[35] In fact, it is fair to state that there is a mainstream movement, a widely-felt need to reconnect with nature, unplug, simplify and nurture that which is organic, natural and animal. The great outdoors. Adventure travel. Extreme sports. Outdoor athleticism – "been there, done that." The desire to head outside and get back to nature is illustrated by the vehicles we drive (sport utility vehicles go off-road), the vacations we take (today you can buy your way to the summit of Mt. Everest), a renewed fascination with the nature-centric cultures of the "First Nations" people (as evidenced, for example, by the popularity of such films as *Dances With Wolves, Last of the Mohicans, Thunderheart,* etc.), and celebrations of rural lifestyle. Even the latest manifestation of daily life-changing technological progress – the Internet – is rife with examples and declarations of this movement.

During a quick search of the Internet, one of my research assistants, Rich Hentz, found many sites dedicated to alternative lifestyles. One such site, *Homesteading,* is dedicated to "people who enjoy the land and want to participate in a more wholesome, less 'instant/automated' life-style."[36] Homesteading is defined as a desire to "encompass the pioneer spirit and a desire to both 'get back to nature' and be more self-sufficient."[37] The *General Homesteading Organizations* site lists no less than twenty-five homesteading organizations throughout the United States.[38]

The rural lifestyle is celebrated in such journals as *Country Connections,* which steps beyond mainstream country life-oriented publications and "present[s] creative, hopeful alternatives in the areas of lifestyle, politics, culture, community, ecology and ethics." This site gives advice to people who want to leave the city for "a simpler life."[39] For further assistance during the big move, there is *Small Town Bound* – perfect for the "urbanite seeking to improve [his/her] quality of life."[40] One need not go on-line, however, to discover such a book, since it has been featured on *The Oprah Winfrey Show* and *Today*, and written about in *Time*.[41]

If you go to the *Simple Living Network*, you will find *Voluntary Simplicity: Toward a Way of Life That Is Outwardly Simple, Inwardly Rich*, which touts the simplified lifestyle as being more purposeful, with a minimum of needless distractions.[42]

Those suffering from spiritual and psychological disconnection from the natural world may find relief at such sites as *Ecopsychology On-Line* and *IGC* (the Institute for Global Communications).[43] The Ecopsychology Institute's on-line library includes essays such as "The Psychological Benefits of Wilderness," which praises "the healing effect of wilderness."[44]

The problem with arguing that Kaczynski was mentally ill because he lived in a primitive cabin in the wilds of Montana is perhaps best articulated by Virginia Postrel:

> This argument is very, very interesting. It says that someone who writes lucidly, who cared for himself for two decades with virtually no outside aid, and who articulates the planning of his crimes and the reasons behind them cannot possibly be sane simply because he lives in the way popular, respected, best-selling environmental theorists say we should all live.[45]

If Kaczynski's lifestyle choice differed from the popular "back to nature" movement, it does so only in degree, not in kind.

The defense psychiatrists didn't see it that way. One wrote that Kaczynski's private journals undermine the claims about why he chose to move to Montana: "The explanations for his chronic social isolation ... were clearly contradicted by Mr. Kaczynski's writings that document his despair over both his inability to establish normal human relationships and his inability to comprehend why he has been unable to do so."[46] A fair translation of this circular psychobabble might be: He was shy, brilliant, lonely, sad and (here is the important part, the part where expert opinions are necessary) these qualities are incontrovertible evidence of mental illness.

Only a uniquely American professional arrogance, and a breathtaking lack of both empathy and respect for worldviews different from one's own, could equate a desire for solitude (Rilke comes to mind) and a return to nature (Thoreau comes to mind) with mental illness. In Eastern cultures, the solitary sage is a figure of respect and a manifestation of courage. Rilke wrote that the best way to express love for other people is to become "guardians of one another's solitude."[47] Thoreau urged Americans to seek "simplicity, simplicity."[48] Buddhists frequently spend long hours in silent contemplation.

It should not be surprising that the mental health experts did not consider these examples when they were evaluating Kaczynski. They did not react well to the Unabomber, or the manifesto's sharp critique of modern psychiatry and its practitioners. Although the Unabomber was not as radical as psychiatrist Thomas Szaz, who believes that mental illness is a "myth," he was acutely aware of the limitations that face psychiatry when describing and explaining the full complexity of human behavior and motivations.[49] Kaczynski argues (correctly, in my view) that a society's notions of mental illness – and mental wellness – are intimately connected to that society's values, norms and mores.[50] Like our laws, the definitions of insanity reinforces values we deem normal and good. This is not a terribly radical supposition (and in fact his understanding of how psychiatry works is far more impressively sophisticated and perceptive than my summary here demonstrates).

Echoing Michel Foucault, the Unabomber wrote: "The concept of 'mental health' in our society is defined largely by the extent to which an individual behaves in accord with the needs of the system and does so without showing signs of stress."[51] As reported in the press, the journals describe his fear that the bombing campaign against technology would be dismissed as the work of a "sickie," noting – correctly, I think – that "many tame, conformist types seem to have a powerful *need* to depict the enemy of society as . . . sick."[52] In another entry, Kaczynski wrote: "If I succeed in killing enough people, the news media may have something to say about me when I am caught or killed. And they are bound to try to analyze my psychology and depict me as 'sick.'"[53] He also noted the Soviet practice of labeling dissidents as mentally ill.[54]

The mental health experts retained by Kaczynski's defense lawyers would respond that he is simply in denial about his mental illness. In the topsy-turvy world of forensic psychiatrists who specialize in the patient's "unawareness of illness" (Kaczynski's lawyers hired a psychologist named Xavier Amador who offered this particular service) Kaczynski's very contempt for psychiatry is itself viewed as evidence of mental illness.[55] Because he denies that he is mentally ill, he must in fact be crazy.

It is also useful to bear in mind that the diagnoses offered by the forensic psychiatrists retained by Kaczynski's lawyers have never been subjected to the crucible of cross-examination or any other form of adversarial testing. I wonder how Kaczynski's experts would have stood up under cross-examination by the prosecution. They certainly would have been challenged. For example, the defense experts diagnosed Kaczynski a paranoid schizophrenic based on the Minnesota Multiphasic Personality Inventory test (MMPI). But a prosecution neuropsychologist found that "since schizophrenia or a 'predisposition to schizophrenia' cannot be diagnosed based on MMPI findings, [the defense's psychologists'] interpretations are erroneous."[56] Dr. Phillip Resnick, another psychiatrist retained by the prosecution, performed an analysis of Kaczynski's journals.[57] Kaczynski had allegedly written: "I intend to start killing people," which suggested perhaps that Kaczynski had a rational agenda for his lengthy bombing campaign.[58] Resnick reportedly wrote in his report that Kaczynski "may have rationally concluded that if he were labeled mentally ill, his political antitechnology agenda would be denigrated . . . It is possible that Mr. Kaczynski is not suffering from a severe mental illness and does not want to be unjustly labeled as mentally ill." Still, Resnick continued, it is "also possible that Mr. Kaczynski is mentally ill and lacks insight into his illness."[59]

Another psychiatrist for the prosecution, Dr. Park Dietz, had also read Kaczynski's journals and reviewed Kaczynski's neurological testing.[60] However, where the defense experts saw "schizophrenia" in the neurological testing, Dietz saw "geek."[61] Dietz explained that Kaczynski's diaries are "full of strong emotions, considerable anger and an elaborate, closely-reasoned system of belief about the adverse impact of technology on society. The question always is: Is that belief system philosophy or is it delusion? The answer has more to do with the ideology of the psychiatrist than with anything else."[62]

To be sure, the prosecution's experts were reportedly hampered by Kaczynski's refusal to cooperate with them. It has also been alleged that potential defense experts were equally hampered by Kaczynski's non-cooperation. Kaczynski himself claimed, with documentary support, that he hampered no one unreasonably.

The conclusions of the forensic mental health experts retained by the defense and prosecution can, to some extent, be dismissed as partisan. Good defense lawyers (and Kaczynski's lawyers were very good) know how to select mental health experts who will give the diagnosis they want.

Dr. Sally Johnson cannot be so easily dismissed. In January 1998, Judge Garland Burrell put the trial on hold and ordered Theodore Kaczynski to be examined by Dr. Johnson. Kaczynski cooperated with Dr. Johnson's exam.[63] After five days of meeting with Kaczynski, Dr. Johnson concluded that he was mentally competent to stand trial.[64] She also made a *provisional* diagnosis that Kaczynski was a paranoid schizophrenic. (The daily press and others missed the fact that Dr. Johnson's diagnosis was provisional.)[65] However, like the defense experts, Dr. Johnson's findings were based on her conclusion that Kaczynski's political ideology was a delusion rather than a philosophy.[66]

Dr. Johnson's analysis reveals more about the values, blind spots and cultural and intellectual biases of her profession than it reveals about Theodore Kaczynski's mental health.

The Circumstantial Evidence

The prosecution's experts would have tried to undermine the defense's experts during the trial. In the battle of the experts that almost certainly would have occurred during Kaczynski's trial, the jury would have had to rely on their own common sense to decide whether Kaczynski was crazy, and if so, just how crazy he was. The jury might well have looked to the circumstantial evidence of Kaczynski's sanity or its absence.

For example, Kaczynski's lawyers placed great emphasis on his reclusive lifestyle in rural Montana. His cabin in Montana was the defense's Exhibit A, a physical proof that their client was crazy. The lawyers even had the cabin transported to Sacramento so they could show it to Kaczynski's jury. But what the lawyers didn't plan to show the jury was the context in which the cabin – and Kaczynski – existed.

Context is everything. Even *The New York Times* waxed poetic about the environs of Lincoln. Theodore Kaczynski bought his land and built his home in a place that "is strikingly beautiful, a mountain woodlands near Stemple Pass, just west of the Continental Divide. Cougars, bobcats, elk and the occasional grizzly bear roam the high country. The Blackfoot River runs through it like a dagger, carrying cutthroat, rainbow and brook trout."[67] During the long winters, "snow lay deep and silent."[68] In summer, "the sun was molten gold, and the rain tapped softly on shingles and gently bent the branches of the trees."[69]

Here was a place to build a home.

Kaczynski's one-room cabin, built with a storage loft and no cellar, was set far back on a dirt road, about a quarter mile from the main road, which was also unimproved. Kaczynski lived without electricity. He obtained a wood stove to provide warmth during the harsh winter months.

In this setting Kaczynski would have the solitude he sought – like many others who moved to the region. "Aside from his taste in books and his rarely displayed articulateness, the usually unwashed Kaczynski did not raise eyebrows around Lincoln, where many people live secluded lives."[70] Where Kaczynski lived – and where I live now, for that matter – a desire for solitude is not considered terribly odd.

Kaczynski strived for self-sufficiency. He baked his own bread.[71] He grew potatoes, parsnips and other vegetables in his garden. For a year or so after coming to Montana, Kaczynski made his own candles. Later, he used something resembling a "slut lamp" fueled with deer fat or paraffin.

As a resident in rural Vermont – "ground zero of the back-to-the-land movement of hippie times" – none of these things seem to indicate mental illness.[72] I don't live off the power grid, but I know people who do. I did not move to Vermont for my modest house any more than Kaczynski moved to Montana for his cabin. I moved here for the mountains and the sky and the trees and the rivers and the air and the solitude. Especially the solitude. There are only about 500,000 people in my adopted state ("more cows than people," according to the bumper stickers), and I have yet to meet most of them.

The people who had interacted with Kaczynski over the years, his neighbors and acquaintances in Montana, did not think he was mentally ill. According to a *Time* magazine article published in November 1997, Becky Garland, co-owner of Garland's Town and Country Store and an acquaintance of Kaczynski said, "I can't imagine anybody saying he's insane. . . You might say that anyone who makes mail-bombs is insane. But insane by law? I don't think he was that."[73] Her sister, who "knew Ted didn't have much of a childhood," also had doubts: "We felt he was normal when he came to town."[74] So did Dan Rundell, who gave Kaczynski a bicycle and got a tour of Kaczynski's garden irrigation system in return: "I always thought that he acted, for a person who was a recluse, well within the bounds of society. He always seemed a little jumpy. But I put that down to the fact that he was not a social person."[75] Similarly, Jack McCabe, owner of a hotel where Kaczynski occasionally stayed, reportedly said "Ted Kaczynski never bothered me any. I figured he was some rancher from up in Lincoln who wanted to get away to the big town for a day or two. Lots of them did."[76]

But perhaps no person claims to have known Kaczynski better than Chris Waits, Kaczynski's neighbor on Stemple Pass Road.[77] Waits allegedly knew Kaczynski during his entire time in Montana.[78] Three days before Christmas 1998, Waits told me: "I've never seen anyone more sane than Ted — he's calculating beyond description. If Ted wants the world to see him as sane, I'll be the national crier for his sanity: I'm his best ally in this."[79] Waits argues that, "Ted *does* care about the environment, but that's not where his motivations came from. He sent the bombs out of hatred and revenge. The hatred might have begun with concern for the environment, but what he really hated were infringements on his own parts of

nature – his privacy, his solitude. He was perfectly willing to litter in parts
of the forest he didn't care about. His motivations are very complex, *he's
very complex* — but not insane."[80]

Consider Theodore Kaczynski's Christmas cards. Kaczynski's eighty-
something-year-old acquaintance, Irene Preston, told *U.S. News and World
Report* magazine that she received Christmas cards from him for nine
years.[81] One holiday season, Kaczynski wrote: "I had a particularly good
crop of carrots in my garden this year."[82] Ms. Preston recalled playing cards
with him, pinochle to be specific, and found him "very kind and gentle."[83]

But however much this may have helped the prosecution, this evidence was not to help raise a mental defect defense. The Unabomber's
defense team reportedly planned to rely on stories from Theodore
Kaczynski's personal and family history as well.[84] Two incidents from
Kaczynski's early childhood were targeted by his family and by investigators as possible catalysts for his future crimes.[85] At the age of nine
months, Kaczynski was hospitalized for an allergic reaction to eggs and,
according to his mother, denied all contact with his parents for a disputed period of time.[86] At age seven, he was allegedly left alone to sob in a
hospital lobby while his father and grandmother were in the maternity
ward visiting his newborn brother David.[87] Kaczynski himself has written a careful and exhaustively documented rebuttal of the picture his
family paints of his childhood. [88]

Portions of the Unabomber's manifesto seem to correspond with
reported events in Kaczynski's early life, and these passages could be
deemed autobiographical. The manifesto argues that because technological society "needs scientists, mathematicians and engineers . . . heavy pressure is put on children to excel in these fields. It isn't natural for an adolescent human being to spend the bulk of his time sitting at a desk absorbed
in study. A normal adolescent wants to spend his time in active contact
with the real world . . . But in our society, children are pushed into study-
ing technical subjects, which most do grudgingly."[89] Perhaps Kaczynski
was describing his own childhood. Perhaps not.

Kaczynski's childhood and early adult life, although working-class, was
far better and more privileged than virtually all of my capital clients.
Kaczynski's personal history was far from perfect. But whose was?
Kaczynski remembers that when his parents became angry at him, they
would shower him with verbal abuse.[90] In particular, they often called him
a "sicko," emotionally disturbed, and they compared him to an acquaintance who had been institutionalized. In contrast, the media has painted a
picture of Kaczynski's parents which makes them out to be solid, hardworking people who loved him, made sacrifices for him and tried to help

him. The jury would seem to be still out regarding the truth here.

Theodore John Kaczynski was born in Chicago, Illinois, on May 22, 1942, the first son born to Theodore Richard and Wanda Kaczynski.[91] His father provided financially for his family.[92]

Ted Sr. committed suicide in 1990 by a self-inflicted gunshot wound to the head.[93] He had been diagnosed shortly before his death with lung and spinal cancer.[94] His mother was well-read and articulate. Ted's mother kept a diary about her son and read to him daily from children's books, then from boys' literature.[95] Throughout his education, his parents suspected that Kaczynski was unhappy, despite his active participation in the school band (playing trombone), the math club, coin club, biology club and German club.[96] They apparently thought this unhappiness stemmed from the fact that he was so much brighter than his peers. Their solution was to accelerate Ted's curriculum, allowing him to skip one year of junior high school and one year of high school. This did little to help Kaczynski's social adjustment, and may have made things worse. He entered Harvard on a full scholarship at the age of sixteen.[97]

Harvard was no picnic for the working-class Kaczynski. He did not fit in, and tended to gravitate toward intellectual boys who shared his developing passion for mathematics and science.[98]

While at Harvard, Kaczynski underwent psychological testing. The Unabomber media implied that Kaczynski needed psychological help during his undergraduate years. In fact, Kaczynski – like many of his Harvard classmates – had consented to be the subject of a psychological study. He participated in one of the many psychological studies conducted during the fifties, which often used Harvard students as subjects.[99] Participants in the study were given code names, and Kaczynski's code name was "Lawful."

During the four years that Kaczynski was an undergraduate at Harvard (1958 to 1962), some fairly weird psychological research was going on there – not all of it with the full consent of the subjects. The Chief Researcher for the Harvard study in which Kaczynski participated was a Lieutenant Colonel during World War II, and worked for the Office of Strategic Services (OSS), the precursor of the CIA. While at the OSS, he conducted experiments on the effect of certain drugs during interrogation.[100]

More to the point, during the 1950s and early 1960s, the OSS, CIA and other military agencies conducted experiments on the effects of LSD using the unsuspecting student-subjects. Writer Alston Chase reports that the Chief Researcher for the Harvard study in which Kaczynski participated was fascinated with LSD, and had been responsible for setting up Timothy Leary at Harvard.[101] Chase hypothesizes that the Harvard experiments must have been CIA operations: The only conceivable purpose of such studies would have been to generate data for the CIA on how to break down stubborn subjects during interrogation. In other words, mind control.

Kaczynski graduated from Harvard in 1962 and headed for the University of Michigan to begin five years of graduate studies. There his intellectual gifts blossomed.[102] To the amazement of his teachers and peers, he began publishing papers in respected academic journals. His article, *Boundary Functions for Functions Defined on a Disk*, was published in the Journal of Mathematics and Mechanics in 1965, and another paper, *On a Boundary Property of Continuous Functions*, appeared in the Michigan Journal of Mathematics a year later. His dissertation was a work of pure theoretical mathematics. It got him the Sumner Meyers Prize for the best mathematics dissertation at Michigan the year he graduated.[103]

Kaczynski was publishing distinguished work, and it landed him a job teaching mathematics at the University of California at Berkeley. Berkeley's Free Speech Movement had spawned the national demonstrations against the Vietnam war, and the campus remained a hotbed of student activism. Even with the activism of the sixties literally under his nose, Kaczynski kept to himself. He seemed to be on the fast-track to tenure there. But in 1969, at the age of twenty-seven, Kaczynski left his teaching post determined to find a simpler life in a rural area. Perhaps Kaczynski hadn't been oblivious to the chaos around him after all. 1969 was the year Neil Armstrong and Buzz Aldrin walked on the moon, but the fragile planet they'd left behind, especially their United States, seemed to be coming apart at the seams.

I don't know what stories Kaczynski's family would have told in court, or if it would have departed much from the above chronology. As mentioned before, unlike many of my own death row clients, Kaczynski was not uneducated. He was not borderline retarded. He did not grow up in poverty, and he probably was not physically or sexually brutalized by his family. Juries routinely sentence people to death who had horrible childhoods, who are retarded, who are crazy.

Personally, I admire Theodore Kaczynski's for his refusal to portray the bombings as the products of a bad childhood and adolescence. In any event, it is unlikely that the "abuse excuse" defense would have won over the jury in the Unabomber case. It is doubtless true that genius-IQ-math-wizards have their sad stories to tell, but I wonder whether a jury of working-class men and women would have found those stories compelling in the Unabomber trial – except perhaps to the extent that the stories may account for the crimes. Although it's impossible for me to evaluate evidence when I have not seen and heard it all, I must wonder whether the stories told by the Kaczynski family stories could outweigh the rest of the circumstantial evidence indicating that, whatever else Theodore

Kaczynski may have been, he did not suffer from a serious mental illness.

Other circumstantial evidence reinforces the idea that Kaczynski's lawyers were "medicalizing" his radical political views and the violent means he used to further his political ideology. The seventeen-year bombing campaign was methodical. The Unabomber eluded the largest and most expensive manhunt in American history.[104] And he took very, very good notes on all of it.

Kaczynski's journals were by all accounts meticulous. The portions of the journals that I have had the occasion to read have not struck me as the writings of a madman. I wish they did. It would make it easier to dismiss him. They are far more chilling than that, far more frightening, and almost clinical in their descriptive content. In coldly sterile language, Kaczynski's notebooks detail his "experiments," and his reasons for conducting them, as well as the specific techniques he used to construct each bomb and plan each attack. After his first fatal bombing, Kaczynski wrote: "Excellent. Humane way to eliminate somebody. He probably never felt a thing. $25,000 reward offered. Rather flattering."[105]

Another important piece of circumstantial evidence was of course the Unabomber's manifesto itself. Don't decide whether the manifesto is the product of a delusion until you have read it for yourself. I read it, all 35,000 words of it, several times. The manifesto's central thesis: that the industrial revolution has done humanity more harm than good. Kaczynski's notion of personal freedom stands at the core of the manifesto, which is an essentially libertarian document. "Freedom means being in control (either as an individual or as a member of a *small* group) of the life and death issues of one's existence: food, clothing, shelter and defense against whatever threats there may be in one's environment. Freedom means having power: Not the power to control other people, but the power to control the circumstances of one's own life."[106] Technology, the Unabomber argues, has brought obvious benefits (electricity, telephones), but the price has been an unacceptable loss of freedom.

In setting out this thesis – and its antidote, a return to nature – the manifesto is tightly reasoned and clear in its assumptions and limitations. The manifesto's tone is sober, and its affect isn't nearly as wild as Zola's *J'Accuse*, Paine's *Common Sense*, or Garrison's *Liberator*. It is far easier to understand than the works of Marx, Engels, Kant, Habermas, or Hegel. It's thoughtful and full of ideas, subtlety and nuance, none of which are beyond refutation but all of which are lucid, and many of which are reasonable.

The Unabomber's critique of technology also is not vastly dissimilar from the ideas articulated by contemporary social critics. One such critic, Kirkpatrick Sale, even criticized the Unabomber's manifesto for unoriginality.[107] And in September 1997, two months before Kaczynski's trial began, *The New York Times* magazine ran a special issue that asked: *What Is Technology Doing To Us?* The magazine concluded that it is making us faster, richer and smarter – as well as "alienated, materialistic and a little crazy."[108] Two months after Kaczynski was sentenced, *The New York Times* op ed pages ran a piece that asked the same question, and answered that we are *Losing our Souls, Bit By Bit.*[109] And then there is the perennial conversation about the destruction of the ozone layer, global warming, the degradation of our rain forests, and all the rest of that crazy environmental stuff.[110] Not only crazy people care about these things.

No matter what Kaczynski's defense team might have argued, it seems clear that the Unabomber's political philosophy was not a delusion. Nor were the violent means he used to further that political ideology a hallucination. The Unabomber is not alone in believing that violent means are necessary to protect the environment.[111] The manifesto explained the Unabomber's violence in this way: "In order to get our message before the public with some chance of making a lasting impression, we had to kill people."[112] If it had not been for the Unabomber's violence, and his threat of further violence if the 35,000-word manifesto was not published in full by *The New York Times* and *The Washington Post*, no major American newspaper would have published it. The Unabomber's reasoning here was coldly manipulative, but it was not crazy.

The prosecution in the Unabomber trial described Kaczynski as being a man motivated more by anger than by his concern for the environment.[113] Both the prosecution's sentencing memorandum, and the recent Chris Waits book, are based on Kaczynski's private journals.[114] Because I do not have access to Kaczynski's journals, I remain agnostic regarding the debate about the motives Kaczynski chronicled there. For my purposes, the rival interpretations of the Unabomber's motives do not really matter. Both accounts of Kaczynski's motives (the Waits/prosecution account, and the manifesto account) are rational and sane. Indeed, Waits has told me that he has tried to demonstrate that Kaczynski is entirely sane in his book.[115] This is, of course, Waits's layman's diagnosis based on an alleged twenty-five-year association with Kaczynski.

I have already suggested that, according to the law, Kaczynski's alleged delusions did not render him mentally incompetent to stand trial. Judge Garland Burrell had no real doubt about the fact that Kaczynski was mentally competent to stand trial, and my reading of the available transcripts leads me to agree. Even when he was under intense pressure, from his own lawyers and Burrell, Kaczynski was poised, and he spoke calmly, rationally and perceptively. His actions in court were rational responses to the circumstances in which he found himself.

Most importantly to me, Kaczynski's own lawyers never seriously seemed to doubt their client's mental competency to stand trial. Of all the participants in Kaczynski's judicial proceedings, his lawyers knew him best; they had worked with him, closely, for a year and a half prior to the scheduled trial. And, so long as Kaczynski followed his lawyers' instructions, they never questioned his competency.

Perhaps Theodore Kaczynski wasn't a paranoid schizophrenic after all. The evidence certainly does not come close to proving that he is a paranoid schizophrenic or otherwise mentally ill in a way that matters in a court of law. I am not arguing that Kaczynski is a normal and well-adjusted American citizen. He isn't. Normal and well-adjusted American citizens don't send deadly, hand-crafted bombs through the mail. Kaczynski exhibited crazy *behavior*, but he is not crazy – again not in any way that matters to the law.

The problem here isn't so much with the soft science of psychiatry; psychiatry is not much better able today to account for a Theodore Kaczynski today than it was able to account for a John Brown in 1859. The problem arises when psychiatry falls into the hands of media-wise defense lawyers in high profile capital cases. Stephen Oates's remark about John Brown's historians is equally true of Kaczynski's lawyers: "It is one thing to learn from what psychology has taught us about human beings. It is quite another for a historian – a layman – to assume the role of the psychiatrist himself . . . and psychoanalyze a historical personality on the basis of controversial evidence."[116]

Apart from the factual question of whether Kaczynski was mentally ill, there remains the advocacy question: Would a jury have been likely to accept his defense counsels' argument that the Unabomber was crazy, and that such craziness mitigated the magnitude of the crimes? This, at bottom, was his defense team's central justification for insisting on a mental defect defense: It was the best chance to save their client's life, and it had a far greater chance of success with a jury than did a political or ideological defense.

This may be true. Juries are the black boxes of our legal system.[117] They are notoriously skeptical of mental defect defenses, even in cases where the illness is clear.[118] I think the jury would have found Kaczynski's alleged mental illness dubious. His ability to evade the largest and most expensive manhunt in U.S. history; his coolly calculating journals; the Unabomber's manifesto – any mental defect defense would have needed to overcome these obstacles, and more. In the end, it is not at all clear to me that a jury (even a jury convinced that Kaczynski did indeed suffer from mental illness) would have found that the mental illness in any way mitigated the cruelty and horror of his crimes. They might very well have decided that he ought to be executed for those crimes.[119] One of Kaczynski's surviving victims, Dr. Charles Epstein, a geneticist and pediatrics professor who lost parts of three fingers to the Unabomber, said it well: "Even if Kaczynski suffers from a mental illness, it doesn't 'excuse' the crimes, and it doesn't take away for me the fact that he is evil."[120]

Although Theodore Kaczynski was "nowhere near the clinical extreme," he will be remembered as a madman, and his writings will be remembered as products of a diseased mind. Even if they would not have been able to persuade a jury of the same thing, Kaczynski's family and his defense team deftly persuaded the media that he was profoundly disturbed.[121] William Glaberson, *The New York Times*' lead reporter at the Unabomber trial, traced Kaczynski's trajectory from anti-technology "man of ideas" to "nut" and "fraud."[122] Glaberson wrote: "It seems hard to believe now, but it wasn't very long ago that the Unabomber seemed like a serious person. To read about him in many newspapers and magazine accounts was to hear of a mysterious philosopher: dangerous yet compelling, brilliant, intriguing. Yes, he was troubled, even evil – but he was a man of ideas."[123] The Unabomber "was once compared in news accounts to Daniel Boone, Henry David Thoreau and characters out of Dostoyevsky . . . an intriguing hybrid of Robin Hood, the Green Hornet and Mick Jagger."[124]

These comparisons seem to me a tad overblown, although, as I have said, some of the ideas articulated in the Unabomber's manifesto strike me as being thoughtful and well-reasoned. But who remembers the ideas in the manifesto any more? "Now he's just a nut. Or, perhaps worse, a fraud . . . material for Jay Leno and the water cooler . . . pathetic . . . a bad sitcom."[125]

The defense team had two powerful allies in their effort to represent Theodore Kaczynski as mentally ill: Ted's brother David and his mother Wanda, aided by David's "media-savvy Washington lawyer."[126] During a media campaign to portray Kaczynski as mentally ill, his family "stayed impressively 'on message'." According to a "key member of the defense team . . . [the family] had learned how to use the press."[127] The media campaign involved long interviews with major newspapers like *The New York Times* and television news magazines such as *60 Minutes.*[128]

Thus, it wasn't just Kaczynski's lawyers who represented their client as mentally ill. Indeed, it was a "bizarre alliance of lawyers he was trying to fire, a family he had renounced, psychiatrists he did not trust or respect (and in some cases had never met), a federal judge who had drastically restricted his right to counsel and seemed to fear (with reason) the trial to come, a press convinced he was a schizophrenic . . . "[129]

Still, in the end, I believe that the principal responsibility for this fiasco remains with Kaczynski's lawyers. They could have shut down the media campaign by Kaczynski's brother and mother or they could have tried to counter it. But the manner in which Kaczynski was represented to the media by his family reinforced the defense team's intended strategy to raise a mental defect case based on the claim that their client was a paranoid schizophrenic.

When Worldviews Collide

[The lawyer] was a good fellow, but his rejoicing at the one little part – in which he was officially interested – of so great a tragedy was an object lesson in the limits of sympathetic understanding.

Bram Stoker, *Dracula*

One significant question about Theodore Kaczynski's alleged paranoid schizophrenia remains. If I am correct about the paucity of evidence that Theodore Kaczynski was indeed seriously mentally ill, then how were his family and his defense team able to convince a generally skeptical press corps and public that the methodical Unabomber was a paranoid schizophrenic?

Part of the answer has to do with the manner in which information was disseminated. Kaczynski's defense team effectively silenced their client by isolating him from the outside world during the eighteen months before jury selection began. During this crucial year and a half, the public conversation about Kaczynski's mental health was dominated by his brother and mother – two people who fervently believed their family member was profoundly mentally ill. When the trial began, he struggled mightily to rebut the family portrait of him as a madman. His lawyers and Judge Burrell silenced him again. The daily press corps did not have access to the transcripts of the closed-door meetings between Kaczynski and his lawyers.

More importantly, however, the public perception of the Unabomber as a profoundly mentally ill person has less to do with the objective evidence of Kaczynski's mental health than with our own expectations, and our need to explain his horrific crimes. The picture of the Unabomber painted by his lawyers – the deranged loner – was what the public expected to see and, perhaps, it was the picture they wanted to see. Proceeding from this presupposition, the Kaczynski defense team gave the nation exactly what it wanted.

Profiles of assassins are embedded in the American psyche. From Lee Harvey Oswald to Russel E. Weston, Jr., the 1998 shooter in the nation's Capitol, we define our assassins as solitary madmen. *Newsweek's* cover story labeled Weston *The Loner*.[130] However, one of the most comprehensive studies ever conducted of American assassins found that the madman or the lonely loser-*cum*-political killer is a myth.[131] The Secret Service studied all eighty-three people who attacked or tried to attack an American political figure or celebrity during the past fifty years; the researchers were able to interview twenty-three of the assassins. They challenged many of the popular stereotypes of assassins in their 1998 report, *Preventing Assassination*: fewer than half of the subjects showed symptoms of mental illness. "None were models of emotional health, but relatively few suffered from serious mental illness that caused their attack behaviors."[132] The assassins were neither loners, nor were they losers.

No matter. The stereotypical lone nut is firmly fixed in the American mind. The portrait painted by the Unabomber's family fit hand-in-glove with that stereotype.

The Unabomber, his manifesto and his journals were like so many cultural Rorschach blots: They gave us insight into our own social psychology as much as the man and his crimes. They gave us what we wanted, or needed, to see. Many Americans expected, wanted and needed to see a madman. The crimes become less threatening if we believe that only a madman is capable of them. There is something comforting in the idea that the Unabomber was a *mad* bomber. What else could have made him do it?

Consider the alternative explanation: Theodore Kaczynski was a perfectly sane, admittedly eccentric, highly educated man who nearly two decades ago decided to devote his life to carefully designing and meticulously constructing bombs. For seventeen years, this cold, sane man caused these bombs to be triggered by a host of victims, all the while outwitting the largest and most expensive manhunt in American history. Had the Unabomber's own brother not turned him in to the FBI, he might well still be sending deadly bombs through the U.S. mail. He wasn't a mad bomber; he was a chillingly sane bomber. The sane bomber, it seems to me, is a far scarier image than the mad bomber.

Lydia Eccles, a Boston artist, anarchist and founder of the Unabomber Political Action Committee (UNAPACK), is right in her supposition that the most obvious evidence of Theodore Kaczynski's sanity, that he was lucid and competent, is the Unabomber's manifesto itself – a document which, although always available to the media and the public, became invisible once the hermit Kaczynski was identified as the Unabomber.[133] She wrote as long as the Unabomber,

> was on the loose, the manifesto was considered a sane political document, and [the Unabomber] was a serious terrorist threat. The suspect

who was arrested lived according to the tenets of the manifesto. What changed to make him 'crazy'? The manifesto was removed from view, and those who wished to discredit [Kaczynski] – his family, the lawyers – were given total control of the podium. The press apparently "forgot" that Kaczynski had written a long and cogent analysis of political reality, something few of them could have accomplished. The media ignored this obvious evidence because it threatened their belief system.

The manifesto blasphemed everything that knits together the worldview of not only the mainstream, but also that of many reformers and radical critics. Many are able to say that Orwell's vision threatens. But they think that to become alert to this danger is to solve the problem. They remain caught up in what Jacques Ellul has called "the illusion of politics" – the belief that in a democracy we actually consciously shape our future through the political process. Many of the Unabomber's anti-mythical ideas are unthinkable to us, more so than the use of violence. Given the right rationale, our society is willing to kill not only guilty people, but innocent ones as well as, and then call it collateral damage. The Unabomber questioned our faith in politics itself, and challenges concepts of self, freedom and happiness. He is a heretic at the deepest level.[134]

One simply can't understand the crimes without understanding the ideas articulated in the manifesto. The manifesto challenges the basic assumptions of virtually every interest group that was involved with the case: the lawyers, the mental health experts, the press and politics – both left and right.

In the end, this may explain how Kaczynski's defense team convinced the media and the public that Kaczynski was crazy, even in the absence of credible evidence. It was an inside job. We outsiders believed it because we *needed* to believe it.

The judiciary, the media and the majority of Americans reacted exactly as the Unabomber's manifesto predicted they would. They decided that the Unabomber was mentally ill, and his ideas were mad. Then they forgot about the man and his ideas, and created a curative tale.

But I'm getting ahead of the story.

CHAPTER TWO

The Unabomber Non-Trial: Kafka Comes to Town

To thrust counsel upon the accused against his considered wishes . . . [means that counsel] is not an assistant but a master; and the right to make a defense is stripped of its personal character . . . An unwanted counsel 'represents' the defendant only through a tenuous and unacceptable legal fiction. Unless the accused has acquiesced in such representation, the defense presented is not the defense guaranteed him by the Constitution, for, in a very real sense, it is not *his* defense.[1]

U.S. Supreme Court (1975)

Kafka Comes to Town

Many months in advance of Theodore Kaczynski's scheduled trial as the accused Unabomber, his attorneys announced to the court that they believed their client to be mentally ill.[2] They went on to aver that a supposition of mental defect was his best defense against the death penalty.

Both Kaczynski and his lawyers seemed to recognize that he would almost certainly be found guilty of murder in the first phase of his bifurcated capital trial. The battleground in the Unabomber case was over the penalty phase of the trial. This was when evidence in support of a "necessity defense" (based on the ideological belief that his actions were necessary per the arguments contained in the manifesto), would have been admissible under the Supreme Court's 1978 decision in *Lockett v. Ohio*.[3] However, Judge Burrell ruled that Kaczynski could not fire his lawyers and that those selfsame lawyers had the legitimate power to raise a defense based on Kaczynski's alleged mental illness – regardless of Kaczynski's adamant refusal to accept such a defense.

Early on in their representation of the Unabomber, Kaczynski's lawyers must have realized two things: First, they must have known that, based on their client's social transformation from promising young mathematics professor at Berkeley University to Montana hermit and alleged Unabomber, their strongest argument to save their client's life would be a mental defect defense. Second, Kaczynski's lawyers knew that their client was dead set against that sort of defense.

For a while, the lawyers were able to finesse the conflict over which defense to raise. During the spring and summer of 1997, Kaczynski's lawyers filed motions to exclude from the trial all evidence found by government agents when they searched Kaczynski's cabin, including Kaczynski's private journals. Kaczynski likely supported such motions, since they were congruent with his personal and political notions of privacy in the face of government snooping. Another thing that occurred was that, months prior to the trial, Kaczynski's lawyers and the prosecution conceded his mental competency to stand trial. Like the evidentiary suppression motions, Kaczynski probably would have been in agreement with his lawyers' position on this score.

In addition to this, five months prior to the beginning of jury selection in November 1997, Kaczynski's lawyers filed a notice of intent stating that they would rely on a mental defect defense. Kaczynski's attorneys apparently did not intend to raise an insanity defense. The federal insanity defense statute rarely has been invoked since it was rewritten in 1984, following its successful use by John Hinckley's lawyers after the attempted assassination of Ronald Reagan. Rather than raising an insanity defense, Kaczynski's lawyers planned to argue that, given his "illness," he was incapable of forming the level of "intent" necessary to hold him culpable for murder.

In June 1997, Kaczynski's lawyers gave notice that they would present expert testimony about Kaczynski's mental condition.[4] Such notices often are summary statements consisting of only a sentence or two. I understand that Kaczynski was aware that his lawyers filed this motion, but unaware, until jury selection had begun in November 1997, that his attorneys intended to base their defense on claims that their client was crazy.[5] My guess is that the lawyers told Kaczynski that filing the notice was a technicality useful for keeping their strategic options open and that, in any event, he would have control over such a defense.[6] I would also guess that the lawyers hoped that when Kaczynski did finally become aware of the magnitude of their intended reliance on a mental defect defense – during the process of jury selection – he would cave in and acquiesce to the one defense that would save his life.

If that was the lawyers' gambit, they grievously misjudged their client's determination to forego the mental defect defense, even if it meant the death penalty. During this time, Kaczynski also explored whether he could be represented by San Francisco Attorney J. Tony Serra, a lawyer with experience raising the political necessity defense in controversial trials. Kaczynski's lawyers never invited Serra to join the defense team, even as an informal associate. The hostility towards him was palpable.

By then, justifiably distrustful of his lawyers' intentions and motives, Kaczynski attempted to exercise the second-to-last option he had to insure that his defense would be the one raised during his trial: He exercised his constitutional right to fire his lawyers and represent himself.[7] But the judge, in flat disregard for the law, refused to honor Kaczynski's invocation of his constitutional right to self-representation.[8] Trapped by his paternalistic attorneys and a judge way out of his depth, he tried to commit suicide.[9] This attempt was unsuccessful and, seeing with crystal clarity that there was only one remaining way to prevent his relentless lawyers from portraying him as a madman, Kaczynski exercised his final option. He pleaded guilty.[10]

Further, if my chronology of events is accurate, then Kaczynski's guilty plea is seriously vulnerable to constitutional attack. If Kaczynski challenges the legality of his plea bargain, it seems to me that he might well succeed. The Unabomber trial may be just beginning.

April 1996 to January 1997:
Kaczynski is Mentally Ill?

For a matter of months preceding the beginning of my trial on November 12, 1997, I had been aware that my attorneys wanted to use a defense that would be based in part on supposed evidence of mental impairment. However, my attorneys had led me to believe that I would have a considerable measure of control over the defense strategy, hence I was under the impression that I would be able to limit the presentation of mental evidence to some items that at the time I thought might have some validity.[11]

Theodore J. Kaczynski

Based principally on court documents and published accounts by first-hand observers of the events described, this is what I believe happened during the Unabomber non-trial.[12]

Soon after Kaczynski's arrest as the alleged Unabomber, the Court determined that he lacked the money to hire a defense lawyer, and appointed Montana federal public defender Michael Donahoe to represent him. Kaczynski formed a quick and close relationship with Donahoe.[13] Five days after Kaczynski's arrest, the well-known Attorney J. Tony Serra wrote to Kaczynski offering to represent him. Serra wrote: "My personal belief systems prompt me to volunteer my services to you. . . I have done many cases with similar symbolic content. I would serve you loyally and well." Serra's letter enclosed a "copy of an article written about me so that you can get the flavor of some of my previous cases."[14]

Serra told Kaczynski that he viewed the case "as one where [Kaczynski's] ideology would be the crux of the defense (not insanity; not a 'whodunit')."[15] After reviewing the letter, Kaczynski decided to stay with Attorney Donahoe. However, Kaczynski remained in touch with Attorney Serra.

When it became clear that Kaczynski would be tried in California, he was appointed federal public defender Quin Denvir as lead counsel. Denvir asked Judge Burrell to appoint Judy Clarke, a passionate opponent of capital punishment, as co-counsel.[16] A third lawyer, Gary Sowards, later joined the defense team. Sowards, a prominent specialist in raising defenses based on mental illness, seemed to be in charge of the mental health aspect of the Kaczynski defense. Sowards had a leading role in selecting the defense's mental health experts, and like any good criminal defense lawyer knew how to select experts who would give him the diagnosis he wanted.

Within the small community of experienced capital defense lawyers, Denvir, Clarke and Sowards are widely regarded by their peers as among the most competent. Long-time opponents of capital punishment, Denvir, Clarke and Sowards have for a professional lifetime fought against the death penalty. Denvir and Clarke could have made far more money in private law practice. Both are federal public defenders by choice. Both are *capital* public defenders by choice, and they are two of the best in the business.

As I have already stated, long in advance of the trial – perhaps as early as May 1996 – prosecutors and defense lawyers had agreed that Kaczynski was mentally competent to stand trial. The defense lawyers were right: Kaczynski clearly was competent to stand trial. Thirty-eight years ago the Supreme Court articulated the legal test for gauging competency to stand trial: To be tried, a criminal defendant must possess "sufficient present ability to consult with his lawyer with a reasonable degree of rational understanding" and a "rational as well as factual understanding of the proceedings against him."[17] Theodore Kaczynski obviously met this easy-going test.

After Kaczynski's arrest on April 3, 1996, the Kaczynski family's lawyer cited his alleged mental illness as a reason the government ought not seek the death penalty in the case. "In his correspondence," the family's lawyer wrote to the prosecutor, "Ted projects his own feelings of anger, depression and powerlessness onto society at large – a society of which he has never really been a member. He blames these ill-effects on a wide variety of external factors, including childhood classmates, teachers and his family as well as the media, chemical and electronic mind control, education, science and technology."[18]

The view of Kaczynski and his life painted by Kaczynski's family is now firmly embedded in the American consciousness. Kaczynski's rebuttal probably would not matter to the news media. Once a simple label has been applied, it becomes a truth regardless of fact. In the American mind, the complexity that is Theodore Kaczynski has been encapsulated by two words: paranoid schizophrenic. I doubt that Kaczynski will ever manage to change the public perception of him, regardless of how much evidence he gathers. That his family and his defense team inaccurately portrayed him, to the court and to the world, is a moot point.

Shortly after Kaczynski's arrest, while he was still housed in Montana, a psychologist named Dale Watson administered a battery of psychological tests to Kaczynski. No report of the evaluation has been made available to the public.[19]

In April 1996, a year and a half before jury selection began, *Time* magazine kicked off the discussion about Theodore Kaczynski's mental health by claiming that he had been "different almost from the start."[20] The magazine reported incidents from Kaczynski's childhood (his hospitalization at age nine months, his alleged isolation and avoidance of human contact) and from his adulthood (his allegedly increasing withdrawal from family members and the outside world in general). Even Robert Bly joined the fray, and set about exploring "the mind of the Unabomber suspect."[21]

In May 1996, *The New York Times* described Kaczynski's mental illness in detail as reported by his family.[22] A segment on *60 Minutes* in September 1996 "featured Mr. Kaczynski's mother and brother and their sympathetic descriptions of him as mentally ill."[23]

On June 15 and 16, 1996, Kaczynski was evaluated by defense psychology experts Ruben and Raquel Gur.[24] Defense psychologist Ruben Gur conducted neuropsychological testing on Kaczynski. He also interpreted the psychological testing conducted by Dale Watson.[25] It was psychiatrist Raquel Gur's impression that Kaczynski met the diagnostic criteria for "Schizophrenia, Paranoid Type," and psychologist Ruben Gur's impression that the testing was not inconsistent with this.[26]

Over the eighteen-month period before jury selection, Kaczynski's lawyers met with his family.[27] To be sure, the lawyers did not wage an overt media campaign. Kaczynski's lead counsel, Quin Denvir was able to say that "you don't try a case to the press. And you don't speak out in court so the press can report it."[28] To be sure. Kaczynski's attorneys had no need to participate *directly* in the family's media campaign to portray their client as mentally ill; the family, guided by their media-savvy Washington lawyer, was doing a great job of staying "on message."[29] When the Unabomber's defense team did opt for a defense that portrayed their client as mentally ill, the foundation had already been well-laid by Kaczynski's brother and mother.

February to November 1997:
What Did He Know, and When Did He Know It?

Everyone has a point of pride, a trait held paramount in defining one-self. Some might have looks or will; Ted Kaczynski prized his brilliance. So it was in a sort of self defense that he refused to allow his mind to be called into question . . . [30]

Time

The Kaczynski family had by now launched a full scale media campaign to portray the Unabomber as a madman. His lawyers declined to comment publicly, refusing to discuss the possibility of a mental defect defense.[31] In February 1997, Kaczynski was interviewed and evaluated by defense psychologist Karen Froming.[32] Froming conducted additional neuropsychological testing, and she reviewed the psychological testing done while Kaczynski attended Harvard. According to Froming, the TAT examination conducted at Harvard indicated themes that consisted mainly of people being dominated by others, and that his responses showed a complete absence of affiliation.[33] Froming concluded that Kaczynski was suffering from paranoid schizophrenia.[34] The linchpin of Froming's diagnosis once again was her treatment of Kaczynski's antitechnology politics, which were seen as a delusional architecture rather than a political ideology.[35]

On June 24, 1997, Kaczynski's lawyers filed a notice pursuant to the federal court rule requiring the defense to provide the prosecution with pre-trial notice of intent to introduce expert testimony "relating to a mental disease or defect or any other mental condition of the defendant bearing upon the issue of guilt."[36] The complete text of the notice filed by Kaczynski's lawyers was as follows: "The defendant, through counsel, hereby gives notice of the intent to introduce expert testimony pursuant to the applicable court rule."[37] In a motion filed July 30, 1997, the prosecution argued that the notice filed by Kaczynski's counsel was insufficiently clear and did not give the prosecutor proper notice about the defense counsels' intentions.[38]

The prosecution reminded the Court of its duty to hold a hearing on the defendant's mental competency to stand trial if there is "reasonable cause to believe that the defendant may presently be suffering from a mental disease or defect rendering him mentally incompetent to the extent that he is unable to understand the nature and consequences of the proceedings against him or to assist properly in his defense."[39] The prosecutors wrote: "Although the government is not aware of evidence rising to the level of the reasonable cause required by the statute, the court may wish to make a preliminary inquiry into the defendant's competency in light of his notice that he will produce evidence relating to a mental disease or defect or . . . other mental condition."[40]

Defense psychiatrist David Foster met with Kaczynski in late 1997. Foster opined that Kaczynski had an aversion to evaluation by psychiatrists and that he suffered from paranoid schizophrenia.[41] The key to Foster's diagnosis was his view that Kaczynski's politics were a delusion, not a philosophy.

Defense psychologist Xavier Amador never met with Theodore Kaczynski, but he was able to diagnose him as a paranoid schizophrenic. Amador claimed that Kaczynski's reluctance to submit to psychiatric evaluations and treatment were hallmarks of schizophrenia.[42] As was the case with Foster and the other experts hired by Kaczynski's defense lawyers, Amador's diagnosis hinged on his belief that Kaczynski's anti-technology politics were a delusion rather than a philosophy.[43]

A New Jersey newspaper ran a story that September with the headline *Unabom Trial Might See Claim of Insanity: Kaczynski's Lawyers Hint at Risky Strategy.*[44] The story reported that "attorneys for Unabomber suspect Theodore Kaczynski are considering using the most precarious defense available to them – not guilty by reason of insanity."[45] The story noted that although Kaczynski's lawyers had given notice of intent to "introduce expert testimony at his trial about a mental illness or condition," they "have refused to state exactly what mental defect they will claim."[46]

At a September court hearing, Kaczynski's lawyers asked the prosecutors to turn over everything they might have on file regarding Kaczynski's mental state: psychological profiles, interviews with family members, neighbors and the like.[47] The prosecutor responded that no psychological evaluations of Kaczynski had ever taken place. This assertion reportedly surprised Judge Burrell and led Kaczynski's lawyers "to charge that the FBI was guilty of misconduct" because "agents had persuaded Kaczynski's brother David to cooperate with their manhunt by telling him that his brother needed treatment."[48] Defense counsel Denvir explained his strategy: "The most important thing we can do in this case is to paint a picture of Mr. Kaczynski's life

... [and to reconstruct] the complex mosaic of a human life, the same life the jury must decide whether to forfeit or spare."[49]

The prosecution had asked the judge to order a mental examination of Kaczynski by the prosecution's own mental health experts. The judge granted the prosecution's motion on September 19.[50] In ordering the examination, the court relied on its inherent authority to order a criminal defendant to undergo mental examination by government experts to "state the mental disease, defect, or condition his expert may seek to establish." The court ordered that the examination occur "no later than 1:00 pm on September 26, 1997."[51] On the evening of September 24, 1997, Kaczynski's counsel filed a motion for reconsideration and for a delay in implementing the court's order. The court granted the delay and gave Kaczynski's attorneys until October 2 to file a brief in support of his motion for reconsideration.[52]

Kaczynski's reported refusal to submit to psychiatric testing was not limited to the prosecution's experts. He also reportedly refused to take tests administered by the experts retained by his own lawyers.[53]

On September 26, the government apprised Kaczynski's attorneys that the mental examination would be conducted by two experts, and would commence on the first weekend of October. The examination would take approximately one week; it would be videotaped; and it would be conducted without counsel present in the examination room.[54] Defense counsel objected to all of the above.[55] On the 29th, the government prosecution asked the judge to force the defense's compliance with the order directing an examination. On the first of October, the court ordered the prosecution to supplement its motion with declarations from the government's experts.[56]

By mid-October the press was reporting that Kaczynski's camp claimed he was a paranoid schizophrenic. The *Sacramento Bee* ran a story that announced *Kaczynski's Mentally Ill, Lawyers Tell Prosecution.* Relying on documents filed by the prosecution, not the defense, the newspaper reported that Kaczynski's defense told prosecutors that he was a paranoid schizophrenic, and that his mental illness rendered him unable to form the intent to commit murder."[57] The *Bee* explained:

> The lawyers apparently contend that Kaczynski suffers from schizophrenia, a mental disorder that can cause delusions of grandeur, hallucinations, deterioration in social functioning and disturbances in thinking and communication. Paranoid schizophrenics think they are being persecuted or plotted against and may react accordingly, medical texts say.
>
> Members of Kaczynski's family have said that he was mentally fragile since childhood, and have pleaded that his life be spared if he is convicted.
>
> David Kaczynski has called his brother "disturbed," and said he cut himself off from friends and relatives while he lived as a hermit in a

house without electricity or running water for nearly three decades.

Among the items that FBI agents seized from Kaczynski's remote Montana cabin in April 1996 was a bottle of Trazodone, an antidepressant.[58]

Similarly, the Associated Press reported that the defense had "indicated that it will claim Kaczynski suffers from paranoid schizophrenia."[59] AP also noted that "lawyers for Theodore Kaczynski said in court documents filed Thursday that they will have mental health experts examine his childhood experiences and his relations with his family – the latest indication he may use an insanity defense."[60]

A few days later, the *Sacramento Bee* reported:

Lawyers for suspected Unabomber Theodore Kaczynski want to bring the one-room plywood cabin where he lived in the Montana woods to Sacramento for his upcoming trial.

In court papers filed Thursday, federal defenders complain that the government, which took custody of the shack after arresting Kaczynski last year, "has refused to assist" them in arranging to transport it to Sacramento.

Kaczynski's attorneys want to show the jury the crude living conditions of the defendant, who graduated from Harvard University and once taught mathematics at the University of California, Berkeley, said federal defender Quin Denvir.

"We feel the cabin represents some of the best evidence of Mr. Kaczynski's background and functioning," Denvir said in an interview. "It's very important for the jury to understand the conditions under which this Harvard Ph.D. and former mathematics professor was living."

Leesa Brown, a spokeswoman for the prosecution team, said the defense has the right to move the cabin to Sacramento. "It belongs to Mr. Kaczynski," she said. But she added the government is under no obligation to supervise the effort.

The cabin is stored in Montana and prosecutors want to introduce a scale model of it.

But Denvir said the jury needs to see the real thing. The 10-by-12-foot shack, where Kaczynski lived for nearly three decades without electricity or running water, will offer "a much different view of him than has been portrayed" in media accounts, he said.

"This is not an A-frame in Tahoe," Denvir said. "This is the rural equivalent of living in a box or out of a shopping cart. This is a very grim way of living."

Asked if the living conditions speak to Kaczynski's mental state, Denvir said: "It speaks to everything about him."

Denvir and his partner in the case, Judy Clarke, have indicated that they may present evidence that Kaczynski suffers from paranoid schizo-phrenia and is incapable of forming the intent to commit the bombings with which he has been charged.[61]

In a motion filed on the fourteenth of October, the prosecution argued: "The government seeks to have two psychiatrists conduct a men-tal examination of the defendant that thoroughly explores his assertion that he suffers from a mental defect sufficient to negate his attempt to commit the charged defenses."[62] Such an examination is "necessary to ensure that the government experts have a firm and reliable basis for their testimony and thus to give the jury a fair and accurate portrayal of the defendant's asserted mental condition. In response, the defendant oppos-es nearly all the conditions that the government psychiatrists find neces-sary to conduct their examinations."[63]

Counsel for the defense relinquished Kaczynski's right to appear at the October 17 oral argument that had been scheduled regarding these motions by filing a waiver. The waiver, which was signed by Kaczynski himself, continued: "Defendant hereby requests the court to proceed dur-ing every absence . . . and agrees that his interests will be deemed repre-sented at all times by the presence of his attorneys, the same as if the defendant were personally present."[64]

The Court rejected defense counsel's objections on the 22nd and ordered the mental health examination by the prosecution's experts to go forward.[65] On the 23rd, the defense informed the government by letter that "Mr. Kaczynski will not be participating in the examination."[66] The following day, when the government expressed its intention to go forward with the exami-nation, the defense responded by noting that "the possible sanction for non-compliance" with the Court's order was an "order precluding Kaczynski from presenting expert testimony on the issue of mental disease or defect."[67]

That same day, the Court convened a telephone conference call during which defense counsel agreed that Kaczynski was "defying [the] orders of September 19, 1997, and October 22, 1997, and that . . . he would not under-go the examination ordered by the Court. Defense counsel further agreed that Kaczynski would have to "live with . . . the consequences. . . of his refusal to comply with the Court's order."[68] The prosecution then moved to pre-clude Kaczynski's attorneys from relying on expert mental health testimony at the guilt/innocence phase of his capital trial and to require Kaczynski to undergo a mental examination before the sentencing phase of the trial.[69] The defense, of course, objected and both sides argued the issue back and forth throughout the months of November and December.

November to Mid-December 1997:
Kaczynski Begins to See the Light

I ask to be excused from the mockery of a trial. I do not know what the design of this examination is. I do not know what is to be the benefit of it to the Commonwealth. I have now little to ask other than that I be not publicly insulted as cowardly barbarians insult those who fall into their hands. [70]

John Brown (1859)

On November 9, 1997, three days before jury selection began in the Unabomber trial, several news organizations reported that Kaczynski's attorneys thought he was a paranoid schizophrenic. The Knight-Ridder News Service reported that Kaczynski's "lawyers favor defense of insanity" and that "Kaczynski's lawyers [were] preparing an insanity defense, portraying a man whose reality was so warped that he was incapable of understanding his actions."[71] The Associated Press reported that Kaczynski suffered "from paranoid schizophrenia, a mental ailment that entails delusions and feelings of persecution."[72] The AP quoted Kaczynski's brother as saying Ted's actions were the result of "illness rather than evil."[73]

On the same day that the AP and Knight-Ridder wire services reported the defense lawyers' belief that their client was a paranoid schizophrenic, the *Baltimore Sun* and *Sacramento Bee* described how Kaczynski's attorneys planned to use their evidence of alleged mental illness. The *Baltimore Sun* reported that the defense lawyers would "describe a paranoid schizophrenic, a man whose illness leaves him incapable of intending, by legal definition, to harm anyone."[74] Kaczynski's lawyers, "according to court papers, [would] argue that his paranoid schizophrenia prevented him from forming an intent to harm – which is part of the legal definition of a crime."[75] Likewise, the *Sacramento Bee*, citing "sources close to the case," reported on the defense team's intent "to demonstrate that mental derangement caused the Harvard graduate and doctor of mathematics to mount a campaign that he hoped would save the world from the evils of technology and scientific progress."[76]

Time magazine joined the fray, and reported that Kaczynski's defense team thought he was a schizophrenic.[77] Adding to the confusion was a *Newsweek* story that came out a week before the above mentioned *Time* article, which cited yet another "source close to the defense." They reported that the Kaczynski's "lawyers had ruled out an insanity defense – that Kaczynski was incapable of understanding his actions. As the evidence mounted – his writings were lucid, his plans methodical – it became clear to his lawyers that no jury would believe he was out of his mind. Though they still maintain he was a paranoid schizophrenic his attorneys believe he is likely to be found guilty."[78]

These conflicting reports actually clarify matters. The attorneys had begun to change their position. They had decided that their only chance of saving Kaczynski from execution was to argue his mental illness during the penalty phase of trial. But more of this later.

On November 10 (two days before jury selection began), the Associated Press reported that "the tiny, primitive cabin – found crammed full of incriminating evidence, including letters, a diary and an unexploded bomb – [would] be trucked to Sacramento by Kaczynski's court-appointed defense lawyers."[79] The AP story explained:

> "You really cannot understand this guy's life unless you can get in that cabin," said Defense Attorney Quin Denvir. "The cabin is 10-by-12 feet and 13 feet tall. It had no running water, no electricity, no toilet – not even an outhouse. And the irony was that a quarter-mile away was electricity and water that he could have hooked into."
>
> Government lawyers oppose the demonstration and want to substitute a scale model of the structure. But in an interview with The Associated Press, Denvir and co-counsel Judy Clarke indicated they will fight to use the actual building – because if Theodore Kaczynski has a defense, it is somewhere in that shack.
>
> "Our goal is to explain the life of Ted Kaczynski," said Clarke, a veteran of another high-profile case – the defense of Susan Smith, who was convicted of drowning her two young sons in South Carolina. But Smith didn't get the death penalty.
>
> Both Clarke and Denvir hiked to the site of the Montana cabin to document and understand the life of deprivation which Kaczynski chose.
>
> "His only heat in the Montana winters was from a potbellied stove," Clarke said. "And he slept on a piece of plywood with a layer of foam on top."
>
> With the defense planning to argue that Kaczynski suffered from a mental disease, paranoid schizophrenia, the cabin offers a window into the darkness that engulfed this once brilliant and promising math professor.
>
> "This is not an idyllic, rustic cabin with a refrigerator and a wet bar,"

said Denvir. "It barely had a window. It was very dark, very cramped and crammed with stuff. And he lived there for almost 25 years."[80]

On the same day *U.S. News and World Report* hit the newsstands with a cover story about Theodore Kaczynski's alleged paranoid schizophrenia. The magazine reported:

> To help convey Kaczynski's lunacy, defense attorneys are hoping to have jurors tour the 10-foot-by-12-foot cabin where he lived without electricity or running water for 25 years. "I think that for the jury to really understand his functioning, you need to understand where this Ph.D. from Harvard and tenure-track professor was relegated to living," says Denvir. "It says a lot about him when you see the cabin and feel the cabin and what it was like for him to live there."

• • •

> Because of the shack's importance, it has become the subject of a bizarre legal struggle. Fearful that curiosity seekers might touch the building or its contents, the government moved the shack in May 1996, a month after Kaczynski's arrest. In a predawn operation, the FBI had the three-ton plywood shack lifted onto a flatbed truck, covered with a green tarp and driven 70 miles north to Malmstrom Air Force Base near Great Falls, Mont. Now, defense attorneys want the shack moved to Sacramento for the trial. Prosecutors are refusing to help. "The government already has generously maintained the cabin for the defendant for the past 17 months and should not be further burdened," they said in a court brief. "We have informed the defense that we have no interest in the cabin and that we will return the cabin to the defendant at its place of storage. However, in so doing, the government wants to be absolved of any further responsibility for the cabin and objects to incurring any additional costs of liability. . . ."
>
> Instead, the prosecution has built its own scale model of the cabin to show the jury in lieu of the real thing. But Defense Attorney Denvir claims it "looks like a Barbie Doll house, or an A-frame. The reality is much closer to a refrigerator box." The defense attorneys had said that jurors should be flown to Montana to see the cabin, but Denvir now says they probably will be able to move the cabin to Sacramento – without the government's help.[81]

The *U.S. News* story included an "exclusive statement on the eve of his brother's trial" by David Kaczynski. The statement read:

I must admit that the government's decision to seek the death penalty for Ted greatly saddens me. There is no way around the fear and sorrow that comes with knowing you may have a hand in causing the death of someone you love. Still, I do not question the fact that it was necessary to turn my brother in to the authorities. The lives of many people already had been devastated by his acts, and I knew that without some kind of confinement Ted's illness was not something I could control or that he could control.

The victims and their families must grieve in their own way, and I would never begrudge them any harsh feelings they may have toward Ted. They have all suffered a terrible and irredeemable loss. I do hope that if people come to know what my mother and I saw over the course of my brother's mental deterioration, there will be some consolation in knowing that these crimes were the product of illness, rather than evil.[82]

The *Newsweek* story had also noted that Kaczynski's lawyers "requested that Kaczynski's dank, foul-smelling cabin be moved" to the trial. The "point was clear: who else but a crazy man would choose to live like that?"[83]

The *Time* article, subtitled *The Accused Unabomber's Lawyers Say He's Schizophrenic, But Can They Use That As a Defense?*, reported that Kaczynski's "stubborn defiance" could "spell disaster for his defense which was in turmoil." The article went on to report "that he initially resisted examination by even his own doctors. This stance might be endorsed by the Unabomber Manifesto, which denounces anyone who attempts to 'control human behavior', but it could seriously jeopardize his attorneys' efforts to save his life."[84]

November 12 marked the first day of jury selection for the Unabomber trial. *The Wall Street Journal* ran a story titled *Alleged Unabomber's Attorneys Press For "Mental Defect" Defense.*[85] The article cited Quin Denvir's belief that his client's refusal to be examined by prosecution psychiatrists was caused by his paranoia.[86]

On the second day of jury selection, the CBS Morning News filed a story titled *Attorneys For Suspected Unabomber Theodore Kaczynski File Papers Claiming He Suffers From Paranoid Schizophrenia.*[87] Anchor Cynthia Bowers reported:

In Sacramento, attorneys for suspected Unabomber Ted Kaczynski have filed papers claiming he suffers from paranoid schizophrenia. In defense papers filed yesterday, an expert who has examined Kaczynski, says he believes he's, quote, "controlled by an omnipotent organization." Jury selection for Kaczynski's trial resumes today. He is accused in the bombing deaths of two Sacramento men and the wounding of two others.[88]

On November 19 (six days into jury selection), the Associated Press reported that defense lawyers have filed court papers which include highly personal accounts by two psychologists who examined the Unabomber suspect. They portrayed him as a tortured genius plagued by schizophrenia but unwilling to acknowledge he was mentally ill.

"Mr. Kaczynski's superior intellect should not be confused with sound mental health," said Karen Bronk Froming, who examined Kaczynski twice.

"Mr. Kaczynski was intent on doing well on the testing and assured me there was nothing wrong with him," she said, but added he was at first unable to make eye contact or even acknowledge her presence.

Another defense expert, Xavier Amador, a Columbia University specialist in schizophrenia, said Kaczynski's refusal to submit to the prosecution testing was proof of his illness.

"The main point here is that high IQ is not mutually exclusive with ... the diagnosis of schizophrenia," he wrote.

According to a statement by the government psychiatrist, Phillip Resnick, Kaczynski allegedly kept a journal to prevent media analysis by writing "an account of my own personality and its development that will be as accurate as possible."[89]

On the 30th, the Newark *Star-Ledger* ran a story that announced, *Contrary Kaczynski Hampers Defense.*[90] The newspaper reported that "Kaczynski, based on claims put forward by his attorneys, suffers from a classic case of paranoid schizophrenia, an irreversible disease characterized by a preoccupation with one or more delusions, or with frequent hallucinations related to a single theme." For the record, the definition of paranoid schizophrenia listed in the leading professional textbook of psychiatric disorders states: "The combination of persecutory and grandiose delusions with anger may predispose the individual to violence."[91]

Everyone seemed to know about the defense Kaczynski's lawyers were preparing for him – everyone, that is, but Kaczynski.[92] He would only find out during jury selection.

The process of selecting a jury began on November 12, and was not finished until December 22. It was a particularly arduous task in the Unabomber trial. Because of the extensive pre-trial publicity, and the prosecution's need to "death qualify" the jury (*i.e.,* to weed out prospective jurors whose personal feelings about capital punishment might prevent them from fairly considering the sentencing evidence presented by the prosecution and defense), six hundred jurors were summoned to fill out extensive questionnaires. Four hundred-fifty jurors filled out the questionnaires.[93] One hundred-eighty-two jurors were brought into court for individual questioning by the prosecution, the defense and Judge Burrell.[94] It was during these proceedings that Kaczynski first began to understand that his lawyers intended to make mental illness a significant feature of his defense.[95]

Prior to November 21, Kaczynski had not been present in court during a single hearing on any of the motions surrounding the defense counsel's filing of the notice of intent to rely on expert psychiatric evidence.[96] It was not until the 21st that the Court directed lawyers for the defense and prosecution, as well as Kaczynski himself, to meet and confer concerning the extent to which the defendant would allow himself to be examined. At that hearing, defense counsel advised the court that they "were willing to speak with Mr. Kaczynski and encourage him to engage in any testing which the government experts find necessary."[97] The Court questioned Kaczynski at the conclusion of the proceedings.[98]

On November 25, Judge Burrell addressed the government's motion to preclude expert mental defect evidence during jury selection. It was at that point, according to news reports, that Kaczynski became noticeably agitated. His anger was warranted. He had just discovered that his lawyers released a psychiatric report to the prosecution and public. He slammed a pen down on the defense table, and it skittered across the table.

Kaczynski's surprise appeared to be genuine. Had Kaczynski's lawyers kept him appraised of their intentions, it is unclear to me why he would have reacted as he did during jury selection.

On December 1, during the process of selecting a jury, Kaczynski wrote a letter to the judge.

To Judge Garland E. Burrell from Theodore J. Kaczynski
Your Honor:

Last Tuesday, November 25, I unexpectedly learned for the first time in this courtroom that my attorneys had deceived me. Specifically:

1. I was told that if I allowed myself to be examined by mental-health experts, the results of the examinations, and even the fact that I had been examined, were covered by attorney-client privilege and would never be known to anyone outside the defense team without my consent. Last Tuesday I learned that much of this information had been made known to the government without my consent.

2. I was told that in the coming trial my attorneys would help me to pursue certain personal concerns of my own, even if these were inconsistent with my attorneys' professional concern to do what they considered to be in my best interest in a legal sense. In particular, I was led to believe that I would

not be portrayed as mentally ill without my consent. But last Tuesday I learned that I had indeed been portrayed as mentally ill without my consent.

3. When I was being urged to consent to a "12.2 b" [mental defect] defense, I was misled as to the nature of such a defense.[99] I was led to believe that it would not necessarily involve an effort to portray me as suffering from mental illness, but was only a legal device to enable a certain mental-health professional whom I know and like to tell the jury what kind of person I am. I was not informed that a 12.2 b defense would require the release of the results of mental-health examinations. Moreover, I was not informed until last Friday, November 28, of the most important results of those examinations.

4. On November 28, when I received, for the first time, copies of the briefs concerning the issue of the government's request for an opportunity to examine me, I discovered that the declarations of the defense's mental-health experts contained statements about me that I believe to be false and misleading.

I have discussed these matters with my attorneys. They admitted that they had deceived me, they expressed regret for having done so, and they promised not to do so again. But, as Your Honor can well understand, I do not find their assurances 100% convincing. I also discussed with my attorneys their future plans for my case, but I am not certain that their plans are in my best interest as I interpret it, and I found their reasoning in support of their plans unconvincing.

I therefore feel strongly the need for legal advice from some source outside my present defense team that would help me to resolve my conflicts with my own attorneys. I need such advice at the earliest possible moment, so as to avoid the risk that certain decisions will become irrevocable.

Can Your Honor help me to obtain such advice?

Theodore J. Kaczynski[100]

Kaczynski's letter did not reach the judge for a number of days.[101] As was proper, Kaczynski did not send his letter directly to the judge; he gave it to his defense lawyers who were then to pass it on to the judge.

The psychiatric report of one mental health expert hired by the defense lawyers provides inadvertent support for Kaczynski's assertion that his attorneys misled him about their intentions regarding the mental defect defense. Psychiatrist David Foster's report noted that Kaczynski thought he was being evaluated for one, narrow reason. Dr. Foster's report also observed that Kaczynski's *lawyers* had asked him to evaluate Kaczynski more generally, and to do so with an eye towards diagnosing Kaczynski as a delusionally paranoid schizophrenic.

As I have already mentioned, Kaczynski's surprise and anger during jury selection seemed genuine to observers.[102] And keeping a "difficult" client in the dark, as Kaczynski claims to have been, is consistent with one model of capital defense lawyering. The idea is to "manage" – *i.e.*, control – the client who resists following the attorneys' marching orders about trial strategy.[103] Recalcitrant clients may bend to arguments, threats, promises or other forms of pressure. Almost always, such techniques succeed in subduing the resistant client.

By keeping their client in the dark about the defense they were planning, Kaczynski's lawyers eliminated his ability to exercise the defense options available to all criminal defendants. Kaczynski could have replaced his court-appointed lawyers with a lawyer willing to present the defense Kaczynski wanted (J. Tony Serra was ready and willing to do so), or Kaczynski could have exercised his constitutional right to act as his own lawyer at trial.

As it turned out, Kaczynski later tried to exercise both of these options – but the judge ruled that Kaczynski did so too late. Burrell ignored the reason why Kaczynski was "too late," which had everything to do with the machinations of his own court-appointed attorneys who had forced him into that position and then, at a critical point in the proceedings, left him with no other alternative.

Kaczynski's Cabin Arrives – Trailed by a Media Caravan

I thought of Ted's cabin, which his lawyers had brought to Sacramento on a flatbed truck, planning to show it to the jury and ask the question: would anyone but a certifiable lunatic choose such a primitive abode? What they did not bring, of course, were the forests and rivers and mountains Kaczynski loved. [104]

William Finnegan

On December 5, 1997, the Montana cabin Kaczynski had built and lived in for over two decades arrived in Sacramento on a flatbed truck after a three day trip.[105] The driver, fearful of leaving his rolling cargo unguarded, had slept in the truck for two nights and even ate his meals there. The truck made the 1,110-miles journey driving only at night.[106] It was trailed by the media.[107]

According to the Associated Press, Kaczynski's lawyers paid to have the cabin transported to Sacramento to provide the trial jury with a window into his mind. The lawyers had claimed that it was the most tangible proof that Kaczynski was mentally ill.

The AP quoted Lead Defense Attorney Quin Denvir as saying: "The cabin symbolizes what had happened to this Ph.D. Berkeley professor and how he came to live . . . When people think about this case, they think about the cabin."[108] Jurors are often taken to view crime scenes but here, Denvir reportedly explained, "it was easier to bring the view to the jury."[109] One reporter covering the trial wrote that the prosecutors "are said to have their own weapons to counter the psychological implications of the cabin. To wit, they are likely to have videotape of the inside of the cabin before it was stripped bare by federal agents. The tape could show an incredibly planned interior space, an organization and order more intense than a crazy person could have contrived."[110]

Until it was needed at the trial, Kaczynski's Montana home would be kept at Mather Field, an old Air Force base near Sacramento.

December 17 - 22, 1997:
Kaczynski Mobilizes; A Fragile Truce

"I'll frustrate them! They shan't rob me! They shan't murder me by inches!"

Bram Stoker, *Dracula* (1897)

The media drumbeat continued to report that Kaczynski was mentally ill. *The Washington Post* reported that "the lawyers for Theodore Kaczynski have a problem, and the problem is their client. His attorneys believe Kaczynski is mad. So do at least two psychiatrists they hired."[111] The allegations of Kaczynski's madness of course influenced the way the outside world perceived and understood both Kaczynski and the coming battles between him and his attorneys. Who would favor a madman's attempt to control his defense? Who would not support Kaczynski's beleaguered defense team in their efforts to call the shots and save his life? They took on a heroic role in the media. When the centrifugal forces of the stand-off between Kaczynski and his lawyers threatened to tear the defense apart, would anyone in their right mind side with the madman?

By now, *The New York Times* was speculating about the existence of "a serious conflict between Mr. Kaczynski and his lawyers over trial strategy."[112] The day before, Judge Burrell had held an unusual closed-door meeting with Kaczynski and his counsel, without any prosecutors present. The judge said afterward that the meeting "involved matters of attorney-client confidentiality."[113]

In a December 16 letter to Kaczynski and his public defenders from Attorney J. Tony Serra, he wrote:

Dear Ted, Quin and Judy:

As everyone knows, I have been in limited contact with Mr. Kaczynski for a longish period of time. I have always represented the following to him:

1.   That I was in a position to represent him *pro bono*; I am of the same mind presently;

2.   That I view his case as one where his ideology would be the crux of the defense (not insanity; not a "whodunit").

More recently, I have represented to him that if he has come to an insurmountable impasse in his relationship with present counsel (wherein there no longer is meaningful communication between attorney and client), he should so notify the Court in a forceful manner, outlining his reasons cogently, and requesting that I substitute into the case.

Beyond the above, I have always wished you all well in the litigation and I continue to do so.

Best regards,
J. Tony Serra[114]

Kaczynski had begun writing a series of letters to the judge. The first such letter was written on December 1. Kaczynski's second letter to the judge was written on December 17. Kaczynski wrote:

Your Honor:

In order to show you that my objection to the [mental illness] defense planned by my attorneys is not frivolous or petty, I have to explain to you my feelings on this subject, which are extremely intense.

Though I object to the [mental condition] defense planned by my attorneys, the nature of that defense in itself is not the most important problem. What I find unendurable is the circumstances surrounding my attorneys' use of that defense.

During my adolescence I was subjected to frequent psychological abuse by both my parents and to bullying by my schoolmates. Perhaps for that reason, or perhaps for some other, the most horrible punishment that I can imagine is to be subjected to anything that I perceive as an injustice and to be completely helpless to defend myself against it or escape from it. And my attorneys are subjecting me to this kind of punishment in its worst form, as I will explain.

During a year and several months preceding my trial, the members of my defense team treated me kindly, they performed many services for me, they professed affection and friendship for me. Since I'd had no close friends during my adult life apart from my brother, I was very susceptible to this treatment and I soon developed strong feelings of friendship toward the members of my defense team. Some of them I even loved.

When locked up in jail, one can do very little for oneself and must depend on people on the outside to do things for one. I had nobody to help me except my defense team, and as a result I became heavily dependent on them.

I do not have a "pathological dread" of psychiatrists, but, as a matter of choice, I am averse to examination by them (unless perhaps under circumstances in which I can set the terms of the interview myself and put limits on it). The reasons are that I do not believe that science has any business probing the workings of the human mind, and that my personal ideology and that of the mental-health professions are mutually antagonistic. One may be willing to bare one's soul to a person whose ideology and values are friendly, but it is humiliating to have one's mind probed by a person whose ideology and values are alien to one's own.

Consequently, when Mr. Sowards asked me to cooperate with Dr. Foster, I was extremely reluctant to comply. Mr. Sowards, who is a very forceful and persuasive talker, subjected me to heavy pressure, which I found very difficult to resist because of my dependence on my defense team and my feelings of affection and friendship for them. But I would have resisted all the same if Mr. Sowards had not told me that the results of the examination would be covered by attorney-client privilege and would never be revealed to anyone outside the defense team without my permission. Later, in order to get me to agree to a 12.2b [mental defect] defense, Mr. Sowards misrepresented to me what that defense entailed. These and other lies, false promises, and misrepresentations were the work of Mr. Sowards, but Mr. Denvir and Ms. Clarke were aware of the most important ones.

On November 25, when I unexpectedly learned in your courtroom that my attorneys had broken the promises that Mr. Sowards had made to me, I was shocked and horrified. The people who I thought were my friends had betrayed me. They had calculatedly deceived me in order to get me to reveal my private thoughts, and then without warning they made accessible to the public the cold and heartless assessments of their experts. Assessments that were not even truthful – and I am not attempting to dispute here the *conclusions* of their experts, I am referring to false statements of *fact* and to ideas from my writings that were taken out of context and reworded to make them sound like paranoid fantasies.

To me this was a stunning blow. I felt then and still feel that it was the worst experience I ever underwent in my life. What made it so terrible was not the assessments of the experts or their public revelation, but the sense of *injustice*. I had been tricked and humiliated by people for whom I'd had warm affection and in some cases love, and with whom I'd worked hard to cooperate. It was made still worse by the fact that, in subsequent discussion with my attorneys, they admitted they had broken their promises, and they said they were sorry for it, but they said they would go ahead with their [mental condition] defense whether I liked it or not, and there was nothing I could do about it.

So there it was – a profound injustice, as I perceived it, and there was nothing I could do to defend myself against it or escape from it. This would have been extremely bad if it had been done to me by a declared enemy; but because it was done to me by people who I thought were my friends and to whom I had given my heart, it was unendurable.

That was why I wrote Your Honor my letter of December 1. I delayed giving it to you in hope of a settlement that would have eliminated the need for a trial. But that settlement has not been reached, and my lawyers again say they are going to force the [mental defect] defense on me whether I like it or not. The [mental defect] defense in itself would be endurable. What is not endurable is my helpless sense of injustice over the way I was tricked into providing the information on which it is based. I would rather die, or suffer prolonged physical torture, than have the [mental defect] defense imposed on me in this way by my present attorneys. I know that that sounds like an exaggeration, but I can assure you that it is literally true.

My feelings on this subject are so intense that there is no conceivable way I can continue to cooperate, or even communicate, with my present attorneys if they go ahead with the [mental illness] defense. There is no way I can cooperate any longer with Mr. Sowards under *any* circumstances. Ever since I learned how he deceived me I have had a strong aversion to him. That aversion has grown stronger every time I remember how eloquently and convincingly he spoke to me of "trust," knowing all the while that the promises he was making me would not be kept. By this time it makes me feel sick just to look at him.

Once again, Your Honor, my refusal to go forward under present conditions is not petty or willful. I simply *cannot continue* to cooperate with my attorneys.

Dec. 18, 1997   Theodore J. Kaczynski[115]

Kaczynski's letters addressed the growing conflicts with his lawyers over their determination to raise a mental defect defense. The letters prompted the judge to hold a series of extraordinary closed-door meetings with Kaczynski and his lawyers from which the prosecutors were excluded. Although the meetings focused on the deteriorating relationship between Kaczynski and his attorneys, they also dealt with Kaczynski's mental competency to stand trial. The competency issue and the representation issue were closely linked, at least in the minds of Kaczynski's lawyers. During the meetings, it became evident that the defense lawyers equated Kaczynski's "mental incompetence" with his resistance to their determination to portray him as mentally ill.

On December 18, there occurred an "unexpected" telephone conference session between Burrell and the defense.[116] The prosecutors did not participate in this conversation.[117]

At that December 18 hearing Lead Defense Attorney Quin Denvir spoke of "a major problem" that had come up between Kaczynski and his defense team. "You just need an opportunity to explore with Mr. Kaczynski and counsel where things are," Denvir began, "and try to figure out where to go from here. We are all very unhappy and sad to be in this position, but we are in the position."[118] Denvir continued to say: We were not requesting competency proceedings.

> As to the question of competency, we were fairly confident that Mr. Kaczynski understood the nature of the proceedings and the role of counsel and the Court and that we had been able to, up to that time, to accommodate his mental illness in preparing and presenting the defense.
>
> I don't think we can tell you, as you can see from the letter, that that is true any further. The question of the mental illness – of course, there's already evidence submitted to you in connection with the preclusion motion, and we believe that what was presented there as to the nature of his illness is, in fact, the problem. We are no longer able to accommodate that in terms of preparing and presenting a defense. As you can see, he is resistant to any defense along those lines, on that basis, [he would like to consider] new lawyers or representing himself.
>
> So I think underlying all this may be – there may be a need of the Court to revisit the issue the Court brought up. We can no longer tell you that we are able to accommodate his mental illness in representing him. But we had not planned on providing any – obviously we would be glad to brief and will have it ready if there are any particular issues, for instance, on competency. I think the Government set forth a certain amount of case authority on that issue in their letter, and I think that part of it – the question of Faretta, we're prepared to address. To the degree Mr. Kaczynski wants to represent himself, we can discuss that at the time; to the degree he's saying there's irreconcilable breakdown in the attorney-client relationship, we can discuss that to the degree you would like. But you may want to have the hearing and first explore the factual basis and then direct us where you would like to have a briefing, or if there's something you would like us to brief in the interim, we can do so. THE COURT: Well, one question centers on who controls the issue that is mentioned in the correspondence. Is that a matter that is controlled by counsel or a matter that is controlled by Mr. Kaczynski?

MR. DENVIR: And we – if you like, we would be glad to brief that overnight. My understanding of the law is that as to the 12.2(a) insanity defense, that that is controlled by the client, if the client is competent, and that is how we have been proceeding, under that understanding of the law, but as to a 12.2(b) defense, since it is consistent with a "not guilty" plea entered by the client, that is part of our authority in controlling what witnesses will be called, what evidence will be presented.

But we could certainly assemble some authority on that and have it ready for the Court hopefully first thing in the morning . . .

THE COURT: I'm now wondering whether I should delay the hearing so that I can look at the Government's authority on the competency issue and also have an opportunity to evaluate any authority you submit on the control issue.

MR. DENVIR: That may be – we would certainly, if you'd like, if you wanted to put it over to the afternoon, we could probably brief – I'll give you further authorities, maybe on competency, maybe if – I haven't reviewed the Government's letter – if it seems like it makes sense. We can certainly talk about the role of attorney and client in these decisions and we might be able to also give you some of the basic law on irreconcilable conflict.[119]

Later that day, the judge held a telephone conference with defense counsel and scheduled an *in-camera* meeting to be held at three thirty the following day. Prior to the meeting, defense counsel, as requested by the Court, filed a brief addressing the need for a hearing to determine Theodore Kaczynski's mental competency to stand trial.[120] In their letter to the judge, Kaczynski's attorneys noted that "under the applicable federal statutes, on the defendant's, the government's, or the court's own motion, the court must order a hearing to determine the defendant's competency to stand trial if there is reasonable cause to believe the defendant is incompetent."[121] Defense counsel did not request a competency examination or determination in the brief.

Kaczynski's counsel continued: "Legal competency is not merely a measure of the function of the defendant's cognitive faculties, such as those that can be quantified or measured by psychological testing. One can be intelligent and articulate, capable of goal-oriented behavior which is internally consistent and yet still have underlying psychiatric and emotional problems which cause incompetence. It is simply not sufficient that an individual has the capacity for rational understanding in the abstract if psychiatric or emotional problems prevent the application of rational faculties to the problem."[122]

At the same time, defense counsel addressed, apparently for the first time, their views on the appropriate allocation of decision-making power and responsibility between the attorneys and their client. In a footnote to their brief, counsel noted that prevailing American Bar Association standards on the control and direction of a case provide that "certain decisions relating to the conduct of the case are ultimately for the accused and others are ultimately for defense counsel . . . [The] decisions . . . to be made by the accused after full consultation with counsel include what pleas to enter, whether to accept a plea agreement, whether to waive jury trial, whether to testify in his or her own behalf; and whether to appeal." The defense counsel's brief argued that "the decision to . . . present a defense based on . . . the defendant's mental condition [as it] bears on guilt falls squarely within the category of strategic decisions that ultimately must be decided by trial counsel.[123] Thus, defense counsel argued that they, not their client (a client who was, in their opinion, mentally competent to stand trial) possessed the legitimate power to gamble with Kaczynski's life by raising a mental defect defense.

As discussed above, Kaczynski himself disagreed. This is documented in the series of letters he wrote to the judge. When Kaczynski's counsel passed these letters on to the judge, Burrell ordered the secret, two-day meeting with Kaczynski and his lawyers.

The Court explained that the closed-door meetings were necessary to "address Kaczynski's concerns with appointed counsel's representation."[124] Burrell wrote: "The purpose for conducting the *ex parte* and *in-camera* proceedings was to make an inquiry adequate for the Court to reach an informed decision about Kaczynski's concerns with appointed counsel's representation."

Another closed-door hearing was held on the afternoon of December 19.[125] This is what happened:

> THE COURT: Okay. Let the record reflect that I'm meeting *ex parte* with the parties that are present. And I'm meeting with the parties in this manner because the defense had requested such a meeting. Before I say anything else, has the status of the matter changed since I spoke to defense counsel yesterday?
>
> MS. CLARKE: Your Honor, we believe that it may change. We've had discussions with Mr. Kaczynski, and I believe he'd like to address that with the Court. There may be a need for a short delay for a final decision-making. But the status could be changing. Am I right?
>
> THE DEFENDANT: Yes. Your Honor, this afternoon my lawyers surprised me by making me what I considered to be a very generous offer,

a very big concession, and I am deciding whether I will do it by Monday morning. The concession is they will withdraw the [mental condition] defense in the guilty/not guilty phase, they would go ahead with mental health mitigating evidence in the penalty phase, and they would minimize my contact with Mr. Sowards.

THE COURT: Okay. Under law I am required to provide you with an opportunity to communicate with me, and perhaps you have just made all the communications you want to make, Mr. Kaczynski, but I'm just making the statements that I'm making to assure myself of that. And if you have made all the communications you want to make, what I'll do is arrange for a time for meeting with you on Monday, if that's what you'd like to have done.

THE DEFENDANT: That's very acceptable to me. I said everything in my letters and in what I've just said now. That's all I have to say for the moment.[126]

Yet another closed-door hearing was held three days later.[127] Again, the judge, defense counsel and Kaczynski were present. Again, no prosecutors were present. The courtroom was closed to the public.

Kaczynski accused his lawyers – particularly Gary Sowards – of deceiving him about their intent to stake his life on a mental defect defense.[128] The defense lawyers did not exactly admit to their client's allegations. They did not exactly deny them, either. They were evasive. Kaczynski was not.

In spite of this, Kaczynski and his attorneys, with the Court's assistance, reached an agreement over the mental defect defense. Kaczynski's lawyers would abandon their efforts to present expert evidence in support of a "mental disease or defect" during the guilty/innocence phase, but they reserved the right to present such evidence at the penalty phase.[129] Kaczynski's lawyers may have been displeased about this compromise, but it did delay the conflict for a while.[130]

The question of Kaczynski's mental competency was brought up once again, at least hypothetically.[131] The judge ruled that there was no evidence of Kaczynski's supposed incompetency. Burrell addressed Kaczynski directly: *"I personally have no doubt about your competency."* And to the counsel: *"I feel that Mr. Kaczynski is competent."*[132]

The following exchange occurred:

THE COURT: I feel that *Mr. Kaczynski factually understands legally everything that has occurred during the proceedings against him;* that he understands he has to make choices. One of the choices that he apparently has made is *the abandonment of the [mental defect] defense.* That abandonment may very well end up with a guilty verdict in this case. You understand that?

THE DEFENDANT: Yes, sir.

THE COURT: *But based upon the intelligent approach he has used in dealing with the issue, the eloquent manner in which he has voiced his opinions, it just seems clear to me that he would rather risk death than to assert that as a defense.* Not to say that that's a necessary result . . .

THE DEFENDANT: (Nods head up and down.)

THE COURT: . . . because you would have to go to the sentencing phase. But it just seems that the only way he would have a chance of avoiding a guilt verdict . . . would be to assert the [mental defect] defense. But he's willing to give that up.

THE DEFENDANT: Yes. Yes, sir.

THE COURT: But I don't see his abandonment of that defense as something that evidences incompetence.[133]

Regarding Kaczynski's ability to "understand the nature and consequences" of the trial proceedings – the core of mental competency to stand trial – Kaczynski's lead defense counsel said, "I don't think there's any doubt about that."[134] The lawyer should have added, "so long as Kaczynski follows our marching orders." Defense counsel explained what they meant when they suggested, always hypothetically, that Kaczynski might possibly be incompetent. As Denvir explained: "Our feeling . . . is that any discussion of competency was merely raised in the context of what Kaczynski wanted to do in representing himself. I think that's what raised the question . . . So any questions of competency were raised only on the hypothetical that he was going to seek to have us discharged and represent himself."[135]

The prosecutor put it more accurately, "the defense argument goes something like this: that in part the defendant is not competent, or they question his competence, because he refuses to go along with the defense that they have chosen. They have kind of equated his refusal with [in]competence."[136]

As the prosecution implied, this circular reasoning did not seem right, and it wasn't. Professor Richard Bonnie, of the University of Virginia, is correct that "disagreement with counsel is not, in itself, evidence of incompetence. Counsel's advice may . . . fail to take adequate account of the defendant's values and preferences . . . [but] unless the defendant is decisionally incompetent, his preferences bind the attorney."[137] In fact, "the purpose of the competence requirement is to establish the minimum conditions for autonomous participation. From this standpoint, the necessary conditions are ordinarily satisfied if the client is aware that she has the prerogative to decline the attorney's advice, and is able to understand the nature and consequences of the decision."[138]

The transcript of this hearing demonstrates that the negotiated truce between Kaczynski and his lawyers was tentative and provisional. The judge said: "Why don't we try it this way first, to see if it works. And if you have difficulty with it, I think you know how to reach me."

Thus, two days of closed-door meetings addressing Kaczynski's competency and his relationship with his attorneys had produced a fragile truce. At the guilt/innocence phase of trial, Kaczynski's lawyers would not present expert evidence that Kaczynski was mentally ill; for this reason Kaczynski would continue with those lawyers. Also, because Kaczynski had dropped his bid to fire his attorneys, they would not challenge Kaczynski's competency to stand trial.

December 23, 1997 to January 4, 1998: The Truce Collapses

> If Jesus had lawyers, I'm sure they said, "Please keep your mouth shut when they ask you if you're the son of God." [139]
>
> Defense Attorney Ronald L. Kuby (1998)

The judge explained his understanding of the December 22 agreement and its subsequent disintegration as follows: "After lengthy discussions in *ex parte, in-camera* proceedings, Kaczynski and his trial counsel made an agreement that he would retain current trial counsel and that his trial counsel would withdraw the [previously filed] notice and not present expert testimony in the guilt phase of the trial." Kaczynski and his attorneys then proceeded amicably until he learned that defense counsel would present non-expert evidence relevant to his mental status at the guilt phase of the trial. A dispute then ensued as to whether it was understood during the December 22 hearing that Kaczynski's attorneys would be presenting non-expert mental status evidence at the guilt phase of trial." [140]

On December 23, the judge ordered defense counsel to file, within ten calendar days, any "notice" that the defense "intends to rely on mental health expert testimony in the sentencing phase of the trial." [141] The notice must contain a "statement evincing whether [the defense] intends to rely on mental health expert testimony to demonstrate the existence of mitigating factors." [142] They were to accompany this notice with a list of all defense experts expected to testify and a description of the substance of their testimony.

On December 29, 1997, defense counsel withdrew its notice stating their intent to introduce expert testimony that Kaczynski suffered from a mental disease or disorder. [143] On the same day, *The New York Times* reported that Kaczynski had offered to plead guilty in exchange for avoiding the death penalty. [144] However, Kaczynski's plea offer came with strings attached: He insisted on reserving the right to appeal the judge's ruling that upheld the legality of the search of his Montana cabin. The plea was rejected by Attorney General Janet Reno's death penalty review committee. [145]

The government's rejection of Kaczynski's conditional plea offer reportedly left Kaczynski's brother David "surprised and distraught."[146]

On the afternoon of December 31, 1997, the judge convened a hearing to explore issues concerning Kaczynski's representation and mental competency to stand trial. The prosecutors and defense counsel were present at this hearing in open court. Kaczynski was not. Judy Clarke observed in passing that Kaczynski's "presence" at the hearing had "been waived."[147]

At the afternoon hearing, Lead Defense Attorney Denvir recounted that the earlier, *ex parte, in-camera* proceedings "were triggered by a letter to the Court or series of letters to the Court from Mr. Kaczynski regarding attorney-client matters."[148] Attorney Denvir explained:

> What I want to point out is that Mr. Kaczynski has court-appointed attorneys. If Mr. Kaczynski were able to retain his own attorneys and he had some concerns about those attorneys that he wanted addressed, he would address those directly to those attorneys and they would be resolved between those two parties. The fact that he is unable to hire his own attorneys means that the court has appointed counsel, and so when there are concerns he must address them to the Court. And that is exactly what he is doing. . . . Now, in the course of these communications, there was a hypothetical question that was intertwined regarding competency . . . it was strictly a hypothetical question. It was not presented to the Court for resolution. The Court did not have to resolve the matter. But it was intertwined in those attorney-client matters . . . It's unfortunate that the Court has to deal with them, but the court has to deal with them. . . . questions of attorney-client communications; [and] trial strategy; and they are simply matters that should remain sealed while this trial is pending. . . . The court indicated . . . that its involvement was strictly to assist with communication difficulties between attorney and client."[149]

The letters the Court had received from Kaczynski presented Judge Garland Burrell with a "conundrum": "Two issues were weighty on my mind as I reflected on that concern. One issue is the 'self-representation' problem. If the situation ever presented itself where I would have to advise your client or any criminal defendant of the [self-representation] admonitions, I think that those admonitions [would have to be] given in public, not in a closed proceeding. And the other problem was the competency question. Although I personally have never had difficulty with the defendant's competency, I still feel obligated to assure myself that no one else has difficulty with his competency. That occurred."[150]

The truce didn't last, probably couldn't last, given the fundamentally antithetical positions taken by Kaczynski and his lawyers. Four days after the lawyers' abandonment of plans to raise a mental defect defense during the first phase of Kaczynski's bifurcated trial, his lawyers notified the prosecution that if Kaczynski was convicted, they would "try to spare him a death sentence by arguing in the penalty phase that he is mentally ill."[151] Further, defense counsel told the prosecution informally that they intended to introduce non-expert, lay testimony, at the guilt phase of trial, to state the case for Kaczynski's mental illness. For example, the defense might show the jury photographs of Kaczynski "before and after" he became a recluse hermit in the wilds of Montana. Kaczynski did not learn of these developments until the evening of Sunday, January 4, the night before the trial was scheduled to begin.

Kaczynski's lawyers had dropped their bid to introduce expert evidence about Kaczynski's mental illness during the first phase of Kaczynski's trial, but nothing stopped them from presenting non-expert evidence. The stage was set for another confrontation between Kaczynski and his counsel.

January 5 and 6, 1998:
Kaczynski Fires Lawyers

[The judge] decided that my attorneys had the legal right to force their defense on me over my objections; that it was too late for me to replace my attorneys with a certain distinguished attorney who had offered to represent me and had stated his intention to use a defense not based on any supposed mental illness; and that it was too late for me to demand the right to act as my own attorney.[152]

Theodore Kaczynski

The drama began the instant Kaczynski entered the courtroom on what had been scheduled as the opening day of Theodore Kaczynski's capital murder trial. There, in the front row, with his arm draped around their eighty-year-old mother Wanda, was Ted's brother David. *The Washington Post* reported that "it is believed to be the first time the two brothers have been face-to-face since David alerted the FBI two years ago that his brother might be the elusive Unabomber." The mother held hands with the brother and wept, as Ted sat only a few feet away, refusing to acknowledge them.[153]

Also present, seated directly behind the prosecution table, were two of the surviving Unabomber victims: Charles Epstein and David Gelernter. David Gelernter, a Yale computer sciences professor, had been outspoken in his views that Kaczynski was an evil coward who deserved to die.[154]

As soon as the judge took the bench to begin the trial, Kaczynski addressed him.[155] Kaczynski, dressed in a bulky knit sweater and blue pants, looked "more like an aging grad student . . . than the wild-haired hermit who was arrested nearly two years ago," wrote one observer.[156] Kaczynski clutched an envelope as he spoke. "Your honor, before these proceedings begin, I would like to revisit the issue of my relations with my attorneys. It's very important."[157]

The judge ushered Kaczynski and his lawyers into his chambers for meetings that dragged on so long that the jurors were sent home.[158] Kaczynski and his counsel met with the judge in closed session for the next four and a half hours. *The New York Times* observed that "it was clear from the defense lawyers' remarks, in a brief courtroom session after the closed door proceeding, that Mr. Kaczynski was continuing to rebel against his lawyers' efforts to portray him as insane."[159]

According to the redacted version of the meeting, it was here that the question of Attorney J. Tony Serra's taking over Kaczynski's defense was raised.[160] Serra had contacted Kaczynski shortly after his arrest.[161] Serra, the real-life inspiration of the 1989 movie *The True Believer*, starring James Woods, is a long-time radical lawyer known for his unpopular clients, his ponytail and his Salvation Army suits.[162] Serra's clients have included both the Hell's Angels and Black Panthers. He also successfully represented two inmates on death row.[163] According to news reports, Serra's resume details the career of a man who is a self-styled legal "warrior" intent on "defending society's outcasts." The 1960s, in Serra's estimation, constituted the "golden age of law."[164]

The judge's question was simple: "What is your goal, Mr. Kaczynski, your ultimate goal as far as Mr. Serra is concerned?"[165] Kaczynski's reply was redacted, what remains of his response was: "for attorney-client privilege and representation matters."[166] The judge noted that one issue on the table "is a representation issue focused on a change of counsel – possible change of counsel – at this stage of the proceeding . . . What I think I should do is maybe appoint another lawyer to assist Mr. Kaczynski with what he has characterized as conflict-type issues. I'm saying that in front of you. And then that way he would have a lawyer to communicate with the Court on these types of issues. He could communicate either personally or through a lawyer . . . I don't foresee that the communications that Mr. Kaczynski has just related should cause a breakdown in the attorney-client relationship."[167]

"To Mr. Kaczynski," replied Denvir, "it *has* caused [a breakdown] or could . . . if it's confirmed. I think that's what he may be conveying to you . . . Mr. Kaczynski . . . would like to know whether Mr. Serra would in fact be available to represent him, and [whether] the Court might consider calling Mr. Serra or having us call him to see if he could make himself available on short notice to resolve that question for Mr. Kaczynski."[168]

The judge asked: "Do you want me to communicate with Mr. Serra's office, Mr. Kaczynski, as your attorney has indicated?"

"I think that would be a very good idea," was Kaczynski's response.

Denvir then repeated the question, "Would you like that? Would that be helpful?" Kaczynski responded, "Yes, it would."[169]

The Court then held a telephone conversation off the record, from which the judge returned to say, "His office doesn't open until around nine. The message center that receives messages for the office didn't have a pager number or any other means of communicating with the people in the office."[170]

While waiting for Serra's office to open, the Court asked Judy Clarke what she thought might happen were he to reach Mr. Serra. "Either Tony Serra [can] come over," Clarke replied, "and meet with Ted and decide whether he could take over the case, [or you could appoint] another lawyer to talk to Mr. Serra [and] Ted . . . to straighten out . . . today's problem. And, you know, I hate to suggest it, but it seems to me, given the state of our affairs right now, maybe we need to take a couple days and see if the Court can find a very skilled and experienced practitioner who can get involved . . . It may not be resolved by a telephone call with Mr. Serra. It may take someone to talk to Mr. Serra and to talk to Ted."[171]

"It's not clear to me, your honor, how that would be more advantageous than me talking to Mr. Serra directly," Kaczynski inserted.[172]

"It would just depend on whether he's available," was Clarke's response, to which Kaczynski conceded, "I see. In that case, I think Ms. Clarke's idea is good and I would agree."[173]

Denvir then implied that the problem between Kaczynski and his lawyers wasn't simply a failure to communicate. It was more basic than that. "I think without going into a lot of detail about it . . . that what you've termed the communication problem may be a much deeper one that goes into the representation problem. I think that Mr. Kaczynski's feelings may be that there's a much more fundamental breakdown in the attorney-client relationship. I'm not sure of that . . ."

Kaczynski interrupted at this point. His answer was an unequivocal "Yes."[174]

Some time later, the Court told Kaczynski: "You have fine lawyers. I've seen a lot of lawyers appear in front of me in criminal cases . . ."

"Your honor, I do not question my attorneys' abilities."

Kaczynski and his lawyers were then asked whether they had a problem with the judge calling in a new lawyer.

"I think it would be very helpful," Denvir replied, "I think Ted would like that".

Kaczynski seconded Denvir's supposition, "I think that would be good."[175]

The above developments seriously threatened to delay the proceedings. "I'm assuming that when I communicate with Mr. Serra's office, it's possible that this matter could be resolved and we could proceed on with the trial. . . ." Judge Burrell had said.

"I don't think it's likely, Kaczynski responded, "that the matter can be resolved that easily. *My lawyers have suggested that I should make it clear to you what I want. And what I'm looking for is a change of counsel.*"[176]

Burrell managed to contact a secretary in Serra's office during the interim. She did not know if Serra would be coming in, and thought he might be away on vacation. Later, the court received a message from Serra's office. Burrell described it as follows: "Zenia Gilg, an attorney from Tony Serra's office, called at 9:40 am. She said Mr. Serra is in Tunia, and they're not sure exactly when he'll be back – today, tomorrow or the day after tomorrow. She knows that he was interested in the case but had a conflict with the Federal Defender's Office and unequivocally withdrew his offer to represent Mr. Kaczynski because of the conflict."[177]

Burrell then suggested another attorney to represent Kaczynski in his dealings with his current counsel and with the Court. Attorney Kevin Clymo arrived, met with the group, and then privately with Kaczynski.

"In my conversations with Mr. Kaczynski," Clymo reported, "I do not get the impression that he has a desire to represent himself . . . that's not what I pick up from my conversations with Mr. Kaczynski. [He has] a communication issue . . . The question would be [whether] Mr. Kaczynski goes forward with his lawyers or states that he has a conflict with those lawyers." Kaczynski explained: ". . . [t]he possibility of changing my representation or representing myself is still very, very nebulous. There's still no definite intention there. It's just a possibility that may arise after present discussions continue. So I don't think change of counsel is yet the issue, though it may become an issue."[178]

While Kaczynski was out of the room, the judge revisited the competency issue with Defense Attorneys Denvir and Clarke, saying "it's my discernment that you had previously indicated that if Mr. Kaczynski took a position that frustrated the defense you were going to assert on his behalf, that maybe that would indicate the need for a competency hearing. And I'm assuming, based on everything I heard, that Mr. Kaczynski may not agree with the defense you are asserting."

"There's the possibility," Denvir returned, "in my mind at least, of the need for a competency hearing, but I'm not in a position, I don't think we are, to tell the court that it's necessary at this time. We may know better after we explore the communication questions . . . with Mr. Clymo and Mr. Kaczynski . . ."[179]

Attorney Clymo first reported that he was making progress, but needed more time. He then suggested without further ado that, "with regard to these proceedings in open court . . . it would be appropriate to continue to have Ms. Clarke and Mr. Quin [Denvir] represent Mr. Kaczynski's interest with the government in public on the record. Is that all right with you?"

Kaczynski: "That's agreeable to me."[180]

The judge also ruled on a pending prosecution motion to preclude Kaczynski from introducing non-expert testimony to show that he had a mental defect.[181] Burrell denied the government's motion.[182] The judge's order implied that Kaczynski's attorneys would be allowed, over their client's vehement objection, to rely on non-expert testimony to establish that Kaczynski suffered from a mental defect.

The transcripts of the closed-door meetings are disjointed, confusing and incomplete. The meetings themselves appear to have been fairly free-form affairs. It is impossible for an outsider to tell, simply from the transcripts, precisely what occurred during those lengthy closed-door sessions.

By parsing language from the transcripts, one could construct a plausible argument that Kaczynski had agreed to go to trial with his current counsel in control of the defense. One could also construct an equally plausible case that Kaczynski had put the Court and his lawyers on notice that their control of his defense was unacceptable.

However, I think what happened during the closed-door meetings was more complicated. I think that Kaczynski, his lawyers and Judge Burrell were all honestly seeking a compromise that would allow the trial to proceed. They all came away from the meetings with very different perspectives about what had been settled during those meetings. When subsequent events exposed the fault-lines in those rival interpretations, the Unabomber defense team fell apart.

January 7, 1998: Judge "Unfires" Lawyers; Kaczynski Attempts Suicide

There is but one truly serious philosophical problem, and that is suicide.[183]

Albert Camus, *The Myth of Sisyphus*

The pressure to acquiesce to what the lawyers and judge wanted Kaczynski to do must have been intense. He was alone. He was isolated. He was a prisoner. He was vulnerable. He must have found it all but impossible to steel his resolve against his lawyers and the judge who had appointed them as counsel.

Kaczynski was beginning to show signs of strain. During the closed-door meetings with the judge on January 7, Kaczynski told the court he was simply too tired to argue his own case and had no choice but to continue with his lawyers.[184] "Your honor," Kaczynski had said, "if this had happened a year and a half ago, I would probably have elected to represent myself. Now, after a year and a half with this, I'm too tired and I really don't want to take on such a difficult task."[185]

At the conclusion of this, the second day of closed-door meetings, Kaczynski stated in open court, for the first time, that he did not want his lawyers to "pursue a mental health defense."[186] But the judge told Kaczynski several times that his attorneys were "in control" of his case and that they would be allowed to introduce non-expert testimony about Kaczynski's alleged mental state.[187]

Although Judge Burrell announced in open court that Kaczynski had agreed to proceed with his present lawyers, the judge also explained that he had received a communication from J. Tony Serra, who had offered to represent Kaczynski for free.[188] According to a note which Serra had written, "If he is successful in recusing his present attorneys, I'm willing to serve on his behalf," and "I wish him well whatever way it goes."[189] According to *The Washington Post*, Serra was en route to Hawaii when the judge read his letter at the trial. [190]

In open court, Kaczynski then told the judge, "I think I would like to be represented by [Serra] . . . since he is not going to pursue a mental health defense."[191] Kaczynski added that Serra would be able to meet with him next week, but conceded that "he would need considerable time to prepare."[192]

Treating Kaczynski's request as a motion to substitute his present counsel with Serra, Burrell told Kaczynski, "the motion is denied." The judge reiterated his prior rulings that it was too late for Kaczynski to change lawyers, reminding him that a jury had been selected, witnesses were ready to go and the trial was about to begin.[193] *The Washington Post* described Kaczynski's reaction: "The alleged Unabomber looked at the judge for an instant, and then began rapidly writing on his legal pads." During the afternoon proceedings in open court, Kaczynski was "alternatively scribbling on his legal pads, shoving notes at his attorneys, or whispering animatedly at them. His brother, David and mother, Wanda, attended the session. But Kaczynski did not look at them."[194]

The prosecution had mobilized. They felt it was necessary to educate Judge Burrell about the governing law. The prosecution filed an excellent brief arguing that the decision to pursue or forego a particular line of defense – such as the defense based on a possible mental disease or defect – belongs to the defendant. It stated in simple terms that, absent a judicial finding that the defendant is incapable of making a competent decision, there was no reason that defense counsel should not respect their client's wishes in this regard.[195]

The prosecution argued that because the Sixth Amendment to the Constitution grants to the accused personally the right to raise his defense, "the government believes that the decision to forego a legally available defense rests with the defendant," rather than with the attorney for the defendant, explaining that:

> any absence of a finding that the defendant is [mentally] incompetent, which defense counsel and the court have expressly and repeatedly rejected, the government sees no reason why the defendant cannot decide whether to pursue a mental defect defense during both the guilt and penalty phases of trial, as long as he is fully advised as to the wisdom of doing so and the potential consequences of ignoring his attorneys' advice. Once the defendant makes a knowing and intelligent decision concerning the defense he wishes to pursue, however, the Government sees no reason why current counsel cannot continue to represent him. Aside from differences over the mental defect defense, there can be no doubt that counsel has been able to represent the defendant vigorously. Indeed, whatever the disagreement between the defendant and his counsel, it is unlikely that substitute counsel could put on a more effective defense or more vigorously represent the defendant."[196]

The inexorable judge was unmoved. Burrell reiterated to Kaczynski that counsel controlled "major strategic decisions," including the decision whether to put on non-expert mental health testimony. Kaczynski became fatalistic, "I've become aware that legally I have to accept those decisions whether I like them or not."[197]

I believe that the prosecution's brief was correct. Burrell's rulings were wrong, although not entirely implausible under the law. What was missing from the judge's reasoning was his failure to ask whether, during the months leading up to jury selection, Kaczynski's lawyers kept him in the dark about the defense they had determined to raise. If this had not been the case, then it was plausible for the Court to refuse Kaczynski's request on the eve of trial. But, if the lawyers had misled their client as he asserted, then the fairest thing would be either (1) to require the lawyers to follow their mentally competent client's decisions about defense strategy, or (2) to dismiss the jury, delay the trial and replace Kaczynski's attorneys with counsel that was more compatible with Kaczynski's values and beliefs.[198] Since delay appeared out of the question for this relentless judge, the most reasonable option was to ask Kaczynski and his lawyers my favorite two questions: What did Theodore Kaczynski know about his lawyers' plans, and when did he know it? If the judge ever asked these questions, it does not appear on the transcripts of the public court records.

By the end of that tedious first day, Theodore Kaczynski must have been in a very bleak mood. In this trial for his life, the only allies in the courtroom – his lawyers – had kept him uninformed and misled him. Now, the judge had authorized his lawyers to raise the issue of mental defect anyway, regardless of Kaczynski's wishes. Firing his lawyers and representing himself was still an option, but for the legally unschooled Kaczynski it must have been a terrifying one. I do not believe that he ever wanted to represent himself. He wanted his lawyers to provide the assistance of counsel guaranteed by the Constitution. Judge Burrell didn't seem to want Kaczynski to represent himself, although the law gave him the right to do so. The Court was willing to deny Kaczynski that right – so there was nothing he could do to prevent his attorneys from portraying him as a raving lunatic.

Sometime during the night of January 7, Theodore Kaczynski tried to kill himself in his jail cell by asphyxiating himself with the elastic of his underpants. Kaczynski's attempted suicide seemed to many observers the final confirmation of his mental illness.[199] I don't think so. Consider it from Kaczynski's point of view. Under the circumstances, suicide was the only rational option open to him. He was utterly alone. He felt betrayed by his lawyers who kept him in the dark until it was too late for him to replace them or to defend himself at trial without a lawyer.[200] The judge was poised to refuse his constitutional right to fire those lawyers and represent himself. For the next few months, he would have to sit in court and listen to his own lawyers build the case that he was mentally ill – and there was absolutely no way he could stop it.

Except for suicide.

Kaczynski's suicide also would have been an act of communication, as Lydia Eccles has pointed out – an act of communication directed at his lawyers.[201] Kaczynski has claimed that his defense counsel made it reasonably clear that suicide was an acceptable option if he found life imprisonment unacceptable. The message implied by his suicide would have been blunt: Your defense is unacceptable.

Kaczynski's lawyers never got the message. Their determination to represent Kaczynski as a schizophrenic remained undeterred.

I followed the meltdown of the Kaczynski defense from my home in Vermont, far away from the Unabomber trial in Sacramento. I generally do not like to second-guess the tactical decisions made by trial lawyers in capital cases (especially high profile capital cases), particularly when I respect the lawyers. The parties in question always know facts about their case that can't be known by outside observers or commentators. Still, it seemed to me that Kaczynski's lawyers were denying their client his day in court.

This prompted me to do something I had never done. I published op-ed pieces arguing that Theodore Kaczynski was being denied his day in court in the *Rutland Herald* and later in *The National Law Journal*.[202] I was pretty sure at the time that I understood why Kaczynski's attorneys had seized control of his defense. They were trying to save his life – from himself, if necessary. But, it seemed to me that by saving his body by any means necessary, his well-intentioned lawyers were simultaneously destroying his life and his life's work, which seemed wrong even in the light of such a morally fraught body of work.

From my far-off observation perch in Vermont, I wondered who would crack first. I didn't think Kaczynski would. He had already sacrificed so much for his political ideology, and I didn't see him giving it all up now to possibly save his life on a mental defect defense that he abhorred. And, given that Kaczynski was obviously competent to stand trial, I couldn't see Kaczynski's lawyers abandoning him to represent himself instead of allowing him to control his own defense. Yet, as the Unabomber non-trial entered its next level of weirdness, that's exactly what his lawyers tried to do.

January 8, 1998: All Hell Breaks Loose

[For a state to] hale a person into its criminal courts, and there to force a lawyer upon him, even when he insists he wants to conduct his own defense [would be] ... to imprison him in his privilege and call it a Constitution. [203]

U.S. Supreme Court (1975)

Over the weeks leading up to the trial, Kaczynski's choices had been narrowing progressively. Now, he had only one realistic option to avoid the mental defect defense. He would have to fire his lawyers and represent himself. Kaczynski clearly did not want to act as his own attorney. He wanted the assistance of counsel in presenting an ideological defense to his jury as a defense against capital punishment. But, if representing himself was the only way to avoid a mental defect defense, he would do it. Kaczynski understood correctly that the law allowed him to do this. In this respect, he understood the law better than Burrell.

On the morning of January 8, Defense Attorneys Denvir and Clarke came to meet with Kaczynski in the holding cell outside the courtroom, just before the session was to begin.

When court resumed at eight in the morning, neither Judge Burrell nor any of the lawyers were aware of the suicide attempt. No mention was made of it during the morning's proceedings. The judge was to hear opening statements, and the prosecutors were preparing to lead. The judge entered the courtroom and assumed the bench. The trial was finally ready to start.

Judy Clarke unexpectedly stood to addressed the Court. She told the judge that her client wanted to represent himself, and that he was ready to proceed immediately.[204]

Clarke continued, explaining that her client's "very heartfelt reaction to the mental defect defense, a situation which he simply cannot endure" made this course of action necessary. Clarke alleged that Kaczynski had "lived with this fear that he would be described as mentally ill," for the majority of his life.[205]

As for the defense lawyers, Clarke explained that they could not, in good faith to their ethical responsibilities, continue as Kaczynski's attorneys without raising a mental defect defense.[206] The lawyers did not explain how their ethical duties allowed them to abandon a capital client on the day of trial – a client they had represented for a year and a half, a client who asserts that his counsel misled him by keeping important information from him regarding their intentions until it was too late for him to do anything *other* than represent himself.

What had happened was really quite simple. There had been a little game of chicken, and Kaczynski's lawyers had counted on him to flinch. But he didn't. When Clarke informed the judge that Kaczynski had insisted on representing himself, Kaczynski's mother Wanda wept, and his brother David was visibly shaken.[207]

Perhaps Kaczynski's lawyers were gambling that Burrell would not allow them to withdraw at this late date – that the judge would, in other words, deny their client his constitutional right to self-representation. Burrell had already ruled that the lawyers, and not the client, controlled all aspects of the defense. Good defense lawyers know their judges, and these were two very good defense lawyers. They might well have been counting on the possibility that the judge would ignore the law and refuse to allow Kaczynski to represent himself at the trial.

Such a ruling would have been attractive to Denvir and Clarke – indeed, it would have given their client an insurance policy of sorts. The lawyers would remain on the case and in control of the defense. If their mental defect defense worked, and Kaczynski's jury voted to spare his life, he would be sentenced to life imprisonment. If it failed, and the jury sentenced Kaczynski to death, the judge's erroneous ruling (that Kaczynski did not have a right to self-representation) would require the appellate courts to throw out Kaczynski's conviction and order a whole new trial. Kaczynski would get a second bite at the apple. They would have a clear conscience. Either way the defense would have won, but day after day in court, Kaczynski would be forced to listen to his own lawyers portray him as a paranoid schizophrenic.

This entire scenario depends, of course, on the judge's willingness to disregard the law and deny Kaczynski his constitutional right to self-representation. As it turned out, the judge was perfectly willing to do so, although not quite yet.

Kaczynski's lawyer stressed again and again to Burrell that Kaczynski was ready to proceed *"without any delay."*[208] Clarke emphasized: "Mr. Kaczynski has advised us he is ready to proceed [as his own lawyer] today. His request to proceed on his own behalf would not delay the trial . . . He is prepared in the sense that he feels he has no choice [but] to go forward today. *He is not asking for any delay.*"[209] Clarke continued, as though she was talking to a brick wall, "I know the timing is a question when a delay is involved. But that is not his position. His position is he will go forward on his own behalf . . . He is prepared. *He is not asking, as the prosecution is, for any delay.*"[210]

I belabor this point – that Kaczynski was not seeking any delay of his trial – because it is extremely important. As subsequent events show, Burrell didn't get it. The judge simply ruled that Kaczynski's mental competency to stand trial and to represent himself would have to be examined and decided.[211] The trial would be delayed, yet again.

Burrell's impatience was palpable. One observer noted that the judge sounded "angry."[212] The Court said Kaczynski "categorically" stated that he did not want to represent himself – a bit of an overstatement, and one that understandably left Kaczynski "shaking his head in disagreement."[213] Then the judge seemed to soften, acknowledging that he may have forced Kaczynski into this problematic situation by ruling that he could not prevent his lawyers from presenting a mental defect defense.[214]

The judge threatened to send Kaczynski to a mental institution for thirty days of observation unless he cooperated with the psychiatric exam. Kaczynski capitulated. The judge's anger and the impact of his actions could not have been lost on Kaczynski. One need not be paranoid to understand what was going on: The judge was angry at Kaczynski for exercising his constitutional right to represent himself. None of the lawyers in the case seriously believed that Kaczynski was even arguably incompetent to stand trial.

Why, then, did Burrell order another delay in the trial for a psychiatric examination that was unneeded? I can't read the judge's mind. But, I have my suspicions. My guess is that he did it to buy himself some time. Kaczynski's invocation of his right to self-representation had left Burrell nonplused. It should have been an easy call: Kaczynski had invoked his right, and he was ready to proceed with the trial "without any delay" (i.e., immediately). The judge should have simply granted Kaczynski's request and let the trial begin. That was the *least* he could do. Remember, there was still Serra. Burrell could, and probably *should* have dismissed the jury and given Kaczynski – or J. Tony Serra – time to prepare a defense that was acceptable to Kaczynski, which he was guaranteed him by the Constitution. However this option, was unacceptable to the judge, who seemed almost obsessed with the need to go forward with this particular jury. He was oblivious to the fact that his rulings had made any verdict of guilty by that jury extremely vulnerable to reversal by an appellate court which would mean a retrial with a new jury.

The judge appeared determined to search until he found a plausible ground for preventing Kaczynski to serve as his own lawyer; this much was evident from his fixation on not "delaying" the trial. William Finnegan suggested a possible explanation. Finnegan hypothesized that Kaczynski's judge was haunted by the experience of Judge Lance Ito during the O.J. Simpson trial, and he was determined not to allow the Unabomber trial to become a circus.[215] Honoring Kaczynski's right to self-representation – and his right to put on an ideological defense – would have risked bringing upon this judge the wrath that had been visited upon Judge Ito.

In short, Kaczynski's judge was determined to be an anti-Ito. Burrell saw the risk that his rulings would lace the trial record with errors so egregious that an appellate court would be forced to throw out any guilty verdict that the jury might produce, and so order a retrial. He was adamant that the proceedings in *his* trial court would be dignified. The defense lawyers would be empowered in their efforts to firmly control their potentially disruptive client. Burrell played the part of an impresario – for this judge, the show must go on; it must go on without delay and it must go on with decorum – even if the cost of such decorum was a mistrial.

So, Burrell needed time to think. He needed a time-out from the trial to come up with a credible reason for denying Kaczynski his constitutional right to represent himself – preferably some reason that could be blamed on Kaczynski himself, and not the attorneys he had appointed as his counsel.

Bear in mind that Kaczynski's lawyers were still unaware of the suicide attempt hours earlier. Around half-an-hour after court opened, Defense Attorney Judy Clarke noticed a red mark on Kaczynski's neck. That was the first inkling the defense had of the botched suicide attempt.

When Burrell ordered Kaczynski to undergo the psychiatric evaluation, he was unaware that Kaczynski had attempted suicide.[216] After Court was recessed, a Sacramento sheriff's department announced that the U.S. Marshals reported a red welt on Kaczynski's neck. In addition, he arrived at the federal courthouse without his underwear. Every day before the court sessions began, Kaczynski changed from his jail uniform into civilian clothes. Every morning he was strip-searched.

An initial search of Kaczynski's jail cell did not disclose the missing underwear, and so authorities believed he had flushed them down the toilet.[217] In a second search, the underwear was found inside a smaller plastic bag inside Kaczynski's trash can.[218] The sheriff's department spokesman announced that, "the underwear appeared to be stretched."[219] Until the suicide attempt, Kaczynski had reportedly been a "model prisoner."[220]

Outside the courtroom, reporters asked Kaczynski's lawyers why he was now willing to cooperate with psychiatric testing. Lead Defense Attorney Quin Denvir's answer was laconic: "He has no choice."[221] What Denvir neglected to say was that his lawyers had deprived him of any other choice.

January 9, 1998: Enter Dr. Johnson

The irony regarding the paternalism of both the lawyers and the psychiatrists cannot be comprehended, nor Kaczynski's reaction understood, unless we recognize the manner in which the Unabomber manifesto explicitly attacked the kind of "benevolent control" they exercised to suppress and discredit him. [222]

Lydia Eccles

On the afternoon of January 9, the judge gathered the parties together to see if they would agree to allow "a psychiatrist to conduct a study and examination of Mr. Kaczynski to determine his competency to stand trial."[223] The Court said that the examination would occur in the Sacramento County Jail, but only if Kaczynski cooperated. "If he's not going to cooperate," Burrell had warned, "I will fly him to a psychiatric institution immediately."[224]

Kaczynski would be examined by North Carolina prison psychiatrist Dr. Sally Johnson, who had tested the competency of John Hinckley, the man who had attempted to assassinate President Ronald Reagan. Dr. Johnson planned to spend five days with Kaczynski, evaluating the records in his case and writing a report, which was to be sealed.

The Court noted that Dr. Johnson's report would include Kaczynski's medical "history and present symptoms . . . description of the tests employed and their results . . . the examiner's findings, [and] the examiner's opinions as to diagnosis, prognosis and whether the [defendant] is suffering from a mental disease or defect rendering him mentally incompetent to the extent that he is unable to understand the nature and consequences of the proceedings against him or to assist properly in his defense."[225] Dr. Johnson's report would be due by seven in the evening on the sixteenth.

On the same day, Burrell appeared to retro-justify his order that Kaczynski undergo psychiatric examination. The Court made it clear that, when he held up the trial for the psychiatric examination, he had not known of Kaczynski's suicide attempt only hours earlier. "After we completed all court proceedings yesterday," Burrell was to announce, "the United States Marshal personnel informed me [of] an allegation that Mr. Kaczynski attempted suicide . . . I knew nothing about the allegations when we were proceeding yesterday."[226] A suicide attempt, the Court reasoned, would be "significant to a determination of the competency issue."[227]

The fact remains, however, that at the time he ordered the competency examination Burrell was trying to quash Kaczynski's invocation of his right to self-representation. Burrell equated Kaczynski's resistance to his counsel's intended defense – resistance that culminated in his coerced decision to represent himself – with possible mental incompetency to stand trial.

At the same time, the Court issued an order stating that "the gist of the conflict between Kaczynski and his counsel relates to whether a mental status defense should be asserted along with communications attendant to that defense."[228] The Court found that "while this conflict presented problems, it [had] not resulted in a total lack of communication."[229] The court explained that the substitution of J. Tony Serra would "be inappropriate in the circumstances" because Kaczynski's request for Mr. Serra was untimely. Furthermore, Kaczynski's conflict with current counsel was not "so great that it [would] result in a total lack of communication, thereby preventing an adequate defense."[230]

The Court appeared to be steam-rollering Kaczynski – in its attempt to appear efficient and in control. The judge already noted that "a lengthy continuance would be required just to allow Serra to coordinate his obligations to his many clients."[231] And the show must go on.

The New York Times' reporter, William Glaberson, and later Judge Burrell, made clear whom they felt was to blame for the disruption of the trial: It was Ted Kaczynski, personally. It was Kaczynski – not his lawyers' game of chicken with their client – who had "reduced his trial to chaos."[232] A few days later the *Times* wrote sympathetically about the lawyers' "nightmare."[233]

January 10-19, 1998:
Kaczynski Undergoes Psychiatric Evaluation

Our society tends to regard as a [mental] "sickness" any mode of thought or behavior that is inconvenient for the system, and this is plausible because when an individual doesn't fit into the system it causes pain to the individual as well as problems for the system. Thus the manipulation of an individual to adjust him to the system is seen as a "cure" for a "sickness" and therefore as good.[234]

Unabomber Manifesto

Dr. Sally Johnson ran a marathon psychiatric examination of Theodore Kaczynski. She questioned Kaczynski for twenty-two hours, on eight separate occasions over five days, and she reviewed transcripts of his conversations with both the lawyers and the judge.[235] Johnson also studied the reports of the defense and prosecution experts, along with other material provided by Kaczynski's attorneys and prosecutors.[236] She spent two days writing her forty-seven-page, single-spaced report and after securing an extra day to file her report, she had a brief, final session with Kaczynski on the afternoon of January 16. A sheriff for the Sacramento Sheriff's Office reportedly said that interactions between Kaczynski and Dr. Johnson had been calm, that Kaczynski was cooperating with the examination, and that "things [were] going smoothly."[237]

Dr. Johnson submitted her written assessment to the judge at nine in the evening on Saturday, the seventeenth.[238] Burrell scheduled a telephone conference for Tuesday, January 20, the day after the Martin Luther King holiday weekend. The judge and lawyers would review Dr. Johnson's report over the long weekend, and decide that Tuesday whether there was any need for a full hearing on Kaczynski's mental competency to stand trial.[239] If needed, the hearing would occur on Tuesday morning, with the trial tentatively scheduled to begin two hours later.[240] There was little doubt that a hearing would not be needed to explore Kaczynski's competency to stand trial.

During this latest delay in the proceedings of the Unabomber non-trial, his lawyers and prosecutors reopened conversations regarding the possibility of pretermitting the trial with a negotiated plea. *The New York Times* reported that the "sticking point" in the negotiations was Kaczynski's insistence that he be allowed to appeal the court's rulings on certain pre-trial motions.[241] (At least one such ruling, allowing the government to use at trial Kaczynski's private journals as evidence, was, in my opinion, a very strong appellate issue for Kaczynski.)

The prosecution filed a legal brief asking for a hearing on issues concerning Kaczynski's representation.[242] This brief was an excellent presentation of the relevant facts and law bearing on the complicated legal and ethical issues before the judge. The prosecution pointed out that, given Kaczynski's mental competency to stand trial, "the Court must face serious questions concerning the defendant's representation. In particular, the Court will have to decide whether to direct defense counsel to follow their client's instructions concerning the mental defect defense or in the alternative to inform the defendant that defense counsel may put on a mental defect defense in some form during both the guilt and penalty phases of trial."[243]

The purpose of the prosecution's brief was to set forth the government's understanding of the Court's options, to sketch the possible consequences of each choice, and to recommend that the Court instruct defense counsel to follow their client's wishes. The brief explained: "Based on the events of January 8, it appears that the defendant will assert his constitutional right to represent himself if the court rules that defense counsel may put on a mental defect defense of any kind during the guilt phase of trial. If the defendant, after proper warning from the court, knowingly and intelligently asserts his [right to represent himself at the trial] and is willing to proceed to trial immediately," the government opined that the Court would have to grant the defendant's request to represent himself.[244]

The brief urged the Court to direct defense counsel to follow their client's wishes concerning the mental defect defense: "Defense counsel have suggested that they have an ethical obligation to pursue a mental defect defense over the defendant's objection. The possibility exists, therefore, that counsel may seek to withdraw if the Court orders them to follow the defendant's wishes.[245] In that case, the Court would have the discretion to deny their request to withdraw. In addition, the Court believes that the Court would have recourse through its civil contempt power to enforce its decision if defense counsel continued to refuse to represent the defendant under these circumstances. Should the Court hold counsel in contempt, they would have the right to [an] appeal to challenge the Court's conclusion that they must follow the defendant's instructions."[246]

January 20, 1998: To No One's Surprise, Kaczynski is Found Competent

> There was, of course, something odd about [the judge's] flying a psychiatrist in from North Carolina for a week to determine the defendant's competency to represent himself, and then, when she found him competent, ruling that he could not represent himself. [247]
>
> William Finnegan (1998)

Dr. Sally Johnson wrote in the cover letter to her report: "It is my opinion that, despite the psychiatric diagnoses described in the attached report, Mr. Kaczynski is not suffering from a mental disease or defect rendering him mentally incompetent to the extent that he is unable to understand the nature or consequences of the proceedings filed against him or to assist his attorneys in his own defense."[248]

The press reports were less detailed: Dr. Johnson had diagnosed Theodore Kaczynski with paranoid schizophrenia. *The New York Times*, citing "a lawyer who had consulted on the case," informed readers that Dr. Johnson had "concluded" that Kaczynski "suffers from serious mental illness, including 'schizophrenia, paranoid type.'"[249] *The Washington Post* lumped Dr. Johnson in with the defense psychiatrists who had collectively "concluded Kaczynski suffers from the grandiose fantasies and delusional rage of an unmedicated paranoid schizophrenic in deep denial."[250] The *Sacramento Bee*, citing "sources close to the case," reported that Dr. Johnson had "found Theodore Kaczynski to be suffering from paranoid schizophrenia."[251] The Associated Press wrote that Dr. Johnson "diagnosed [Kaczynski] as a paranoid schizophrenic."[252] It was unanimous.

But the fact remains, Dr. Johnson made a *provisional* diagnosis of paranoid schizophrenia and paranoid personality disorder.[253] Dr. Johnson's findings with respect to Kaczynski's mental competency to stand trial – especially her chronology of events – require quotation at some length:

Mr. Kaczynski was arrested on 4/03/96 and initially was in custody at the a county jail in Montana. At that time he was represented by Michael

Donahoe, of the Federal Defenders' Office. Mr. Kaczynski describes forming a quick and close relationship with Mr. Donahoe. He identifies that throughout the several months he was held in Montana, he received a variety of letters through his attorney from private attorneys indicating an interest in representing him. He reports that Mr. Donahoe sorted through these letters and brought a letter from Tony Serra to his attention, as one he might look at seriously. After reviewing the letter, Mr. Kaczynski determined that he would continue to utilize Mr. Donahoe. He believed that Mr. Donahoe would continue with his case even after he was moved to Sacramento. As the time approached for that move, Mr. Donahoe told him that he would not be continuing with his case. This precipitated an angry response from Mr. Kaczynski, although he claims that he was able to modify that the next day.

Upon arrival in Sacramento, Mr. Kaczynski was assigned to the team of Federal Defenders currently working on his case. He describes developing a close personal relationship with his defense team including the investigators and paralegals. He describes them as taking the place of his family. He indicates that his friendship with his attorneys has been excellent, but he has serious conflicts with them about his case. He is able to name the members of his defense team and identify them by sight. He indicates that someone from the team visits him once every few days and someone from the office sees him daily except weekends. Members of the team take messages to and from him.

Mr. Kaczynski indicates that early on he identified that he did not want to use a mental health defense in his case. He describes that nonetheless the question of psychiatric evaluation arose early in his period of detention. He did not like the idea of talking to a psychiatrist because he believes that "science has no business probing the workings of the human mind." Early on, he reluctantly agreed to some psychiatric and psychological evaluation by defense experts because he believed by taking neuropsychological tests he could prove that he was not mentally ill. He also indicates his belief that information obtained from those evaluations would remain an attorney-client work product and would not be released.

He believes that the question of competency to stand trial in his case arose because of his suicide attempt and because he expressed the conflicts he is having with his attorneys. His recent upset stemmed from his belief that he had been deceived by his attorneys in that declarations from their experts had been made available to the prosecution and information from those declarations came out in a hearing in November

1997. Observations by the prosecution and defense attorneys indicate that at the time Mr. Kaczynski became aware of this, he became agitated in the courtroom and threw a pen across the table. He subsequently addressed a letter to Judge Burrell expressing his wish for legal advice from an outside source to help him resolve conflicts with his attorneys. He also expressed his wish for his attorneys to be prevented from using a [mental defect] defense and to have Mr. Soward removed from his defense team. He admitted that he had originally given his consent for a 12.2(b) defense but expressed his wish to withdraw that consent. He proposed that he might represent himself, with stand-by counsel, or that a new attorney could be appointed to replace his present team. He further discussed why he could not endure the use of a 12.2(b) defense, indicating that because of the impact of the frequent psychological abuse by his parents and schoolmates . . . he was now feeling subjected to a similar situation where he was subject to something he perceived as an injustice and was feeling helpless to defend against it or escape from it. He claimed that his attorneys were subjecting him to the same type of punishment that his parents had.

Mr. Kaczynski waited several weeks before submitting his letters (three) to Judge Burrell and indicates he did so in order to await completion of negotiations between the prosecution and defense, which could have resulted in the lack of necessity for a trial. He submitted the letters after the negotiations fell through. In these letters he also expressed his belief that his attorneys had originally promised to help him pursue "certain personal concerns of my own, even if these were inconsistent with my attorneys' professional concerns to do what is in my best interest in a legal sense. In particular I was led to believe that I would not be portrayed as mentally ill without my consent." Through the use of a conflict resolution attorney, Mr. Clymos, these issues appeared to be resolved in the eyes of the attorneys and the Court. On 01/05/98, at the beginning of the first day of the trial, Mr. Kaczynski provided information to Judge Burrell indicating that he needed to talk to him about a serious matter. He stated, "Your Honor before these proceedings begin, I would like to revisit the issue of my relations with my attorneys. It's very important, I haven't stood up because I'm under orders from the Marshals not to stand up." An *ex parte* and *in-camera* discussion was held, wherein Mr. Kaczynski was able to identify that he did not want what followed in the discussion to constitute a waiver of any part of his attorney-client privilege. He provided the judge with his written account of his history of his relationship with Attorney Tony Serra. He indicated his perception that again his attorneys had been less than honest with him. He referenced the earlier dispute with his attorneys which he claimed arose from the fact they had deceived him, and asked the Court to contact Mr. Serra to determine whether he was willing to represent him. Mr. Kaczynski presented the position that if his information was not accurate, he would apologize to his attorneys, but if it was correct then the conclusion would be inescapable that his attorneys have continued to deal with him in an underhanded fashion and in that case he could not cooperate with them because he could not rely on the truth of what they told him.

Mr. Kaczynski accused his attorneys of deliberately deceiving him in order to sabotage his attempts to consider a change of counsel. He went on to claim that that issue was not the only problem creating conflict. He expressed his concern that although the 12.2(b) defense had been withdrawn, his attorneys still intended to present evidence of mental illness through the use of lay witnesses at the guilt/innocence phase of the trial. He claimed that one of the sources of conflict between him and his attorneys was the fact that their values and attitudes were contrary to his and that he was under the impression that Mr. Serra's attitudes and values would be much more similar to his own. The Court then determined to appoint Mr. Kevin Clymos to represent Mr. Kaczynski's interest on the issue. Mr. Kaczynski indicated that his wish was to change counsel but then indicated that he was not sure he would want Mr. Serra as a replacement because he had not yet had the opportunity to speak to him. He continued that the root of his problem was that his attorney (Ms. Clarke) thought he was crazy and that is why she was insistent on representing him as crazy. The Court indicated that they would put Mr. Kaczynski's statement in the record and he objected, saying that his statement was conjecture and highly speculative. After speaking with Mr. Clymos, Mr. Kaczynski indicated that . . . (redacted)

In the 01/07/98 hearing, continued discussion took place and Mr. Kaczynski indicated that he was willing to permit his attorneys to go ahead with the mental health defense in the sentencing phase because that was the best agreement he could get and he did not want to break up the defense team. He was going to defend himself with what was essentially "a symbolic victory" by eliminating the mental health defense in the guilt/innocence phase of the trial. During extended discussion at that hearing Mr. Kaczynski first indicated his intent to proceed with present counsel, even though he disagreed with the defense in the guilt/penalty phase. At the end of the hearing he expressed his wish to consult with Mr. Serra about representation.

On 01/08/98 Defense Attorney Clarke addressed the Court indicating that Mr. Kaczynski was making a request that he be permitted to proceed in the case as his own counsel. He expressed that it was a difficult decision but believed he had no choice but to go forward as his own attorney. Ms. Clarke indicated this was a very "heartfelt reaction to the presentation of the mental illness defense, a situation which he simply cannot endure, so it is requested the Court permit him to proceed on his own behalf." Mr. Kaczynski did not request a delay in the trial and indicated that he would go forward on his own behalf as soon as the jury was sworn. After extended discussion regarding several issues of law, the Court determined that a competency evaluation should be conducted to assist in determining Mr. Kaczynski's competency to stand trial and represent himself. The defense indicated their position that he not only was wishing to refuse to allow them to present a mental illness defense at the penalty phase of the trial, but it was their impression that he could not bear for them to present that defense. Mr. Kaczynski voiced his opinion that he objected to having a competency evaluation because it was his position that he was competent. The Court subsequently indicated that it would proceed with ordering the evaluation and did.

Limited observations were available concerning Mr. Kaczynski's behavior in court, in that he waived his presence at most court hearings prior to jury selection. Prosecution observations during jury selection were that he was attentive and interacted with his attorneys. Defense attorneys did not raise the question of competency during the jury selection process. They were on record with their opinion that they had been able to accommodate Mr. Kaczynski's mental disorder and viewed him as competent to stand trial.

In discussion with Mr. Kaczynski about the issue of jury selection, he expressed a clear understanding of the selection process and indicated that he had provided his comments and review to his appointed counsel. He expressed his understanding of how the jury in his case had been selected and was able to discuss the pros and cons of the jury process in resolution of a legal proceeding. He expressed his preference to have a trial by jury even a situation where he would have the option to be tried by the judge. [sic] He also expressed his understanding that in a trial involving a potential death penalty, that the trial would have to proceed with a jury.

In specific discussion with Mr. Kaczynski around the issue of competency to stand trial, he was able to clearly articulate the problems in his relationship with defense attorneys in regard to choosing a defense in his case. He expressed an understanding why psychiatric issues, including a psychiatric evaluation, might arise in his case, by again noting his history of psychological verbal abuse beginning in adolescence that had continued as an issue for decades. He indicated that his mother and brother, in their interviews with the media, had portrayed him as mentally ill in an effort to cover up the history of abuse in his family. He believed that his attorneys portraying him as mentally ill would indicate that they were helping his brother, an individual against whom he was experiencing considerable anger. He also indicated that his attorneys had used deception to get him to see the psychiatrist and psychologist defense experts. He indicated his own goal of refuting the image the family had portrayed of him since his arrest.

Mr. Kaczynski further indicated that he was aware of these potential conflicts with his attorneys much earlier but had focused with the defense team on the motion to suppress evidence during the first several months of 1997, knowing that should that be successful, the issue of mental illness would not need to be pursued. At present he indicates that he was not claiming that he was free of any psychiatric disorder and he would not object to the issue of a psychiatric disorder being raised; what he was concerned about was that the information would not be portrayed accurately and some of the facts that had been presented in declarations were already incorrect. He felt his statements had been taken out of context to make him sound paranoid. It was also his belief that his attorneys, in their wish to win the case and try for minimum penalty, were adamant about presenting a mental illness defense. He indicated his own goals were to also receive the least penalty possible and to be acquitted if possible, but he could only pursue this goal through something like a mental illness defense if he had an 80% chance of succeeding and being released. He indicated if that was the case, he would concede to a mental illness defense but it would be by his choice. He did not view himself as having an 80% chance of success. At present he felt his attorneys were forcing that defense upon him. He expressed a clear understanding of the 12.2(b) defense as not being an insanity defense and clearly articulated an understanding of the statute as allowing use of information regarding mental disease and defect bearing on the issue of guilt.

Mr. Kaczynski was able to explain a clear understanding of the insanity defense and was aware that his attorneys would require his permission to give notice of that defense. He claimed an ability to consider the use of the insanity defense, qualifying it by stating he would only consider that if he had a reasonable belief that in a short period of time (five years) he could be released. It was his impression, however, that if found to be insane he would spend his life in a prison hospital facility, an outcome he was unwilling to accept. He expressed a preference for death over life in prison, but at the same time denied having an interest in being put to death.

Mr. Kaczynski is also aware that his attorneys are capable and are perceived by the judge and prosecution as being such. He regretted his initial statement to the judge that he would not represent himself and felt that post his unsuccessful suicide attempt and a period of time to rethink the issue, he now had the energy to commit to attempting to represent himself adequately. He had no doubt that his skills would fall short of those of his present attorneys, but expressed his firm belief that although he could elect to use a mental illness defense, he was choosing not to do so. He realized that his chance at success of being acquitted were slim, but felt that he could vindicate himself by saying he was not crazy in court. In that way, he felt he would only have one strike against him instead of two. He was able to compare the impact of having the prosecution present him as mean and dangerous versus the presentation by the defense of him being mentally ill and less than capable. He believed that the jury would somewhat discount the prosecution's presentation, as it was to be expected, but the mental illness presentation was potentially far more damaging to him personally.

During extended discussions, Mr. Kaczynski did indicate his belief that his attorneys were conventional and "part of the system." He imagined that Mr. Serra, who had been portrayed as much more of a rebel proba bly had views that were more against the system and had more in common with him. . . . he persisted throughout the evaluation period in expressing interest in exploring representation by Mr. Serra as a possibility. At the same time he realized that it was late in the trial process to change attorneys, and that the Court was not willing to appoint new counsel at this time. It was his perception that it would take Mr. Serra numerous months to prepare for trial. He also expressed his wish to resolve his legal situation in a prompt manner. He viewed his choices as self-representation or continuing with his current attorneys. He indicated he could not do the latter if they were able to proceed with a 12.2(b) defense over his objection.

Mr. Kaczynski was able to outline other conflicts he had with his attorneys, including the issue of publicity. He had been interested in writing letters to counter the image being presented by his family of him in the media. He discussed this with his attorneys and although he felt some pressure to conform, he had agreed with them not to write letters to the media and draw additional public attention to him at this point in the trial process. Nonetheless he spent approximately four months preparing a rebuttal to all he perceived as inaccurate in the public portrayal of him, and focused extensively on portraying his brother David in a negative light in these writings. He denied any intent on his part to attempt to delay the trial by making a suicide attempt. He described his perception that a successful attempt at the time he tried (the evening before trial) would have "made a statement," but that the opportunity for that was passed, in that he would now be too closely watched. He expressed his own opinion that he was competent to stand trial and his wish to be found as such, although he considered that, if found incompetent, the four month restoration period would potentially allow time for Mr. Serra to prepare a defense. He was able to consider the two schools of thought about legal representation, which included representing the client's best interest versus representing the client's expressed interest. It was his belief that representation should support the client's expressed interest.

Discussion with Mr. Kaczynski about his case revealed that he has an accurate understanding of the charges against him and the possible penalties if convicted. He explained the role of various participants in the legal process in some detail. This included the role of the judge, jury, prosecutor and defense attorney. He expressed a full understanding of the plea bargaining process. He reviewed his own capabilities for self-representation and indicated that he had debated one of his attorneys in a hearing situation and felt he had bested him. He also claimed he had some teaching experience to fall back on in addressing the jury. He admitted his own perception that he would not do as well handling things extemporaneously as he could if he had time to prepare his responses. He expressed an understanding of the evidence available in his case. After much consideration he was able to respond to the question of what image he wished to present of himself during the trial. Initially he had only been able to protest against the image to be portrayed by the defense attorneys. It took him some time to be able to determine that he wanted to present himself as rational; a person having a valid point to make; a decent person who felt cornered; as socially vulnerable; in some ways a victim personally and via the system; an individual who had his back against the wall; a person who lived a beautiful way of life in the woods; and a person whose psychiatric disorder could serve as a mitigating factor. When questioned as to how this image differed from that potentially planned to be presented by the defense attorneys, he was unable to articulate a difference, but focused on his concern that his attorneys would not accurately present the facts. In essence, he wanted to present his slant on the factual information. This appeared consistent with his voluminous writing, wherein he attempts to dispute the descriptions and "facts" of the information provided by the media and his family. He was able to understand that his plan in presenting the image outlined above would require use of the 12.2(b) defense at least at the penalty phase, if that was reached.

Mr. Kaczynski expressed an awareness of the order of presentation in a trial such as his. He understood that he would have to listen through the prosecution's presentation of details of the alleged offenses, and expressed his opinion that he could tolerate that, although it might anger him. He had an understanding of the burden of proof and that he could choose to testify. He indicated he would prefer not to testify and denied any interest in using the courtroom to espouse his views. He was able to articulate that although his chances of acquittal were slim, he still wished to attempt acquittal. He recognized that although he could avoid any portrayal of him as mentally ill or chance of denigration of his life style by equating it with mental illness, by pleading guilty and not going to trial, he recognized that a trial was necessary to proceed with an appeal on the suppression issue. The latter still offered a glimmer of hope, which he intended to pursue.

• • •

In regard to the issue of competency to stand trial, it is my opinion that at the present time, despite the presence of significant mental illness historically and residual evidence of such problems at the present, Mr. Kaczynski is able to understand the nature and consequences of the proceedings against, and is able to assist his attorneys in his defense. Thus, I view him as competent to stand trial. Extensive interviewing around the issue of competence to stand trial in conjunction with the diagnostic assessment and review of extensive collateral material, support that Mr. Kaczynski does have an excellent factual understanding of the legal proceedings against him and has an adequate rational understanding of these proceedings. He does have the ability to assist his attorneys in his own defense and the capacity to choose whether he will opt to assist them in presenting his defense. Mr. Kaczynski does describe goals for the trial process that might be viewed as somewhat inconsistent with maximizing the potential success of a defense to support his plea of innocence. It appears, however, that his motivation for his decision making in regard to his legal situation is not primarily his wish to clear his name and set the record straight about his family. His decision making, instead, appears to take into consideration a realistic review of the probability of various outcomes in his case, and supports his lack of interest in spending his life in prison as an alternative to being put to death if found guilty.

As described in detail above, Mr. Kaczynski has superior intelligence; he has the ability to read and interpret complex writing; he can contribute to review of documents; he has a full understanding of the roles of the various court personnel; he understands the charges against him and potential penalties if found guilty; he appreciates the nature of the proceedings and understands the likely sequence of events in a trial. Mr. Kaczynski has formed an unusual relationship with his defense team, in that he has quickly come to regard them as "friends and family." In some ways he has idealized his relationship with them, and at times can as easily devalue the relationship with individual members of the team. Nonetheless, he retains an awareness that they are a skilled group of individuals, who have provided him with good legal advice and maneuvering to date. He recognizes that continuing to utilize them in his defense would provide him with a higher level of representation than self-representation. He continues to wish to make the crucial decisions in his case, even if they could lead to less likelihood of a more lenient outcome.

Through the review of *in-camera* proceedings, it was evident that Mr. Kaczynski was able to track the rather complicated discussion regarding legal issues in an area where the law was unclear. He supplied information and opinions at appropriate times, and was able to contain his verbalizations appropriately within that setting. Although his ambivalence about the future course of action was evident, he was able to demonstrate the capacity to arrive at a decision from available material. There was not evidence that his behavior became disruptive or aggressive during these stressful proceedings.

The opinion that Mr. Kaczynski is competent to stand trial despite the diagnoses that have been rendered, does take into consideration that, at present, he is not demonstrating significant overt psychotic symptomatology. There is clearly evidence of *residual delusional ideas*. [my emphasis] Upon extensive interviewing throughout this evaluation, Mr. Kaczynski has been able to challenge his beliefs to some degree and to consider alternative explanations for some of his claimed beliefs. This is not to say he has relinquished his ideas, but that he is capable of processing alternative explanations in regard to these areas as they impact on his case.

It is likely that Mr. Kaczynski will present some challenges during the trial process, regardless of whether he is represented by counsel or proceeds *pro se*. He will continue to focus on detail and be reluctant to separate out useful detail from unnecessary detail. He will continue to demonstrate his ambivalence and suspiciousness, and is likely to overvalue some information that may arise. His interactions regarding the possibility of resolving his current conflicts by acquiring new representation is an example of this issue. He does not have much insight into the fact that acquiring new representation will not necessarily resolve the types of conflicts he currently has with this defense team, who remain his main support system at this time.

In interacting with Mr. Kaczynski, it may be prudent to maintain awareness of his psychological functioning during interpersonal interactions with him. It is extremely important for him to feel included in the process and those interacting with him need to be aware of his tendency to suspect that others may be deceiving him and to read hidden meaning into benign remarks or events. An effort should be made to help him sort through his perceptions that any specific information is designed to attack his character.

In regard to Mr. Kaczynski's recent suicide attempt, it is not my impression that the attempt resulted from significant depression. Instead it appeared to be a considered action in response to a difficult situation. He will remain at risk of choosing suicide as an option throughout the remainder of the legal proceedings. It is unlikely that he will share his ideas on this subject with anyone. He has expressed his belief that he sees no disadvantage to death over life in prison. Should he be convicted and incarcerated, his risk of suicide would, in all likelihood, be a chronic issue. Those interacting with him should also be aware that he tends to form rapid attachments and overvalue relationships. It is important to be very clear with him what the purpose and intent of your interactions are with him, and for individuals to clearly define their roles in those interactions.[254]

Like every mental health expert hired by the defense, the linchpin for Dr. Johnson's diagnosis of schizophrenia was her conclusion that his politics were a delusional architecture, not a philosophy. Johnson wrote:

Mr. Kaczynski presented a clearly organized belief system that he was being harassed and harmed by modern technology. He stated that he believed that the system as it exists is bad and rebellion against it is justified. He further stated that freedom and personal dignity have greater importance than comfort and security. This belief system was explored at length with Mr. Kaczynski and it was evident that it had developed in his early 20s, during a period of time when he was feeling particularly isolated. This appears to stem from his acceptance of a variety of ideas that he had culled from reading books such as the "Technological Society" referenced above. It is interesting that he had not only latched onto the ideas that were presented, but had expanded them to the extreme and accepted the suggestions and premises, many of which were only opinions stated by the authors, as if they were fact. He has subsequently devoted his activities and time in rebellion against a future as he accepted it would be. In essence, the ideas that he collected and wrote about in the early 1970s remain the basis for his current belief system. He feels compelled to live a life of extreme isolation and to focus his energy against the aspects of society that are attempting to control the masses. This includes a focus on advertising, genetic engineering, computer technology, business, certain aspects of education, chemical companies, etc. He expresses philosophical and personal concerns about these issues and feels personally threatened by the potential advances in these areas. Included in this is his inability to critically read newspapers, magazines and books to determine if statements carry any actual merit. He tends to collect pieces of literature, opinions and comments that support his views and use them as justification for continuation of his ideas. Mr. Kaczynski has intertwined his two belief systems, that society is bad and he should rebel against it, and his intense anger at his family for his perceived injustices. He talks openly about his ability to direct his anger from one set of ideas to the other quite fluidly.

. . .

It does appear that Mr. Kaczynski's investment and convictions about the outcome of modern technology and the alleged abuse by his family are consistent with fixed belief in that he does not challenge them in response to new information. Both of these systems could be viewed as meeting the criteria of nonbizarre delusional beliefs. The certainty of this, however, is clouded by the duration of these beliefs and the adaptation he has made by extreme social isolation.

Mr. Kaczynski adamantly denies any experiences of thought insertion, thought broadcasting, mind control, or command hallucinations. He does describe a variety of fantasies and nightmares, and it is unclear through this evaluation, whether his report of those as occurring only while he is sleeping is accurate. Some of his writings discuss his ability to use his will to control the outcome of these experiences, and raises the question as to whether these are actually hallucinatory experiences rather than dreams and fantasies as he labels them.[255]

The conclusions of the mental health experts retained by the defense and prosecution can, to some extent, be dismissed as partisan practitioners of advocative medicine. Dr. Johnson cannot be dismissed so easily. Although she is an Associate Warden for a federal prison, she has a reputation for fairness and being even-handed. In particular, I believe her chronology of primary, historical facts is fairly reliable.

However, Dr. Johnson's report contained much *less* than meets the eye. Despite the abundance of irrelevant, superficial and salacious detail that she managed to pack into the forty-seven page report, her provisional diagnosis of paranoid schizophrenia rests on only two dubious presuppositions. The first is that Kaczynski's politics were a delusion rather than a philosophy, and that his decision in the early 1970s to return to nature indicated mental illness. The second was Kaczynski's feeling that his parents were responsible for his discontent and unhappiness as an adult – a commonplace idea that is discussed every day with countless psychiatrists across America.

Like the mental health experts hired by Kaczynski's defense lawyers, Dr. Johnson's report reveals more about Johnson's biases and values than it does about the mental health of Theodore Kaczynski.

It seems reasonable to assume that Johnson was under tremendous pressure to find Theodore Kaczynski mentally ill in some way or another. The defense lawyers wanted this outcome for obvious reasons. Burrell also must have wanted it, because a crazy Kaczynski would provide him with more ammunition to justify the denial of Kaczynski's right to self-representation. The prosecution also wouldn't have been displeased with a finding of mental illness, since the judge would probably allow Kaczynski's lawyers to control the defense. The media and public didn't figure in the equation since they had already decided that Kaczynski was crazy.

On the Tuesday following the holiday weekend, Kaczynski's lawyers reiterated the obvious point that they had conceded since 1996: that their client was mentally competent to stand trial.[256] Because prosecutors had always maintained that Kaczynski was competent, this latest concession by Kaczynski's lawyers resolved the issue without any ruling from the judge.[257]

The Judge ruled that the issue of Kaczynski's representation would be decided in open court between eight and ten in the morning of the 21st, with the opening statements of the trial to commence at ten.[258] Burrell noted that "the question" at tomorrow's hearing would "center on self-representation." He again revealed his bias when he added that "currently I'm not inclined to bring in new lawyers."[259]

January 21, 1998:
The Defense Team's Game of Chicken

> So the paradox, as his case neared trial, could not have been lost on Kaczynski. His own lawyers, talented idealists intent on saving his life, were striving mightily to label him mentally ill. The prosecutors, meanwhile, intent on having him executed, were ready to accept him as the dead-serious dissident and violent anarchist that his writings said he was.[260]
>
> William Finnegan (1998)

According to the letter of the law, Burrell's decision regarding Theodore Kaczynski's right to self-representation should have been a no-brainer. Dr. Johnson, the defense lawyers and the prosecution all agreed that Kaczynski was mentally competent to stand trial. This meant Kaczynski was sufficiently competent to decide whether he would go to trial without the aid of a lawyer.

The law was clear. Any mentally competent defendant has a constitutional right to represent himself at trial, so long as he has been warned and understands the risks and disadvantages of self-representation. The judge must explain those risks and disadvantages, but the final choice lies with the defendant. It does not matter that the judge thinks the defendant is making a terribly stupid decision in foregoing his right to a lawyer. The law states that it is the defendant's decision to make, and not the judge's.

In order for Judge Burrell to deny Kaczynski's clear constitutional right to self-representation, he would have to find a procedural technicality. The Honorable anti-Ito Garland E. Burrell seemed to be scrambling to find a reason, any reason, to keep Kaczynski's lawyers on the case and in control of the defense. The procedural pretext the court came up with was delay: Kaczynski had waited too long to invoke his right to self-representation, and his invocation of that right was only designed to further delay the trial.

The judge's reasoning flatly contradicted the public record in the case. Kaczynski had invoked his right to self-representation more than a week earlier, at the very latest he did so on January 8. At that time, as Kaczynski's lawyers had hammered home again and again, Kaczynski was seeking no delay: He was ready to go ahead with the trial *immediately.*

Burrell's opinion that Kaczynski had asked to represent himself too late, and then only in order to delay the trial, was a position supported by neither the facts nor the law, as both the prosecution and the defense pointed out to the judge in briefs filed on January 21.[261] The government's January 21 brief summarized the relevant history as follows:

> As the government understands the record, the defendant first raised the issue that later caused him to invoke his [right to self-representation] on December 22, before the jury was impaneled. He had no reason to assert his [self-representation] rights at that time because he believed the issue was resolved to his satisfaction. Presumably, the defendant learned that the issue was not resolved to his satisfaction on or after January 2, 1998, when the government filed a motion to preclude the defense from using non-expert testimony to show a mental defect defense. The defendant then immediately raised the issue again with the court when he next appeared in court on January 5, 1998. *In-camera* proceedings followed. During these proceedings the defendant learned that the issue would not be resolved to his satisfaction. The redacted transcripts of these proceedings indicate that at one point on January 7, the defendant was informed by the court that he had the right to represent himself, but the defendant declined to do so. The next day, the defendant, through counsel, invoked his right to represent himself in open court.[262]

The prosecutors wrote in their brief: "As the government understands the sequence of events in this case, we cannot say that the defendant's assertion of his right to represent himself was untimely or for purposes of delay."[263]

The defense agreed with the prosecution – a fairly uncommon event in a hard-scrabble capital trial. The defense's brief agreed that Kaczynski was not trying to delay the trial. He had said in open court that he was ready to proceed immediately when he asked to represent himself. In their January 21 brief, Kaczynski's defense attorneys argued that his request to represent himself "was timely because the request was made before the jury was empaneled and sworn . . . Moreover, the request was clearly not made to delay the trial since Mr. Kaczynski announced he was ready to proceed with the trial as scheduled and did not seek any delay . . . Mr. Kaczynski first moved to represent himself on January 8, 1998, and he has not wavered in this request."[264]

Defense Attorneys Denvir and Clarke threatened to withdraw from the case. "Indeed, ethical obligations may cause defense counsel to seek to withdraw from representation in this case if ordered to forego what counsel believes is the only viable defense in favor of one that would lead to Mr.

Kaczynski's conviction and execution," the defense lawyers wrote.[264]

Indeed. It was a telling development. Kaczynski's attorneys reportedly threatened civil disobedience should Judge Burrell cede to the prosecution's claim that Kaczynski's attorneys were required to follow their client's instructions.[266] To outside observers, the defense lawyers' court filings suggested that they might disobey such an order as a violation of the lawyers' rules of professional responsibility.

Kaczynski's lawyers argued that the "prosecution [had taken] the unprecedented step of asking the Court to order defense counsel . . . to forego counsel's own judgment of the best defense to present at trial, and . . . to follow the wishes of a defendant, whom experts have diagnosed as suffering from paranoid schizophrenia, in pursuing a defense that will assist the prosecution in convicting and executing the defendant."[267] The defense lawyers continued, revisiting a familiar theme: "The decisions [as to] whether and how to present a mental status defense in the guilt phase (other than an insanity defense) and what witnesses to call in the penalty phase of a capital trial fall squarely within the category of strategic decisions that ultimately must be decided by trial counsel."[268] Further, "the government's argument that defense counsel would not render ineffective assistance in this case by following the defendant's wish that no mental health evidence be presented at trial is a red herring. It means little that defense counsel might pass muster under the minimal standards of performance required under the Sixth Amendment if counsel should decide to accede to a defendant's request not to present certain evidence at trial . . . It is unconscionable for the government to ask the Court – in a capital case – to order defense counsel to forego the only defense that is likely to prevent the defendant's conviction and execution. In fact, the government's improper interference with defense counsel's choice of a defense and [their] relationship with Mr. Kaczynski infringes his Sixth Amendment right to counsel."[269]

Yale Law School ethics professor Geoffrey Hazard characterized the defense attorneys' argument as "twaddle."[270] I agree.

In addition to the materials submitted by the defense lawyers and prosecutors, Theodore Kaczynski himself wrote to Burrell on January 21.

To The Honorable Garland E. Burrell, Jr.
From Theodore John Kaczynski

Your Honor:
   In court on January 20, 1998 you cited a passage from the December 22, 1997 *ex parte* hearing in support of your belief that my agreement with my attorneys allowed them to use mental-health evidence provid-

ed by non-expert witnesses. This passage reads as follows (according to pages 38, 39 of my copy of the reporter's draft, which is marked "Not proofed or certified – do not cite").

"MR. DENVIR: . . . I want to make sure . . . we . . . agree . . . that at some point soon we would withdraw the [mental condition defense notice] and would not present any mental health expert testimony at the guilt phase . . . "

In response to this I would offer the following arguments.

1. Your Honor seems to feel that the statement, "we would withdraw the [mental defect defense notice] and would not present any mental health expert testimony" is equivalent to a statement that withdrawing the [mental defect defense notice] means nothing more than not presenting mental-health expert testimony.

But it is not at all clear that the two statements are equivalent. I personally do not feel that they are equivalent, and from the passage cited, I do not understand that withdrawing the [mental condition] defense means no more than not using mental-health expert testimony.

2. The validity of Your Honor's argument depends on the exact wording of the passage cited, and court reporters do not always achieve word-for-word accuracy. Your Honor may recall that my last words at the bench conference on January 20 were, "I have no objection to that." Later on January 20, Mr. Clymo showed me the reporter's draft of the bench conference, and I pointed out to him that the reporter had put down my words incorrectly. Mr. Clymo answered, "I think you're right," and added that such errors on the part of court reporters are common.

3. In the case of a written agreement it is reasonable to expect adherence to the exact wording of the agreement, because the parties can study the wording with the necessary care. In the case of an *oral* agreement, it is unrealistic to expect adherence to the exact wording of the agreement unless the words in question are repeated and strongly emphasized; for, inevitably, much of the detail in oral communication is not absorbed by the listeners.

Your Honor yourself – trained in legal matters – at first interpreted my agreement with my counsel to mean that all mental-health evidence would be omitted from the guilt phase of the trial. You did not find and interpret the passage cited above until after the dispute arose between me and my counsel over the substance of our agreement. Hence it is not reasonable for you to expect that I should have understood from that passage what my counsel was promising me.

4. It was on Friday, December 19, that my attorneys first offered to withdraw the [mental defect defense] notice. They and I discussed the

matter at length over the weekend in preparation for the *ex parte* hearing on December 22. Thus they had plenty of opportunity to make clear to me that they still intended to use lay testimony on mental-health issues in the guilt phase; yet they failed to make this clear to me.

5. I would call Your Honor's attention to a passage that appears in my (uncertified) copy of the reporter's draft, just shortly after the passage cited earlier (page 39 of my copy). Mr. Denvir said that part of the agreement was:

". . . that we will keep the defendant apprised of the case as it develops, what we're going to put on in the case.

"THE DEFENDANT: In other words, Your Honor, that they won't spring any more surprises on me."

Yet my lawyers still did not inform me until the evening of January 4 – the eve of the opening of proceedings on January 5 – that they intended to use lay testimony in the guilt phase. Thus they sprang a very big surprise on me and failed to keep me "apprised of the case as it develops, what we're going to put on in the case." So they failed to keep that aspect of the agreement.

• • •

Your Honor, I recognize that you are an unusually compassionate judge, and that you sincerely believe yourself to be acting in my best interest in seeking to prevent me from representing myself. In an ordinary case your course would be the most compassionate one, and the one most likely to preserve the defendant's life. But I beg you to consider that you are dealing with an unusual case and an unusual defendant, and that preventing me from representing myself is not the most compassionate course or the one most likely to preserve my life.

Theodore John Kaczynski
January 21, 1998 [271]

January 22, 1998: Kaczynski Forced to Plead Guilty

This put me in such a position that I had only one way left to prevent my attorneys from using false information to represent me to the world as insane: I agreed to plead guilty to the charges in exchange for withdrawal of the prosecution's request for the death penalty. . . I am not afraid of the death penalty, and I agreed to this bargain only to end the trial and thus prevent my attorneys from representing me as insane . . . [272]

Theodore Kaczynski

What turned out to be the final day of the Unabomber's non-trial began with Burrell's ruling that Kaczynski's had made his request to act as his own attorney too late. In a rambling order, the Court said that allowing Kaczynski to represent himself would amount to providing him with a "suicide forum." The judge said that Kaczynski must have known that his public defenders planned to portray him as mentally ill (the judge did not explain how Kaczynski could have known this prior to the beginning of jury selection on November 12, 1997). There was also the accusation that Kaczynski was trying to delay the trial.[273] Once again, an observer wrote that the judge seemed "angry" at Kaczynski for refusing to follow his lawyers' directions.[274]

These rulings, understood correctly, can only be called bizarre. Not only had the prosecutors conceded that Kaczynski's request to represent himself was timely, the defenders thought so too. It is difficult for me to grasp how the judge could have reasonably found otherwise. Again, the law is clear that defendants have a constitutional right to handle their own case. The only requirement is that the Court warn the defendant of the risks, disadvantages and dangers of self-representation (a colloquy analogous to the familiar *Miranda* warnings that must precede custodial interrogation of a suspect). These warnings typically require about half an hour of court time. Kaczynski had made his request to represent himself without a legal counsel on January 8. Fourteen days later, following

Johnson's psychiatric evaluation, Burrell concluded that Kaczynski's request had come too late.

Burrell's decision that Kaczynski's request was designed to delay the trial is equally weird. On January 8, Kaczynski said that he was ready to proceed as his own lawyer "without any delay," and his lawyers reiterated this in their January 21 filing.[275] "Without any delay" means without any delay.

Burrell's January 22 ruling is the fullest articulation of his reasoning on the self-representation issue, and as such, it bears discussion in some detail. Burrell began by criticizing Kaczynski for sending him a letter, dated January 21. The letter covered two issues, according to the judge: "his desire to represent himself;" and his understanding of the notice of intent, filed by his lawyers, to use mental health experts during the sentencing phase of the trial.[276] Although the court had in the past received letters from Kaczynski regarding these matters, this time he found it "an inappropriate *ex parte* communication with a jurist" because "it contained advocacy which should have been made through counsel."[277] Burrell drove this home when he added, "Mr. Kaczynski does not represent himself, at least not yet."[278]

"Mr. Kaczynski," Burrell continued, "[has moved] to exercise his right of self-representation. A criminal defendant has a Sixth Amendment constitutional right to self-representation if it is [asserted in a timely manner] and the assertion is not a tactic to secure delay."[279] The judge held that Kaczynski's request was both untimely and constituted a manipulative bid for delay.

Regarding the timeliness of Kaczynski's request, the court found that his "first unequivocal request for self-representation occurred on January 8, 1998, seventeen days after the jury had been empaneled. Although the subject of self-representation was discussed several times over the course of the *ex parte, in-camera* proceedings [between December 18 and January 7] Kaczynski never made a statement that could even remotely be construed as an *unequivocal* request to represent himself."[280]

Of course he didn't. Kaczynski never *wanted* to represent himself. He wanted to be provided with the *assistance* of counsel to raise a defense against the charges. Before January 8, Kaczynski hoped to be able to work out some sort of compromise with his lawyers. Only when it became evident that this would be impossible did he ask to represent himself, and to proceed "without any delay." His decision to represent himself was a last ditch resort forced on him by his relentless lawyers and Judge Burrell.

In addition to the problematic ruling that Theodore Kaczynski's request for self-representation was entered too late, came the judge's dubious opinion that it was a "tactic to secure delay."[281] Burrell evidently thought that "without any delay" meant something like "with lots and lots of mean-spirited delay." "Although Kaczynski did not accompany his request [to represent himself] with a motion [for delay to allow him time to prepare], granting Kaczynski's request at this stage [would] undoubtedly result in a substantial impediment to the orderly process of this capital case."[282] According to Burrell, Kaczynski would need time to prepare. This was not Kaczynski's understanding. Regardless, the preparation cited by Burrell would take time. The resulting delay would require the selection of a new jury. The judge then opined what almost seemed a non-sequitur, that Kaczynski could not have been ignorant of the fact that his lawyers intended to raise a defense against capital punishment based on his alleged mental illness.

At the end of his ruling, the judge did pay lip service to "the paramount principle at the heart of [the right of self-representation]," and he tipped his hat to, "the freedom of the accused to personally manage and control his own defense in a criminal case." But in this case, "if Kaczynski abandons the mental health defense, he will forego the only defense that is likely to prevent his conviction and execution," which would convert his courtroom into a "suicide forum."[283]

Quoting from the *dissenting* opinion – i.e., the losing side – of the leading Supreme Court case on self-representation, Burrell reasoned that the "system of criminal justice" cannot be used as "an instrument of self destruction."[284] Since Kaczynski's judge quoted from the dissenting opinion in the leading self-representation case, it seems to me an appropriate time to consider exactly what the *majority* of that court had to say in this landmark case of *Faretta v. California*.

Many legal doctrines are fuzzy, unclear and difficult to apply in a practical situation. The right of self-representation is not one. There is really but a single case that one need read and understand. *Faretta v. California* was an old case that closed in 1975 when it reached the Supreme Court from the California courts.[285]

Anthony Faretta was charged with grand theft. Mr. Faretta was dissatisfied with the California state public defender assigned to represent him by the Court. He requested to represent himself. The judge, after initially allowing self-representation, held a hearing to determine Faretta's "ability to conduct his own defense."[286] The court then ruled that Faretta must be represented by the public defender. He was represented by public appointed counsel, and he was convicted.

The Supreme Court in Anthony Faretta's case framed the issue in this way: Does a defendant "[have] a constitutional right to proceed *without* counsel when he voluntarily and intelligently elects to do so. Stated another way, the question is whether a state may constitutionally hale a person into its criminal courts and there force a lawyer upon him, even when he insists that he wants to conduct his own defense." The Court ruled that "a state may not constitutionally do so."[287]

The Court reasoned that the "right of self-representation – to make one's defense personally – is necessarily implied by the structure" of the constitutional source of the right to counsel, (*i.e.*, the Sixth Amendment). "The right to defend is given directly to the accused; for it is he who suffers the consequences if the defense fails."[288]

The Sixth Amendment itself speaks of the "assistance" of counsel. The Supreme Court explained that "an assistant, however expert, is still an assistant. The language and spirit of the Sixth Amendment contemplate that counsel, like the other defense tools guaranteed by the Amendment, shall be an aid to a willing defendant – not an organ of the state interposed between an unwilling defendant and his right to represent himself personally."[289]

"To thrust counsel upon the accused, against his considered wish, thus violates the logic of the Amendment" the Supreme Court continued.[290] In such a case, counsel is "not an assistant, but a master; and the right to make a defense is stripped of the personal character upon which the Amendment insists. It is true that when a defendant chooses to have a lawyer manage and present his case, law and tradition may allocate to counsel the power to make binding decisions on trial strategy in many areas. This allocation can only be justified, however, by the defendant's consent, at the outset, to accept counsel as his representative ... Unwanted counsel 'represents' the defendant only through a tenuous and unacceptable legal fiction. Unless the accused has acquiesced in such representation, the defense presented is not the defense guaranteed him by the Constitution for, in a very real sense, it is not *his* defense."[291]

The Supreme Court in Anthony Faretta's case recognized that virtually all defendants would be better off with counsel: as the old saw has it, "the person who represents himself has a fool for a lawyer." Any criminal attorney will tell you this is almost always true. Still, the Court in Faretta's case also recognized that individual free will must trump the paternalistic values of compulsory representation. As the Court put it: "Whatever else may be said of those who wrote the Bill of Rights, surely there can be no doubt that they understood the inestimable worth of free choice."[292] A defendant's choice to represent himself, so long as he is "made aware of the dangers and disadvantages of self-representation," must be honored. His choice "must be honored out of that respect for the individual, which is the lifeblood of the law."[293] Kaczynski's lawyers, in concert with Burrell, had imprisoned a man in his privileges and called it the Constitution.[294]

And thus, the Kaczynski trial never came to be. Immediately after the judge's clearly erroneous rulings, Lead Defense Attorney Denvir asked to approach the bench. At the sidebar, Denvir said: "Your Honor, Mr. Kaczynski would like to offer the government that he would plead guilty . . . if the government would withdraw the death penalty notice. We have not been authorized to make that offer before."[295]

All they needed was an hour, defense counsel said: "just an hour."[296]

Burrell didn't bite. "Judge," Denvir continued, "we can resolve this case." "You'd better do it [in less than] an hour," Burrell replied.[297]

With the judge's emphatic one-hour deadline, the defense team then met privately, to work out terms of the plea agreement. For the first time, Kaczynski agreed to plead guilty with no strings attached, except a reprieve from a death sentence. The plea negotiations apparently took less than an hour.[298]

Cornered by Burrell's erroneous rulings, and by his own lawyers' apparent willingness to disobey a court order that would have allowed him to take control of his own case, Kaczynski finally caved in to the pressure. Kaczynski pleaded guilty. The plea agreement hinged on one issue, that, "in return for the defendant's guilty plea, the government agrees that it withdraw the Notice of Intent to Seek the Death Penalty . . ."[299] During the process of pleading guilty, Kaczynski acknowledged publicly that he was the Unabomber, and that he was responsible for the series of bombings between 1978 and 1995.[300]

> THE COURT: Mr. Kaczynski, please state your full and true name for the record.
>
> THE DEFENDANT: Theodore John Kaczynski.
>
> THE COURT: How old are you?
>
> THE DEFENDANT: Fifty-five years old.
>
> THE COURT: How far did you go in school?
>
> THE DEFENDANT: I have a Ph.D. in mathematics.
>
> THE COURT: What is your occupation?
>
> THE DEFENDANT: That's an open question right now. My occupation, I suppose, now is Jail Inmate.
>
> THE COURT: Okay. What past occupations have you held?
>
> THE DEFENDANT: I was once an Assistant Professor of Mathematics. Since then I have spent much time living in the woods in Montana and have held a variety of unskilled jobs.
>
> THE COURT: Have you ever been treated for any mental illness or addiction to drugs of any kind?
>
> THE DEFENDANT: No, Your Honor.

• • •

THE COURT: Mr. Kaczynski, are you fully satisfied with the counsel, representation and advice given you in this case by Mr. Denvir and Ms. Clarke as your attorneys?

(Discussion off the record between Ms. Clarke and Mr. Kaczynski).

THE DEFENDANT: I am satisfied except as reflected otherwise in this record.

THE COURT: You need to explain that, sir.

THE DEFENDANT: All right, Your Honor. You know that I have had certain dissatisfactions in my relationship with my counsel. And those dissatisfactions are reflected in the record. Apart from those dissatisfactions that are reflected in the court record, I have no other dissatisfactions with my representation by counsel.

(Discussion off the record between Mr. Denvir and the Kaczynski.)

THE DEFENDANT: I am willing to proceed for sentencing with present counsel.

THE COURT: My understanding of your dissatisfaction with present counsel is that there was a disagreement as to the assertion of the mental status defense and you had some problems with present counsel concerning communications surrounding the presentation of mental status-type evidence.

THE DEFENDANT: Yes, Your Honor.

THE COURT: Is that what you are referencing?

THE DEFENDANT: Yes, Your Honor. That is what I am referring to.

THE COURT: Are you referring to anything other than that?

THE DEFENDANT: No, Your Honor.

THE COURT: Is it your understanding that your attorneys had discussions with the attorneys for the government in this case concerning your change of plea?

THE DEFENDANT: Yes, Your Honor.

THE COURT: Does your willingness to plead guilty result from those discussions?

THE DEFENDANT: Yes, Your Honor.

THE COURT: Are you entering this plea of guilty voluntarily because it is what you want to do?

(Discussion off the record between Ms. Clarke and the defendant.)

THE DEFENDANT: Yes, Your Honor.[301]

William Finnegan, who was present during these proceedings, described the denouement of the Kaczynski non-trial:

Next, the prosecutors laid out some of the facts that they would be prepared to prove at trial. The recitation lasted nearly an hour. It was gory

– shrapnel piercing a heart, hands blown off – and what was particularly horrifying were the decoded "lab notes" from Kaczynski's journals, in which he recorded the results of his "experiments." "Excellent" was his judgment on the swift, bloody death of Hugh Scrutton, a young computer-rental-business owner. "A totally satisfactory result," he wrote of the murder of Thomas Mosser, a New Jersey father of two.

After each horror story – and all sixteen bombings were described – the judge asked Kaczynski, "Do you agree with the factual representation just made by the Government's attorney?"

And Kaczynski answered, in a clear, unreadable tone, "Yes, Your Honor."[302]

Relatives of Kaczynski's victims who were in court wept. As her son confessed publicly for the first time, Wanda Kaczynski wept as well. She and her son David leaned into one another for comfort. Theodore Kaczynski studiously ignored them, as he had done since the non-trial didn't begin on January 5.[303]

Why did the prosecutors agree to the plea bargain? Largely, no doubt, they agreed for the reason they gave; Kaczynski, for the first time, was willing to plead guilty with no strings attached. Also, perhaps the prosecutors were reasonably worried that the apparent errors already committed by the judge, especially his denial of Kaczynski's right to self-representation, would have rendered any jury verdict of guilt highly vulnerable to reversal on appeal. Equally important, I think, the prosecutors must have understood that any death sentence obtained in Judge Burrell's court would have been highly vulnerable to attack on appeal – not only for Burrell's erroneous denial of Kaczynski's constitutional right to self-representation (discussed above), and for the judge's questionable rulings that Kaczynski's private journals were admissable into evidence against him, (discussed below in Chapter Seven), but also perhaps because of the prosecutor's own alleged violation of the basic constitutional duty to disclose the discovery of all exculpatory information in the government's possession to the defense.[304]

If any of the above scenarios unfolded, the case would have to go back to the beginning: a new trial with a new jury. Kaczynski's guilty plea, and all the pre-trial motions that proceeded it, would be null and void.

The reason the defense jumped at the plea bargain was obvious. From the start, they had identified their goal as a life sentence for Kaczynski. The plea gave him that.

Less clear was why Kaczynski accepted the plea. Perhaps he accepted it to avoid a death sentence. Perhaps he took the plea to prevent his lawyers from portraying him as mentally ill. That's what he said.[305] Perhaps both reasons, combined with exhaustion and isolation, came into play.

Reports on the plea from the media repeated, with thudding predictability, their incorrect statement that Dr. Sally Johnson had pronounced – as opposed to *provisionally* diagnosed – Kaczynski a paranoid schizophrenic. *The Washington Post* wrote that Dr. Johnson had "concluded" that Kaczynski "suffers from the grandiose fantasies and delusional rage of an unmedicated paranoid schizophrenic in deep denial."[306] *Time* magazine entitled their piece *Crazy Is As Crazy Does*, and reported that Johnson had "found that he was a delusional paranoid schizophrenic."[307]

The New York Times, treating this misconception as a truism, reported that after Johnson had "diagnosed [Kaczynski] as a paranoid schizophrenic," his "struggle seemed more and more to highlight the legal system's difficulties in dealing with the mentally ill."[308] That same day, the *Times* emphasized the psychiatric evaluation done by Dr. Johnson. The editorial averred that Johnson's "sealed report, according to people who have seen it, says that he suffers from schizophrenia and has delusions of persecution that can lead to violence. Dr. Johnson's diagnosis is in accord with the defendant's own [sic] psychiatric experts, who have said he is severely mentally ill."[309]

While the media circus whirled around the topic of Kaczynski's supposed illness, formal sentencing was deferred until May 1998. Between the time Kaczynski pleaded guilty in January and his formal sentencing in May, he continued to be represented by Public Defenders Quin Denvir and Judy Clarke. He did not challenge the legality of his guilty plea or revisit the manner in which his lawyers represented him during the time leading up to the plea. Kaczynski's lawyers objected to the prosecution's filing of a brief on sentencing, which Burrell overruled. The prosecution's sentencing brief is a singularly powerful document on the harm wrought by Kaczynski's bombing campaign, and the methodical records Kaczynski himself kept about that campaign.

All this gives rise to a question. If Theodore Kaczynski was stampeded by his lawyers and the judge into pleading guilty on January 22, why is it that, at the sentencing on May 4, Kaczynski did not challenge the plea? Kaczynski had an opportunity to speak to the judge in open court during sentencing – a courtroom filled with reporters. Why did the "professed" Unabomber not try to challenge or withdraw his plea? At the very least one wonders why he passed on this very public opportunity to attack the legality of his plea and the actions of his attorneys, as well as the judge which had forced him into that plea.

Kaczynski's answers are fascinating. Shortly before the May 4 sentencing hearing, Kaczynski told his attorneys that he wanted to withdraw his plea at the sentencing hearing. The lawyers told Kaczynski that they weren't sure that was a good idea, but that they would think about it and speak with him on that subject before court began on May 4.

On the morning of May 4, the lawyers persuaded him not to withdraw the plea. Denvir and Clarke argued that if Kaczynski tried to withdraw the plea, Burrell would use it as additional evidence that he was "manipulating the judicial process" and this would hurt Kaczynski's chances of being able to withdraw his plea later.

Judgment Day: Life Without Parole

... one has to balance struggle and death against the loss of freedom and dignity. To many of us, freedom and dignity are more important than a long life or avoidance of physical pain. Besides, we all have to die some time, and it may be better to die fighting for survival, or for a cause than to live a long but empty and purposeless life.[310]

Unabomber Manifesto

The prosecutor's sentencing brief, reproduced in part in the appendix to this book, described the pain caused by Kaczynski's bombing campaign. For this reason, the brief, as well as the haunting memoir of one of his victims, should be required reading for anyone tempted to view Kaczynski's crimes in a sympathetic light.[311]

On May 4, 1998, Theodore Kaczynski was formally sentenced to four life terms plus 30 years – life imprisonment without possibility of parole, ever. On that day, Kaczynski spoke. He also listened – to the witness borne by those people he maimed and the families of those the Unabomber had killed. "May your own eventual death occur as you have lived, in a solitary manner, without compassion or love," said Lois Epstein, whose husband was disfigured by one of the Unabomber's devices.[312] "Lock him so far down that when he does die, he'll be closer to hell," said Susan Mosser, whose husband's body was torn apart by a devastating bomb.[313] Kaczynski appeared unmoved.

Then it was Kaczynski's turn to speak:

THE COURT: Does the defendant wish to make a statement before I pronounce sentence?
THE DEFENDANT: Yes, Your Honor. Your Honor, may I come to the podium?
The COURT: You may.
THE DEFENDANT: My statement will be very brief.

A few days ago the government filed a sentencing memorandum, the purpose of which was clearly political. By discrediting me personally, they hope to discredit the ideas expressed by the Unabomber. In reality, the government has discredited itself. The sentencing memorandum contains false statements, distorted statements and statements that mislead by omitting important facts. At a later time I expect to respond at length to the sentencing memorandum and also the many other falsehoods that have been propagated against me. Meanwhile, I only ask that people reserve their judgment about me and about the Unabom case until all the facts have been made public.

THE COURT: Let the record reflect Mr. Kaczynski has finished making his statement and returned to counsel table.[314]

The victim-impact evidence was not the aspect of the prosecution's brief that seemed to bother Kaczynski the most. What bothered him was the brief's use of his private journal: The passages cited in the brief portrayed Kaczynski, not as a principled neo-Luddite warrior trying to protect society from technology, but rather as a petty, childish murderer who killed to extract "personal revenge" (as Kaczynski wrote in his journal) on the kinds of people who annoyed him: loggers who disturbed his peace; business travelers who flew in the planes above his home; campers who wandered onto his property. This was the *real* Theodore Kaczynski, the prosecution had argued.

Kaczynski promised an eventual reply: "At a later time I expect to respond at length to the sentencing memorandum. Meanwhile, I only ask that people reserve their judgement about me and about the Unabom case until all the facts have been made public."[315]

Winners and Losers: The Meaning of Life

The Medieval martyrs did not *seek* execution. They were executed because they refused to recant. It was worth sparing Ted Kaczynski to burn the manifesto at the stake – and there was community interest in doing so.[316]

Lydia Eccles

I believe that Kaczynski pleaded guilty in exchange for life imprisonment without the possibility of parole, not because he feared the death penalty, but because he simply had no other choice.[317] It was the only way he could prevent his lawyers from portraying him as crazy and his manifesto as the ravings of a madman.[318]

Theodore Kaczynski was denied his day in court. The lawyers he ultimately tried to fire had forced him into a defense that he would have rather died than raise. In the guise of providing him with the constitutional right to the assistance of counsel, Kaczynski's judge and his court-appointed lawyers stripped him of the only power he had left as an American citizen: the power to have his case raised against the indictment in a manner that was personally acceptable to him. Kaczynski was, after all, the main player in a judicial proceeding where his life was on the line. His life, his liberty – not his lawyers' life, not his judge's life.

Both the prosecution and the defense can claim Kaczynski's guilty plea as a victory. The defense lawyers won, because their client would not be executed – an outcome few would have predicted at the time jury selection began. The prosecutors won, because the confessed Unabomber would never take a breath as a free man. The judge won, because the plea means no appeal, and no appeal means no reversal by the appellate courts – and a reversal was a very real possibility, given the multitude of errors Burrell had made even before the trial began. The justice system won, because it was spared the spectacle of a trial that had degenerated into farce even before opening statements had been made.

Did the Unabomber's victims and their families win? I wonder. They were spared the uncertainty of a jury trial, but the prosecution's evidence of Kaczynski's guilt was so solid that the jury almost certainly would have convicted him of murder.[319] Kaczynski would have been sentenced to life imprisonment without the possibility of parole at the very least, which was his sentence under the plea agreement. Kaczynski might have been sentenced to death, which was a very real possibility regardless of the defense raised by Denvir and Clarke. There was at least one Unabomber victim, David Gelernter, who was outspoken in his wish that Kaczynski die for his crimes.[320] Gelernter wrote that "we execute murderers in order to make a communal proclamation: that murder is intolerable . . . A deliberate murderer embodies evil so terrible that it defiles the community."[322] The Unabomber deliberated on his murderous campaign for seventeen years.

Did American society as a whole win in the Unabomber plea? Thirty-eight states, the federal government and the overwhelming majority of the public supports the death penalty for the most heinous murderers. Jeff Jacoby, an eloquent supporter of capital punishment, gave powerful articulation to why so many Americans support capital punishment:

> Life is not the ultimate value. Otherwise no nation would send young men to fight for honor, or against tyranny, or in defense of freedom. Life is sacred, but some things are more sacred. And if that is true of innocent life, how much more so is it true of guilty life – of those whose hands are slick with the blood of others?
>
> It is for the good of society that assassins ought to die – that we may declare, to ourselves and to the world, that the crime of stealing life is worse than any other crime and deserves a penalty worse than any other penalty.
>
> It is up to the law to speak for [the victims of crime] – to speak for all grief-stricken survivors confronted with the butchery of someone near and dear. Capital punishment says to them: We, the community, take your loss with the utmost seriousness. We know that you are filled with rage and pain. We know that you may cry for vengeance, may yearn to strangle the murderer with your bare hands. You are right to feel that way. But it is not for you to wreak retribution. As a decent and just society, we will do it. Fairly. After due process, in a court of law.[323]

If American society did win in the Unabomber's plea, that victory carried a high price tag. The Kaczynski prosecution, which did not even include a trial, cost a million-and-a-half dollars, which does not include the one-million dollar reward given to David Kaczynski for turning in his brother.[324] The Unabomber saga has been called the most expensive case in American history, because it involved numerous federal agencies for two decades. Some have estimated the cost of the case to be as high as fifty-million dollars (almost as much as the Starr report), but the actual cost has never been calculated.[325] Still, the Unabomber is in prison. That's a win.

And Theodore Kaczynski? Did he win? Once again, I wonder.

His lawyers won Kaczynski the right to spend the rest of his natural life (he was age 55 at the time of his non-trial) in a federal "Supermax" prison that boasts the very latest in detainment technology. This means that Kaczynski is locked in his cell for twenty three hours a day – a cage slightly smaller than his cabin.[326] Solitary. A tiny, little cage. All his own, for the rest of his life. Except for legal correspondence, all his mail is read. For any American, this would not be much of a life. For Theodore Kaczynski, who prized freedom and privacy above all else, it must be a living hell. "Freedom" and "autonomy" weren't just words to him, they *were* him.

Not that he doesn't deserve it; perhaps he should get worse treatment. However, the point is that this is what his lawyers *won* for him. This was the victory for which they seized control of his defense and, along with the judge, forced him into pleading guilty.

Denvir and Clarke could not have succeeded in their efforts to take control of Kaczynski's defense without Burrell's help. It was the judge who ruled that they "controlled" the case. It was the judge who insisted that Kaczynski was seeking to delay the trial, even though Kaczynski was ready to proceed without delay. It was the judge who blamed Kaczynski, not his lawyers, for disrupting the trial. Burrell was the one who relentlessly demanded that the show go on regardless of the Sixth Amendment and the fundamental fairness that is its foundation.

Of all the judge's rulings regarding the hostile takeover of Kaczynski's defense, the most erroneous was the judge's rulings that Kaczynski did not have a constitutional right to fire his lawyers and represent himself. As discussed above, both the defense and the prosecution agreed that Kaczynski had a right to self-representation and that he had exercised that right in a timely fashion.

Burrell's ruling turned the right to the assistance of counsel on its head. He transformed a constitutional protection designed to shield the defendant's constitutional rights into a sword with which to kill Kaczynski's right to a trial before his peers. The whole purpose of the right to the assistance of counsel at criminal trials – a right recognized since the infamous Scottsboro case of 1932 – is to *empower* the citizen-accused whom the state has decided deserves to die.

Again, the constitutional language is "assistance." Theodore Kaczynski's lawyers, however well-intentioned and paternalistic, were not "assisting" him. They were controlling him. They strong-armed a man on trial for his life – a man who they had long conceded was mentally competent to stand trial. This finding of competency to stand trial meant that Kaczynski was competent to make the important decisions in his case – such as whether he would testify, whether he would accept a guilty plea and whether to stake his life on a mental illness defense, a defense with little chance of success in this or any other high profile serial murder case.

Kaczynski never should have been forced into the position of having to choose between no legal counsel and a defense team determined to raise a mental defect defense. Kaczynski's lawyers forced this Hobson's choice on their client, and they did it on the eve of the trial for his life. And he was blamed for their brinkmanship.

The deepest soul searching should have been done by Kaczynski's court-appointed lawyers before they seized control of their client's case. They should have specifically thought long and hard about their decision, months before trial, to agree with the prosecution regarding Kaczynski's mental competency. They are at least partially responsible for the events that culminated in Kaczynski's coerced guilty plea. They knew from the outset that mental illness was their best defense, and they also must have known that their client opposed that defense. Their apparent hope was that by forcing Kaczynski to choose – on the eve of his trial – between going with their defense or representing himself, their client would relent and allow them to control the defense.

It was a gamble, and they lost.

The hard part of playing chicken is knowing when to flinch.[327] Theodore Kaczynski never flinched. Given the choices with which his lawyers had left him, he chose to exercise his constitutional right to represent himself. The judge denied him even that.

As elsewhere in the Unabomber case, the real issue here is power: Should it be the man whose life hangs in the balance, or his court-appointed lawyers who decide whether to raise a mental defect defense? I believe the choice belongs to the accused.

His lawyers' job was to represent him – not to manage him, not to control him. And not to silence him.

Of course this case certainly did present Kaczynski's lawyers with an ethically awkward conundrum. Both are dedicated opponents of capital punishment, and Kaczynski was asking them to present a defense that surely would have won him a death sentence – and would have won his lawyers the anger and contempt of their peers in the capital defense bar.

I do know that defense lawyers regularly confront conflicts between their own private morality and their duties to their clients – in that conflict, either the client should prevail or the lawyer should withdraw from the case due to the conflict of interest.

A few years ago, I found myself in an ethical situation similar to that facing the Unabomber's attorneys.[328] My client was Paul Hill, who was then (and remains now) on Florida's death row for murdering a doctor and his escort in front of a Pensacola clinic that performed abortions. Hill's cause was anti-abortion, not anti-technology. I am personally adamantly pro-choice. I also thought that Hill might be mentally ill, but I followed his instructions not to raise mental issues in his case. Rather, I agreed, and actually wrote, a lengthy legal argument that Hill should not be executed because his views on abortion were correct. Notwithstanding my personal pro-choice beliefs, I was ready to stand up in the Florida Supreme Court and argue that because life begins at conception (a notion endorsed by the Pope, among others), Hill's crime was justified because, in taking two lives, he was acting reasonably because his actions saved more than two unborn lives. I never had a chance to make the argument. Hill fired me because he thought, erroneously, that I intended to portray him as mentally ill.[329] He was represented by a pro-life movement lawyer who probably made Hill's argument with warmer zeal than I would have. The Florida Supreme Court rejected those arguments and affirmed Hill's death sentence; he will probably be executed sometime in the next few years. The Hill case (and the Unabomber case) are extreme examples of the sort of conflicts that defense lawyers deal with all the time.

I believe that Kaczynski's lawyers were acting in what they honestly believed to be their client's best interests legally. But that was not the point, and that was not their job. They had one client and only one client; that client clearly was competent to stand trial, and his lawyers knew it.

Even if Kaczynski's lawyers had felt he was too crazy to stand trial – something they obviously did not believe – they should have asked the judge months before trial to explore that issue in a serious way. Once their client had been found competent to stand trial, they were ethically and morally obligated to either (1) put on the defense their client wanted them to put on, or (2) move to withdraw when other counsel could take the case over with reasonable time and resources to prepare for trial.

Abandoning Kaczynski to represent himself was not a legitimate ethical option for the defense lawyers in this case. Kaczynski did not want to represent himself – and for very good reasons. He wanted lawyers willing to abide by his wishes.

Kaczynski's lawyers managed to save his body – they succeeded in keeping it off the lethal injection gurney. But in so doing, they robbed him of his life. Even his lawyers believed that the manifesto was nothing more than the scribblings of a madman.

There are, of course, rules and regulations that purport to codify the ethics of the legal profession. These rules and codes are exquisitely vague on the questions of power and control at issue in the Kaczynski case, which is evidenced by the reliance of Kaczynski's lawyers and the prosecutors on the same rules and interpretive case law to support their respective positions. The American Bar Association Standard 4-5.2 provides:

CONTROL AND DIRECTION OF THE CASE

(a) Certain decisions relating to the conduct of the case are ultimately for the accused and others are ultimately for defense counsel. The decisions which are to be made by the accused after full consultation with counsel include:

> (i) what pleas to enter;
> (ii) whether to accept a plea agreement;
> (iii) whether to waive jury trial;
> (iv) whether to testify in his or her own behalf; and
> (v) whether to appeal.

(b) Strategic and tactical decisions should be made by defense counsel after consultation with the client where feasible and appropriate. Such decisions include what witnesses to call, whether and how to conduct cross-examination, what jurors to accept or strike, what trial motions should be made and what evidence should be introduced.

(c) If a disagreement on significant matters of tactics or strategy arises between defense counsel and the client, defense counsel should make a record of the circumstances, counsel's advice and reasons, and the conclusions reached. The record should be made in a manner which protects the confidentiality of the lawyer-client relationship.[30]

Unless the client is disabled, Model Rule 1.2 requires that a lawyer shall "abide by a client's decisions concerning the objectives of representation . . . and shall consult with the client as to the means by which they are to be pursued." Ethical consideration 7-7 is similar: "In certain areas of legal representation not affecting the merits of the cause of substantially prejudicing the rights of a client, a lawyer is entitled to make decisions on his own. But otherwise, the authority to make decisions is exclusively that of the client and, if made within the framework of the law, such decisions are binding on his lawyer." Model Rule 1.14 provides that "when a client's ability to make adequately considered decisions in connection with the representation is impaired . . . the lawyer may . . . take . . . protective action only when the lawyer reasonably believes that the client cannot adequately act in the client's own interest." Further, as the comment to Rule 1.14 notes, the law recognizes intermediate stages of competence: Even clients lacking general competence often possess the ability to "understand, deliberate upon and reach conclusions about matters affecting . . . [their] own well-being."

These codifications are vague, and what directive content they do possess seems to me illusory.[331] One difficulty is the indeterminacy and malleability of the language used here. Another difficulty is that the black letter codes of professional ethics themselves reflect competing, even conflicting, values. This jurisprudential "personality disorder," in turn, reflects the drafting histories of the codes and rules. At critical points, when one is most in need of rules with directive content, there are none: The final language is an effect of the negotiation and compromise processes from which the language came. They were, after all, drafted by lawyers. The rules offer enough wiggle room to justify the actions of Theodore Kaczynski's trial lawyers. But that's only part of the problem, and it's the easier part.

The deeper problem is law culture in general. Ironically, the Unabomber manifesto anticipates the professional forces that forced Kaczynski's lawyers to act as they did with respect to the mental defect defense. Kaczynski was the victim of a cultural phenomenon that the manifesto calls "oversocialization": "The oversocialized person is kept on a psychological leash and spends his life running on rails that society has laid down for him."[332]

Shortly after pleading guilty, Kaczynski demonstrated a clear understanding of why his lawyers did what they did to him. He wrote: "Perhaps I ought to hate my attorneys for what they have done to me, but I do not. Their motives were in no way malicious. They are essentially conventional people who are blind to some of the implications of this case, and they acted as they did because they subscribe to certain professional principles that they believe left them no alternative. These principles may seem rigid and even ruthless to a non-lawyer, but there is no doubt my attorneys believe in them sincerely."[333]

Lawyers wear masks.[334] Kaczynski got this exactly right. His lawyers were immersed in the culture of lawyering in general and capital defense lawyering in particular. Law culture has its own specialized morality, norms and values. We all know, even without attending law school, that lawyers operate according to their own code of ethics. These ethics are variously described as "role morality," or "role differentiated behavior." [335] Essentially, lawyers live by an ethical code that is different from the rest of the world (including the rest of *our* world, when we're not acting like lawyers). To some extent, we leave our "everyday ethics" at the threshold of our respective office doors each morning when we show up to work. We do things – we're ethically required to do things – that, if they were done by others, outside the profession, would be deemed wrong or immoral (keeping certain kinds of secrets, for example, even when revealing those secrets would prevent other people from suffering harm). Law students are taught to "think like lawyers," and lawyers are taught to act like lawyers, without questioning the foundational values on which our specialized role morality is based.

The general problems of ethical role morality are magnified in capital cases where the stakes are life and death. Criminal defense lawyers fight hard for their clients; capital defense lawyers fight harder. Criminal defense lawyers sometimes act paternalistically to save a client from himself; capital defense lawyers do so more often. I have argued elsewhere that capital punishment warps the law and deforms the lawyers and judges who apply the law.[336] Capital punishment not only warps, it deforms the professional ethics of those who work in the legal profession.

CHAPTER THREE

Considerations

I will not debate my soul with strangers.

Andrew Hudgins, *After the Lost War*

The Unabomber Speaks

After the chronology of events set out in the previous chapter had been drafted, I heard about Theodore Kaczynski's January 26 statement, which gave his account of the battles with his lawyers.

Kaczynski wrote the statement four days after he pleaded guilty. The statement reads as follows:

INFORMATION CONCERNING THE CASE OF THEODORE J. KACZYNSKI, ACCUSED OF BEING THE UNABOMBER.

For a matter of months preceding the beginning of my trial on November 12, 1997, I had been aware that my attorneys wanted to use a defense that would be based in part on supposed evidence of mental impairment. However, my attorneys have led me to believe that I would have a considerable measure of control over the defense strategy, hence I was under the impression that I would be able to limit the presentation of mental evidence to some items that at the time I thought might have some validity.

The first weeks of the trial were devoted to selection of a jury, a process that told me little about the defense that my attorneys planned to use. But in late November I discovered that my attorneys had prepared a defense that would virtually portray me as insane, and that they were going to force this defense on me in spite of my bitter resistance to it.

For the present I will not review in detail what happened between late November, 1997 and January 22, 1998. Suffice it to say that the judge in my case, Garland E. Burrell, decided that my attorneys had the legal right to force their defense on me over my objections; that it was too late for me to replace my attorneys with a certain distinguished attorney who had offered to represent me and had stated his intention to use a defense not based on any supposed mental illness; and that it was too late for me to demand the right to act as my own attorney.

This put me in such a position that I had only one way left to prevent my attorneys from using false information to represent me to the world as insane: I agreed to plead guilty to the charges in exchange for withdrawal of the prosecution's request for the death penalty. I also had to give up all right to appeal, which leaves me with a virtual certainty of spending my life in prison. I am not afraid of the death penalty, and I agreed to this bargain only to end the trial and thus prevent my attorneys from representing me as insane. It should be noted that the defense my attorneys had planned could not have led to my release; it was only intended to save me from the death penalty.

By concealing their intentions from me and discouraging me from finding another attorney before it was too late, my attorneys have done me very great harm: They have forced me to sacrifice my right to an appeal that might have led to my release; they have already made public the opinions of supposed experts who portray me as crazy; and they have caused me to lose my opportunity to be represented by a distinguished attorney who would have portrayed me in a very different light.

Perhaps I ought to hate my attorneys for what they have done to me, but I do not. Their motives were in no way malicious. They are essentially conventional people who are blind to some of the implications of this case, and they acted as they did because they subscribe to certain professional principles that they believe left them no alternative. These principles may seem rigid and even ruthless to a non-lawyer, but there is no doubt that my attorneys believe in them sincerely. Moreover, on a personal level my attorneys have treated me with great generosity and have performed many kindnesses for me. (But these can never compensate for the harm they have done me through their handling of my case.)

Recent events constitute a major defeat for me. But the end is not yet. More will be heard from me in the future.

Theodore J. Kaczynski

January 26, 1998[1]

Theodore Kaczynski's January 26 statement was the first – and as of this writing remains the only – communication Kaczynski has made publicly since his non-trial about his experience during the proceedings. It is of interest for that reason alone, but there are several other reasons as well.

As we have seen, the existing public record would suggest that Kaczynski's assessment of what happened to him is accurate, perceptive and correct.[2] As discussed above, the court files do indeed support Kaczynski's contention that, prior to jury selection in November 1997, his lawyers kept him (but not the court or the prosecution) in the dark about the defense his lawyers planned to raise.[3] Judge Burrell and Kaczynski's lawyers did indeed back him into a corner, from which he had only two possible routes via which to extricate himself: plead guilty or allow his own lawyers to portray him as mentally ill and his manifesto as delusional. For the proud, Harvard-educated Berkeley professor, this was no choice at all. He pleaded guilty, not to save himself from capital punishment, but rather to save himself from having his own lawyers portray him as a lunatic. His statement demonstrates Kaczynski's understanding of the situation.

And Kaczynski's January 26 statement suggests something else. Written only four days after being stampeded into the guilty plea, a time when the most sound of mind would have been pushed to the meniscus of their mental and emotional fortitude, it shows that Theodore Kaczynski was competent by a country mile. He understood the charges against him. He understood what his trial was about. He understood what his lawyers were doing to him. He understood what his options were, and he understood, better than many of the players involved, precisely who had radically limited those options.

Robert Graysmith, in the excellent epilogue to *Unabomber: A Desire to Kill* argues that the disruption of the Unabomber trial was all part of Kaczynski's "master plan" to use his trial as a political soapbox. I think Graysmith is incorrect: The transcripts of the closed-door meetings between Kaczynski, his lawyers and the judge, show, that Kaczynski was the one being manipulated, not the other way around. Still, Graysmith was present at the non-trial, and I was not. On the other hand, I have had access to the closed-door transcripts, and to Kaczynski's own interpretation of the events swirling around him, which Graysmith, I believe, did not. Only Kaczynski himself knows for sure. Since his account seems to square with the existing documentary evidence available to me, I believe the chronology set out in this book to be accurate.

Kaczynski's Case May Have Just Begun

> Law enforcement agencies are frequently inconvenienced by the consti-
> tutional rights of suspects and often of completely innocent persons,
> and they do whatever they can do legally (or sometimes illegally) to re-
> strict or circumvent those rights. Most of these educators, government
> officials and law officers believe in freedom, privacy and constitutional
> rights, but when these conflict with their work, they usually feel that
> their work is more important.[4]

> Unabomber Manifesto

The facts set out in Kaczynski's January 26 statement and the chronology
are of more than academic or historical interest: The Kaczynski legal
drama may well be far from over. As of this writing, Kaczynski has been
trying to vacate his guilty plea. If Kaczynski's statement and the chronology of events set out earlier in the previous chapter are accurate, then he has
a powerful legal claim that his guilty plea is illegal and should be set aside.

Kaczynski's guilty plea is seriously vulnerable on at least three independently sufficient constitutional grounds. First, Kaczynski has a powerful claim that his plea was coerced by Burrell's erroneous legal rulings
(particularly the ruling that Kaczynski had exercised his right to self-representation "too late"). Then there is of course Denvir and Clarke. As the
federal appeals court for the Ninth Circuit recently reiterated, "a criminal
defendant may be asked to choose between waiver and another course of
action so long as the choice presented to him is not constitutionally offensive."[5] In that case, the court ruled that a defendant on trial for his life
"could not have been forced to choose between incompetent counsel and
no counsel at all."[6]

Several courts, including the Ninth Circuit, have indicated that coer-
cion by *the accused's counsel* can render a plea involuntary.[7] At the core of
Kaczynski's coerced guilty plea was the representation he received from
Attorneys Clarke and Denvir. Both attorneys were well aware, from the

beginning, that Kaczynski vehemently opposed a mental defect defense and would do anything to avoid being portrayed as a "madman." Kaczynski continuously refused mental examinations, diligently pursued the possibility of acquiring Attorney J. Tony Serra (who would present a "political" defense), attempted to commit suicide the night before trial, and petitioned the Court to represent himself *pro se*. All of these actions were done for one simple reason; to avoid a mental defect defense. Despite Kaczynski's *clear* objection to a mental defect defense, Denvir and Clarke continued to believe that such a defense was the only way to spare Kaczynski's life. Although they may have ultimately been correct, the defense was inconsistent with the way Kaczynski chose to make his defense, a choice which is protected by the Sixth Amendment to the Constitution.[8]

A second factor which led to Kaczynski's involuntary guilty plea centered on the judge's questionable interpretation of the law; that it was counsel's decision whether to pursue a mental defect defense. The Ninth Circuit has held that in determining the voluntariness of a guilty plea, "[t]he district court should consider such factors as the amount of time remaining *before* trial when [the defendant] plead[s] guilty."[9] After Kaczynski exhausted all possible avenues to avoid a mental defect defense, he was left with no choice but to plead guilty on January 22, 1998, the morning on which trial was set to begin. In fact, immediately after the judge denied Kaczynski's motion to proceed *pro se* Denvir approached the bench and communicated Kaczynski's intentions to plead guilty. As Kaczynski himself explained,

> this put me in such a position that I had only one way left to prevent my attorneys from using false information to represent me to the world as insane: I agreed to plead guilty to the charges in exchange for withdrawal of the prosecution's request for the death penalty . . . I am not afraid of the death penalty, and I agreed to this bargain only to end the trial and thus prevent my attorneys from representing me as insane . . .[10]

In sum, both the United States Supreme Court and the Ninth Circuit have held that a guilty plea must be the defense counsel's voluntary expression of *the defendant's* own choice. Kaczynski's guilty plea was the expression of Denvir and Clarke (it was consistent with their ethical beliefs regarding capital punishment) and it was an expression of the Court, which faced intense pressures by the public to bring the case to an end. It was never the voluntary expression of Theodore Kaczynski. While it is true that under oath and in court, Kaczynski informed the judge that he was pleading guilty voluntarily, the totality of the circumstances indicate otherwise. In fact the totality of the circumstances indicate one basic point; Theodore Kaczynski pleaded guilty in order to avoid being portrayed as mentally ill.[11]

Once upon a time, decisions about whether to raise a mental defect defense rested with the lawyer, not the defendant. "Within the past twenty years, however, the governing legal norm has shifted decisively . . . [These recent cases have established] that the defense attorney must adhere to the wishes of a competent defendant who [declines] to raise the [insanity] defense."[12]

In addition to this, Kaczynski has a strong claim that his lawyers, in demanding to raise a defense that their client would rather die than raise, rendered his assistance of counsel constitutionally ineffective – which offers grounds for voiding Kaczynski's guilty plea all by itself.[13] The argument here would be that Kaczynski's rights were disabled by some species of conflict – a conflict of interest between the fundamental goals of the defense that caused a structural defect in the attorney-client relationship that, in turn, caused counsel to effect a hostile takeover of the defense.

It must also be borne in mind that Kaczynski was represented by public defenders. Had he the resources to hire his own lawyer, Kaczynski could have simply fired his counsel and found a lawyer who was willing to respect his wishes. He could only ask the judge for help. When the judge sided with the public defenders, Kaczynski tried to exercise his right to self-representation, and the court refused that, too. Kaczynski couldn't do what a client able to hire his own lawyers could have done: replace his disloyal attorneys months before the trial.

Any attempt to invalidate Kaczynski's guilty plea would be an uphill effort, particularly since he did not attempt to do so at his sentencing, four months after he pled guilty. Retaining a lawyer to represent him in this effort, which he has done, proved very difficult because the obvious pool of qualified counsel – the experienced capital defense bar – were understandably squeamish about providing assistance to a long-shot litigation campaign that would, even if successful, only expose Kaczynski to a death sentence.[14] The flipside is that Kaczynski would get a trial – a real day in court, which he was denied the first time around.

Giving the Unabomber his day in court, before a jury, would be a dramatic cultural event. But the more significant event would be a judicial determination that even the Unabomber has a right to receive his day in court – and that his right cannot be usurped by court-appointed lawyers, no matter how well-intentioned. The Unabomber case thus could result in a judicial ruling that redefines the essential nature of the attorney-client relationship in death penalty cases. That *would* be a landmark in American law.

With Kaczynski's guilty plea, the judicial system, the media and the public closed the book on the Unabomber case. I believe they were premature in doing so. As discussed above, the pressures that forced Kaczynski into pleading guilty – exerted on him by his own lawyers and the judge – have left the guilty plea seriously vulnerable to constitutional challenge by the Unabomber.

That, perhaps, is the saddest aspect of the Unabomber's non-trial: It isn't over yet. It is the birthright of every American, no matter how despicable, that he is constitutionally entitled to have his day in court. The Unabomber has not yet had his.

And who is the "real" Theodore Kaczynski? Unless he gets his day in court – at the conclusion of which he might well be sentenced to death and executed – we may never know.

The Political Trial That Wasn't:
Kaczynski, McVeigh and Hill

> A man's spirit can be marked most clearly in its passage from the reform
> to the revolutionary impulse at the moment he decides that his enemy
> will not write his history.

> Murray Kempton

Timothy McVeigh and the Waco massacre; Paul Hill and abortion;
Theodore Kaczynski and anti-technology – we seem to live in an age when
some Americans are ready and willing to kill other Americans to make an
ideological point. It almost makes one nostalgic for the days when court-
marshal defendant Captain Howard Levy, M.D. presented evidence to try
to prove that the United States was following "'a general policy or pattern
or practice' of war crimes in Vietnam," or when the Winooski 44 "tried"
America's policies in Central America.[15]

McVeigh, Hill and Kaczynski all faced trials for their lives. Kaczynski
never got his trial. Hill and McVeigh did, although their respective court-
appointed attorneys responded very differently to their clients' wishes
regarding their defenses – against the imposition of capital punishment –
by raising defenses that were based on their political ideologies. Hill wanted to invoke a little-used defense to argue that his killings were justifiable
homicide – or at least motivated by a sincere desire to prevent a greater
harm – because he was saving the lives of the "unborn."[16] When Paul Hill's
trial judge denied him the counsel of his choice (an anti-abortion attorney
who wanted to argue that the murders were justifiable homicide), he fired
his court-appointed public defenders and represented himself. After the
judge ruled that his "political necessity" defense evidence was inadmissible, Hill stood mute.[17] His jury unanimously recommended that Hill be
put to death. On appeal, Hill was represented by the anti-abortion lawyer
he had been denied at trial. The state Supreme Court, rejecting Hill's
"necessity" defense, unanimously affirmed Hill's death sentence.

Like Paul Hill, Timothy McVeigh was sentenced to death. However, unlike Hill (and Kaczynski), McVeigh's trial lawyers did mount a vigorous political defense against a death sentence. In his opening statement at the penalty phase of McVeigh's bifurcated capital trial, McVeigh's lawyer told the jurors that the defense would reveal to them a Timothy McVeigh who had been a model soldier deeply disturbed by the federal government's botched raid at Waco, Texas. McVeigh's attorney told the jurors he would ask them to consider "what Mr. McVeigh believed happened at Waco." After Waco, McVeigh thought that "the federal government that we rely on to protect us, serve us, had turned the tables, had become master, had declared war on the American people."[18] He tried to spark the jurors to empathize with McVeigh's misplaced passion. "You will hear," McVeigh's lawyer closed, "that the fire in Waco did keep burning in McVeigh. He is in the middle of it."[19]

McVeigh's lawyers showed the jury magazine articles and videotapes about Waco – where about 80 people (including children) died in the catastrophe at the Branch Davidian complex near Waco, which burned to the ground on April 19, 1993, exactly two years before McVeigh bombed the Federal Building in Oklahoma City that killed 168 people, including many children.[20] McVeigh's lawyers called the author of some of the *Soldier of Fortune* magazine articles that had impressed McVeigh as a witness.[21] The defense tried to paint McVeigh's outrage and political sentiments to the jury in a vivid light. The author of a book titled *Ashes of Waco* "summarized what McVeigh might have gleaned from other articles and videos critical of the Government's role" in Waco and Ruby Ridge.[22] In closing arguments, McVeigh's lawyers, seeking to spare him, reiterated that the bombing was political."[23]

One can only speculate how the presentation of evidence struck the jurors. I think I can imagine how revolted I would have been had I served as a member of the McVeigh jury listening to this sort of evidence and argument – I know how I would feel if Judge Vance's assassin had offered political swill as an "excuse" for the deadly bomb he mailed to Judge Vance's home.[24] Unsurprisingly, the McVeigh lawyers' strategy backfired and left the lawyers open to harsh and very public criticism. "Legal experts" denounced the lawyers' "bizarre strategy" that may well have "persuaded the jury to impose a sentence of death rather than life in prison."[25] *Newsweek* interviewed some of McVeigh's jurors, and proclaimed that the defense strategy was a "catastrophe."[26] However, *Newsweek* also reported that all 12 McVeigh jurors "accepted," as mitigating evidence, the defense's "depiction of McVeigh's deep hostility toward the federal government after Waco and the FBI shoot-out at Ruby Ridge."[27]

They agreed that McVeigh believed the federal government's "ninja-warrior tactics in those incidents were 'leading to a police state.'"[28]

One commentator opined: "The strange calculation of the defense in presenting Mr. McVeigh as politically motivated seemed [to be] forced by Mr. McVeigh himself."[29] However, the decision to base McVeigh's defense against capital punishment on his political reasons for committing the crime was apparently a choice made by his lawyers. In an interview, one of McVeigh's trial attorneys was asked: "Did Mr. McVeigh instruct you to bring a penalty phase that portrayed this as a political act? Was this a way of painting himself as a martyr?"[30] The lawyer responded: "Tim doesn't want to be a martyr. He was an active participant, but we [*i.e.*, the lawyers] made all the final decisions. This was not a conventional capital case; it needed unconventional tactics. The government prosecuted Tim because of what he believed happened at Waco. We turned that on its head. We said, 'Let's talk about Waco.' In the end, all 12 jurors said Waco and Ruby Ridge were mitigating factors."[31]

It is not likely that Theodore Kaczynski (or Paul Hill, for that matter) would have fared any better than McVeigh with a political defense. Arguing the political bases of his crimes would have increased the likelihood of a death sentence. Still, the evidence could have been admissible during the penalty phase of the trial, for the same reasons it was admissible in McVeigh's.

The precedent here is of course the *Lockett* doctrine, which is based on the 1978 case of *Lockett v. Ohio*.[32] The *Lockett* doctrine is a sort of Magna Carta that obliges a capital sentencing body to hear, and to be allowed to consider, any mitigating evidence that has bearing on any aspect of the defendant's character, record, or crime. "Mitigating evidence," the *Lockett* doctrine provides, is any "fact about the defendant's character or background, or the circumstances of the particular offense, that may call for a penalty less than death."[33] As Louis Bilionis has demonstrated, the definition of what counts as "mitigative evidence' in *Lockett* is broad:

> *Lockett*'s definition extends constitutional protection to the kind of evidence that must be taken into account at sentencing to produce a morally appropriate sentence. Any evidence about the offender or the offense that might support a conceivable moral argument against the death sentence in a particular case is protected under the *Lockett* definition. Mitigating evidence might include, for instance, evidence that a death sentence would be unjust because the defendant's personal responsibility for the offense is lessened by youth, stunted intellectual and emotional growth, mental retardation or impaired capacity, mental or emotional

disturbance, provocation by others, insanity, the influence of alcohol or drugs at the time of the offense, or to shared or limited participation in the actual crime. *Lockett's* definition of mitigating evidence also would embrace evidence in support of a claim that the defendant suffered tragic or horrible circumstances in his or her formative years, such as abuse, neglect, poverty, or domestic turbulence, that might explain the defendant's failure to develop into a fully normal and law-abiding citizen. Evidence tending to show that a death sentence would be too harsh because the defendant in the past has succeeded in making a well-behaved and peaceful adjustment to prison life, is prone only to isolated incidents of violent behavior that can be controlled or minimized in prison, has been willing to confess or cooperate with authorities in some way, or otherwise has good prospects for rehabilitation would find protection in *Lockett's* definition. So, too, would evidence of some of the defendant's positive traits – such as remorse, general good character, hardworking nature, success in overcoming considerable hardships, service to the community or the military, or relatively minor criminal record – that distinguish the defendant from truly incorrigible murderers and commend restraint in imposing the harshest sentence.[34]

The core questions on the table during the penalty phase of a capital case – whether the defendant has lost his moral entitlement to live, whether he deserves to die – are essentially moral, not legal questions. To be sure, the sentencing jury must be provided with a legal framework with which to structure their moral inquiry (set out by legislators in statutory lists of "aggravating" and "mitigating" circumstances, for instance). Still, the ultimate decision – life or death – is a moral one. Capital defendants have a constitutional right to present any relevant mitigating evidence that might cause the sentencing body to choose life over death in that particular case. The motivation for a murder is directly relevant to that moral calculus, even when that reason is a political ideology, as the judge in the Timothy McVeigh trial agreed. Perhaps Burrell would have agreed as well, had he been willing to consider and hear all of the relevant evidence.

Notes On an Anti-Technology Defense

But we seldom hear . . . a Luddite point of view. Not that they left a lot to work with: In 1812, unions themselves were illegal – not until 1824 were they allowed to negotiate on wages and working hours; not until 1871 could they strike – and machine-smashing was a capital offense. To put anything down on paper was suicidal. And it was almost as dangerous, later on, to reminisce. No firsthand account of Luddite activity has survived for historians to construe, no periodicals, Minute Books or memoirs. "Luddism," as E.P. Thompson reminds us, "ended on the scaffold." [35]

John Leonard

If Theodore Kaczynski had made the defense he wanted all along, how would it have worked? Of the three recent would-be political martyrs under discussion (McVeigh, Hill and Kaczynski), Kaczynski had the most fully and publicly developed political ideology.

The Unabomber manifesto would have formed the core of any ideological defense against the death penalty. The defense would have situated the manifesto within an intellectual, cultural and historical tradition. Eminent political scientists would then be called to interpret the manifesto, line by line, paragraph by paragraph, in excruciating detail.

The prosecution probably would have attacked Kaczynski for being unoriginal. There were many people who felt this way. Kirkpatrick Sale, after lamenting the prose style and lack of intellectual originality of the manifesto, wrote:

The Unabomber stands in a long line of anti-technology critics where I myself have stood, and his general arguments against industrial society and its consequences are quite similar to those I have recently put forth in a book on the people who might be said to have begun this tradition, the Luddites.[36]

The defense would have argued that the ideas in the manifesto were too heretical for much of mainstream society – including law, psychiatry, science, the press, academia and radical activists on the left and right – and that this would make people feel the need to define Kaczynski as a delusional madman. According to this argument the "mental defect" label would be little more than a smokescreen that obscured the political ideas articulated in the manifesto. Even the label "anti-technology," Lydia Eccles has pointed out is "reductive of how comprehensive his heresy is."[37]

Eccles categorized Kaczynski's ideology as follows:

Technology and Progress: The manifesto attacks the idea that technological progress is a natural, benevolent force as promoted by those on the front lines of technological research and development; especially those with a vested interest such as the media industry and pharmaceutical and biotech corporations. It also counters the more mainstream idea that technology is a neutral tool. Beyond that, it dismisses the possibility that technology might be a "mixed blessing," or a counter-cultural tool for anarchists.

Standard of Living: The manifesto asserts that independence is more important than security and comfort. (Kaczynski's repudiation of modern conveniences was considered *ipso facto* evidence of insanity, and his defense team strategy included the display of his uprooted cabin to drive the point home.

Materialism: The manifesto not only attacks consumerism (which is merely the tip of the iceberg) but also the scientific ethos, which reduces reality to the material and quantifiable. Materialism denies the qualitative, subjective, experiential – as opposed to behavioral – aspect of life (*e.g.*, Marxists who define social welfare as the equal distribution of material goods, anti-death penalty workers who define saving a life as saving a body, psychopharmacologists who define mind as brain).

Freedom, Rights, Democracy: The manifesto debunks these core assumptions of our national identity. The abstract concept of freedom conceals the fact that in our daily lives we actually have less and less freedom of action. Democracy is an illusion. Politics merely deal with the details once the important decisions are made beyond the realm of participatory politics. Individual rights protect us from government but not from market forces, leaving us open to other forms of interference with our freedom. The First Amendment cannot protect us from social control by propaganda.

The Counter-culture: Leftists are not necessarily the rebels they appear to be. They are prone to being unconsciously submissive to authority, masochistic, guilty, self-serving and opposed to the true spirit of freedom. The Unabomber credits street gangs and militia groups for being a greater threat to authority. The manifesto does not strategize in terms of mass movements and unified actions, but instead urges individual action of any kind. It does not invoke political theory, but instead objectively discusses the observable behavior of large complex systems. Personal opinions are qualified as such. The manifesto makes the minimum truth claims; instead of being a flaming rant, it is a proof: Technology and freedom inevitably collide.

Nature Worship: The manifesto does not consider Earth to be more important than humans, but rather discusses the environment from the standpoint of human autonomy. It advances the idea of wild nature as opposed to benevolently managed nature.

Productivity: The manifesto ridicules the belief that paid work is a meaningful and socially valuable activity.

Academia: Instead of seeing academics as disinterested and above politics, the manifesto targets them as the biggest political threat, since they have an ego-investment in their careers. They rationalize the development of new techniques regardless of the long-term consequences to human freedom.

Medicine, Psychiatry, Social Work: Regarding the main claims of modern medicine, the manifesto posits that longevity should not be highly prized, since it measures life quantitatively, not qualitatively. Psychological therapy and social work, including projects spearheaded by leftist reformers, embody various forms of social control.

The Right/Left Divide: The real axis is technology. The choice is between simple small-scale autonomous existence and an alienated existence of dependency within a large-scale complex technological system of centralized social control. The manifesto inverts Marxism: technological development will not inevitably lead to revolution and liberation, but to absolute social control. The more time that passes, the less our capacity to rebel.

Experts: Whether they are academics, industry scientists, politicians, or business professionals, experts define and further strengthen social norms by virtue of "certified" authority.

Political Revolution/Utopia: The manifesto considers and weighs the possible consequences of various responses to our situation and unromantically concludes that an ideal outcome is unattainable. Rather than invoking utopia, the manifesto proposes to place stress on the system to cause its collapse as a calculated risk: the benefits outweigh the costs.

The Cloak of Intention: The manifesto challenges the idea that we are in control of our history; that history is a contest of heroes and villains in a conflict of will. Instead it shows how benevolent human intentions amplified by increasingly powerful technologies inevitably tend toward totalitarian control: history is a side-effect.[38]

In addition to situating Kaczynski's politics within an intellectual, cultural and historical context, Kaczynski's defense against the death penalty would situate his politics within his own personal history. *The New York Times* has already published a blueprint of the sort of penalty phase defense that I am suggesting. A massive article (almost as long as the Unabomber manifesto) titled *The Tortured Genius of Theodore Kaczynski*, painstakingly traced the course of Kaczynski's life.[39] Interlarded throughout the piece were relevant excerpts from the manifesto.

Ironically, the most powerful witness against capital punishment for Theodore Kaczynski is a witness Kaczynski himself would not allow to testify – his brother David. Since turning his brother in to the FBI as the suspected Unabomber, David Kaczynski has been trying to save his brother from a death sentence.[40] The spectacle of David Kaczynski's divided soul – struggling to save the life of the big brother he once idolized and in the end turned in – might provide a jury with the strongest reason to spare Kaczynski's life.

An ideological defense would almost certainly fail for the Unabomber, as it failed for McVeigh, and for the same reasons. But that's not the point. The point is that it's *his* defense. It's *his* life. It's his day in court. And the choice of the grounds upon which to stake that life ought to be his and his alone.

The Supreme Court has said repeatedly that the legality of death penalty trials must be judged by the "evolving standards of decency that mark the progress of a maturing society." Consider how our standards of decency have "evolved" from 1859 to today. Consider John Brown and his lawyers.

CHAPTER FOUR

John Brown's Body

Read as you will in any of the books,
The details of the thing, the questions and answers,
How sometimes Brown would walk, sometimes was carried,
At first would hardly plead, half-refused counsel,
Accepted later, made up witness-lists,
Grew fitfully absorbed in his defense,
Only to flare in temper at his first lawyers
And drive them from the case.
                              Questions and answers,
Wheels creaking in a void.[1]

Steven Vincent Benét, *John Brown's Body*

Introduction: Why John Brown?

John Brown was the son of Ohio abolitionists, a divinity school drop-out, father of twenty children and the presiding spirit of the killings at Pottawattomie in "Bleeding Kansas." He was also a self-flagellating, secretive, pious, stiff-necked man whose hatred of slavery led him to kill for its abolition. His acquaintances included Thoreau and Emerson, and he was an intimate of Frederick Douglass and Harriet Tubman.[2] John Brown spearheaded a coup that succeeded in ousting the pro-slavery majority who ran the United States government. Leading a raiding party of eighteen white and African American men (with three men held in reserve as a rear guard), Brown seized control of the federal arsenal at Harper's Ferry, Virginia.[3] He believed that northern abolitionists and southern slaves would join him, thereby initiating mass political tactics to bring about the end of slavery. It didn't happen as Brown had planned. The slaves didn't rise up; the town did. Brown, and most of his surviving followers, were captured the next day, thirty-six hours after the raid began. They were tried by the Commonwealth of Virginia for treason, murder and inciting slave insurrection. Brown's court-appointed trial lawyers wanted him to raise an insanity defense, and indeed, the circumstantial evidence that Brown was crazy – his single-minded fixation on freeing the slaves by any means necessary, his doomed raid on Harper's Ferry, some evidence of mental illness in the family – would have made such a defense highly credible. But Brown refused to allow his lawyers to write off a lifetime of work as the by-product of a diseased mind, and his attorneys honored their client's wishes. He was convicted and condemned to die. Brown was hanged on December 2, 1859. Emerson proclaimed Brown a new saint in the calendar. Thoreau described him as an angel of light.[4] Victor Hugo proposed an epitaph: "Pro Christo sicut Christus."[5] Melville wrote that "Weird John Brown" was the "meteor of the war" between the states.[6]

Or so goes the heroic view of John Brown. On the polar-opposite side of the John Brown continuum, there is the demon: a lunatic psychopath, a mercenary who cynically manipulated the incendiary politics of slavery to manufacture his own martyrdom – and all with the assistance of counsel.[7] As is the case with many latter-day, would-be martyrs, both views probably contain some truth. John Brown was neither a madman nor a martyr. But, in a way, he was both.

Confronted with the impossible task of representing a would-be political martyr who was on trial for his life, Brown's lawyers chose to proceed in a manner that was very different from the tack taken by Kaczynski's counsel. Both cases provide insight into what one historian of John Brown has aptly called in a somewhat different context, the "politics of insanity."[8]

I believe that, of the two groups of lawyers I will explore, John Brown's lawyers served him better than their historically distinct successors served Kaczynski. These are of course matters about which reasonable people of conscience can and will disagree, even when the respective parties to the conversation possess all the facts, which in this instance I certainly do not. Like all good history, this can only be read as a cautionary tale.

Kaczynski does not consider John Brown to be his historical antecedent or role model – nothing in his voluminous writings ever mentions Brown. But while the men may differ, there are remarkable parallels between their two cases.

My interest in Brown dates from childhood and was reinforced by the years I spent in capital post-conviction litigation, which is the law-world counterpart of guerrilla warfare. I was fascinated by the tactical and strategical insights of those who had studied how a small force might defeat a much larger and better equipped one, particularly Stonewall Jackson in the Valley ("always mystify"), Robert E. Lee (at Chancellorsville), Nathan Bedford Forrest (everywhere), James Longstreet (offensive in strategy; defensive in tactics) and John Brown, whose plan itself never seemed to me unsound, but whose successful conclusion required rapid extrication of his raiding party from Harper's Ferry once the job was done.

John Brown makes sense in the context of the Unabomber trial because of the historical, and therefore emotional, distance it affords us. In 1995, Robert McGlone could write that "the question of Brown's mental state still bedevils us. Echoes of the politics of insanity resonate in the literature of the coming of the Civil War."[9] Virtually every major historian of Brown has had to grapple with the "bedeviling" question of Brown's sanity – and with the "politics of insanity."[10] The validity of John Brown's politics was proven in the crucible of war; the Unabomber's may not be proven until the next century, if it ever is. Thus Weird John Brown's case is more amenable to neutral examination: Kaczynski, and his anti-technology politics, are still too close and too present to make this possible. Another curiously "bedeviling" facet of Brown's trial is the fact that most of the professional ethics issues raised by it still resonate today – particularly in juxtaposition with the Unabomber non-trial.

Before discussing the similarities between John Brown's trial and the Unabomber case, it should be made clear that Brown's lawyers possessed sufficient evidence to assert that Brown was mentally ill. I do not believe that Brown was in fact mentally ill. To be more precise, I do not believe that the existing evidence on this score is sufficient to support such a conclusion one hundred and forty years after the fact. Stephen Oates is right to contend that the evidence itself is unreliable, because it was produced by Brown family members and other interested lay people whose primary goal was to save Brown's life by showing him to be mentally ill. Oates is also right that "insanity" and related notions are culturally defined ideas that must be understood within the cultural context in which they appear.[11]

> To begin with, the word "insanity" is a vague, emotion-charged and clinically meaningless term. Modern psychology has long since abandoned it in describing mental and emotional disorders. And historians should abandon it as well. As C. Vann Woodward has reminded us, the term even in historical context is misleading, ambiguous and relative – it has meant different things to different peoples in the past, and what seems "insane" in one period of time may seem perfectly "sane" at other times. Even in nineteenth century parlance, "insanity" was a catchall term used to describe a wide range of odd or unacceptable behavior, including epilepsy and multiple sclerosis. Consequently, when Brown's relatives and friends talk about instances of "insanity" in the family we do not know what sort of disorders they were describing. Maybe some of the cases were epileptics or mentally retarded.[12]

I am certainly unwilling to treat the raid itself as evidence of mental illness: On the matter of slavery, Brown wasn't crazy. He was right. The only realistic method to rid the nation of slavery at that time was war. Brown was right again. In short, I do not believe that John Brown suffered from a delusional disability. To the contrary, I believe he saw the situation far more clearly than did the vast majority of his contemporaries. Mental illness can be a hard thing to diagnose in a society such as ours. In the *Boston Strangler*, Gerold Frank described the psychologist Leo Adler's reflection on some of his patients:

> If a depressed patient walked into his office and said that the world was so grim that he could not face it, he had to treat him as a sick man. Actually, the patient was right . . . He no longer had the normal illusions that keep us sane.[13]

Weird John Brown and the Mad Bomber

The Constitution makes no distinction between property in a slave, and other property. [14]

> The Supreme Court of the United States
> *Dred Scott v. Sanford* (1857)

John Brown, the slavery abolitionist whose 1859 raid on the federal arsenal at Harper's Ferry, Virginia, was, at least in the minds of most historians, critical in galvanizing public opinion in ways necessary to make war possible and likely, if not inevitable. When the Commonwealth of Virginia hanged John Brown, he was transformed into a celebrated martyr in the North. At the same time, the South became convinced that compromise on the slavery issue was impossible. Secession (and war) was inevitable. Brown himself had hoped and planned that just this would occur.[15]

The Brown case and the Kaczynski case do indeed possess eerie similarities. Like Kaczynski, Brown committed intentional murder in aid, he claimed, of what he believed to be a higher purpose. Like Kaczynski, Brown was implacably determined to base his defense upon that higher purpose even if that meant a virtually certain death sentence.[16] The initial public reaction to John Brown's crime was that he must have been crazy.[17] "Old John Brown had to be crazy. That was the almost universal supposition after his capture . . ."[18]

> Sometimes rebuked for his 'wild' scheme to free the slaves, sometimes depicted as a 'poor demented old man' deserving clemency, Brown was everywhere the subject of widespread bewilderment. As friends and foes alike began to grasp the political ramifications of Brown's raid, his 'crazy' act ignited public debate of an unprecedented nature. At Brown's trial . . . the claim that he was legally insane upset the calculations of prosecutors and defense attorneys alike."[19]

Like Kaczynski, Brown's lawyers wanted to raise a mental illness defense and there was arguably enough evidence of Brown's insanity to make such a defense credible.[20] Robert Penn Warren writes that Brown's lawyers:

> possessed one powerful defense for their case. When the proceedings opened on Thursday morning they had in their hands a telegram from Akron, Ohio, testifying that insanity was hereditary in the Brown family. John Brown absolutely refused to avail himself of the defense. It would have meant a repudiation of himself, and in comparison to such a thing the danger of the noose was inconsequential; it would have meant that he himself was nothing, and all his life, since the youthful period of doubt when he felt a "steady, strong desire to die," had been spent in a ruthless, passionate attempt to prove to the world that he, John Brown, was something. In refusing the plea he was simply risking his life once more to establish that desire for which he had already risked his life so many times before.
>
> With the plea of insanity eliminated, [Brown's lawyers] could only declare their belief in the nobility of John Brown's intentions and indicate some of the atrocities which he might have, but had not, committed.[21]

Brown was willing to waive an insanity defense to keep his life's work from being dismissed as the product of a diseased mind.[22] Perhaps the strongest argument against Brown's insanity was the careful planning of his crime and the lucidity and morality – if not the legality – of his political reasons for committing murder. Brown was willing to die for his cause. As if foreshadowing the Kaczynski trial, the governor ordered – against Brown's wishes – a mental health professional to examine him in order to determine his sanity.[23] Unlike Kaczynski's case, the psychiatric evaluation never took place.[24]

But Brown's family did try to save him from himself: "to save him, they gladly laid bare some sad family secrets" as evidence of his insanity: [25]

> These affidavits [from Brown family members and others] varied so far as John Brown himself was concerned, from statements that he was occasionally insane, of an "unbalanced mind," a monomaniac, to outright assertions that he had been clearly insane for the previous twenty-four years. But on the family record they all agreed. These generous admissions of nearest of kin proved that, aside from other cases of less serious derangement, Brown's grandmother on the maternal side, after lingering six years in hopeless insanity, had died insane; that of his grandmother's children, Brown's uncles and aunts, two sons and two daughters were intermittently insane, while a third daughter had died hopelessly lunatic; that Brown's only sister, her daughter and one of his brothers were at intervals deranged; and that of six first cousins, two

were occasionally mad, two had been discharged from the state lunatic asylum after repeated commitments, while two more were at the time in close restraint, one of these being a hopeless case. This is a fearful record, and one surely grave enough to have warranted the employing of alienists to make certain that Justice, in her blindness, did not execute an irresponsible man. But the Governor failed to act. It was then too late for the issue to be raised legally, for there was no procedure by which the question of sanity could be raised after the sentence had been confirmed by the Court of Appeals.[26]

At critical moments during his trial, Brown appeared to be the calmest person in the courtroom. When Brown's jury filed back into the court-room, after only forty-five minutes of deliberation, to announce their ver-dict of guilt, "the least moved [in the jammed courtroom] was John Brown, as indomitable and iron-willed as ever in his life."[27] His detractors have hated John Brown and argued that he was neither crazy nor a martyr – that his asserted ideology was nothing more than a cynical cover for sim-ple murder, a convenient excuse exploited by a violent sociopath.[28] But commentators as diverse as Virginia's Governor Wise and Oswald Harrison Villard agreed that Brown was "sane, and remarkably sane if quick and clear, if assumed rational premises and consecutive reasoning from them, if cautious tact in avoiding disclosures and in covering con-clusions and inferences, if memory and conception and self-possession are evidence of a sound state of mind."[29] Of John Brown's alleged insan-ity, Oswald Garrison Villard wrote:

> No historian of John Brown can fail to take note of the facts in the affi-davits, and to scrutinize the life of his subject in the light thus cast upon his inheritance from one line of his progenitors. If it could be roundly declared that he was partially or wholly deranged, it would be easy to ex-plain away those of his acts which at times baffle an interpreter of this remarkable personality, – the Pottawatomie murders, for instance. But this cannot be done. Governor Wise was correct in his estimate of John Brown's mentality; the final proof is the extraordinary series of letters written by him in jail after his doom was pronounced. No lunatic ever penned such elevated and high-minded and such consistent epistles. If to be devoted to one idea, or to a single cause, is to be a monomaniac, then the world owes much of its progress toward individual and racial freedom to lunacy of this variety. If John Brown was insane on the sub-ject of slavery, so were Lucretia Mott and Lydia Marie Child, while Gar-rison and Phillips and Horace Greeley should never have been allowed to go at large. That their methods of advancing their joint cause differed

from John Brown's violent ones, in no wise argues that he went beyond the bounds of sound reason in his efforts for freedom for the blacks. If John Brown was the victim of an *idée fixe*, so was Martin Luther, and so were all the martyrs to freedom of faith. But, examining his record day by day, weighing all the actions of a life of great activity, and reading the hundreds of letters from his pen which have survived to this hour, the conclusion is inevitable that, however bad his judgment at times, however wild the planless assault on Harper's Ferry, John Brown himself had escaped the family taint, – and this despite the kindly affidavits of those who wished to save him from the gallows. Moreover, while lunatics have often for a time imposed their will upon weaker intellects, persuaded them that fancied wrongs were real, and nerved them to acts of violence, John Brown lived too long and too intimately with many men to have been able to mislead them always. The paranoiac invariably betrays himself at last. But the man who sacrifices business prospects, a quiet orderly life, his family's happiness, and the lives of himself and his children, in a crusade which the world has since declared to have been righteous as to its object, cannot, because of his devotion to that purpose, be adjudged a maniac – else asylums for the insane have played too small a part in the world's history. Dr. Starry, the gallant physician of Harper's Ferry, said, years after the raid, that such devotion as Brown's followers had for him he, Dr. Starry, had never beheld before or since. "They perfectly worshiped the ground the old fellow trod on." The hard-headed, able Americans, like Stevens, Kagi, Cook and Gill, who lived with John Brown month in and month out and were ready to die with him, worshiped no lunatic.[30]

Of course, the mavens of modern psychiatry could counter that Villard's understanding of Brown's mental status does not account for today's knowledge of the subtleties and nuances of mental illness, and it should be noted that some historians have indeed diagnosed Brown as being mentally ill.[31] But I have worked with a fair number of contemporary mental health experts, and I doubt that the soft science of psychiatry can truly account for John Brown – or Theodore Kaczynski or Timothy McVeigh or Paul Hill, for that matter.[32]

The Lawyers: A Study In Contrasts

If the cases of John Brown and the Unabomber share some fascinating similarities, the ways the respective trial lawyers dealt with their would-be martyr clients could not have been more different. Brown's trial lawyers respected their client's wishes – although a later group of lawyers, beholden to Northern abolitionists, did not – and Brown was executed.[33] Kaczynski's lawyers informed the court prior to trial, that they believed their client was suffering from a serious mental illness and that they wanted to base their defense on that mental illness. Even when Kaczynski tried to fire them, his lawyers stuck to their guns. In the end, Kaczynski's lawyers, and the trial judge, pressured Kaczynski into a guilty plea to avert the mental defect defense against the death penalty.

Sure, Kaczynski *may* suffer from some form of schizophrenia; "mental health *is* a continuum."[34] "But [Kaczynski] is nowhere near any clinical extreme" – as his lawyers' misleadingly told the Court during the non-trial, and as one of Kaczynski's former public defenders continues to assert even after the trial.[35]

It seems to me that Quin Denvir and Judy Clarke were largely responsible for Kaczynski's denigration into a pitiful laughingstock. They were motivated by high ideals and good intentions. They wanted to save his life. Yet, again it seems to me that by saving his body they destroyed his life. They had no legal or moral right to do so. These lawyers conceded from the outset that their client was mentally competent to stand trial. In this they were clearly correct.[36]

Consider John Brown's trial lawyers (as opposed to his self-appointed clemency lawyers). John Brown did not place much faith in the legal machinery associated with the justice system. Brown initially acquiesced to the counsel that the government chose to provide him.[37] After his trial began, Brown "rose and denounced his counsel."[38] Unlike Kaczynski's two court-appointed lawyers, Brown's two court-appointed lawyers "announced that they could no longer act in behalf of the prisoner, since he had declared that he had no confidence in them," even though this left their capital client's life in the hands of an inexperienced attorney, at least for a short time.[39] The following account details how Virginia Attorney Lawson Botts was appointed to represent Brown in this manner:

> Sheriff [Campbell] read the commitment of the prisoners on the charge of treason and murder, when Mr. [Harding], the State's attorney, asked that the Court might assign counsel for the prisoners if they had none.
>
> The Court inquired if the prisoners had counsel, when Brown addressed the Court as follows:
>
> "Virginians: I did not ask for any quarter at the time I was taken. I did not ask to have myself spared. The Governor of the State of Virginia tendered me his assurance that I should have a fair trial; and under no circumstances whatever will I be able to attend a trial. If you seek my blood you can have it at any moment without the mockery of a trial. I have had no counsel. I have not been able to advise with one. I know nothing about the feelings of my fellow-prisoners, and am utterly unable to attend in any way to my own defence. My memory don't [sic] serve me. My health is insufficient, although improving. There are mitigating circumstances, if a fair trial is to be allowed us, that I would urge in our favor. But if we are to be forced, with a mere form of a trial, to execution, you might spare yourselves that trouble. I am ready for my fate. I do not ask a trial. I plead for no mockery of a trial – no insult – nothing but that which conscience gives or cowardice would drive you to practice. I ask to be excused from the mockery of a trial. I do not know what the design of this examination is. I do not know what is to be the benefit of it to the Commonwealth. I have now little to ask other than that I be not publicly insulted as cowardly barbarians insult those who fall into their hands."
>
> The Court assigned Messrs. [Charles J. Faulkner] and [Lawson Botts] as counsel for the prisoners.
>
> After some consultation with the prisoners, Mr. Faulkner, addressing the Court said:
>
> "I was about to remark to the court that although I feel at any time willing to discharge any duty which the court can legally and by authority of law devolve upon me, I am not, in the first place, aware of any authority which this court has, sitting as an examining court, to assign counsel for the defence. Besides, it is manifest, from the remarks just made by some of the prisoners, that he regards the appearance of counsel under such circumstances not as a *bona fide* act, but rather as mockery. Under these circumstances I do not feel disposed to assume the responsibility of that position. I have other reasons for declining the posi-

tion, connected with my having been at the place of action, and hearing all the admissions of the prisoners, which render it improper and *inexpedient* for me to act as counsel . . . "

Mr. Botts said he did not feel it his duty to decline the appointment to the court . . .

Capt. Brown: There were certain men, I think Mr. Botts was one of them, who declined acting as counsel, but I am not positive about it; I cannot remember whether he was one, because I have heard so many names. I am a stranger here and do not know the disposition or character of the gentlemen named. I have applied for counsel of my own, and doubtless could have them if I am not, as I said before, to be hurried to execution before they can reach here. But if that is the disposition that is to be made of me, all this trouble and expense can be saved.

Mr. Harding: The question is, do you desire the aid of Messrs. Faulkner and Botts as your counsel? Please to answer yes or no.

Capt. Brown: I cannot regard this as an examination under any circumstances. I would prefer that they should exercise their own pleasure. I feel as if it was a matter of little account to me. If they had designed to assist me as counsel, I should have wanted an opportunity to consult with them at my leisure . . . [40]

The proceedings next day went as follows:

Before the reading of the indictments, Mr. Hunter called the attention of the Court to the necessity of appointing additional counsel for the prisoners . . . After consulting with Capt. Brown, Mr. Botts said that the prisoner retained him and desired to have Mr. Green assist him . . . The Court requested Mr. Green to act as counsel for prisoners, and he consented to do so.

Capt. Brown then rose and said: I do not intend to detain the Court but barely wish to say that, as I have been promised a fair trial, I am not now in circumstances that enable me to attend to a fair trial, owing to the state of my health. I have a severe injury in the back . . . which enfeebles me very much, but . . . I only ask for a very short delay of my trial . . . [My] hearing is impaired . . . in consequence of the wounds I have about my head . . . I could not hear what the court has said this morning . . .

Mr. Hunter said that the arraignment could be made, and this question could then be considered.

The Court ordered the indictment to be read so that the prisoners could plead guilty or not guilty, and said it would then consider Brown's request. The prisoners were compelled to stand during the arraignment – Capt. Brown standing with difficulty and Stevens being held upright by two bailiffs. The reading of the indictments occupied about twenty minutes. The prisoners each responded to the usual question, "Not Guilty," and desired to be tried separately.

Mr. Hunter: The State elects to try John Brown first.

The Court: His condition must first be inquired into.

Mr. Botts: Brown . . . is mentally and physically unable to proceed with his trial at this time. He has heard today that counsel of his own choice will be here soon, whom he will of course prefer. He asks only for a delay of two or three days . . . and I hope the Court will grant it.

Mr. Hunter: I do not think it the duty of the prosecutor . . . to oppose anything that justice requires . . . Yet . . . to delay the trial of John Brown for one, two, or three days, they deemed it their duty that the Court, before determining the mater, should be put in possession of all the facts . . . judicially, that they were aware of in the line of their duties as prosecutors. His own opinion was that it was not proper to delay the trial of this prisoner a single day . . . He alluded to the circumstances by which they were now surrounded being such as rendered it dangerous, to say nothing of exceeding pressure upon the physical resources of our community growing out of the . . . affair for which the prisoners were to be tried; and that the State law, in making special provisions for allowing a briefer time than usual in the case of conviction of such offenders, within the discretion of the Court, between condemnation and execution, evidently indicates indirectly the necessity of acting promptly and decisively, though always justly, in proceedings of this kind . . . [He] asked the Court not to receive the unsupported statements of the prisoner . . . but that the jailor and *physician* be examined . . . impediment had been thrown in the way of the prisoners procuring such counsel . . . able and intelligent counsel had been assigned to them here, and . . . there was but little reason to expect the attendance of those gentlemen from the North who had been written to. There was also a public duty resting upon them to avoid . . . the introduction of anything likely to weaken our present position and give strength to our enemies abroad, whether it issues from the jury in time or . . . comes from the mouth of prisoners or any other source. It was their position that had been imperiled and jeoparded, as they suppose, by enemies.[41]

On the third day of trial, the matter of counsel and delay came up again:

Several witnesses for the prisoner were here called and did not answer. It was stated that the subpoenas had not been returned. Capt. Brown here rose from his mattress, evidently excited. Starting upon his feet, he addressed the Court as follows: "May it please the Court . . . I gave the names, as soon as I could get them, of the persons I wished to have called . . . and was assured they should be subpoenaed. I wrote down a memorandum to that effect, saying where these parties were. But it appears that they have not been summoned, so far as I can learn. And now I ask, if I am to have anything at all deserving the name or the shadow of a fair trial, that this proceeding be deferred until tomorrow morning, for I have no counsel, as I have before stated, on whom I feel that I can rely. But I am in hopes that counsel may arrive . . . I have nobody to do any errand for me, for my money was taken from me when I was sacked and stabbed, and I have now not a dime . . . " Brown then laid down again, drew his blanket over him and closed his eyes, and appeared to sink in a tranquil slumber.

Mr. Hoyt, of Boston, who had been sitting quietly all day at the side of Mr. Botts, now rose, amid great sensation, and addressed the Court as follows: "May it please the Court, I would add my voice to the appeal of Capt. Brown, although I have had no consultation with him, that a further hearing of the case be postponed until morning. He said he would state the reason for this request. He was informed and had reason to believe that Judge Tilden, of Ohio, was on the way to Charlestown, and would undoubtedly arrive . . . tonight . . . He had taken measures to secure that gentleman's arrival at this place tonight if he reached the Ferry. For himself, he had come from Boston, traveling night and day, to volunteer his services in the defence of Capt. Brown, but he could not take the responsibility of undertaking his defence as now situated . . . I have not read the indictment through; have not, except so far as I have listened to this case and heard the counsel this morning, got any idea of the line of defence proposed. I have no knowledge of the criminal code of Virginia, and have had no time to read it. . . . [For] all these reasons I ask a continuance of the case till morning.[42]

Green, one of Brown's appointed counsel, "rose to state that [Botts, the other appointed counsel for Brown] and himself would now withdraw from the case, and could no longer act in behalf of the prisoner, he having got up and declared that he has no confidence in the counsel who have been assigned."[43] Following the prosecutor's objection to any delay to allow new defense counsel time to enter the case, Brown's other court-appointed attorney then said: "[There] is now a gentleman from Boston who has come on to volunteer his services for the prisoner. I suggest to the Court to allow him this night for preparation. My notes, my office, and my services shall be at his command. I will sit up with him all night . . . I cannot do more."[44] The judge grudgingly agreed: "The Court will not compel the gentlemen to remain on the case and accordingly granted the request

... and at six o'clock adjourned."[45] The next morning, the Northern counsel arrived and took over Brown's defense as best they could under the circumstances. Like Kaczynski's judge, Brown's judge refused to delay the trial further to allow new counsel to come up to speed: The "inexorable judge ordered the trial to proceed. [Brown] had had able counsel and ample defense; he had chosen to make a change, for which the responsibility was on his own shoulders."[46]

John Brown "understood clearly what was at issue in the clamor over his sanity" as well as Kaczynski. If he was adjudged mad, "his sacrifices would be for naught, his passion to end slavery would be dismissed as madness."[47] The issue of Brown's alleged insanity "had political as well as legal implications."[48] When they began working with Brown, the Northern abolitionists hoped that "if Brown were insane – adjudged legally irresponsible for his actions – that judgment" would also "absolve his accomplices of responsibility."[49] However, Brown's own actions during and after his trial shifted the center of gravity of the politics of insanity: "As Brown's words and conduct in prison began to win widespread admiration in the North . . . other abolitionists and supporters exalted the 'Old Hero' in a world gone mad."[50] One Brown historian observed that if John Brown's raid was "the private product of his own disordered mind, then it had "no political context, no social bearing . . . If Brown was insane, he was not representative of anyone but himself."[51] Another historian put it more bluntly. "Only a sane Brown belonged in history."[52] Building on the work of Oates, McGlone writes: "The forms of mental illness are at least in part socially defined, and the content of the delusions of mental patients is culturally determined. If Brown's contemporaries could not agree whether he was mad, many recognized in him the social type of the 'Puritan warrior.'"[53] And: "In the final analysis, the politics of insanity was part of a process of cultural transformation, blurring older distinctions between madness and reason and domesticating political violence in the republic."[54] Similarly, the definition of Kaczynski as a deranged person "domesticated" his political violence and made it easy to dismiss the ideas espoused in the Unabomber manifesto: Kaczynski refused a mental defect defense for precisely this reason.

This is, however, where Theodore Kaczynski and John Brown part ways. Brown got his day in court – assisted by trial counsel. "With the plea of insanity eliminated" – per the insistence of John Brown himself – his trial lawyers "could only declare their belief in the nobility of John Brown's intentions and indicate some of the atrocities which he might have, but had not committed."[55] Brown had "prepared an outline for his counsel," and the defense lawyers called witnesses who "established every point in question" raised in Brown's outline.[56]

Before the death sentence was pronounced, John Brown had an opportunity to speak. Brown "addressed, not the men who surrounded him [in the courthouse] but the whole body of his countrymen, North, South, East and West."[57] This is what John Brown said:

> I see a book kissed, which I suppose to be the Bible, or at least the New Testament, which teaches me that all things whatsoever I would that men should do to me, I should do even so to them. It teaches me, further, to remember them that are in bonds as bound with them. I endeavored to act up to that instruction. I say I am yet too young to understand that God is any respecter of persons. I believe that to have interfered as I have done, as I have always freely admitted I have done, in behalf of His despised poor, I did no wrong, but right. Now, if it is deemed necessary that I should forfeit my life for the furtherance of the ends of justice, and mingle my blood further with the blood of my children and with the blood of millions in this slave country whose rights are disregarded by wicked, cruel and unjust enactments, I say, let it be done.
>
> Let me say one word further. I feel entirely satisfied with the treatment I have received on my trial. Considering all the circumstances, it has been more generous than I expected. But I feel no consciousness of guilt. I have stated from the first what was my intention, and what was not. I never had any design against the liberty of any person, nor any disposition to commit treason or encouraged any man to do so, but always discouraged any idea of that kind.
>
> Let me say, also, in regard to the statements made by some of those who were connected with me, I hear it has been stated by some of them that I have induced them to join me. But the contrary is true. I do not say this to injure them, but as regretting their weakness. Not one but joined me of his own accord, and the greater part at their own expense. A number of them I never saw, and never had a word of conversation with, till the day they came to me, and that was for the purpose I have stated.
>
> Now, I have done.[58]

One eyewitness, Judge Thomas Russell, wrote in November 1859 that Brown delivered his speech "speaking with perfect calmness of voice and mildness of manner, winning the respect of all for his courage and firmness. His self-possession was wonderful ..."[59]

Brown's trial lawyers had allowed him to maintain his dignity – his personal dignity and the dignity of the beliefs for which he was willing to die. Brown's "behavior during and after his trial had much to do" with the transformation of Northern opinion about Brown from "misguided, wild and apparently insane" into "a perception of Brown as a martyr to a noble cause."[60] In Brown's trial "testimony, letters, interviews and, above all, in his closing speech to the court, he exhibited a dignity and fortitude that impressed even Virginia's Governor Henry Wise and the fire-eater Edmund Ruffin."[61]

I have no doubt that the Unabomber's mitigation specialists, family historians and mental health experts could have worked their magic to portray John Brown and his crime as the work of a raving madman, in much the same way as they succeeded in portraying Kaczynski's manifesto as the product of a diseased mind. (In so doing they exaggerated the magnitude of Kaczynski's alleged mental illness.)[62] First, there is the evidence of a long history of insanity in the Brown family, especially on his mother's side.[63]

After Brown's trial and sentence, new lawyers, purporting to act on Brown's behalf, sought commutation of Brown's death sentence. McGlone writes: "Contrary to Brown's wishes and instructions to his initial counsel," a "new team of Northern-supported attorneys undertook to win clemency."[64] The basis of the clemency application was that "on questions connected with slavery and the liberation of the slave, [Brown] is insane."[65] Robert Penn Warren wrote:

> At his trial John Brown completely rejected the plea of insanity, but the issue did not die there. Now, along with the other demands for clemency, came further evidence tending to prove that John Brown was irresponsible. As a supplement to the information contained in the telegram from Ohio, George Hoyt secured nineteen affidavits from citizens of the region about Akron and Hudson, and presented this material to Governor Wise.[66] The affidavits recorded nine cases of insanity in the immediate family of John Brown on his mother's side, and six cases among first cousins. To this could be added the two instances among his own children, whose mother, however, had died insane. Those relatives back in Ohio now wanted to save their kinsman even if it meant exposing a family infirmity and losing a martyr to the cause which claimed their sympathy. "Oh, that we had known the amazing infatuation which was urging you on to certain destruction before it was too late!" wrote one of them. "We should have felt bound to have laid hold upon and retained you by violence, if nothing short would have availed. You will not allow us to interpose the plea of insanity in your behalf; you insist that you were never more sane in your life, – indeed, there was so much 'method in your madness,' that such a plea would be of no avail."[67]

A psychiatrist hired by a modern capital defense team would probably single out Brown's paranoia regarding slavery. If paranoia is defined by delusions of grandeur or persecution fantasies, Brown arguably had both: He saw himself as the sword of God. And this soldier of the Lord took his orders directly from the Almighty himself. He believed vehemently that America was in the grip of a vast slavocracy, a slavocracy that controlled the Supreme Court (the *Dred Scott* decision and the *Abelman v. Booth* decision) and Congress (the Fugitive Slave Act of 1850 and the series of slavery compromises between 1820 and 1855). It employed slave catchers, bounty hunters and lobbyists to extend their influence even into the abolition-minded North.[68] (A modern student of the period might not view these as delusions, but rather as a fairly reasonable and accurate understanding of the factual reality of America in the late 1850s.) Again, Robert Penn Warren:

> Undoubtedly, it would be possible to construct an argument for paranoia from certain facts: the matter of heredity; the "steady strong desire to die" in the earlier years of his life; his talent for putting other people in the wrong by adopting the part of an abused and deceived victim; and his egotism, his conviction of being an instrument of Providence, and his delusions of grandeur. But there is other material which does not fall so neatly into the argument. Certainly John Brown was not normal – whatever that may mean. His egotism, his enormous force of will, his power of endurance, his deliberate cruelties, his deliberate charities, his intolerance, his merciless ambition and the element of religious fanaticism which worked regularly as a device of self-justification – all these things made up an intensity of nature which appeared, beyond doubt, as abnormal. The issue of responsibility remains, and, pragmatically, it is not begging the question to say that John Brown was as responsible for his actions as are the general run of criminals who have suffered similar penalties; that is another problem.[69]

And then, there is crazy Captain Brown the Old Testament prophet who was willing to impoverish his own family – and in the end allow three of his sons to be killed.[70] Like Kaczynski, Brown built his small home in a setting of surpassing natural beauty. If Brown's cabin in Lake Placid, New York is a bit bigger than Kaczynski's cabin in Lincoln, recall that Brown shared his cabin with a wife and as many as ten children. Still more fuel for the clinician's crucible, there is some circumstantial evidence (albeit flimsy) that Brown's vision of himself as God's avenger might have been brought about by his failures as a businessman.[71] But, Brown was a fairly good businessman during most of his adult life, and when he did suffer setbacks, he was far from alone, since they occurred during periods of general economic instability.[72] Last but not least, there is Brown's propensity for violence in aid of his mission from God – which was his justification for the murder of pro-slavery people in Pottawattomie, Kansas and the doomed raid on Harper's Ferry.[73] Brown's raid seems in retrospect as hopeless as Kaczynski's one-man war against technology. This holds out the only carrot that could lead one to dismiss their respective acts and ideologies as the froth of madness. Brown and Kaczynski were willing to kill in the name of an ideological cause to which most of their countrymen at the time did not subscribe. At the time of the raid, it was not at all clear that the violence would succeed in achieving the goals that inspired it. History had not yet passed judgment. Stephen Vincent Benét's lines on Robert E. Lee come to mind: "Taking enormous risks again and again . . . Mocking at chance and all the odds of war/with acts that looked like hairbreadth recklessness – we do not call them reckless, since they won."[74] Since Brown's raid seemed crazy, Brown himself seemed crazy.

An insanity defense for John Brown would have played well in the Virginia that tried and executed him.[75] Doubtless the courts would have ruled that some circumstantial evidence was admissible. The plantation culture of the South would have loved to dismiss Brown as a lunatic. Barring that attractive option, they would be forced to confront something far more frightening – the possibility that Brown's terrifying actions (and nothing terrified the South more than the possibility of armed slave insurrection) might have at least the implicit support of the Northern abolitionists. Walter Kirn put it well: "Beside his abolitionist contemporaries – Quaker pacifists, Boston philosophers and New York journalists – Brown was a crude and primitive avenger in a world of feeble moral dilettantes. If John Brown was sane, then so were the most radical of the Northern abolitionists."[76]

Stephen Oates, once again, eloquently captures the situation: "Perhaps some day in the future, when the science is more exact, an expert psychiatrist will tell us what Brown's 'mental disorder' was. Or maybe he will conclude, when all the evidence is in, that Brown was no sicker than most of his countrymen, remembering, as one must, the words of Karen Horney that in times of social injustice it may be the passive individual, not the reformer, who is mentally disturbed."[77] Oates explains:

> All this is not to argue that Brown was a "normal," "well-adjusted," "sane" individual. These terms are meaningless too. That he was a revolutionary who believed himself called by God to a special destiny (a notion that stemmed from his Calvinist beliefs), that he had an excitable temperament and could get carried away with one idea, that he was inept, egotistical, hard on his sons, afflicted with chronic attacks of the ague, worn down from a lifetime of hardship, and enraged enough at his

"slave-cursed" country to contemplate destroying it, that he could have five men he regarded as his enemies assassinated in cold blood (after proslavery forces had murdered six free-state men in cold blood), and that he wanted to become either an American Spartacus at the head of a slave army or a martyred soldier who was the first to die in a sectional war over slavery – all this is true. Yet to dismiss Brown as an "insane" man is to ignore the tremendous sympathy he felt for the suffering of the black man in the United States; it is to disregard the fact that at a time when most Northerners and almost all Southerners were racists who wanted to keep the Negro at the bottom of society, John Brown was able to treat America's "poor despised Africans" as fellow human beings. And to label him a "maniac" out of touch with "reality" is to ignore the piercing insight he had into what his raid – whether it succeeded or whether it failed – would do to sectional tensions that already existed between North and South. Nor can John Brown be removed from the violent irrational, and paradoxical times in which he lived. A man of "powerful religious convictions" who believed to his bones that slavery was "a sin against God," he was profoundly disturbed that a nation which claimed to be both Christian and free should condone, protect and perpetuate that "sum of villainies." It was not only Brown's angry, Messianic mind, but the racist, cave society in which he lived – one that professed "under God" to provide liberty and justice for all – that helped bring John Brown to Harper's Ferry.

"John Brown may be a lunatic," *The Boston Post* declared, but if so "then one-fourth of the people of Massachusetts are madmen" and three-fourths of the ministers of the Gospel. At a time when thousands of Northerners remained indifferent to the contradiction of slavery in a self-proclaimed "free and just" Republic, at a time when Christians, scientists and politicians (in North and South alike) heralded Negro slavery as "enlightened" and "inevitable," at a time when thousands of Southerners were plagued with fears of a black republican invasion and haunted by nightmares of Negro rebels raping "our wives and daughters," it was indeed (as Wendell Phillips said) "Hard to tell who's mad."[78]

Indeed, it is "hard to tell who's mad."

In the next chapter, I will take another look at Kaczynski's defense team, and why his experience was so different from that of John Brown.

CHAPTER FIVE

The Politics of Insanity

They could kill [John Brown], but they could not answer him. [1]

Frederick Douglass (1879)

Life as Memory, Memory as Life

The execution of John Brown in 1859 ignited a conflagration that engulfed America from 1861 to 1865. Neither Brown's life – he failed in much, save how he chose to die – nor even the hopelessly doomed raid on the federal arsenal at Harper's Ferry can be cited. His death provided the spark. The raid was quickly suppressed, and the slaves did not rise up, as Brown and his followers had planned, but two of Brown's own sons did die in the raid.

Regardless of Brown's failures, his death – and his actions during the six weeks between his crime and being executed – succeeded beyond even his wildest dreams. Brown foresaw – in ways his lawyers and many of his followers did not – just how much power a trial and execution would have in shaping memory and fostering debate. The reaction to Brown's execution, North and South, was extraordinary, "at the very hour Brown was hanging, officials in Albany, New York, were firing a 100-gun salute to honor his martyrdom; and church bells were tolling in commemoration from New England to Kansas." Thoreau, America's quintessential non-violent pacifist, eulogized the "crucified hero," and William Lloyd Garrison told a large crowd that Brown had converted him into a proselyte of violence.[2] "In the weeks that followed Brown's execution, Northern writers, poets and intellectuals enshrined him in an almost endless procession of poems, songs, letters, essays and public addresses."[3] These events did not pass unnoticed in the South, where men and women for whom secession had seemed a laughable idea six months earlier now spoke openly of its likelihood.[4] More importantly, the militia movement in the South, previously a joke, began developing rapidly and in deadly earnest.[5] This armed and minimally trained force became the embryo of the Confederate Army.

Then came the war – John Brown's war. Stephen Vincent Benét's 1928 narrative poem of the Civil War, aptly titled *John Brown's Body*, remains my favorite assessment of Brown and the law ("yardstick law," Benét called it) and the war that his encounter with Virginia's yardstick law ignited: "For fifty-nine unsparing years/ Thy Grace has worked apart/ to mould a man of iron tears/ with a bullet for a heart."[6] And:

Sometimes there comes a crack in Time itself.
Sometimes the earth is torn by something blind.
Sometimes an image that has stood so long
It seems implanted as the polar star
Is moved against an unfathomed force
That suddenly will not have it any more.
Call it the *mores*, call it God or Fate,
Call it Mansoul or economic law,
That force exists and moves.

                  And when it moves
It will employ a hard and actual stone
To batter into bits an actual wall
And change the actual scheme of things.

                        John Brown
Was such a stone – unreasoning as the stone,
Destructive as the stone, and, if you like,
Heroic and devoted as such a stone.
He had no gift for life, no gift to bring
Life but his body and a cutting edge,
But he knew how to die.

                   And yardstick law
Gave him six weeks to burn that hoarded knowledge
In one swift fire whose sparks fell like live coals
On every state in the Union. [7]

John Brown's was a political trial – in part because his trial lawyers allowed it to be. Political trials are different from normal criminal trials. Perhaps Daniel Berrigan made this point best in the elegant introduction to his powerful play *The Trial of The Catonsville Nine*.[8] In explaining why he wrote the play, Berrigan wrote:

> The trial was finished, the judge's gavel had pounded us into true shape, and the thing was done, lost, given over, run like veins aground; in the shape of the body, in the shape of man.
>
> The facts of the case are perhaps known by now. "An FBI agent estimated that at least 600 individual draft files were in the two huge wire baskets carried by nine defendants from local board number 33 in Catonsville, Maryland, on May 17, 1968, and set afire in a parking lot" (A.P. Wire). The trial evidence brought forward a more modest figure of ruin: some 378 files. In any case, the damage was something more than symbolic, as the judge insisted several times. The damage exceeded $100,

and the prosecution proved it to the hilt. So our crime stood under a Federal statute.

The trial of the "Catonsville Nine" was held in a Baltimore Federal court, October 5-9, 1968. A verdict of guilty was returned against each defendant on each of three counts: destruction of U.S. property, destruction of Selective Service records and interference with the Selective Service Act of 1967.

It was not however a matter merely of a record. It was a matter for us of life and death. For each of us, the spring had wound tight in the weeks of discernment and scrutiny and long, patient sharing which preceded Catonsville. There was a danger that intensity and passion would be dissipated in the routine of the trial itself, in the obeisance paid to legal niceties and court routine, in the wrangling and paper shuffling which threatened to obscure the firmness and clarity of the original deed. This work had but one purpose therefore: to wind the spring tighter.[9]

The Catonsville Nine was a political trial. John Brown's was also political. Theodore Kaczynski's trial was not political – it wasn't even a trial.

Committing a crime at the right point in history and having the right lawyers would seem to make all the difference. By forcing Kaczynski to raise a mental defect defense, his attorneys determined how their client, and his life's work, would be remembered. Their actions were very much informed by the legal climate in which they were made.

One of the more interesting things about John Brown – besides the subsequent vindication of his "crazy" abolitionist views – was the way he carried himself during the trial and the fact that his lawyers respected his wishes.

Brown knew exactly what he was doing when he raided Harper's Ferry: He was trying to incite a rebellion. The plan was far-fetched, but not crazy (at least not to Virginia and the South, in the wake of the Nat Turner, Denmark Vesey, Gabriel Prosser and other slave uprisings).[87] If Brown was crazy, so were a number of Northern abolitionists and certain percentage of the Southern elite. After his trial and condemnation, Brown categorically scotched any plan to orchestrate his escape from Virginia. Brown was adamant: His execution would do far more for the cause than anything he might do later. Brown was absolutely right.

Unlike John Brown, the Unabomber's crimes did not hit a nerve that was already near the surface of the American political psyche. This can be explained to some extent, by taking a look at the differences between Brown's intended victims – guards defending a federal arsenal – and Kaczynski's victims, who were at best obscurely connected to the technological state he sought to smash. The political differences between the anti-slavery movement in 1859 and Kaczynski's anti-technology views of today necessarily mean that Kaczynski's execution would possess little of the cultural impact caused by Brown's execution. I agree with Lydia Eccles that Kaczynski's execution would have come too soon in America's evolving understanding of technology and the environment. His execution would not have hit an American nerve.

But the execution of Paul Hill might. Hill now resides on Florida's death row for the shotgun-killing of an abortion doctor and his escort.[88] Hill does consider John Brown to be his historical role model. Like Kaczynski and Brown, Hill refused to allow his trial lawyers to use a mental illness defense at his capital trial. Like Brown, and unlike Kaczynski, Hill was sentenced to death, and that sentence has been upheld on appeal. Hill's views about the evils of abortion – albeit not his means for advancing those views – *are* shared by many Americans. Hill's execution might hit a nerve.[12]

I am not qualified to say whether the Unabomber is another John Brown. The difference between the statements these two men gave prior to sentencing – Kaczynski's rather narrow complaints, and Brown's masterful articulation of his antislavery politics – suggests to me that Theodore Kaczynski is no John Brown. Neither was his cause, in my view, comparable, since it lacks the same obvious moral magnitude. Slavery was intrinsically evil; technology is not.

Any comparisons of modern day social ills with North American slavery make me squeamish, for the same reasons that comparisons with the Holocaust do. Slavery is different. It is difficult for me to imagine that as recently as the middle of the last century, some Americans owned other Americans as property: that people were property – a concept enshrined into law by the United States Congress and given the constitutional imprimatur by the United States Supreme Court, and indeed the United States Constitution itself. It is difficult for me to imagine that the issue of ownership of human beings was ever treated as an *issue* of public policy in this nation – like issues of taxation – and that serious people made serious arguments, in Congress and elsewhere, that slavery was anything other than unalloyed evil wherever it existed, and especially evil in these United States of America, founded on the Declaration of Independence and the Bill of Rights. It is difficult for me to believe that my South, where I was reared, the South I love, that produced the great Army of Northern Virginia and the General Lee who commanded it – fought a bloody war to retain slavery.[13]

With the advantage of 20/20 hindsight, I agree both with Brown's ends and his means – although I am not at all certain I would have agreed with the latter had I lived in 1859. I am ambivalent about the mixed blessing of technology at this moment in history. Although I don't know how to use a computer, my personal heroes include the astronauts and cosmonauts of the 1960s and 1970s. There are ideas in the Unabomber manifesto that I admire, and there is much with which I cannot agree.

My personal appraisal of Brown's politics, and Kaczynski's ideology, is something that history will sort out, and is of little interest here. What interests me is the dramatic difference between the way Brown's trial lawyers and Kaczynski's lawyers responded to their respective clients' ideological motives. Brown's lawyers honored his. Kaczynski's lawyers hobbled his in their single-minded effort to save his life.

Why the difference in the way the two different groups of lawyers, separated by one hundred and thirty-eight years, understood their professional roles as lawyers and the professional values that animated those understandings? It is not because the codifications of professional conduct we have today did not exist in 1859. Today's codes and rules are exquisitely vague on power struggles between the client and lawyer, as was evidenced by the reliance of both the defense and prosecution in the Unabomber non-trial on the same codes to support their adversarial positions. John Brown's lawyers appeared to be following a view of client autonomy consistent with the views set out by John Stuart Mill in *On Liberty*. According to Mill, the only justification for infringement upon a sane adult's freedom is to prevent harm to others. The modern professional rules and codes "build upon principles that John Stuart Mill elaborated" in *On Liberty*.[14] Both Mill and the modern rules of professional responsibility recognize certain exceptions to this general principle.

Nor can the difference between Brown's lawyers and Kaczynski's lawyers be adequately explained, it seems to me, by the ascendancy in modern times of psychiatry as a social force. The Bible was the national religion in John Brown's time; psychiatry is the national religion at the close of the twentieth century. Still, with respect to people like John Brown and Theodore Kaczynski, psychiatry isn't much better today than it was in 1859. The labels are different: Brown was a "monomaniac" on the issue of slavery, and Kaczynski was called a "high-functioning paranoid schizophrenic."[15] But what *really* indicated such a diagnosis for Kaczynski?[16] Whence Kaczynski's "systemized paranoid delusions," and what were they exactly? "Anti-technology . . . His view of technology as the vehicle by which people are destroying themselves and the world."[17]

Substitute "slavery" for "technology," and Kaczynski's 1990s psychiatrist essentially diagnosed Kaczynski a "monomaniac." In this instance, I prefer the old nomenclature to the modern DSM cartography of the human mind, heart and soul. The different labels for the disease affecting John Brown do not obscure the core reality: one hundred thirty-eight years have passed, and psychiatry isn't much better able to account for sane, rational, intelligent people who commit murder in aid of a political cause.

Even though psychiatry in 1859 was still in its infancy, lunacy was a tool that Brown's trial lawyers had in their arsenal – and, given the history of alleged insanity in Brown's family history, it would have been a potent tool. Brown's lawyers simply chose not to use that tool – presumably, at least in part, because Brown himself would have fought their attempts to portray him as a madman. Again, Brown might indeed have been insane, as some picklock biographers of him have suggested.[18] But Brown's lawyers honored their client's wishes, even though such a course virtually guaranteed Brown a death sentence and execution.

Then there are the differences between Brown and Kaczynski, differences between the men and their crimes and their victims and their reasons for committing those crimes. Brown's understanding of slavery as a kind of poison (not his antidote) was not foreign to people from important abolitionist circles in the North. Kaczynski's views are not widely held, and his execution would have little of the cultural impact that Brown's had. Perhaps this difference justifies, or at least mitigates, the course of action pursued by Kaczynski's attorneys.

Further, as the Marxist historian Herbert Aptheker has persuasively demonstrated, "the concept of militancy – of the propriety and justice of armed resistance by the slaves – was widespread within the abolitionist movement by the 1850s. Indeed, it had become a dominant view within the movement by the decade preceding the Civil War."[19] Although the examples cited by Aptheker might not be representative, they do suggest that Brown's violence was not the aberration most historians would have us believe, and they offer a possible explanation for the public transformation of Brown from madman to martyr. Theodore Kaczynski's anti-technology politics do not tap into the same cultural feelings mined so successfully by John Brown.

In addition, as a host of Brown biographers have noted, Brown truly saw African-Americans, and treated African-Americans, as fully equal to himself. Brown genuinely cared for the people he was fighting to free – and he cared with a depth almost unheard of in his own time and which is sadly rare in ours. W.E.B. Dubois put it best: "John Brown worked not simply for Black Men – he worked with them; and he was a companion in their daily life, knew their faults and virtues, and felt, as few white men have felt, the bitter tragedy of their lot."[20] Perhaps Theodore Kaczynski felt as deeply for technology's victims, but his cause, and the way he went about fighting for it, do have the arid feel of a mathematical theorem.

There is yet another important difference between Kaczynski and Brown, which concerns the relative clarity with which the two men sought martyrdom. Stephen Vincent Benét captured, I think, the sense of fatalism that overtook Brown even before the raid began: He must have known it would fail unless he withdrew his small force from the town posthaste. He waived at least three opportunities to avoid capture, as well as the possibility of escape from custody after he had been apprehended.[21] In short, Brown seemed to want to be captured and, once he was behind bars, he wanted to be executed.[22] By contrast, Kaczynski applied tremendous effort to avoid detection by law enforcement, and he showed every sign of hating his brother for turning him in. Brown sought martyrdom; Kaczynski did not. Perhaps *this* explains the actions of Kaczynski's lawyers.

Regardless of the explanation, the Unabomber's non-trial made clear that the capital defense lawyers of today are a different breed from the ones who represented John Brown. If psychiatry was in its infancy in 1859, the contemporary organized capital defense bar – of which Theodore Kaczynski's court-appointed attorneys were members – had not yet been born, and neither had the modern specialty of "mitigation investigation," a field pioneered by Scharlette Holdman, Kaczynski's mitigation specialist.[23]

Constitutional challenges to the legality of capital punishment did not begin in earnest until the 1960s.[24] Today, a small cadre of criminal defense lawyers are as committed to the abolition of capital punishment as anti-slavery abolitionists were committed to their cause in the 1850s. These "abolitionist" lawyers specialize in the hardball defense of people on trial for their lives. Some of these lawyers are motivated to do death work by a personal opposition to capital punishment. And sometimes, in my experience, these diehard attorneys – and for a long time I was one – allow their personal views on capital punishment to displace their duty of undivided loyalty to their clients. I know this can happen, because it happened to me during my own fourteen years of death work. I think this is what happened to Kaczynski's lawyers. It is a trap into which John Brown's trial lawyers did not fall – although his clemency lawyers did, and their reasons were as laudable as those of Kaczynski's lawyers. They believed that their highest duty was to save their client's body, even if that meant destroying his life. These are not decisions lawyers have the moral or professional right to make.

The difference between then and now perhaps reflects little more than the changes in the lawyer-client relationship generally and paternalistic advocacy – with the added presence of an ideologically-driven abolitionist capital defense bar.[25] In common parlance, paternalism usually has a negative connotation, suggesting one who is overbearing and condescending, no matter how well-intentioned. Deborah Rhode, in *Professional Responsibility*, uses the term in a more precise sense, to mean interfering with others' liberty for their own good. In this sense, paternalistic interventions need not have a pejorative cast. A paradigmatic case might be John Stuart Mill's bystander who prevents a person from crossing an unsafe bridge.

The paternalism of Kaczynski's lawyers was beneficent and sincere – they did what they genuinely felt was best for him. Still, I am left with nagging doubts about the validity of the role that personal politics and ideology played in the choices Denvir and Clarke made. Ironically, their ideology seems more problematic than Kaczynski's "delusional" theories.

It seems pretty clear that Kaczynski's lawyers strongly oppose capital punishment. Like myself, that opposition has led them to make career decisions that many in the legal profession might view as a bit crazy.

In John Brown's day, he was called a "monomaniac" on the subject of slavery. Kaczynski could be labeled a monomaniac on the subject of technology. I have been called a monomaniac on the subject of capital punishment. Like Kaczynski's lawyers, I passed on jobs at prestigious law firms in order to help people who most of my neighbors and friends (most Americans, I'd guess) feel have little right to a lawyer at all, much less a good one – and all in aid of a political ideology that proposes to abolish capital punishment.

It would be deliciously interesting to see the outcome were Kaczynski's defense team – or any other zealous opponents of capital punishment – to subject themselves to the battery of tests to which Kaczynski was subjected by his lawyers. I wonder whether the whole lot of us "abolitionists" might then have been labeled, as Kaczynski was, "high-functioning paranoid schizophrenics," which would of course place us at the least-ill end of schizophrenia, where obvious symptoms are often absent."[26] Many of us are just as monomaniacal as the Unabomber and John Brown when mounted on our hobby horses.

As Wendell Phillips said: "Hard to say who's mad."[27]

What Would Clarence Darrow Do?

> When every other man has turned against him, the law provides that he
> should have a lawyer, one who cannot only be his lawyer, but his friend. [28]

> Clarence Darrow (1928)

The sort of diehard death abolitionists who represented Kaczynski simply
did not exist in 1859, although fierce opposition to death as a punishment
did. Clarence Darrow, perhaps the most thoughtful and most courageous
criminal defense attorney this nation has yet produced, provides a useful
perspective on John Brown's lawyers and Theodore Kaczynski's lawyers,
even though he was writing four decades after Brown's execution and eight
decades before Kaczynski's non-trial. Darrow opposed capital punishment.[29] Yet, in a lecture about John Brown that Darrow regularly gave, he
never faulted Brown's trial lawyers because they didn't save his life by any
means necessary.[30] Darrow was a master of putting more on trial than the
simple guilt or innocence of his clients – he put racism on trial, he put cap-
italism and suppression of labor unions on trial, he put fundamentalist
religion on trial and he put the law itself on trial.[31]

Darrow also pioneered the use of psychiatry as a defense in capital trials.
His now classic defense of Leopold and Loeb – the first modern capital
trial during which Darrow pleaded his clients guilty to murder, and made
punishment the sole issue in the trial. He based the post-guilt defense testimony on psychiatrists (they were called "alienists" then), and those
alienists got life sentences for the "thrill killers" in what we now refer to as
the first "crime of the century."[32] Darrow's speeches about John Brown
argue that his trial was about far more than a crazy raid on the federal
arsenal at Harper's Ferry.[33] Darrow argued that John Brown's crime
against Virginia was a crime against slavery and that Brown's capital murder trial had everything to do with slavery.

In the end, this is perhaps the most useful frame of reference when
judging the actions of John Brown's trial lawyers, and the Unabomber's

lawyers, too: What would Clarence Darrow have done? In John Brown's case, the answer to this question seems to me fairly clear: Darrow, the paradigmatic attorney for the damned, who hated capital punishment, would have done as Brown's trial lawyers did. I also believe, although I can't be sure, that Darrow would not have done what John Brown's clemency lawyers did – or what the Unabomber's lawyers did.

If Theodore Kaczynski succeeds in voiding his guilty plea, he will be put on trial (for the first time) and the stakes will be life and death.[34] Kaczynski himself, and not his lawyers, should be allowed to choose what defense to assert at that trial. In deciding to honor Kaczynski's choice, his new lawyers might find a persuasive precedent in the 1859 story of John Brown and his trial lawyers.

CHAPTER SIX

Live Free or Die (You Decide)

Do I contradict myself?
Very well then I contradict myself,
(I am large, I contain multitudes.)

I concentrate toward them that are nigh, I wait on the door-slab.

Walt Whitman, *Song of Myself*

Allowing Theodore Kaczynski to represent himself at trial would be legally sanctioned suicide.[1]

David Kaczynski's Lawyer

The Suicide Mission

In many ways, the Unabomber case was about loyalty. When should a brother's duty of loyalty to his sibling yield to his obligations to society? When should a capital defense attorney's duty to empower his capital client give way to his obligation to save his client's life? And what about suicide?

The issue of suicide was at the core of the Unabomber case. The matter of suicide, and the duties of a lawyer with a suicidal client, permeated the reciprocal bonds of loyalty that connected Kaczynski to his lawyers.

Soon after Kaczynski's public defenders were appointed to represent him, he informed them that he would prefer to be sentenced to death if he was found guilty. In essence, Kaczynski was asking his lawyers to aid him in state-assisted suicide. Denvir and Clarke would not acquiesce to this. On the eve of his trial, Theodore Kaczynski made a serious attempt to kill himself.

The *Newsweek* headline was in large, stark type: "Suicide Mission."[2] The story dealt briefly with Kaczynski's jailhouse suicide attempt on January 7, 1998, the night after Judge Burrell ruled "that Kaczynski's lawyers could do the one thing he dreaded most – proclaim to the world" that he was mentally ill.[3] But the focus of the *Newsweek* piece was more simply that Kaczynski's claim to the constitutional right to represent himself was the same thing as suicide.

Judge Burrell had said that Kaczynski was seeking a "suicide forum" when he denied Kaczynski his constitutional right of self-representation.[4] His lawyers had made similar noises about the wisdom of a political defense rather than one based on mental defect. As a matter of trial tactics and strategy, they were probably right. But assuming they were correct, did it justify their hostile takeover of Kaczynski's defense?

For me, the answers to these questions, in the specific context of the Unabomber case, are relatively easy. Kaczynski's lawyers had a client who was obviously competent to stand trial. The evidence that he was sufficiently ill to preclude a death sentence was problematic at best. Given the methodical nature of the Unabomber's seventeen-year bombing campaign, and the ruthless detail with which Kaczynski himself documented his crimes, a death sentence would have been likely. Kaczynski was by all appearances guilty. But assume, hypothetically, that Kaczynski was in fact innocent – that the evidence against him was an elaborate invention á la Oliver Stone – that he was a patsy who couldn't prove it.

Theodore Kaczynski had decided to let the state kill him. It was an informed decision. Does that mean Denvir and Clarke should have given effect to their client's wishes? One might argue that they would be respecting the inmate's human dignity and his right to make a most personal and intimate life choice, one of the few such choices permitted to death row prisoners. But maybe they would be simply abetting the inmate's suicide, which would probably make it easier for the state to execute other prisoners who do *not* want to die. How does an attorney balance the choices and desires of one's suicidal client with the interests of other death row inmates in resisting executions – particularly when some of those other non-suicidal inmates are also clients of that selfsame attorney? These questions are neither hypothetical nor rhetorical.

Some of these issues have been dealt with, extensively and excellently, in the existing academic literature.[5] However, by definition that literature was written by academics and is read mostly by academics. It is also somewhat dated; the capital postconviction landscape is vastly different than it was in the 1980s and early 1990s when most of that literature was published. This chapter brings to its enterprise my fourteen-years of experience as a full- or part-time attorney for death row prisoners.

A Paradox

"Euthanasia" is an excellent and comforting word! I am grateful to who-
ever invented it." [6]

Bram Stoker, *Dracula*

It is paradoxical that only the very dregs of our society have the legal right
to commit suicide with the state's assistance – a right which I will suggest in
this chapter includes the right to the assistance of an attorney in seeking
that outcome. My topic may appear narrowly-focused, but in fact it implicates a constellation of issues at the core of the attorney-client relationship:
the lawyer's duty of undivided loyalty to his client, the duty to maintain
client secrets and confidences and, perhaps most fundamentally, locating
the appropriate balance of power between counsel and the condemned
client. The ethical rub can arise at any stage of the capital punishment
assembly line: during the trial, on appeal, or in the post-conviction process.

In 1997 the United States Supreme Court held that the Constitution
does not provide terminally ill people with a right to assisted suicide –
regardless of whether that assistance be provided by a physician or spouse
or other loved one.[7] Neither terminally ill cancer patients nor AIDS
patients in chronic and excruciating pain have the constitutional right to
professional, medical assistance in aid of suicide.

But since Gary Gilmore's consensual execution in 1977, the law has
been fairly settled that a condemned prisoner – and no one else in
America – *does* have a right to forego challenges to the legality of his execution, so long as such prisoner is deemed by the courts to be mentally
competent to make the decision and he has done so voluntarily: And,
when he does, the state will provide him with all the "assistance" he needs
to die, including a custom-built machine and the technicians necessary
to make it work. In other words, a death row prisoner who is mentally
competent and fully informed of the risks and consequences of his
actions, has a legal right to die. That right, I will suggest below, includes

the right of attorney assistance when necessary to enforce it.

This thesis goes to the heart of the attorney-client relationship. The issue of a capital defense attorney's appropriate response to a client who wants to volunteer for execution is as controversial as it is fundamental. The issue bitterly divided the Florida capital public defenders office at which I worked as an attorney during the mid-1980s. Virtually all of the experienced attorneys and investigators in the offices held the passionate belief that an attorney's duty was to oppose – in court, if necessary – a client's decision to waive challenges to the death penalty and consent to his own execution. Given the crushing pressures of death row, the argument ran that no prisoner's "choice" to die could ever be a genuine, voluntary exercise of free will. Our highest duty as defense lawyers was to protect our clients from capital punishment, even when that required protection from the client's own self-destructive will.

Like many hard questions regarding the scope of the attorney-client relationship, this one turns on issues of loyalty and power. The familiar paradigm is that a lawyer, especially a criminal defense lawyer, owes an absolute duty of loyalty to his client and to carrying out the wishes of that client with zeal, while remaining "within bounds of the law." In reality when we consider the actual hearts of lawyers representing actual death row prisoners with actual execution dates – the lawyer's duty of undivided loyalty becomes far more complicated. Sure, the ultimate duty is to the client. Yet that loyalty must also be balanced against that lawyer's duty to the integrity of the criminal justice system; the implied duty to other con-demned clients who do *not* want to die, but whose executions might become more likely if the client in question gets his way (this was the American Civil Liberties Union's position in the Gary Gilmore case).[8] Then there is the most difficult issue, the duty to the lawyer's own con-science, which may include a moral conviction that capital punishment is wrong or lawless. As a death-work friend once told me, "I didn't go into death row defense work so I could help the state kill my clients."

Fair enough, but an outdated position. My friend made her comment in the mid-1980s, when we were both working for Capital Collateral Representative, the state agency created by the Florida legislature in 1985 to provide legal aid for Florida's death row population. Then – and certainly at the time of Gary Gilmore's execution in 1977 – capital appellate attor-neys could honestly say, to their clients and to themselves, that fighting in the courts would (1) delay their clients' executions for a decade or more, and (2) provide a fairly high probability of winning substantive relief, in the form of retrial or resentencing. By 1983 the federal courts were throwing out death sentences at a rate of sixty percent. This number dropped to forty percent during the years following 1983, and it would drop further as the United States Supreme Court and Congress began gutting *habeas corpus* in an effort to shut down federal judicial review of death cases.[9] A lawyer at CCR during the 1980s – under the leadership of the ferociously brilliant Mark Olive and Scharlette Holdman – was at a dangerous law firm, one that provided the best death row legal aid in the nation.

What a difference a decade can make. By 1995, Olive and Holdman were gone from CCR, and the agency had devolved into a hack public defense office.[10] The federal courts were in a lockdown; between Clinton's crime bills and a federal judiciary packed to the rafters with Reagan and Bush cronies, *habeas corpus* had ceased to exist in the 1990s realm of deregulated death. The few state courts inclined to give serious appellate review to the legality of death sentences were intimidated by threats of political reprisals, reprisals that removed three justices from the California Supreme Court in 1986 and one Tennessee Supreme Court justice in 1996.[11]

Factual innocence itself had been reduced by the Rehnquist/Thomas/Scalia court to a mere technicality. In the 1993 *Herrera v. Collins* decision, a majority of the United States Supreme Court actually held that executing an innocent person does not violate the Constitution.[12] Absurdity prevailed. And it is the law that capital post-conviction defense attorneys must follow and accept if they want to continue practicing law.

In the Supreme Court's 1992 *Herrera* decision, Justice Harry Blackmun had written a dissenting opinion. Execution of an innocent would come "perilously close to simple murder," Blackmun wrote. If Blackmun's characterization is accurate then a number of justices, judges and prosecutors are in fact murderers. The same goes for defense lawyers who participate in the rites of capital punishment as a legal system.

In other words, in 1977, or 1983 or even 1995, lawyers could believe that their skill and sweat and experience might well save a guilty client's life. Today, a lawyer can't even count on saving an *innocent* client's life. By even trying to do so under the aegis of a legal system so rigged against the client, the lawyer must wonder whether he, too, is an accomplice to murder.

This is the real world of capital post-conviction litigation as America approaches the *fin de siècle*. This is the judicial and political environment within which lawyers must operate, if we choose to operate as lawyers at all. This is the landscape in which we must decide whether to honor our client's wishes, and to acquiesce to their own electrocution, hanging, gassing, shooting or lethal injection.

The world of capital punishment is a madhouse. In this madhouse, you must decide whether your client's choice to be killed is mad or sane.

Representing Socrates, Imagining Death Row

The hour of departure has arrived, and we go our ways – I to die and you to live. Which is better, God only knows.[13]

Socrates

Given the moral, ethical and jurisprudential complexity of my topic, it may be of some use to enact a hypothetical situation. In what follows, I have attempted to craft the strongest case *against* lawyer-assisted suicide, in order to demonstrate that in some instances it is indeed justified if not required.

Assume you are an experienced capital post-conviction attorney. Personally, you oppose capital punishment. You work at a public defender's office that exists for only one purpose: to provide top-flight legal aid to your state's death row population. You now represent thirty-five condemned prisoners. During your fourteen-year career in death-work, you have worked personally with about seventy capital clients.

Assume that of your seventy or so death row clients, there has been only one case where you were absolutely convinced that your condemned client was totally innocent of murder – although neither you nor he can prove it. I mean innocent the old-fashioned way – he didn't do it; they got the wrong guy. In a rational world you would be able to present your proof of innocence, and your client would be set free by the courts. Fifteen years ago, when the federal courts kept a tight reign on this nation's capital punishment systems, your client might have had a shot.

But not today. Today, innocence is irrelevant to the United States Supreme Court. You know it, and so does your client, whose name is Theodore Kaczynski. It would seem that in the absence of a determining trial, the best your client can hope for is a delay of his execution. There is always the possibility that your client will see justice done in his case. Lightning strikes every once in a while, even during the reign of the Rehnquist/Thomas/Scalia regime. Having said that, there isn't a thinking person out there who would be willing to bet on it. You know it, and so does your client.

Given the likelihood that Kaczynski would be executed eventually for crimes he did not commit, he has made a decision. After careful consideration, he has decided that he wants to drop his appeals and other possible challenges to the legality of capital punishment in his case. He doesn't really want to die right now. If his eventual release from prison were a realistic possibility (and for this client it is not) he might choose to stay alive and fight. But in today's legal and political climate, it is *not* a realistic possibility for many convicts. In the real world your client has only two options: The state can kill him now, or it can kill him later. He wants to be killed now.

Your Client Chooses Death

> I beg, as a favor, that I may be immediately led to execution. I know that you have predetermined to shed my blood, why then have this mockery of a trial? [14]
>
> A follower of Gabriel Prosser's Rebellion of 1800
> the day before he was hanged

Is execution necessarily a worse fate than life imprisonment, without the possibility of parole, in a maximum security prison? For my own part, the prospect of spending the rest of my days in a maximum-security prison would be far worse than death by lethal injection, the electric chair, hanging, gassing, or a firing squad. I have never been incarcerated as a prisoner, but I have, over my years as a capital public defender, spent many hours visiting my clients in Florida's maximum-security prison. I have been close enough to know the fear and despair of the place. I have witnessed the utter lack of privacy and solitude that would be, for me, perhaps the worst part of living in that world. The sound of the electronically-operated gates clanging shut produces a feeling that cannot be conveyed with words. It affected me deeply even though I was free to leave at will.

Anyone who has been inside the high-tech fortresses of America's death row can perhaps appreciate why your client might feel death to be preferable to the uncertainty of death row, or even to life imprisonment. [15]

We all have our private terrors – at the siege of Sebastopol, Tolstoy jumped from the trenches and ran towards the bastion under heavy fire from the enemy (he was horribly afraid of rats, and had just seen one). Anyone who has seen *Raiders of the Lost Ark* will remember the intrepid explorer's aversion to snakes. For many, the worst part about living on death row is the *noise* of the place. William Styron has written that exhaustion combined with sleeplessness is a rare torture. [16] Your client is living this rarity.

As it turns out, your client's decision has everything to do with the untenable situation in which he has been placed. The conditions in his maximum security prison are pretty bad, but not intolerable. What he finds intolerable is the waiting – the slow death by degrees. To illustrate the point, your client, who is highly educated and very well-read, sends two books to you. The first is Albert Camus' *Reflections on the Guillotine*. He has dog-eared the following passage:

> What is capital punishment if not the most premeditated of murders, to which no criminal act, no matter how calculated, can be compared? If there were to be a real equivalence, the death penalty would have to be pronounced upon a criminal who had forewarned his victim of the very moment he would put him to a horrible death, and who, from that time on, had kept him confined at his own discretion for a period of months. It is not in private life that one meets such monsters.
>
> Here again, when our official jurists speak of death without suffering, they do not know what they are talking about, and furthermore they betray a remarkable lack of imagination. The devastating, degrading fear imposed on the condemned man for months or even years is a punishment more terrible than death itself, and one that has not been imposed on his victim. A murdered man is generally rushed to his death, even at the height of his terror of the moral violence being done to him, without knowing what is happening . . . For the man condemned to death, on the other hand, the horror of his situation is served up to him at every moment for months on end. Torture by hope alternates only with the pangs of animal despair.[17]

The other book he sends you is by Kafka. Your client analogizes his situation to those executed by Kafka's death machine:

> When the man lies down on the bed and it begins to vibrate, the harrow is lowered onto his body. It regulates itself automatically so that the needles barely touch the skin . . . As it quivers, its points pierce the skin of the body . . . The long needle does the writing and the short needle sprays a jet of water to wash away the blood and keep the inscription clear . . . [The harrow] keeps on writing deeper and deeper for the whole twelve hours . . . so that the actual progress of sentence can be seen.[18]

Your innocent client further articulates argument. He wants to join the immortal ranks of John Brown and Socrates. He wants to become a martyr to his political cause. His cause is the obliteration of modern technology. He reasons that the execution of a wrongly condemned neo-Luddite would prove that no neo-Luddite is able to get a fair trial in America. Further, execution of a person who was later pronounced innocent might succeed in challenging the validity of capital punishment where scores of death row lawyers have failed. After all, in the 1950s just such a case led to abolition of capital punishment in England. Your client's execution would not only advance his own cause, it might also inadvertently serve yours. This possibility would never make you fight any less fiercely for your client's life, were he to want that fight. But this client wants you to fight for his death.

Your client reminds you that Socrates himself was a volunteer for execution in ancient Athens after refusing to raise the one argument that might have saved his own neck.[19] Like John Brown, he then rejected the increasingly insistent demands of his disciples that he escape his execution by fleeing the city. In the *Crito*, Socrates argues that "not life, but a good life, is to be chiefly valued."[20]

Socrates' defense at his bifurcated capital trial is reported by Plato in the *Apology*. Socrates made clear that he would not make any "shameful" argument to win acquittal, and that he would not bring in witnesses to that end. He set out "not to debase himself," and announced "I care not a straw for death."[21]

Death before dishonor, in other words. In one of the most beautiful passages in the *Apology*, Socrates says: "Someone will say: Are you not ashamed, Socrates, of a course of life which is likely to bring you to an untimely end? To him I may fairly answer: There you are mistaken; a man who is good for anything ought not to calculate the chance of living or dying; he ought only to consider whether in doing anything he is doing right or wrong – acting the part of a good man or of a bad."[22]

Socrates scoffs at "men of reputation" who plead to live at any cost; such men "were a dishonor to the state."[23] They are arrogant as well, because "fear of death is indeed the pretense of wisdom, and not real wisdom, since no one knows whether death, which they in their fear apprehended to be the greatest evil, may be the greatest good. Is there not here conceit of knowledge, which is a disgraceful sort of ignorance?"[24]

Your client reminds you that, according to Socrates, death is an unknown. Socrates argued that one should not fear the unknown: "Those of us who think that death is an evil are in error . . . There is great reason to hope that death is good."[25] At any rate, it is "one of two things: either death is a state of nothingness and utter unconsciousness, or . . . a migration of the soul from this world," and whatever happens to be the case, "to die is gain: for eternity is [either] a single night," or it is a journey that would enable Socrates to continue his "search into true and false knowledge."[26]

I.F. Stone powerfully demonstrates how Socrates could easily have won a sentence of less than death, if not outright acquittal. He then encapsulates the issue with which you have been confronted by your client: "Neither in war nor yet at law ought any man use every way of escaping death."[27] Athenian juries were "notoriously susceptible to graceful rhetoric and pity."[28] But Socrates chose to antagonize the jury at every turn. Stone calls it Socrates' "determination to die."[29]

Socrates leaves his judges with a warning, that resonates with your client's stance vis-à-vis his inevitable execution. "I am about to die, and that is the hour in which men are gifted with prophetic power. And I prophesy to you, who are my murderers, that immediately after my death, punishment far heavier than you have inflicted on me will surely await you. Me you have killed because you wanted to escape the accuser, and not to give an account of your lives. There will be more accusers of you."[30]

Modern Medicine Has No Cure For Despair

We are unutterably alone. [31]

Rainer Maria Rilke

Your client is understandably anxious and depressed, but he is not crazy. Indeed, his decision to pursue his action was animated in part by the fervent desire *not* to be driven insane by the uncertainties of life in a maximum security prison. He'd seen it happen to others, cellmates and friends, who were able to keep their minds intact during their first few years in lock down. But no one lasted forever. The years of monotony and boredom are punctuated only by the sheer terror of having a death warrant signed and an execution date. Maybe someone wins an eleventh-hour stay from the courts. He gets another few years to wait. Another warrant comes down the pike, and so on. A few rounds of that, and who *wouldn't* go mad?[32]

Your client has obtained a copy of the 1997 moot court brief written by Vermont Law School students Paul Perkins and Mike Whipple. I suppose this might be a stretch, but let's run with it. The moot court problem assigned to Perkins and Whipple was *Vacco v. Quill*. The United States Supreme Court rejected the argument raised by the brief and denied the constitutional right of mentally competent, terminally ill patients to hasten death – to die with dignity – including the right to physician assistance in aid of suicide. The argument for physician-assisted suicide is not perfectly analogous to the issue at hand – doctors, unlike lawyers, swear by the Hippocratic Oath to preserve human life – but there is some value to be found here. In particular, your client argues that "life" on death row is no better than "life" as a terminally ill, but mentally competent, patient. He passes over the fact that he is being punished for a crime he did not commit (and for which he will not be acquitted). Your client quotes Perkins and Whipple:

> New York's interest in denying mentally competent patients in the final stages of terminal illness the benefit of hastening death with physician

assistance is not reasonable because these patients have no life to preserve. When the potential for a patient's life diminishes, the state's interest lessens. By extension, when a patient has virtually no life left to preserve, a law requiring that patient to endure the final stages of dying
does not preserve life. Rather, it prolongs death.

Terminally ill patients [will be defined as those who] will die in less
than a year from an affliction that cannot be alleviated. The respondents
here do not wish all mentally competent, terminally ill patients to receive
the benefit of physician assistance in hastening death. If so, then there
might be a year or more of life to preserve. This benefit should accrue only
to persons in the final stages of terminal illness, to those persons whose
deaths are imminent, who will die – as the original plaintiffs in this case
did – within a very short, painful and humiliating period of time.

The state does not preserve life at all with its current policy. Rather,
it lengthens decay. This is not a case in which the state wants to prevent
death in order that the patient may live on as a productive, emotional,
spiritual, physical being. These patients have lived those lives. There is
no chance that medical science can present them with lives to preserve.
All that is left is death. These patients choose only to shorten the time.
Therefore, since mentally competent patients in the final stages of terminal illness face imminent death, New York's penal statutes, designed
to preserve all life, do not serve that interest.

New York's penal statutes violate the Equal Protection Clause because
they single out one class of terminally ill patients and deny to them the
benefit of physician assistance in hastening death. Although the state argues that it has a legitimate interest in preserving the life of its citizens, it
has failed to demonstrate it with its double standard statutes. Yet even if
the state did have a legitimate interest in preserving life, the penal statues
do not serve that interest because they only lengthen decay.[33]

Indeed, your client argues, his claim on your assistance is stronger than
that of a terminally ill patient for physician-assisted suicide. Not only are
you not bound by the physician's Hippocratic Oath to preserve life in the
eyes of society and its law, but in the eyes of society and its law, the terminally ill patient's life still has value: The patient still deserves to live. By
contrast, in your client's case the law has already decided that he deserves
to be killed by the government. The law has already annihilated your
client's "right" to life.

To hell with that, your client tells you. He wants to die with some sem-
blance of dignity. He could hang himself in his cell, but he tried that once
before and failed. He wants a more certain method. The law gives him the

right to drop his appeals, but only if he's mentally competent. He wants you to help prove his mental competency to the courts. You know, of course, that as a practical matter you would be able to find a psychiatrist willing to question your client's mental competency. However, it wouldn't take the prosecution long to blow your psychiatrist out of the water. It might delay the execution for a short while, but at the end of the day your client would be allowed to drop his appeals. Again, your efforts would buy your client some time – but he doesn't want it.

The Courage of Your Client's Convictions

Last night suicide was on my mind. Not whether, but how. Tonight it will be on my mind again . . . I sit in my underwear at this unblinking fool of a computer and try to wrap words around a few horrid truths . . . I have just taken my first drug of the day, a prescription drug, Oxazepam, which files the edge off anxiety. Thing is I'm not anxious. I'm slop. This is despair. This is a valence of horror that Vietnam never approximated. If war is hell, what do we call hopelessness? [34]

Tim O'Brien (1994)

Your client shows no indications of being delusional about life in prison. His reality principle is working fine with regard to his chances of ever being released from prison. To the contrary, his arguments for legal suicide strike you as not the least irrational. You recall from your college days that many philosophers did not categorically reject suicide – the Stoics, Socrates, Plato, Epicurus, Seneca, Cato the Younger, Pliny the Older, Marcus Aurelius, Voltaire, Hume, to name but a few.[35]

These folks weren't crazy (and they were not slated to spend the rest of their natural lives in a maximum-security prison). They also weren't cowards. Neither was Randall Jarrell, Vincent van Gogh, Virginia Woolf, Arshile Gorky, Hart Crane, Vachel Lindsay, Sylvia Plath, Mark Rothko, John Berryman, Jack London, Ernest Hemingway, Diane Arbus, Paul Celan, or Anne Sexton. They all committed suicide. The list is William Styron's, and he rightly notes that it could go on and on.[36]

Include Primo Levi. Styron notes that only a special species of arrogance would even consider characterizing Primo Levi as a coward because he committed suicide: Levi had survived Auschwitz and written some of the best books about the qualities of resilience, courage and luck necessary to survive Hitler's death camps. How *dare* anyone call Primo Levi a coward?

Far from being a source or a sign of weakness, suicide – and the thoughts of suicide – can for some people become a source of strength. As Herman Hesse wrote in *The Steppenwolf*:

> As every strength may become a weakness (and under some circum-
> stances must) so, on the contrary, may the typical suicide find a strength
> and a support in his apparent weakness. Indeed, he does so more often
> than not. The case of Harry, the Steppenwolf, is one of these. As thou-
> sands of his like do, he found consolation and support, and not merely
> the melancholy play of youthful fancy, in the idea that the way to death
> was open to him at any moment. It is true that with him, as with all men
> of his kind, every shock, every pain, every untoward predicament at once
> called forth the wish to find an escape in death. By degrees, however, he
> fashioned for himself out of this tendency a philosophy that was actual-
> ly serviceable to life. He gained strength through familiarity with the
> thought that the emergency exit stood always open, and became curious,
> too, to taste his suffering to the dregs. If it went too badly with him he
> could feel sometimes with a grim malicious pleasure: "I am curious to see
> all the same just how much a man can endure. If the limit of what is bear-
> able is reached, I have only to open the door to escape." There are a great
> many suicides to whom this thought imparts an uncommon strength.

So your client isn't a coward. That doesn't necessarily mean that he is a model of courage, but you have to wonder. Execution would be like acquittal in his case. While trying to sort it out, you remember an interest-ing definition of courage in Tim O'Brien's 1969 memoir, which in turn takes you back to Plato and Aristotle.

O'Brien was looking for "proper courage," during his tour in Vietnam, the sort of courage "exercised by men who know what they do is proper." Proper courage, O'Brien continues, is "wise courage. It's acting wisely, act-ing wisely when fear would have a man act otherwise. It is the endurance of the soul in spite of fear – wisely."[37]

Socrates, in the dialogue *Laches*, distinguished between "foolish endurance" and "wise endurance." He said: "only the wise endurance is courage." Building upon *Laches*, O'Brien argues that "men must *know* what they do is courageous, they must *know* it is right, and that kind of know-ledge is wisdom and nothing else. Which is why I know few brave men. Either they are stupid and do not know what is right. Or they know what is right and cannot bring themselves to do it. Or they know what is right and do it, but do not feel and understand the fear that must be overcome."[38]

Aristotle defined courage as "what enables you to do what is right, habitually."[39] Courage is partly experience and partly reflection on that experience. O'Brien's heroes in Vietnam "had been out long enough to know; experienced and wise . . . Realistic and able to speak the truth. Conceited? Never. And, most strikingly, each of the heroes *thought* about courage, *cared* about being brave, at least enough to talk about it and wonder to others about it."[40] The French have a phrase, *courage sans peur* (courage without fear), which highlights that you can do something with your heart (coeur), and then you can do this fearlessly.

If your client wants to drop his appeals knowing that he is innocent, in the face of a likely execution, your inquiry should go beyond considerations of your client. He is willing to sacrifice his life in aid of his cause. As John Brown put it, "I am almost fully persuaded that I am worth more to hang than for any other purpose."[41] Your client might be wrong; his execution might not have any effect whatsoever on the world at large. He may disappear without a trace. He can't know that in advance; neither can you; neither could John Brown himself. The fact remains that he's willing to forfeit his life in the face of the above uncertainty.

And what are *you* willing to forfeit by allowing the state to kill your client for a crime he didn't commit? Lifetime excommunication from the community of abolitionists, a community you have regarded for years as your family? The dignified distance of lawyers who once treated you as a respected colleague? Disbarment for selling your client down the river? When the definitive proof of your client's innocence finally does come to light – after he's executed – the person who will bear the brunt of any wrath won't be the police or the prosecutors or the judges or the jury or the media. *You* will take all the blame. Which raises the question: How much courage do *you* have?

Are you worthy of the task your client would have you perform on his behalf? Your client has the courage of his convictions. Do you have the courage of yours?

Deciding Who Decides

> Die at the right time.
>
> Nietzsche (more or less)

You now feel that your client does have plausible reasons to acquiesce in the state's will to execute him for a crime he didn't commit. You might even admire his willingness to sacrifice his life, for the same reasons you've always admired John Brown and Socrates. Although your client has denied having any desire for martyrdom, martyrdom may well be the resulting interpretation some years down the line. You've often wondered how you would feel if you were John Brown's lawyer instead of playing counsel to your usual capital client base of convenience-store murderers and gang-bangers. The usual suspects have very little to look forward to: a few years of uncertainty, followed by electrocution, gassing, hanging, firing squad or a lethal injection gurney.

But for your client, death isn't a punishment. It's a release. (Remember, he isn't guilty.)

Although your client's reasons sound plausible to you, you feel uncomfortable *evaluating* them. You feel paternalistic, and you behave in an arrogant manner. But who are you? You are an over-educated professional from a Top-Ten law school who could be earning big bucks at a Wall Street law firm with no jurisdiction over the decisions made by a brilliant neo-Luddite, who has experienced, up close and personal, life among the living dead. You can't even imagine the world your client wishes to escape. So, who are you, to sit in judgment of your client's reasons? So long as your client is not delusional, why shouldn't his reasons be enough for you? You know he isn't delusional. He sees the reality and the truth of his situation with remarkable clarity, a clarity perhaps born of his proximity to death and the serenity sired by the choice he has made. As Socrates said, "Those about to die are given the gift of prophecy."

In the past, this client's trust in your loyalty has been something in which you've taken great pride. Without that trust, you cannot function effectively as counsel to a person on death row. If your client doesn't trust you, he won't tell you everything, and you can't do your job without all the facts. Building up that sort of trust takes a lot of time; gaps of class, race, ideology and education must be bridged. In this case, your hard work has paid off. Your client trusts you with information he wouldn't even tell his spouse, mother, child, best friend, or minister. He trusts you implicitly.

Until now. It so happens that your public defender's office overrode another prisoner's death wish. Despite the strong protests of the condemned prisoner, your office opposed the execution by claiming mental incompetency.[42] The office lost, but not before a bitter conflict involving the client's family developed. Your client did not make peace with them before he was executed.

What do you do? The days are gone when you might have thwarted your client's goal, confident that you would be able to get your client acquitted, or at least make arrangements for a retrial. No longer.

You might also find comfort in the knowledge that his decision was not the uncoerced effect of free will, given the manifold pressure and stress of life on death row. Most capital appeals lawyers and commentators would counsel you to override your client's wishes and fight his death wish – to refuse to assist your client's desire for state-assisted suicide.

Although acquiescing to one's own execution shares characteristics with suicide, the two modes of life termination are in important respects different. One difference concerns the participation or interference of the state in a citizen's decision that life is no longer worth living. The state believes that your client has lost his moral entitlement to live. It agrees that your "volunteer" should die, but the state's reasons for wanting him dead differ radically from your client's rationale. The intrusion of the state into private decision concerning personal autonomy and sovereignty allows one to harmonize two antithetical propositions: that the state cannot legitimately forbid suicide, and that death row prisoners can volunteer for execution. In both instances the state is not allowed to thwart the will of the individual who has decided to die.

In the following sections I shall attempt to articulate why you might come to the opposite conclusion, and assist your client in his effort to die for a crime he didn't commit. The hypothesis has everything to do with matters of loyalty and power – the very matters I believe Kaczynski's lawyers got so terribly wrong.

Tangled Loyalties: Three Conflicts of Interest

> Some of the strongest moral epithets in the English language are re-
> served for the weak who cannot meet the threshold of loyalty: They
> commit adultery, betrayal, treason.[43]

> George Fletcher

On the topic of loyalty, George Fletcher writes that one way to understand its importance in our civilization is to focus on its opposites: disloyalty and betrayal. Betrayal is more than simply the absence of loyalty. Betrayal is "one of the basic sins of our civilization. Dante reserves a special place in hell for those who betray trust . . . In Blackstone's eyes, treason '[i]s the highest civil crime which (considered as a member of the community) any man can possibly commit.'"[44]

The idea of loyalty is at the heart of the attorney-client relationship, at least as defined by the United States justice system. Most of the characteristics we think of as essential to the attorney-client relationship are themselves grounded by notions of loyalty: the duty of attorneys to keep secrets in confidence, and the provision that makes it impossible for an attorney to represent conflicting interests. These responsibilities belong to a code of ethics. The rules, regulations and norms that govern the professional ethics and behavior of lawyers were themselves drafted and enforced by lawyers. There are predictably many loopholes that provide lawyers with wiggle room when applying their professional mores to specific situations. Still, the unifying credo of lawyers in America is loyalty.

This does not mean an unalloyed, undivided loyalty to your client alone. Indeed, your interlocking loyalties have come to resemble the patchwork of European peace treaties in the years leading up to World War I. At the outset, you are expected to be loyal to your client. But you must also be loyal to your other thirty four capital clients, and the consensual execution of your innocent client might contribute to an atmosphere more amenable to the execution of your *other* clients. (As I've mentioned, this was the unsuccessful argument made by the ACLU in Gary Gilmore's case in 1977.)[45] So, the first potentially disabling conflict lies between your innocent client and your other clients.

As an officer of the court you must also be loyal to the integrity of the criminal justice system; thou shalt not perpetrate a fraud on the court. This gives rise to a second potential conflict between your client and the legal system whose integrity you have sworn to uphold. This duty isn't implicated here, because your client wants you to do nothing more than enforce his legitimate legal right to drop his appeal and die.

Finally, you must remain loyal to your own conscience including, perhaps, your own abolitionist convictions. This, in my view, is the one conflict of loyalties that is outcome-determinative in this hypothetical situation. The first two conflicts can be finessed; the applicable ethical rules and norms regulating the behavior of attorneys provide you with all the flexibility and discretion to locate or avoid a disabling conflict of interest. You know that the courts will back up your choice either way. Although in civil and noncapital criminal cases, the justices enforce the rules prohibiting attorney conflicts of interest, in capital cases the court will more or less ignore those rules, in the apparent belief that death row inmates had better be satisfied with whatever lawyer the state, in its generosity and grace, chooses to foist on them.[46]

But the third conflict of interest – between your client's wishes and your conscience – cannot be finessed. The manner in which you resolve the third conflict will animate and drive the resolution of the first two. Your conscience will inform your opinion regarding any "disabling" conflicts between the loyalty that you espouse for your innocent client, your other clients and the integrity of the judiciary system.

The third conflict thus becomes the hardest one. And it explains why Kaczynski's lawyers seized control of their client's case.

Resolving the Third Conflict:
Attorney-Assisted Suicide

Choose the right enemy.

Nietzsche (more or less)

I oppose the role played by capital punishment in the American legal system. I would therefore try to persuade my hypothetical client to change his mind and to permit me to fight on his behalf against his execution. I would satisfy myself that my client understands and appreciates the consequences of dropping his appeals – the consequences to himself, but also to his family, friends, lawyers and colleagues on death row, including my other clients. The Model Code of Professional Responsibility instructs that "in assisting his client to reach a proper decision, it is often desirable for a lawyer to point out those factors which may lead to a decision that is morally just as well as legally permissible."[47] As Richard Dieter correctly observes, however, "persuasion has its limits."[48] What must/should/can a lawyer do when his client proves immune from the lawyer's powers of persuasion?

Dieter and others suggest that a lawyer in such circumstances has at least two options, both of which I would reject were I representing this client. First, the lawyer may withdraw as counsel.[49] Dieter notes correctly that, given the scarcity of experienced capital post-conviction attorneys, exercising the withdrawal option might mean, as a practical matter, that the client ends up with no lawyer at all. In addition, by withdrawing, you would only be dropping your moral and ethical dilemma into the lap of another lawyer. This solves your problem, but it only exacerbates the client's dilemma. So, let's say you reject the escape hatch offered by Dieter.

Dieter notes that "another option open to the attorney is [to pursue] a declaration of incompetency."[50] You are satisfied that your client is mentally competent to stand trial. You do not agree with those who "maintain that for any physically healthy person to hasten his own death is a form of mental illness and grounds for questioning competency."[51]

You are not a psychiatrist, but mental competency in this context is not a medical determination – it is a legal determination, based on medical facts. You cannot accept the Catch-22 logic that anyone who wants to be executed (or to commit suicide by other means) must perforce be crazy. You are not prepared to conclude that Socrates and John Brown were insane any more than you are willing to conclude that Primo Levi was a coward.

If I were in your shoes, I'd use my legal skills and experience to carry out my innocent client's death wish. Two issues are central to my conclusion. The first is whether following my client's wishes constitutes "state-assisted suicide." Resolution of this question turns on my own personal views regarding the moral legitimacy and wisdom of suicide. The second issue central to my conclusion has to do with power, specifically self-determination and client empowerment.

Your resolution of this hypothetical Unabomber fact pattern is inseparable from one's personal beliefs about suicide. Indeed, some commentators on consensual executions seem to treat this complicated problem as resolvable by means of labeling. If consensual executions are "state-assisted suicide," then they're bad and ought to be banned. If they're called something else, then they may be legitimate in certain tightly-controlled circumstances.

Richard Dieter argues that "the ethical standards which direct the attorney to follow the client's instructions are conditioned by the requirement that the client's interests be legitimate."[52] Whether a client's wish to die is "legitimate," Dieter argues, will depend on whether the attorney is being asked to assist in suicide. A client with a life sentence who wants legal help to die shouldn't get it, because "assistance with suicide to avoid a life sentence" is "not a legitimate client interest." By contrast, a death row inmate seeking such legal aid should receive it – unless the attorney "might be legitimately convinced that passively allowing one's client to hasten his own death is also to assist suicide."

The late Henry Schwarzschild argued in 1993: "The important thing to remember about 'consensual' executions is that they are *not* 'state-assisted suicides' . . . They are *homicides*, like all other executions; they are prisoner-assisted homicides, to be sure, but nothing like suicides at all."[53] Prisoners may not cheat the executioner – "after all, the prisoner's *dying* is not the point of the execution; we shall die, with or without" the active assistance of the state. "A 'consensual' execution has nothing to do with the prisoner's preference about living or dying but is a consequence only of the state's decision to kill him."[54]

For its part, the *state* surely perceives a difference between suicide and execution. Robert Brecheen was a model prisoner during his twelve years on Oklahoma's death row. But a few hours before he was scheduled to be killed by lethal injection, he attempted suicide with an overdose of sedatives. Doctors had to pump his stomach at a local hospital and make sure he was mentally fit to be executed. Then they brought him back to the prison. Forty minutes later, the execution squad strapped him to a gurney and executed him.[55] Prisoners in phase two of deathwatch in Florida are placed on similar round-the-clock suicide watch. When Theodore Kaczynski attempted suicide in January 1998, he was placed under 24-hour-a-day video surveillance. In short, the government sees a vast difference between execution and suicide, and the state goes to great lengths to prevent the condemned from cheating the executioner.

Thus, the state has its reasons for refusing to allow condemned people to "cheat the executioner." However, the state's reasons need not be *our* reasons. The mere fact that the state insists on doing the killing itself ought not necessarily resolve for us, as lawyers, whether we ought to acquiesce in the state's – and our client's – desire for execution in this particular instance.

To pretermit the tyranny of labeling, and to call the thing by its real name, I concede that my client is seeking "state-assisted suicide." The question then becomes whether I, as an attorney, should assist the state in its will to execute my innocent client. I answer this question in the affirmative.

I believe that every adult who is mentally competent (to stand trial, for instance) has a sovereign right to end his life at the time of his choosing – without interference by the government for that person's "own good." His reasons for suicide are his and his alone. Regardless of whether the government deems his reasons good, bad, or nonexistent, the government lacks the legitimate power to second-guess or sit in judgment of those reasons.

As a lawyer, counselor and friend of death row prisoners, my defining goal is client empowerment. My overriding aim is to empower the client, to serve as his ambassador to a legal system bent on killing him regardless of what he does or says, and regardless of what I do or say on his behalf – and this would include any new evidence of innocence that I beg the sleepy sharks on the bench to at least consider.

His lawyers are the client's only allies and friends in this howling sea of hostility. In today's political and judicial climate, the most we can offer him is a leaky life raft that is taking water on fast, a flimsy structure that may delay the inevitable, but not for long. Neither my client nor myself possess the wherewithal to improve his situation in any appreciable way.

From the moment he was charged with a capital crime, the fix was in. Sure, the state gives him a public defender to go through the motions of arguing legal issues on appeal, so the courts can go through the motions of considering those issues before they rubber stamp the legality of the death sentence, so the judges and the politicians and the people who put them there can all maintain their comfortable illusion that capital punishment can be tamed by the rule of law. I know it and so does my client.

From the time the death sentence was handed down, virtually all my client's choices have been made by others. The courts decide when and under what circumstances he will be killed – on what specific date, at what specific time and at what designated place. The prison decides how he will live – if that's the right word for it – in the meantime, right down to the last detail of his day-to-day existence.

The law has stripped him of the power to determine the quality and quantity of his remaining time on earth, in all respects save one: Right or wrong, the constitutional law does empower him to choose death over what passes for life in a maximum security prison. As a mere lawyer, I won't take that final choice away from him. I would help our government kill my innocent client.

The hypothetical fact pattern leads me to the conclusion that it is right to provide Theodore Kaczynski with attorney-assisted suicide. Kaczynski's lawyers should have honored their mentally competent (and factually guilty) client's decision not to stake his life and reputation on a defense he would rather die than raise. Even if that would have been tantamount to attorney-assisted suicide. Even if that would indeed have *been* suicide.

From the beginning, the Unabomber case was about power. Theodore Kaczynski understood this better than his lawyers or his judge. Perhaps the Kaczynski case might yet result in a landmark judicial decision that re-defines the essential nature of the attorney-client relationship and the ethical duties of capital defense lawyers. That would not be too bad a legacy for the Unabomber.

CHAPTER SEVEN

The Missing Link

He thought of things as a man might think
Of certain things by a river-brink,
Seen in a flash from a passing train,
And, before you could look at them, gone again.
It was important to eat and drink
Than give the pain or suffer the pain
And life was too rapid for memory.

Stephen Vincent Benét, *John Brown's Body* (1928)

The Unabomber's Journals

At the Unabomber's capital trial in federal court, our government would have attempted to convict Theodore Kaczynski and send him to death row based on certain "admissions" in Theodore Kaczynski's private journals, which were found when the FBI searched his cabin in Florence Gulch.[1]

The journals were a major stumbling block during the trial. Kaczynski's refusal to accept a guilty plea was based in part on his desire to challenge, on appeal, the government's search of his cabin and its intended use of his private journals to convict him. These were the strings that Kaczynski had attached to his guilty plea. Eventually, his lawyers and Burrell pressured him into giving up his right to appeal in exchange for a plea bargain. But no treatment of Kaczynski's non-trial could be complete without a discussion of the appellate issue he forewent by agreeing to this "bargain."

The Unabomber case first caught my attention because of the journal issue. For years, my constitutional law courses at Vermont Law School have included a classroom hypothetical fact pattern based on a serial killer who kept a diary detailing his crimes. When *The New York Times* reported that Kaczynski kept a diary, I used the story as a final exam question. I contacted the Kaczynski defense team, during the summer of 1997, to obtain copies of their court filings on the journal issue, for my class that Fall. That contact led to a series of communications with Judy Clarke about the journal issue. Kaczynski's lawyer made my informal advisory role in this narrow aspect of the Kaczynski defense a matter of public record.[2] The prosecution's sentencing brief demonstrated the importance of Kaczynski's private journals to the prosecution.

Let's go back to basics: Theodore Kaczynski was charged with offenses connected to four bombings that occurred between 1985 and 1995. According to a government pre-trial motion, these four bombings were part of a seventeen-year campaign during which Kaczynski mailed or placed sixteen bombs.[3] The government had also planned to use evidence relating to thirteen bombings that had not been listed in the indictment.

The motion described in some detail the complex geometry of evidence against Theodore Kaczynski. The prosecution's evidence against Kaczynski fell into "three categories."4 The first category consisted of Kaczynski's own writings, which were seized during the extensive search of Kaczynski's cabin. The government's second category of proof consisted of "non-documentary physical evidence found at the various UNABOM crime scenes, [which included] Kaczynski's cabin."5 The government's third and final category of proof included "documentary and testimonial proof showing the defendant's resources and opportunities to travel from his Montana cabin to the locations where he placed or mailed his explosive devices."6

At a hearing held on September 20, 1996, Lead Prosecutor Robert Cleary emphasized the critical value of the journals to his case:

> Those documents . . . are the backbone of the Government's case. It will be the documents that we're going to rely upon in proving the charges in the indictment. We will then round out our proof and corroborate our proof with other evidence. What are those documents? Those are documents, by and large, in Mr. Kaczynski's handwriting, in which he's keeping day-to-day journals of his activities for years and years. Many of them are just, you know, my day in the woods, what I ate for dinner – that sort of thing. A much, much smaller set of those documents, a stack maybe this big (indicating), and I'm holding my hands about a foot apart, are what we call the key documents in the case.7

The capital prosecutor was not exaggerating the importance of the journals to the government's case. In its motion the government had observed: "One of the foundations of the government's case will be the defendant's written admissions to the charged offenses, contained in the documents seized from his cabin."8 The motion described Kaczynski's "extensive handwritten journals," which "consist of thousands of pages of handwritten material in English, Spanish and a numeric code."9 The earliest entry is dated 1969; the latest is February 1996. "In the late 1970s," the government continued, Kaczynski recorded the details of his first bombing, and he continued memorializing his bombing activities through the final entries."10

"The journals contain extensive discussions of Kaczynski's . . . ideology and motivations, and expressions of his intent to kill his victims," the prosecutor went on.11 "Briefly stated," the government argued that the journals would show that Kaczynski "despised anyone who interfered with the solitude he craved, and he harbored a deep-seated hatred of certain aspects of modern technology and industrial society."12 Again and again throughout their motion, the government refers to and emphasizes that Kaczynski's writings contain *admissions*.13

In some passages of the motion it is not clear whether the "written admissions" attributed to Kaczynski occur in his journals or in his other writings, such as letters.[14] In many instances, however, the government was clearly relying on "admissions" drawn from Kaczynski's journals, although most citations from the journals have been redacted from the motion. In one place, a footnote to an otherwise blank page explains: "This admission, as well as several others the government seeks to introduce, is from Kaczynski's coded journals."[15] Eight pages later, under a rubric titled "Corroboration of Kaczynski's Admissions to the Charged Bombings," the government notes that, "in particular the government will seek to emphasize those admissions" (i.e., "the defendant's written admissions to the charged offenses contained in the documents seized from his cabin") "that provide specific, previously undisclosed details about the construction of the bombs."[16] One page later, the government's motion observes that "in journal entries dated August 21, 1978 and May 31, 1979, Kaczynski describes . . . two bombings in detail."[17]

The government had a mountain of circumstantial evidence against Kaczynski, but Cleary was steadfastly fixated on the journals, which held Kaczynski's "detailed admissions" of the bombings and expressed his "desire to kill."[18] *The New York Times* characterized the journals as "handwritten confessions."[19]

In this chapter, I make several factual and legal assumptions solely for purposes of clearly framing the journal issue I wish to discuss. First, I assume and sincerely hope that the FBI had a legal right to be present in Kaczynski's cabin, and the search of the cabin was conducted with a valid search warrant issued by a federal district court with sufficient probable cause. In other words, I assume that the procedural requirements of the Fourth Amendment were satisfied.

On April 3, 1996, the United States District Court for the District of Montana issued a search warrant of Theodore Kaczynski's cabin in Lincoln, Montana, at the request of agents for the FBI. The application for a search warrant was supported by a one hundred fourteen page affidavit describing the results of the Unabom investigation. The search warrant was signed on April 3, 1996. The search continued through April 11, 1996. A second search warrant for Kaczynski's property was issued on May 9, 1996.

In a Notice of Motion and a Motion to Suppress Evidence and Accompanying Memorandum of Law filed on March 3, 1997, counsel for Kaczynski moved to exclude the evidence obtained from the two searches of his cabin. The suppression motion "moves to suppress this evidence [of the searches of Kaczynski's cabin] on the ground that the evidence was obtained as the result of an unlawful search of his cabin and property in violation of the Fourth Amendment, for the reasons set forth in the accompanying Memorandum of Points and Authorities in Support of Defendant's Motion to Suppress."[20] The memo notes:

> The affidavit presented the results of the Unabom investigation in a deliberately misleading manner in an attempt to create the illusion that the government had evidence establishing probable cause to believe that Mr. Kaczynski was the Unabomber and that there was a legal basis for searching his cabin. To create this illusion, the government relied on misstatements, omissions, speculation and pages and pages of essentially meaningless minutiae. The affidavit attempted to seduce the reader by its detail, but it really was like a spinning compass, not pointing in any true direction.[21]

• • •

By hiding exculpatory DNA evidence, misrepresenting evidence of an alibi for the December 11, 1985 bombing, and concealing an eyewitness description that did not match Mr. Kaczynski, along with many other false statements and material omissions set forth below, FBI agents intentionally duped the judge into issuing a search warrant by concocting the appearance of probable cause, where none existed. If the FBI had been frank with the judge, the affidavit would have shown beyond all dispute that the agents lacked probable cause to believe that Theodore Kaczynski was the Unabomber.

CIRCUMSTANCES SURROUNDING APPLICATION FOR AND ISSUANCE OF THE SEARCH WARRANT

The affidavit in support of the search warrant consists of two hundred thirty numbered paragraphs, which consume one hundred and four pages of double-spaced type. It is supported by six exhibits and six attachments, including an eighty-page copy of "Industrial Society and Its Future" (two hundred thirty-two numbered paragraphs, thirty-six paragraphs of footnotes and two pages of corrections), a twenty-three page typewritten essay and a fifty page comparison of "T" (Ted) and "U" (Unabomber) documents. The completed document is one and one quarter inches thick.

• • •

Although the affidavit was rife with false and misleading statements, and omitted significant evidence tending to show that Theodore Kaczynski was not the Unabomber, even on its face, probable cause was missing. The first fifty-eight pages of the affidavit presented information to show that a single person known as the Unabomber placed or mailed a series of explosive devices across the United States over a period of almost seventeen years. The remaining portion of the affidavit attempted to show that FBI agents had evidence constituting probable cause that it was Mr. Kaczynski who was the Unabomber. This evidence fell within three general categories: (1) DNA evidence; (2) a "comparative analysis" by an FBI agent of documents believed to be written by Mr. Kaczynski and documents written by the Unabomber; and (3) evidence purporting to show that Mr. Kaczynski had the opportunity to commit the Unabom crimes or could not be excluded as the Unabomber. This evidence was wholly insufficient to establish probable cause that Mr. Kaczynski was the Unabomber.

First, the affidavit stated that, based on an analysis of the DNA found on one Unabom letter, Mr. Kaczynski was included among the pool of persons who could have been the source of the DNA — as were three percent of all Caucasians, three percent of all Blacks, five percent of all Southeastern Hispanics and two percent of all Southwestern Hispanics — almost 7,000,000 people in the United States. Second, the affidavit summarized the belief of an FBI agent, who lacked any training in linguistic analysis, that defendant's personal writings contained a number of so-called "similarities" with Unabom documents. Third, the affidavit set forth voluminous information concerning bus schedules, banking records, hotel stays, employment, education, etc., that tended to show only that Mr. Kaczynski could not be excluded as the Unabomber. Indeed, the affidavit stretched to implicate Mr. Kaczynski by his use of the correct (and commonly used) phrase "You can't eat your cake and have it, too."

In short, the affidavit simply failed to provide any trustworthy information that would convince a reasonably prudent person that Mr. Kaczynski committed the Unabom crimes. As explained in detail below, the "comparative analysis" showed only superficial, insignificant similarities between the Unabom manuscript and Mr. Kaczynski's known writings, by an agent with no training in such analysis. The FBI's analysis failed to point to a single detail in more than 150 of defendant's letters that only the Unabomber would have known. Moreover, like Theodore Kaczynski, millions of persons could have been potential contributors of the DNA reportedly found on one Unabom letter and could have had the opportunity to commit the Unabom crimes – and thus potentially could have been labeled as a Unabomber suspect and subjected to an intensive search of their homes by a swarm of FBI agents. At most, the affidavit indicated that Mr. Kaczynski could not be definitively excluded as the

Unabomber, as was true of much of the United States population.

As set forth more fully in the Argument section below, the FBI also misled the judge by including in the affidavit numerous false and misleading statements and by omitting crucial, exculpatory material. For instance, FBI agents deliberately failed to disclose to the judge that the FBI lab's DNA testing firmly excluded Theodore Kaczynski as being the source of DNA found on a third Unabom letter. The affidavit suggested that DNA evidence linked Theodore Kaczynski to a Unabom letter, when an accurate portrayal of the evidence that the FBI possessed would have told the judge that DNA testing excluded or tended to exclude Mr. Kaczynski as the Unabomber. This evidence alone – if it had not been hidden from the judge who issued the warrant – would have eliminated any possibility that the judge would have found probable cause.[22]

Burrell denied the motion.

The Fourth Amendment questions aside, I assume that Kaczynski's journals do indeed constitute a "diary" for purposes of the constitutional questions raised here. I also assume that Kaczynski's journals contain admissions that could be legally construed as confessions, at least regarding some of the bombings attributed to the Unabomber. I further assume that these confessions are, as the government has argued, an essential ingredient in the government's case: Without them conviction would have been problematic and condemnation would be difficult and perhaps inappropriate.

Regardless of the above considerations, it may well be that the contents of Kaczynski journals are entitled to absolute protection from governmental intrusion – regardless of how much probable cause the prosecution possessed, and regardless of how many procedurally valid search warrants the government obtained. In other words, the Constitution marks out an inviolate zone of privacy, into which the government may not intrude, regardless of the government's compliance with the procedural requirements (i.e., that they had both probable cause and a search warrant).[23] Given the members of our Supreme Court, this inviolate zone of privacy has only one possible occupant; when the private journals of a citizen-accused include inculpatory information that can be interpreted as "confessions," and which the government wants to use against the citizen-accused at his capital trial in federal court. The jurisprudential basis for this inviolate zone of privacy is the 1886 case of *Boyd v. United States.*[24]

The Unabomber capital prosecution presented an issue of federal constitutional law as breathtakingly simple as it was fundamental to questions of jurisprudence. Has the time come for *Boyd* to be overruled, and if so, should the Supreme Court give this landmark case a decent burial? In the modest pantheon of decisions in constitutional criminal procedure that can truly be called landmarks, *Boyd* was the first and arguably the greatest – at least as foundationally important as *Miranda v. Arizona* and *Gideon v. Wainwright*.[25]

For all the cultural chatter about "defining moments," the Unabomber prosecution genuinely was one in the history of our judicial system. Declaring *Boyd* dead, in the context of a capital prosecution in federal court, would be a judicial act of transcendent significance.

The Gap Between the Fifth
and Fourth Amendments

It is something to show that the consistency of a system requires a particular result, but it is not all. The life of the law has not been logic: it has
been experience. [26]

Oliver Wendell Holmes (1881)

Based upon prevailing constructions of the Fifth and Fourth
Amendments, the government appeared constitutionally able to convict
and condemn Theodore Kaczynski based on the admissions contained in
his journal; or at least that was Judge Burrell's ruling. The Fifth
Amendment's prohibition against compelled self-incrimination did not
present an insurmountable obstacle to the government, because, as the
Supreme Court held in *Schmerber v. California*, "the privilege protects an
accused only from being compelled to testify against himself, or otherwise
provide the State with evidence of a testimonial or communicative
nature."[27] The compulsory blood test at issue in *Schmerber* was held not to
have been "testimonial" or "communicative" in nature. Justice Brennan's
opinion for the court in *Schmerber* explained:

> A dissent suggests that the report of the blood test was "testimonial" or
> "communicative," because the test was performed in order to obtain the
> testimony of others, communicating to the jury facts about [the] peti-
> tioner's condition. Of course, all evidence received in court is "testimo-
> nial" or "communicative" if these words are thus used. But the Fifth
> Amendment relates only to acts on the part of the person to whom the
> privilege applies, and we use these words subject to the same limitations.
> A nod or head-shake is as much a "testimonial" or "communicative" act
> in this sense as are spoken words. But the terms as we use them do not
> apply to evidence of acts noncommunicative in nature as to the person
> asserting the privilege, even though, as here, such acts are compelled to
> obtain the testimony of others.[28]

In addition, records "voluntarily committed . . . to writing" do not constitute the sort of "compelled" self-incrimination that is prohibited by the Fifth Amendment.[29] The Fifth Amendment does not exist to shield private writings from the prying eyes of government, but rather "applies only when the accused is compelled to make a testimonial communication that is incriminating."[30] In effect, the focus of Fifth Amendment jurisprudence focuses, not on privacy, but rather on the process of compulsion.[31] Unless the "act of producing evidence in response to a subpoena" possesses "communicative aspects of its own, wholly aside from the contents of the papers produced," the Fifth Amendment is not violated.[32]

Today's Fourth Amendment also appears to allow Kaczynski's journals to be introduced into evidence. If the assumptions set out earlier are valid, the government complied with the procedural requirements of the Fourth Amendment. The FBI presumably had probable cause to search the cabin and its contents, including the journals. A valid search warrant had been obtained.

So, Kaczynski's journals most likely are admissible evidence under what Anthony Amsterdam aptly calls the "monolithic" approach to the Fourth Amendment.[33] Similarly, under the balance of interest approach – at least as it has been applied by the Burger and Rehnquist Courts – the government would win as a practical matter. When the present justices "balance" interests, the government's interests in stopping crime are typically found weightier than the citizen's interest in being left alone.

However, as a theoretical matter this need not necessarily be so and, in at least one case, it was not. Justice Byron White's opinion for the Court in *Zurcher v. Stanford Daily* held that "prior cases do no more than insist that the courts apply the warrant requirements with particular exactitude when First Amendment interests would be endangered by the search."[34] Justice White also observed that the press is "not easily intimidated – nor should it be" and, indeed, *Zurcher* generated federal and state legislative action.[35] We doubt that America's diary-writers would have the organizational lobbying muscle to do the same.

In *Zurcher*, the First Amendment values at issue were placed in the balance against the government. Even though the government satisfied the procedural requirements of the Fourth Amendment, and the search of the *Stanford Daily*'s newsroom was held proper, at least two commentators have suggested that "the existence of a warrant supported by probable cause will not necessarily be sufficient to make a search reasonable."[36]

The First Amendment overtones of *Zurcher* suggest that the scale might slide the other way when considering the government's decision to allow Theodore Kaczynski's journals as evidence.[37] At least one court has "balanced" to require greater Fourth Amendment protection the procedural minima when a private diary was at issue.

Similarly, police searches of an attorney's law office might require that the Fourth Amendment's "sliding scale" of protection slide the other way – to require *more* than governmental compliance with the procedural minima of the warrant requirements and probable cause requirement. Such raids are rare but not unprecedented. Once such example would be when agents of the FBI and DEA raided the home law office of Vermont civil rights attorney William Hunter. Hunter's wife, April Hensel, described the nighttime raid:

> At 3 a.m. on Friday morning, I was awakened by a loud banging on the front door of our home. My first thought was that one of our dogs had been barking and had awakened the neighbors. In fact, in trooped seven federal agents, some wearing bulletproof vests, bearing a search warrant. My husband and I were dumbfounded that the government would use such a technique to obtain files from an attorney's office.
>
> My husband looked at the search warrant and complied, pulling the requested files from their cabinets and providing them to the agents. The agents videotaped the rooms in the house and in my husband's office, which is downstairs, shone flashlights in the bedrooms of my three sleeping children and visiting parents and followed me around while I made Ovaltine and my daughter's lunch to take to school.
>
> Once I saw that they were not going to brandish any weapons, I bemusedly introduced one agent to the two turtles in the upstairs bathroom and had to keep reminding them to shut the door to the basement so that the cats wouldn't come up and bother the baby chicks in my daughter's bedroom. After several hours of searching, they left with the client files identified in the warrant, as well as four computers my husband uses daily in his business.
>
> Later that day, we were shocked to learn from a Free Press reporter that my husband was suspect in a money-laundering operation. We were even further jolted the next day when a friend called to read us the article, which quoted federal agent James Bradley as saying, "It is clear that (Frank) Sargent and Hunter had worked together to launder Sargent's money and that they used CRT (Connecticut Realty Trust) for that purpose."[38]
>
> Hunter's neighbors were stunned.[39] The raid of an attorney's law office was unprecedented in Vermont. [40]

For two years following the raid, the government investigated the allegations that Hunter laundered drug money. Although the investigation was called "confidential," leaks to the media were not uncommon. Almost two years after the raid, Hunter was finally indicted – but not for laundering drug money – he was indicted on ten counts of mail fraud and one count of bankruptcy fraud (an idea his prosecutors got perhaps from the Tom Cruise character in the movie *the Firm*). He pleaded guilty to a single count in June 1998.[41]

Although the trumped-up circumstances surrounding the Hunter incident are not comparable to the Unabom case, Hunter's experience does serve to illustrate the sliding scale of government interest vis-à-vis a citizen-accused. One can only assume that the scales are even further loaded in a federal capital case. But the Supreme Court could indeed rule in Kaczynski's favor to address the relevant societal interests at stake. That is both the beauty and the curse of interest-balancing as it figures in Fourth Amendment adjudication: Unless one identifies *in advance* the relative weights to be allocated to the various interests in the scales, balancing is nothing more than an intellectual artifice used to clothe the desired outcome in something that looks neutral and rational.

The balance of interests is, as Amsterdam quipped, little more than an "immense Rorschach blot."[42] It does not provide a sufficiently principled manner of deciding the journal problem.[43] However, *Zurcher's* use of the First Amendment in the ostensibly Fourth Amendment context does provide a useful clue. One can interpret the *Zurcher* case in such manner that it makes an "intimate connection" between the First and Fourth Amendments with regard to the search of a newsroom. Similarly, the confluence of values that inform the First and Fifth Amendments suggest a further connection. The classic listing of the "policies and purposes" underlying the Fifth Amendment privilege against self-incrimination is that provided by Justice Goldberg in his opinion for the Court in *Murphy v. Waterfront Commission*.[44] The *Murphy* Court's fifth cited policy was "our respect for the inviolability of the human personality and of the right of each individual to a private enclave where he may lead a private life."[45]

Thus, one could argue that the journal question suggests a connection between First, Fourth and Fifth Amendment interests. For over a century, the Supreme Court has recognized an "intimate connection" between the Fourth and Fifth Amendments.

Theodore Kaczynski's journals appear to fall between the constitutional benches. Something else is needed to bridge the gap between the two amendments.

Bridge Over Troubled Waters: *Boyd v. United States*

> *Boyd v. United States* is a case that will be remembered as long as civil lib-
> erty lives in the United States.[46]
>
> Louis Brandeis, dissenting in *Olmstead v. United States*

Between the creation of the Republic and its Bicentennial in 1976, the prevailing rule in our Supreme Court was that "the Fifth Amendment privilege against compulsory self-incrimination protects an individual from
compelled production of his personal papers and effects as well as compelled oral testimony."[47] This principle, which had its genesis in the
English tradition preceding the adoption of the American Constitution,
was endowed with explicit constitutional stature more than a century ago,
during the proceedings of *Boyd v. United States*, when the Supreme Court
held that "any forcible and compulsory extortion of a man's own testimony or of his private papers to be used as evidence to convict him of crime"
was a violation of the Constitution.[48] "Papers are [the owner's] dearest
property," the Court reasoned, and forcing their production "would be
subversive of all the comforts of society."[49]

Boyd and Sons were charged with federal tax fraud. They failed to pay
import tax on thirty-five cases of plate glass. The government wanted the
invoices for the plate glass. Since those invoices were in the Boyds' possession, the government went to court for an order compelling the Boyds to
produce the invoices.

When the *Boyd* case reached the United States Supreme Court, the
Boyds won. A very conservative Supreme Court held that the Boyds could
not be compelled to produce the incriminating invoices. It was a nice
result for the Boyds, but that's not why the case is important here. The case
is important because of the reasons for Boyd's victory in a court that was
just slightly to the political right of the Star Chamber.

The Boyds didn't win based on either the Fourth Amendment's guarantee against unreasonable searches or seizures or on the Fifth Amendment's

guarantee against compelled self-incrimination. The Boyds won because of the "intimate relationship," as the *Boyd* Court put it, between the Fourth and Fifth Amendments: The government was trying to use the Boyds' words (which was their property) to convict them. The *Boyd* Court explained:

> We have already noticed the intimate relation between the two amendments. They throw great light on each other. For the "unreasonable searches and seizures" condemned in the Fourth Amendment are almost always made for the purpose of compelling a man to give evidence against himself, which in criminal cases is condemned in the Fifth Amendment; and compelling a man "in a criminal case to be a witness against himself," which is condemned in the Fifth Amendment, throws light on the question as to what is an "unreasonable search and seizure" within the meaning of the Fourth Amendment. And we have been unable to perceive that the seizure of a man's private books and papers to be used in evidence against him is substantially different from compelling him to be a witness against himself. We think it is within the clear intent and meaning of those terms.[50]

The "intimate connection" between the two amendments led the *Boyd* Court to recognize two zones of privacy, one located in the core of the other.[51] Think of it as a Venn diagram. Beyond the outer limit, the government can do whatever the hell it wants, even without probable cause or warrants. If the governmental activity isn't a "search" or "seizure," the Fourth Amendment simply doesn't apply. Beyond the outer perimeter is the Wild West.

Within the outer limit, but not at the overlapping center, is an intermediate zone of privacy. This zone isn't inviolate; if the government satisfies the procedural requirements of the Fourth Amendment (probable cause and warrant), then it can search and seize within this zone. In the nomenclature of the Fourth Amendment, searches or seizures are "reasonable" in this intermediate zone of privacy, with "reasonableness" being defined by the government's compliance with probable cause and warrant requirements.

At the center of these graduated zones of privacy was the inviolate zone of privacy which decided the Boyds' dispute. The government may not intrude into this inner sanctum of citizen privacy. No matter how much probable cause; no matter how many warrants, this inviolate zone of privacy is protected by the "intimate relationship" between the Fourth and Fifth Amendments. The Court decided that the Boyds' invoices fell within this zone. So would their diary. And so would Ted Kaczynski's journals.

To understand why Kaczynski's journals would probably fall within this inviolate zone of privacy requires an extensive discussion of doctrinal and jurisprudential history that lies beyond the scope of this book. Briefly, the hundred years since *Boyd* was decided have seen a gradual severing of the "intimate connection" between the Fourth and Fifth Amendments, along with an expansion of the intermediate zone of privacy and a concomitant contraction of the center's inviolate privacy. Today, this center is inhabited by a single occupant: a United States citizen's private diary.

The *Boyd* Court defined the center of our Venn diagram in terms of property rights: The inviolate zone of privacy was coextensive with property rights. Because your property was part of you, the government couldn't force your property to "testify" against you.

This "you are your property" idea made historical sense, because the rights of property and contract were of paramount importance to the *Boyd*-era courts.[52] They were of course the forebears to the *Lochner* era, when the court enjoined Eugene Debs's American Railway Union and struck down the minimum age working laws as offensive to "substantive" due process.[53] In other words, if the citizen-accused had a superior property interest in the item (an invoice, say, or a journal), then it fell within the zone of inviolate privacy. If the government had a superior property interest, it didn't.

With the demise of the *Lochner* era of substantive due process as a protection of fundamental economic interests, the property-based principle of *Boyd* became a casualty. *Boyd*'s "intimate connection" idea was finally done in by two landmark decisions of the Warren Court. In *Warden v. Hayden* and *Schmerber v. California*, the Court purported to bury *Boyd*.[54] No longer would property law define the limits of constitutional protections against unreasonable searches and seizures. The Constitution "protects people, not places," was the epitaph inscribed in memory of *Boyd*.[55]

Justice William Brennan's opinion for the Court in *Schmerber v. California* further compromised the "intimate connection" between the Fourth and Fifth Amendments provided by *Boyd*. The language and logic of the *Schmerber* opinion divide the two amendments. But the structure of Brennan's opinion brought the point home most graphically. Each constitutional amendment received its own separately-captioned and separately-numbered place in the *Schmerber* opinion. "Divide and conquer."

To be sure, the Burger Court inexorably but carefully narrowed the *Boyd* rulings on privacy. In the 1976 case of *Fisher v. United States*, the Court held that the Fifth Amendment is not abridged by compelling the production of records by the defendant's accountant.[56] *Fisher* involved a subpoena that required a defendant to produce an accountant's work papers in the taxpayer's possession. The logic behind this decision was that the accountant's work papers did not belong to the taxpayer, were not prepared by him and contained no testimonial declarations by him. The

Court concluded that the subpoena did not violate the Fifth Amendment, regardless of how incriminating those papers might be to the taxpayer, because "the privilege protects a person only against being incriminated by his own compelled testimonial communications." In addition, inasmuch as their preparation was "wholly voluntary," the records cannot be said to contain compelled testimonial evidence."[57]

Justice White, who wrote the principal opinion in *Fisher*, asserted that "several of *Boyd*'s express or implicit declarations have not stood the test of time."[58] Among them, White continued, was "the pronouncement in *Boyd* that a person may not be forced to produce his private papers."[59] That this portion of *Boyd* had been repeated in subsequent decisions was mere "dictum," according to Justice White.[60] Such dictum of dictum was not persuasive to White: the "prohibition against forcing the production of private papers has long been a rule searching for a rationale that is consistent with the proscriptions of the Fifth Amendment against compelling a person to give 'testimony' that incriminates him."[61]

Of course the private papers rule *did* have a rationale; it was set out in *Boyd*, and it was based on the confluence of both the Fifth *and* Fourth Amendments. As to purely private papers, such as a diary, Justice White's *Fisher* opinion regarding *Boyd*'s death was itself dictum (third-degree dictum at that). The *Fisher* opinion acknowledged the diary exception: "Special problems of privacy which might be presented by subpoena of a personal diary are not involved here."[62]

Yet Justice Marshall, in his concurring opinion, stated that the majority's opinion may provide the most complete protection yet against compulsory production of private papers.[63] The majority was concerned that if the government were to compel the production of certain documents, the act of production itself would establish their existence, making it, not the documents, testimonial. The existence of personal documents is *not* proven solely by the act of production, but the existence of business or other non-personal documents is sufficient proof.[64] Because of the inverse relationship between the privacy of a document and the possibility of assuming its existence: the more personal, the less possible it is to verify its existence.[65] Therefore, although keeping a diary may not be incriminating, the Fifth Amendment would protect the diary only to the extent that it would incriminate the diarist.[66]

Likewise, in the 1984 case of *United States v. Doe*, the Court held that compelled production of "business records" does not offend the Fifth Amendment, nor does compelling a bank to produce an individual's account records, as the Court held in *United States v. Miller* in 1976.[67] On the Fourth Amendment front, the Court held that the Fourth Amendment did not preclude seizing a person's business records with a valid search warrant.[68]

In separate concurring opinions, Justices O'Connor and Marshall (joined by Brennan) were not in agreement as to whether *Doe/Fisher* applied to private papers as well as business records – and thus the continued existence of *Boyd* became a matter for debate. Justice O'Connor observed: "I write separately . . . to make explicit what is implicit in [the majority's opinion]: that the Fifth Amendment provides absolutely no protection for the contents of private papers of any kind. The notion that the Fifth Amendment protects the privacy of papers originated in *Boyd v. United States*, but our decision in *Fisher v. United States* sounded the death-knell for *Boyd*."

"Sounding the death-knell" would seem to aver that Boyd is dead.

Justice O'Connor seems to think so, and her penchant for overturning constitutional cases has not diminished to this day. Justice O'Connor concurred in *Doe* to revisit her concurrence in *Fisher* where she originally declared *Boyd* dead. Yet the Court itself had never made such a declaration, and in *Fisher*, no other justice joined her opinion. Further, at least one federal appellate court has declined to use her concurring opinions to challenge the majority opinions in *Fisher* and *Doe* because in them she was joined by no other justice.[69]

Justice Marshall, also concurring in *Doe*, shot back: "This case presented nothing remotely close to the question that Justice O'Connor eagerly poses and answers." Like *Fisher*, the documents at issue in *Doe* were business records, "which implicate a lesser degree of concern for privacy interests than, for example, personal diaries." If the majority opinion possessed any of the implications O'Connor found in it, Marshall noted "I would assuredly dissent."

Doe and *Fisher* have spawned an academic literature, much of it excellent, some of it awful, filled with doctrinal analyses of the Fifth and Fourth Amendments.[70] In a superb article published in the *Michigan Law Review*, a student concurred with O'Connor's opinion that *Boyd* was dead.[71] I do not think that *Boyd* is quite dead yet – dismembered, diminished, disrespected by some members of the current Supreme Court, but not dead.

As the First Circuit observed in a wry understatement, only four years after *Doe*, "The lower courts, interpreting *Doe*, have expressed diverging opinions" regarding Justice O'Connor's conclusion that *Doe* "sounded the death knell of *Boyd*."[72] This should not be surprising. After all, "only Justice O'Connor 'sounded the knell of *Boyd*."[73] The Court's opinions in *Fisher, Doe* and *Miller* took pains to distinguish *Boyd* by pointing out that the writings in question were *business* records – not the "private papers" of the persons whom they incriminated.[74]

The lower courts, struggling to sort out *Boyd, Fisher, Andresen, Doe* and the difference between "private papers" and non-private papers (such as business records) have mirrored the opacity of the Supreme Court's opinions. By 1986, only two years after *Doe* was decided, the Fourth Circuit lamented that the "[once]-clear line between the production of papers with personal content and corporate content has been blurred by recent court decisions shifting the focus away from the privacy interest of an individual in his personal papers and toward protection against testimonial self-incrimination." The Court then noted that "circuits have split over the proper application of *Fisher* and *Doe* to the question of private papers."[75] Perhaps most notable about the way various circuit courts have treated this issue is the squeamishness they seem to experience when confronted by it. For example, in a 1991 opinion, the Eleventh Circuit observed that "although a few circuits have held that even personal papers are subject to [the reasoning of *Doe and Andresen v. Maryland*], this circuit has not yet addressed the remaining vitality of *Boyd* with regard to private documents. The Supreme Court's own reluctance to overrule *Boyd*, and the government's failure to press this point here, counsel in favor of continuing to leave [the] question open in this circuit."[76] A well-reasoned 1993 Second Circuit opinion on a ruling that effectively killed *Boyd* drew an equally well-reasoned dissent that argued *Boyd*'s relevance to purely private papers.[77] In addition to that Second Circuit case, at least two other circuits have concluded that the Fifth Amendment does not protect the contents of voluntarily prepared documents, business or personal.[78]

Other courts, before and after *Doe*, have grounded the Fifth Amendment's protection of "private papers" firmly in *Boyd*. In an excellently articulated and widely cited 1981 case, *In re Grand Jury Proceedings*, the Third Circuit held that "the Fifth Amendment protects an accused from government-compelled disclosure of self-incriminating private papers, such as purely personal date books."[79] The court noted that "although some commentators have predicted the demise of [*Boyd*], we explicitly reject the prophecy."[80]

The constitutional firewall between private papers and business records "can hardly be characterized as novel," the Third Circuit wrote.[81] Quoting the Supreme Court's opinion in *Bellis v. United States*, and citing *Boyd*, this court noted: that "the Supreme Court has said that 'the Fifth Amendment privilege against compulsory self-incrimination protects an individual from compelled production of his personal papers and effects . . . '"[82] The court explained:

No case has held to the contrary.[83] In *Fisher v. United States*, the Supreme Court held that production of an accountant's papers did not violate the taxpayer's Fifth Amendment rights. Plainly, the question whether the compelled production of the taxpayer's own papers would have violated his Fifth Amendment was not before the *Fisher* court. The Fifth Amendment doctrine protecting an accused from producing incriminating private papers manifests its vitality by virtue of the *Fisher* court's explicit efforts to distinguish its facts from the facts in *Boyd*.

Moreover, the policies underlying the Fifth Amendment proscription against compelled self-incrimination support protection of an accused from having to produce his private papers. One well recognized policy stems from "our respect for the inviolability of the human personality and of the right of each individual 'to a private enclave where he may lead a private life'. . . ." *Murphy v. Waterfront Commission*. The Fifth Amendment "respects a private inner sanctum of individual feeling and thought and proscribes state intrusion to extract self-condemnation." *Couch v. United States*. The Fifth Amendment in its self-incrimination clause enables the citizen to create a zone of privacy which government may not force him to surrender to his detriment. *Griswold v. Connecticut*.

Nor are these expressions of allegiance to the concept that a man ought not to be compelled to produce his private papers for use against him in a criminal action without relevance to modern American society. Our society is premised on each person's right to speak and think for himself, rather than having words and ideas imposed upon him. This fundamental premise should be fully protected. Committing one's thoughts to paper frequently stimulates the development of an idea. Yet, persons who value privacy may well refrain from reducing thoughts to writing if their private papers can be used against them in criminal proceedings. This would erode the writing, thinking, speech tradition basic to our society.

But it is not the policies of privacy alone which underlie our refusal to permit an accused to be convicted by his private writings. We believe that the framers of the Bill of Rights, in declaring that no man should be a witness against himself in a criminal case, evinced "their judgment that in a free society, based on respect for the individual, the determination of guilt or innocence by just procedures, in which the accused made no unwilling contribution to his conviction, was more important than punishing the guilty."[84]

The idea that an accused is entitled to certain rights developed slowly. But the Anglo-American theory of criminal justice has taken many steps, albeit one at a time, since the day of Star Chamber and the High

Commission.[85] In *Entick v. Carrington,* an English decision issued in 1765, the foundation was laid disallowing conviction on the basis of government-seized private papers of the accused.[86] It was not just the intrusion of the search which offended the Court, but the compelled use of a man's private papers as evidence used to convict him.[87] As Lord Camden, writing for a unanimous court recognized, "papers are often the dearest property a man can have."[88]

The American origins of this right may be seen as early as 1776 in the Constitution of Virginia. Section 8 of the Virginia Declaration of Rights, in the midst of the enumeration of the rights of criminally accused, declared: Nor can he be compelled to give evidence against himself. Since an accused person at that time in Virginia was not permitted the right to testify at his trial, "he could neither be placed on the stand by the prosecution nor take the stand if he wished," the guarantee secured by the Virginia constitution would have been meaningless, unless it meant that by not being "compelled to give evidence against himself" that an accused could not be forced to give his private writings to be used as evidence against him in a criminal trial.

But even if the somewhat obscured origin of this right dates back only one century, to the decision in *Boyd,* it has been staunchly heralded as a basic right of an accused. We believe that failure to continue to preserve this right, which we believe basic, would be a step forward in what has been a long and bitterly contested battle to accord rights to persons who stand accused of crime.

Therefore, we do not believe that the government can compel production of the pocket date books of Johanson, which are his wholly personal papers, without violating his guarantees under the Fifth Amendment. These books were his own, kept on his person, with all entries recorded by him, not by third persons. We believe he had a rightful expectation of privacy with regard to these papers. His Fifth Amendment privilege is transferred to protect the same documents when in Johanson's attorneys' hands by an effective merger with the attorney-client privilege. For this reason, we affirm the district court decision to quash the portion of the subpoena *duces tecum* ordering production of Johnson's private papers, his personal date books.

A case decided shortly after *Doe* further elaborates this delicate issue of privacy. The Sixth Circuit observed that although *Fisher* and *Doe* had "eroded" *Boyd,* the court did "not read either of these cases as holding that the contents of private papers are never privileged, it is evident from the dialogue between Justices Marshall and O'Connor, in their concurring opinions in *Doe*, that if contents are protected at all, it is only in rare situations where compelled disclosure would [as Marshall put it] break "the heart of our sense of privacy."[89] Because the records at issue were "not so intimately personal as to evoke serious concern over privacy interests," the bankruptcy records were held not privileged.[90]

The Ninth Circuit, the very same court that would have decided the Theodore Kaczynski journal issue, implied in the 1985 post-*Doe*, post-*Fisher* case of *In re Grand Jury Proceedings (Terry)*, that because a subpoena demanding "personal journals, files related to the purchase of fishing boats, stock transactions, escrow statements and receipts could . . . relieve the government of proving the existence, possession or authenticity of the records, and thus could be incriminatory, the act of production would violate the Fifth Amendment.[91] The *Terry* Court also opined that "private papers" received no special constitutional protection. Similarly, in *United States v. MacKey*, a 1981 case that was decided after *Fisher* but before *Doe*, the Ninth Circuit relied on the distinction between private papers and business "entity" papers, particularly a corporate executive's "diary" planner and desk calendar.[92] The court held that, notwithstanding some "indicia that might point to a conclusion that the documents were MacKey's personal papers, other facts persuade us that they are properly discoverable corporate papers."[93] The papers were not personal because they "were kept in his office there [at the corporation] and used by him in the day-to-day management of the corporation." MacKey had "used the diary and calendar to record business meetings and transactions he conducted as an executive" of the corporation.[94] The fact that he also made some personal notations of a non-business nature was not deemed sufficient to shroud them with the Fifth Amendment protection reserved only for purely private papers."[95] In recognizing that the Fifth Amendment does indeed "shroud" papers that are "purely private," the Ninth Circuit in *MacKey*, perhaps unwittingly, anticipates *Doe* and the constitutional line separating truly private papers from business records.[96]

Several cases stand for the proposition that if a criminal defendant creates inculpatory writings in a diary without being compelled to do so, and the government obtains them without compelling that defendant to authenticate or vouch for those writings, then the Fifth Amendment is not violated, and neither is the First Amendment.[97]

Yes, but . . .

Notwithstanding their sometimes passionate defense of *Boyd*'s inviolate zone of privacy, these cases seem to miss the central teaching of the *Boyd* opinion. The constitutional source of this privacy is neither the Fifth

Amendment nor the Fourth Amendment alone, but rather the intersection – or "intimate connection" – between these Amendments. When the branched roots of *Boyd* are separated, the inviolate core of privacy withers.

The problem here is that these circuit cases tend to treat *Boyd* as nothing more than a Fifth Amendment case. The decisions usually turn on whether a subpoena compels the act of production of private (or business papers). In Kaczynski's case, however, he was not being compelled to "produce" his private journals. He had already produced them, over a period spanning many years. The government didn't need him to "produce" the journals, it already *had* them.[98] It had this evidence ever since the FBI searched and ransacked his home pursuant to a search warrant that had been issued based on sufficient probable cause. Thus, a court might forget the private nature of the journals and rule against Kaczynski under the Fifth Amendment alone because he wasn't "compelled" by the government to "produce" the diary. He has no protection under the Fourth Amendment alone because the procedural requirements of the Fourth were met: There had been a warrant and probable cause.[99]

Theodore Kaczynski's journals were not subpoenaed. Government agents seized them. In the aforementioned cases, the courts decided whether the government could merely *subpoena* documents. The Court has not yet determined whether the government could seize them. Yet concern for privacy should be even greater in seizures because subpoenas fall within the category of searches and seizures, albeit "divested of many of the aggravating incidents" to which search and seizure give rise.[100] Subpoenas contain the "substance and essence," and "effect [the] substantial purpose" of the incidents of searches and seizures.[101] They constitute a "figurative" or "constructive" search.[102]

The cases that we examined suggest that, although certain kinds of papers might be difficult to pigeonhole as either "personal" or "business," *Boyd* and the Fourth and Fifth Amendments still carve out an inviolate zone of protection for purely private papers even in the post-*Fisher* and *Doe* world. The issue for us now becomes this: If such an inviolate zone of privacy exists, can it accommodate a personal diary?

The Court has never expressly overruled *Boyd.* If the Court is confronted with a case that left the justices without an escape hatch – a case in which, for the Court to rule in the government's favor, *Boyd* would have to be overruled once and for all – I do not think they would do so.

Theodore Kaczynski's diary would be just such a case. If any vestige remains of *Boyd,* the sole occupant of that tiny zone of privacy would be a citizen's private journals which the federal government wants to put forth as the basis of a death penalty.

To a great extent, the Warren court and its successors have indeed buried *Boyd*. Today, in almost all instances, Fourth Amendment "reasonableness" is defined solely in terms of the manner in which the government satisfies the *procedural* requirements of the Fourth Amendment. In other words, as long as they have probable cause and a warrant, any search and seizure is "reasonable" and therefore constitutional. In case after case, the Supreme Court has narrowed the privacy of personal papers established by *Boyd*. But the journal issue – the core of this inviolate zone, so to speak – has never gone before the Court.

Boyd's Last Stand

> ... the essential principle of *Boyd* – that the compulsory production of a man's private papers to establish a criminal charge against him violates the Fifth Amendment – has been frequently reaffirmed by the United States Supreme Court. [103]
>
> Maine Supreme Court (1990)

The United States government rarely seeks to base capital prosecutions on the private diaries of a defendant. In at least one recent murder trial in federal court the government succeeded in introducing into evidence a diary in a non-capital murder prosecution.[104] This was the trial of Walter Leroy Moody for the mail-bomb assassination of Eleventh Circuit appellate Judge Robert S. Vance. According to the reported opinion in the case, Moody's appellate counsel did challenge the use of the diaries (which may not even have been genuinely private).[105] Moody's challenge, however, was based solely on the First Amendment – not the Fourth Amendment or Fifth Amendment or *Boyd*. Diary-dependent capital prosecutions are just as rare in state courts. Perhaps the rarity of such cases indicates a widespread societal repugnance towards the governmental practice.[106]

The most germane case that I was able to find was the Main Supreme Court 1990 judgment, *State v. Andrei*.[107] The Maine trial court had ruled that the introduction of Hope Ann Andrei's diary would violate her constitutional rights under the Fifth Amendment.[108] The trial judge cited *Boyd* "for the proposition that the production of a defendant's private papers against her will is compelling that defendant to be a witness against herself within the meaning of the Fifth Amendment."[109]

The Maine Supreme Court reversed the ruling, holding that Ms. Andrei had not been "compelled" to incriminate herself because of the manner in which the police came into possession of her diary. (Her husband had given it to them, pointing out the inculpatory passage.)[110] Because the diary "was delivered to the police in the absence of any form of coercion," the Court held that her Fifth Amendment rights were not implicated.[111]

In an interesting digression from the legal issue thus raised, the *Andrei* Court found it "worth noting" that "the essential principle of *Boyd* – that the compulsory production of a man's private papers to establish a criminal charge against him [is a violation of] the Fifth Amendment – has been frequently reaffirmed by the United States Supreme Court."[112] The defendant's challenge "focus[ed] on a reading of *Boyd* that would extend Fifth Amendment protection to a document obtained in the absence of some form of 'compulsion.'"[113]

In the recent, rather forgettable debacle over former Senator Robert Packwood's diaries, many diarists in America were outraged that the government could so easily profane their secrecy.[114] Yet the outrage was premature: The former senator consented to handing over the diaries.[115] He testified about the diaries in response to questioning by the Ethics Committee, and he apparently did not have the staying power necessary to oppose the subpoena from the Senate Ethics Committee. He flaccidly agreed that the *Boyd* principle had eroded.[116]

It seems odd to articulate a neutral, legal, rational principal that distinguishes diaries from business papers. Charles Black, editing a brief in *Brown v. Board of Education,* made this point with spare eloquence:

> These infant appellants are asserting the most important secular claims that can be put forward by children, the claim to their full measure of the chance to learn and grow, and the inseparably connected but even more important claim to be treated as entire citizens of the society into which they have been born. We have discovered no case in which such rights, once established, have been postponed by a cautious calculation of conveniences. The nuisance cases, the sewage cases, the cases of the overhanging cornices, need not be distinguished. They distinguish themselves.[117]

Boyd is very much the product of late nineteenth-century law. It did not rely on constitutional rhetoric or the conceptual framework of "privacy" so familiar to us today. The view that our Constitution provides a fundamental "right to an unmolested private life" – a right to privacy – can be traced to the famous *Harvard Law Review* written by Brandeis and Warren in 1890, four years after *Boyd* was decided.[118]

Still, the postulation of tiered zones of privacy as illustrated by the Venn diagram does have a contemporary resonance about it. The diarist's claim to *Boyd*'s core zone of inviolate privacy should be comparable to a woman's constitutional right to an abortion during the first trimester of pregnancy – a right that cannot be encumbered by direct or indirect governmental regulation, which was recognized in *Roe v. Wade* and reaffirmed in *Planned Parenthood v. Casey.*[119] Later in the developmental stages of fetal life, the Constitution does allow limited governmental regulation – much as *Boyd's* zone of intermediate privacy allows governmental intrusion (but only if the procedural requirements of the Fourth Amendment are satisfied).

In *Griswold v. Connecticut,* Justice William O. Douglas wrote that "[v]arious [constitutional] guarantees create zones of privacy," among them the "Fourth Amendment": The Fourth Amendment explicitly affirms the "right of the people to be secure in their persons, houses, papers and effects from unreasonable searches and seizures."

Justice Blackmun seems to have been on the same wavelength in *Roe v. Wade* when he wrote: "The Constitution does not explicitly mention any right of privacy. [But] the Court has recognized that a right of personal privacy, or a guarantee of certain areas or zones of privacy, does exist under the Constitution. In varying contexts, the Court or individual Justices have, indeed, found at least the roots of that right in the First Amendment; in the Fourth and Fifth Amendments."

The talk of "penumbras" and "emanations" from explicit constitutional guarantees in the *Griswold* and *Roe* cases have made those privacy decisions by the Court jurisprudentially controversial.[120] But the constitutional quicksand in which *Griswold* and *Roe* grounded the right to contraception and abortion ought not obscure the fact that, in the *Boyd* context, the rights being protected *are* rooted in the specific textual language and history of the reasonably clear Fourth and Fifth Amendments to the United States Constitution.

The modern Court's privacy cases are, of course, controversial among legal scholars, largely because of the lack of textual support for the generalized right to one's privacy that are recognized in *Roe, Griswold* and their progeny.[121]

Griswold addressed the banned distribution of contraceptives by doctors to married people; *Eisenstadt v. Baird* invalidated bans on contraception to unmarried people.[122] Even if *Griswold* was not simply a "substantive due process" decision, *Eisenstadt* seemed to have been exactly that.[123]

The most persuasive critiques of "substantive due process" as a conceptual and analytical device focus on its vagueness – and the perceived tendency that this empowers judges to impose their own personal views on the organic document that is arguably one of the supreme laws of our land. This was the critique of the *Lochner* Court by progressives, it is the critique of *Roe* by the religious right, and it is the Court's own self-critique.

The Court, most notably in the infamous *Bower v. Hardwick* decision, hesitated to expand the scope of due process to privacy rights.[124] Often the

Court relies on history to support its rationale. Yet "[h]istorical evidence alone is not a sufficient basis for rejecting a claimed liberty interest" in privacy.[125] Furthermore, "neither the Bill of Rights nor the specific practices of states at the time of the adoption of the Fourteenth Amendment marks the outer limits of the substantive sphere of liberty which the Fourteenth Amendment protects."[126]

Bowers is riddled with weaknesses. The case was decided by a five-to-four margin. Former Justice Powell has repeatedly announced his regret for supporting the opinion.[127] The Court has refused to apply the central holding of *Bowers*.[128] One significant commentator has suggested that the decision was based on animus rather than principled grounds, posing "less of a threat to other privacy precedents than would otherwise be the case."[129]

Substantive due process – whether deployed at the turn of the century to protect the economic rights of capitalists, or today to protect the privacy rights of adult women who have decided to terminate early pregnancies – is powerful as a legal concept because it does indeed lack directive content. Gunther writes that the question with substantive due process is "whether due process authorizes the Court to resort to fairly open-ended modes of constitutional adjudication: to pour into the due process clause fundamental values not traceable to constitutional text or history or structure."[130]

But we are *not* concerned here with values that are "not traceable to constitutional text." Indeed, *Boyd* provides a careful and persuasive analysis of *two* provisions in the constitutional text, as well as a treatment of the historical circumstances that gave rise to those two provisions, a history that, in 1886, was much closer in time to the justices who decided *Boyd* than it is to us today.

The language and history of the organic document that is the Fourth Amendment do support a citizen's right to be free of unreasonable searches or seizures by his or her government – a right to one's private life and safety in the face of unreasonable governmental intrusion. Indeed, when the court in *Griswold* and *Roe* were searching the constitutional text for "penumbras" from enumerated rights that might support a generalized right to privacy, the Court turned to the Fourth Amendment.

Boyd was written in the language of property rights because during in the nineteenth century property was the heartland of personhood. The twentieth century has brought about a shift in the heartland, so that definitions of privacy have become central to the concept of personhood. It is not surprising that *Katz v. the United States* substituted privacy for property as the touchstone of Fourth Amendment protection. In the wake of *Katz* – and in the face of the future forecast by Orwell's *1984* and Sinclair Lewis's *It Can't Happen Here* – Anthony Amsterdam's 1974 law review article offers the best framing device: "The ultimate question [regarding permissibility of any peculiarly invasive criminal surveillance or investigative practice is ultimately concerned with the possibility that if] the particular form of surveillance ... [were] permitted to go unregulated by the constitutional restraints, the amount of privacy and freedom remained to citizens would be diminished to a compass inconsistent with the aims of a free and open society."[131]

Boyd is not the only aspect of the Fourth Amendment that today finds itself gasping for breath, or barely making it on life support. The procedural protections of the Fourth Amendment – as defined by the Burger and Rehnquist Courts – are simply inadequate to vindicate the privacy interests of an American citizen whose government wants to send him to death row based on "admissions" they found in his private diary. This Supreme Court's disrespect for the Fourth Amendment is no longer news, and over the past two decades the Court has inexorably deregulated police procedures with regard to searches and seizures. Today, the procedural protections of the Fourth Amendment – the probable cause and warrant requirements – have less life in them than *Boyd*. It has become a commonplace that the police need neither probable cause nor a warrant to conduct searches and seizures. When they do need to prove probable cause we find a legal environment where the Fourth Amendment has been defined out of existence. Such precedent is available, although legal precedent may not even be necessary since the exceptions to warrant requirement were swallowed up by its multifarious exceptions long ago.

Some commentators have suggested that the procedural safeguards created by the Fourth Amendment have become so many casualties of the war on drugs.[132] Yet even here, there are limits that even the U.S. Supreme Court may recognize. In 1997, the Court did the unthinkable: It struck down Georgia's drug-testing policy. The policy required candidates for public office to submit to drug testing, regardless of probable cause or articulable suspicion.[133] Georgia's policy was laughable, but it is still significant that the *Rehnquist* Court struck it down.

If Georgia's candidates for public office have some legal shelter, maybe there is still hope for our private diaries. Perhaps the Court will recognize that a citizen's private papers are fundamentally different from a vial of crack cocaine.

I have to believe that even the justices of the United States Supreme Court – five of them, anyway – understand that diaries should be off-limits. And they are different in precisely the ways articulated by the language of the *Boyd* opinion itself. Much of the *Boyd* court's rhetoric – the property rights stuff, for instance – sounds quaintly archaic today. But not when it's read with a personal diary in mind. Listen to *Boyd*:

The principles laid down in this opinion affect the very essence of constitutional liberty and security. They reach farther than the concrete form of the case then before the Court, with its adventitious circumstances; they apply to all invasions on the part of the government and its employees of the sanctity of a man's home and the privacies of life. It is not the breaking of his doors and the rummaging of his drawers, that constitutes the essence of the offence; but it is the invasion of his indefeasible right of personal security, personal liberty and private property, where that right has never been forfeited by his conviction of some public offence, – it is the invasion of this sacred right which underlies and constitutes the essence of Lord Camden's judgment. Breaking into a house and opening boxes and drawers are circumstances of aggravation; but any forcible and compulsory extortion of a man's own testimony or of his private papers to be used as evidence to convict him of crime or to forfeit his goods, is within the condemnation of that judgment. In this regard the Fourth and Fifth Amendments run almost into each other.

"Diary in Fact — Diary in Form"

[Mary Chestnut's book *A Diary From Dixie*] is an extraordinary document – in its informal department, a masterpiece . . . [The] Diary is
more genuinely literary than most Civil War fiction.[134]

Edmund Wilson

What is a diary? Why do people keep them? Whence diary in fact – diary
in form?[135]

To understand the continued viability of *Boyd*, the question of what
counts as a diary becomes an issue of some doctrinal and jurisprudential
importance. For Kaczynski – and for all of us who call our diaries "jour
nals" or something other than the magic word "diary" – the issue is of profound significance. Kaczynski called his diary a "journal." Does this label
matter? And what is a diary anyway?

The word "diary" descends from the Latin *diarium* meaning daily
allowance.[136] The word first appeared in 1581: "Thus most humbly I send
unto yor good Lored this last weeks Diarye."[137] The word was first used in its
modern sense, conveying the uniquely personal nature of diaries in 1791:
"We converse with the absent by letters, and with ourselves by diaries."[138]

In literature, the word denotes "a day-to-day record of the events in a
person's life, written for personal use and pleasure, with little or no
thought of publication."[139] Diarists record themselves in words, to fashion
their lives secretly, lest anyone know them better than themselves. Nellie
Ptaschkina writes, "[My diary] is a record of my thoughts and feelings. It
was the wish to write them down that gave me the idea of this diary . . . "[140]
Emily Carr: "Yesterday I went to town and bought this book to enter scraps
in . . . to jot me down in, unvarnished me, old me."[141]

A diary is both confessor and confessional. It alone receives his purga-
tion, lest he betray himself or another. The diaries of Saint Augustine and
of Jean-Jacques Rousseau are naturally titled *Confessions*, and others,
though not necessarily in title, have declared their entries so many shrifts.

Florida Scott-Maxwell: "I should like this to be accepted as my confession."[142] Katherine Mansfield: "[My diary] is more restful than conversation, and for me it has become a companion, more a confessional."[143]

Yet every confession is not truth. Like the people who write them, diaries are loaded with contradictions, equivocations and outright lies. Marie Bashkirtseff: "I find [my diary entries] full of vague aspirations toward some unknown goal. My evenings were spent in wild and despairing attempts to find some outlet for my powers."[144] Kathe Kollwitz: "Recently I began reading my old diaries . . . I became very depressed. The reason for that is probably that I wrote only when there were obstacles and halts to the flow of life, seldom when everything was smooth and even . . . I distinctly felt what a half-truth a diary presents . . . "[145] Fyodor Dostoyevsky: "But there are other things which a man is afraid to tell even to himself, and every decent man has a number of such things stored away in his mind . . . A man's true autobiography is almost an impossibility . . . man is bound to lie about himself."[146] George Bernard Shaw: "All autobiographies are lies. I do not mean unconscious, unintentional lies: I mean deliberate lies. No man is bad enough to tell the truth about himself during his lifetime . . . And no man is good enough to tell the truth to posterity in a document which he suppresses until there is nobody left alive to contradict him."[147]

Diaries record what alone out of his life the diarist chooses to keep to himself. Naturally then, a companionship is felt towards diaries that is not extended to anything, or anyone else. "I hope I shall be able to confide in you completely," Anne Frank wrote, "as I have never been able to do in anyone before, and I hope that you will be a great support and comfort to me."[148] When Frank was preparing to go into hiding, she wrote, "Margot and I began to pack some of our most vital belongings into a school satchel. The first thing I put in was this diary . . . memories mean more to me than dresses."[149]

Anne Frank's decision to bring her diary with her also demonstrates the kernel of terror a diarist conceals and which would explode should one profane her secrecy. "I used to write diaries when I was young but if I put anything down that was under the skin I was in terror that someone would read it and ridicule me, so I always burnt them up before long."[150]

That motivations that cause a diarist to write are entwined with the goods that drive every writer. Perhaps the German poet Rainer Maria Rilke, put it best in his *Letters to a Young Poet* : "Can you avow that you would die if you were forbidden to write? Above all, in the most silent hours of your night, ask yourself this: *Must* I write?"[151] That, I believe, in the end is why writers write and why diarists keep diaries. It is why Anne

Frank kept her journal while hiding from the Third Reich.

The English and American language and legal lexicographical definitions of "diary" maintain a common theme: A diary is what a diary provides space for. This theme determines, in customs law, what the size, shape and number of pages an item must have in order to be characterized as a diary.

In English usage, diary means "[a] daily record of events or transactions, a *journal*; specifically, a daily record of matters affecting the writer personally, or which come under his personal observation."[152] It also denotes "[a] book prepared for keeping a daily record or having spaces with printed dates for daily memoranda and jottings . . ."[153]

The word has the same two meanings in American usage. The first, a record of events personal to the author: "A daily record, especially a personal record of events, experiences and observations; a journal."[154] The second, anything suitable for writing that is prepared with the intent of keeping such personal entries: "A book for use in keeping a personal record, as of experiences."[155]

Courts in customs decisions have relied on the second of these definitions to give legal meaning to the word: "Judicial authority . . . has adopted the crux of the lexicographic definitions that the 'particular distinguishing feature of a diary is its suitability for the receipt of daily notations.'"[156] Courts distinguish between substance and form in determining whether a particular item is a diary. So long as the book or compilation of papers is suitable for personal entries, it need not be in any particular manufactured form to fit the legal definition of diary. In close cases, courts query whether the item's "diary" portion is "essential or indispensable."[157] And "[e]ssential means something more than convenient, desirable, or preferable."[158] In other words, the "essential" test cannot rest "on outward appearances only;" rather, "[t]he resemblance to be essential must pertain to 'essence,' and . . . essence is 'that which makes something what it is.'"[159]

No matter the form it takes, the essence of a diary is its provision for the daily notation of personal observations, reflections and feelings as described in the dictionary definitions: "[T]he particular distinguishing feature of a diary is its suitability for the receipt of daily notations."[160] The test for "suitability" is one of common-sense: can one make such notations in the space provided? For example, "a space of no greater size than three-eighths of an inch by two inches scarcely serves as a sufficient area for a register of daily events; a record of personal experiences or observations; or even a place for personal notes or memoranda."[161] Likewise, a bound item containing "fifty three calendar pages, each bearing the month at the top and includ[ing] seven separate blocks of space devoted to one day of the week[,]" when the "space allocated to each block is . . . one-inch by 4 13/16 inches . . . obviously was not intended to be used primarily for extensive notations" and is not, therefore, a diary.[162]

To meet the suitability test, the diary must contain sufficient space for personal writings. For example, a book in which "there are more blank pages, used for recording events and appointments, than there are pages containing information [printed by the manufacturer]" measuring "4 1/4 by 7 3/8 inches in dimensions" . . . with all but the first few pages consisting of "ruled pages allocated to the days of the year and the hours of the day and each headed with calendars for the current and following months . . . is a diary in fact and in law."[163]

A diary, then, is more than just a daily allowance, as its Latin name denotes. It is a place to record one's personal reflections, observations and thoughts. The diary, in the words of Disraeli, is a private matter for the author, in which he communicates with himself, not with absent others. And customs courts agree with this definition, requiring sufficient space to be allocated in the pages of one's diary in order to record these very personal writings to oneself.

No American who has ever kept a diary should fail to intuit the differences between diaries and business invoices or other such sorts of private papers – not even personal letters intended to be read only by the intended recipient. This is stated eloquently in an essay titled *Fifth Amendment First Principles*:

> [W]hat protection should diaries enjoy? Unlike bodies, diaries are clearly communicative and testimony-like. At a minimum, the search for and seizure of diaries should be governed by a Fourth Amendment reasonableness test. This test should be informed by the probability that a search for a diary will be intrusive, the broad freedom of thought principles of the First Amendment, and the special treatment the Fourth Amendment accords to "papers." What's more, reading a person's diary (even if lawfully obtained) in open court, civil or criminal, can be seen as an additional invasion of privacy – an incremental "search" of a man's soul, an additional "seizure" of a woman's most intimate secrets – that once again calls for a careful judicial inquiry into the reasonableness of this public reading. Above and beyond these Fourth Amendment concerns is a key Fifth Amendment concept – reliability. Writers of diaries often fantasize or write in a personal shorthand easily misinterpreted. Though not compelled testimony in exactly the same way that forcing the witness to take the stand is compelled testimony, diaries may raise sufficiently distinct reliability issues to justify treating them differently

from all other voluntarily created documents that the government wants to search for or subpoena. Therefore, we can see why the Court has intuited that diaries might differ on Fifth Amendment grounds from, say, voluntarily created business records.[164]

There is something special about a diary, and there's something wrong-headed about sending a man to death with a court-ordered drug overdose, on the basis of his diary. Diaries aren't invoices. Diaries are very different from business records. As Steve Thayer wrote in his elegant novel *The Weatherman*:

> [Capital prosecutor] Jim Fury stormed back to the evidence table and grabbed the diary. He waved it in the air. "This book I hold in my hands is not a diary. This is a road map to the murders of seven women, maybe more. A map drawn in code by the mind of a psychopath and then followed to the last inch. The sick demented mind of Dixon Graham Bell. A schizophrenic, clairvoyant weatherman."
>
> [Capital defendant] Dixon Bell made no attempt to match Jim Fury in volume, but he more than made up for it in raw intensity. "Go ahead and start a diary, Mr. Fury. Write down what you truly think of your wife, or your neighbors, or your boss. Put into words your real politics, believing in your heart that nobody will ever see those words. Then I'll take your words and I'll leak them to the newspapers one page at a time. I'll read your words with a sarcastic voice on national television and we'll see if you don't sound like a madman. Let's see how long you keep your job. You've perverted my diary. You've used my words in a way that should be illegal. People don't read books anymore. They watch television." He pointed at the camera, the red light glowing like a warning. "The words you read from my diary are probably the only reading most of these couch potatoes will get all year." He turned his attention to the jury box. "If you jurors are going to judge me by what I wrote in my diary, for God's sake read the whole book. Read it yourself. Crawl into bed with it at night and turn the pages. That's how books are meant to be read. That's the spirit I wrote it in."[165]

The poet Andrew Hudgins put it more succinctly when he proclaimed: "I will not debate my soul with strangers."[166]

Mary Chestnut, the incomparable Civil War diarist, referred to her diary as "journals" and "notes." Married to a high-ranking member of the Confederate government, Chestnut traveled in aristocratic, patriarchal and slave-owning circles. She had a horror of slavery and called herself an abolitionist since early youth. Against male domination, she denounced it in some of the most passionate feminist writing of her time.

Mary Chestnut was uniquely positioned to watch the South's headlong rush into a war it could not possibly win. "It was a way I had, always, to stumble on to the *real show*."[167] She saw a lot. And she took good notes.

She took very good notes. After the war, she used them to write a book she called a "Diary." When Mary Chestnut's *Diary* was published it went through several editions, and it was a critical success.[168] "What the critics had before them," the historian C. Vann Woodward wrote, was "clearly entitled a diary and was presented as such . . . moreover, it bore all the familiar characteristics of the genre."[169] The *Diary* "proceeded from the start under dated entries."[170] Other than one fifteen-month gap, the diary runs from February 1861 to July 1865. Apart from the gap, "the diary form is consistently maintained through forty-eight copybooks of more than twenty five hundred pages, the diarist is narrator of her own experiences, and they are 'real-life' experiences – flesh and blood people, real events and crises, private and public, domestic and historic. Recording them in dated entries, Mary Chestnut adheres faithfully to the style, tone and circumstantial limitations of the diarist and conveys fully the sense of chaotic daily life."[171]

Most importantly, "[t]o all appearances she represents the Latin meaning of *diarium* and its denial of knowledge of the future . . . Over all hangs endless speculation, suspense and anxiety about the fortunes of the war and the outcome of the struggle for Southern independence. The diarist agonizes over the uncertainties [of the world around her]."[172] Mary Chestnut's *Diary* "therefore appears to embody the cherished characteristics peculiar to the true diary – the freshness and shock of experience immediately recorded, the 'real life' actuality of her subject matter, the spontaneity of perceptions denied knowledge of the future . . ."[173] There is one problem: We now know that the version of this work known to the public as the *Diary* was composed between 1881 and 1884, twenty years after the [chronicled] event."[174]

This is not to say that Mary Chestnut never kept a true diary. She did. She simply called it something else. "Mary Chestnut did keep an extensive diary intermittently during the years of the Confederacy, though she preferred to call it her 'journal' or 'notes.'"[175] It was clear to Woodward "that the Journal was never intended for publication and equally clear that from its inception the [*Diary*] book was."[176] Unlike the *Diary* book, the journal was "kept in tight security, under lock and key, and was clearly intended for no eyes but her own, not even those of her husband."[177]

In Kaczynski's case, one aspect of the government's response to the defendant's *Boyd* motion is worth noting. In a footnote to its brief, the government asserts that portions of Kaczynski's journal "addresses 'the reader,' suggesting that he intended to disseminate or publish the documents at some point."[178] Does a diarist's apparent intention that the diary address a third person, by, for example, use of language such as "The reader will note" evince an intent, or at least a knowledge, that the journal will someday be read by others – thus possibly diluting a privacy claim grounded in *Boyd*?

I don't think so. My own journals contain some such language, although its purpose is to serve as reminders to the journal's *author*. When he is reading over his own journals, he is indeed "the reader" rather than "the writer" he was when he wrote the journal in the first place. They are notes to myself – a self which, in this instance, has a poor memory. Hence the principal reason for keeping the journals or "memory books."

The history of the Anne Frank diaries reinforce my view on this score. Anne Frank wrote her diary entries to "Kitty," her name for her diary. A typical day's entry began "Dear Kitty" (or sometimes "Kit") and ended, "Yours, Anne." The daily entries suggest that Anne Frank was writing *to* her diary.[179] In an early entry to her diary (June 6, 1942), Anne Frank explains:

> It's an odd idea for someone like me, to keep a diary; not only because I have never done so before, but because it seems to me that neither I – nor for that matter anyone else – will be interested in the unbosomings of a thirteen-year-old schoolgirl. Still, what does that matter? I want to write but more than that, I want to bring out all kinds of things that lie buried deep in my heart. There is a saying that paper is more patient than man; it came back to me on one of my slightly melancholy days while I sat chin in hand, feeling too bored and limp even to make up my mind whether to go out, or stay at home. Yes there is no doubt that paper is more patient and as I don't intend to show this cardboard-covered notebook, bearing the proud name of diary to anyone, unless I find a real friend, boy or girl, probably nobody cares.
>
> And now I touch the root of the matter the reason why I started a diary; it is that I have no such real friend.
>
> Let me put it more clearly, since no one will believe that a girl of thirteen feels herself quite alone in the world, nor is it so. I have darling parents and a sister of sixteen. I know about thirty people whom one might call friends, I have strings of boy friends, anxious to catch a glimpse of me and who, failing that, peep at me through mirrors in class. I have relations, darling aunts and a good home, no I don't seem to lack anything, save "the" friend. But it's the same with all my friends, just fun and joking, nothing more. I can never bring myself to talk of anything outside the common round or we don't seem to be able to get any closer, that is the root of the trouble. Perhaps I lack confidence, but anyway,

there it is, a stubborn fact and I don't seem to be able to do anything about it. Hence, this diary. In order to enhance in my mind's eye the picture of the friend for whom I have waited so long I don't want to set down a series of bald facts in a diary like most people do, but I want this diary, itself to be my friend, and I shall call my friend Kitty. [180]

Although Anne Frank's actual diary includes such apparent references to "the reader," she clearly intended neither her parents nor her neighbors – one of whom turned her and her family in to the Nazi occupiers – to read her diary. Her actual diary contained intimate, sometimes sexual, information that she never would have wanted her parents to read. Indeed, when, after the war and Anne's extermination in a Nazi death camp, her father Otto Frank published Anne's diary – but only after censoring it of personal information he considered offensive, in bad taste, or otherwise inappropriate for a book.[181]

Like the above examples, the information contained in Mary Chestnut's journals "go far in explaining her concern" that "no one see it but herself."[182] While the diary book "became noted for its candor in many respects, her journal often goes much further."[183] In her journal, "Mary Chestnut permitted herself great frankness and freedom in expressing her feelings about friends, neighbors, in-laws, relatives and immediate family, including her husband and his parents. It is here we learn, for instance, of her suspicion that her father-in-law, for whom she had mixed feelings, sired children by one of his slaves."[184] But "[p]erhaps most closely guarded of all . . . were those secrets of Mary Chestnut's journal that concerned herself, particularly revelations of her vanity or evidence of her conceit, arrogance and ambition."[185] Mary Chestnut "was likely to mince no words in recording the quantity of human folly, pomposity and charlatanary she encountered."[186] The journals are nastier and more self-aggrandizing than her published diary. Such is the nature of diaries – *real* diaries, regardless of whether their authors label them "diaries," "journals," or "notes."

Mary Chestnut finished *The Diary* in 1884. Two years later, the Supreme Court decided *Boyd*. Ten years after that, Warren and Brandeis published their classic right to privacy article in the *Harvard Law Review*. The Justices of the *Boyd* era would never have approved the ransacking of Mary Chestnut's home by police, the seizure of her "journal," and the use of the journal to convict her of a crime, whether the crime happened to be murder or petty vanity.

If the federal government deems it appropriate to convict and condemn Theodore Kaczynski to death based on his journals and notes, then *Boyd* is truly, and most lamentably, dead.

"The Right to Be Let Alone"[187]

... what you really need is simply this – aloneness, great inner solitude. [188]

Rainer Maria Rilke

There are two timelessly brilliant law review articles that are indispensable to any meaningful understanding of the Fourth Amendment. Both are old, which is to say they are time-tested. The first is Anthony Amsterdam's 1974 article *Perspectives on the Fourth Amendment*. In an area of constitutional law that changes rapidly and fundamentally, his 1974 piece remains the best single articulation of basic Fourth Amendment principles. The second article, which is not solely concerned with the Fourth Amendment, is *The Right to Privacy*, written by Warren and Brandeis in 1896.

It is no exaggeration to posit that the constitutionalization of the right to privacy has been the most important innovation in American jurisprudence during the last quarter of the twentieth century. It is also no exaggeration to situate the genesis in *The Right to Privacy*. It is perhaps no accident that the conceptual genesis of the constitutional right to privacy focused on diaries – a diary is perhaps the most potent metaphor for that which our government ought most clearly and completely "leave to its own devices."

Like most law review classics, the Warren and Brandeis piece was short. Unlike most classics, it was published in the *Harvard Law Review*. *Boyd* was only four years old at the time.

Although published more than a century ago, the Warren and Brandeis article sounds strikingly contemporary. The piece begins:

That the individual shall have full protection in person and in property is a principle as old as the common law; but it has been found necessary from time to time to define anew the exact nature and extent of such protection. Political, social and economic changes entail the recognition of new rights, and the common law, in its eternal youth, grows to meet the demands of society. Thus in very early times, the law gave a remedy only for physical interference with life and property, for trespass *vi et armis*. Then the "right to life" served only to protect the subject from battery in its various forms; liberty meant freedom from actual restraint; and the right to property secured to the individual his lands and cattle. Later, there came a recognition of man's spiritual nature, of his feelings and his intellect. Gradually the scope of these legal rights broadened; and now the right to life has come to mean *the right to enjoy life, – the right to be let alone*; the right to liberty secures the exercise of extensive civil privileges; and the term "property" has grown to comprise every form of possession – intangible, as well as tangible.[189]

And, in a passage that today's reader might reasonably think referred to the *National Enquirer* – or the trial by media of Bill Clinton – Warren and Brandeis write:

Recent inventions and business methods call attention to the next step which must be taken for the protection of the person, and for securing to the individual what Judge Cooley calls the right "to be let alone."[190] Instantaneous photographs and newspaper enterprise have invaded the sacred precincts of private and domestic life; and numerous mechanical devices threaten to make good the prediction that "what is whispered in the closet shall be proclaimed from the house-tops." For years there has been a feeling that the law must afford some remedy for the unauthorized circulation of portraits of private persons; . . . and the evil of the invasion of privacy by the newspapers, long keenly felt, has been but recently discussed by an able writer . . . The alleged facts of a somewhat notorious case brought before an inferior tribunal in New York a few months ago . . . directly involved the consideration of the right of circulating portraits; and the question whether our law will recognize and protect the right to privacy in this and in other respects must soon come before our courts for consideration.

Of the desirability – indeed of the necessity – of some such protection, there can, it is believed, be no doubt. The press is overstepping in every direction the obvious bounds of propriety and of decency. Gossip is no longer the resource of the idle and of the vicious, but has become a trade, which is pursued with industry as well as effrontery. To satisfy a prurient taste the details of sexual relations are spread broadcast in the columns of the daily papers. To occupy the indolent, column upon column is filled with idle gossip, which can only be procured by intrusion upon the domestic circle. The intensity and complexity of life, attendant upon advancing civilization, have rendered necessary some retreat from the world, and man, under the refining influence of culture, has become more sensitive to publicity, so that solitude and privacy have become more essential to the individual; but modern enterprise and invention have, through invasions upon his privacy, subjected him to mental pain and distress, far greater than could be inflicted by mere bodily injury. Nor is the harm wrought by such invasions confined to the suffering of those who may be made the subjects of journalistic or other enterprise. In this, as in other branches of commerce, the supply creates the demand. Each crop of unseemly gossip, thus harvested, becomes the seed of more, and, in direct proportion to its circulation, results in a lowering of social standards and of morality. Even gossip apparently harmless, when widely and persistently circulated, is potent for evil. It both belittles and perverts. It belittles by inverting the relative importance of things, thus dwarfing the thoughts and aspirations of a people. When personal gossip attains the dignity of print, and crowds the space available for matters of real interest to the community, what wonder that the ignorant and thoughtless mistake its relative importance. Easy of comprehension, appealing to that weak side of human nature which is never wholly cast down by the misfortunes and frailties of our neighbors, no one can be surprised that it usurps the place of interest in brains capable of other things. Triviality destroys at once robustness of thought and delicacy of feeling. No enthusiasm can flourish, no generous impulse can survive under its blighting influence.[191]

· · ·

The common law secures to each individual the right of determining, ordinarily, to what extent his thoughts, sentiments and emotions shall be communicated to others. Under our system of government, he can never be compelled to express them (except when upon the *witness-stand*); and even if he has chosen to give them expression, he generally retains the power to fix the limits of the publicity which shall be given them. The existence of this right does not depend upon the particular method of expression adopted. It is immaterial whether it be by word or by signs, in painting, by sculpture, or in music. Neither does the existence of the right depend upon the nature or value of the thought or emotion, nor upon the excellence of the means of expression. The same protection is accorded to a casual letter or an entry in a diary and to the most valuable poem or essay, to a botch or daub and to a masterpiece. In every such case *the individual is entitled to decide whether that which is his shall be given to the public. No other has the right to publish his productions in any form, without his consent.* This right is wholly independent of the material on which, or the means by which, the thought, sentiment, or emotion is expressed. It may exist independently of any corporeal being, as in words spoken, a song sung, a drama acted. Or if expressed on any material, as a poem in writing, the author may have parted with the paper, without forfeiting any proprietary right in the composition itself. The right is lost only when the author himself communicates his production to the public, – in other words, publishes it.[192]

. . .

These considerations lead to the conclusion that the protection afforded to thoughts, sentiments and emotions, expressed through the medium of writing or of the arts, so far as it consists in preventing publication, is merely an instance of the enforcement of the more general right of the individual to be let alone. It is like the right not to be assaulted or beaten, the right not to be defamed. In each of these rights, as indeed in all other rights recognized by the law, there inheres the quality of being owned or possessed – and (as that is the distinguishing attribute of property) there may be some propriety in speaking of those rights as property. But, obviously, they bear little resemblance to what is ordinarily comprehended under that term. The principle which protects personal writings and all other personal productions, not against theft and physical appropriation, but against publication in any form, is in reality not the principle of private property, but that of *an inviolate personality*.[193]

. . .

It may be urged that a distinction should be taken between the deliberate expression of thoughts and emotions in literary or artistic compositions and the casual and often involuntary expression given to them in the ordinary conduct of life. In other words, it may be contended that the protection afforded is granted to the conscious products of labor, perhaps as an encouragement to effort. This contention, however plausible, has, in fact, little to recommend it. If the amount of labor involved be adopted as the test, we might well find that the effort to conduct one's self properly in business and in domestic relations had been far greater than that involved in painting a picture or writing a book; one would find that it was far easier to express lofty sentiments in a diary than in the conduct of a noble life. If the test of deliberateness of the act be adopted, much casual correspondence which is now afforded full protection would be excluded from the beneficent operation of existing rules. After the decisions denying the distinction attempted to be made between those literary productions which it was intended to publish and those which it was not, all considerations of the amount of labor involved, the degree of deliberation, the value of the product and the intention of publishing must be abandoned, and no basis is discerned upon which the right to restrain publication and reproduction of such so-called literary and artistic works can be rested, except the right to privacy, as a part of the more general right to the immunity of the person, – the right to one's personality.[194]

. . .

We must therefore conclude that the rights, so protected, whatever their exact nature, are *not rights arising from contract or from special trust, but are rights as against the world*; and, as above stated, the principle which has been applied to protect these rights is in reality not the principle of private property, unless that word be used in an extended and unusual sense. *The principle which protects personal writings and any other productions of the intellect or of the emotions, is the right to privacy*, and the law has no new principle to formulate when it extends this protection to the personal appearance, sayings, acts and to personal relation, domestic or otherwise.[195]

. . .

The right of one who has remained a private individual, to prevent his public portraiture, presents the simplest case for such extension; the right to protect one's self from pen portraiture, from a discussion by the press of one's private affairs, would be a more important and far-reaching one. If casual and unimportant statements in a letter, if handiwork, however inartistic and valueless, if possessions of all sorts are protected not only against reproduction, but against description and enumeration, *how much more should the acts and sayings of a man in his social and domestic relations be guarded from ruthless publicity*.[196]

The late twentieth century might pass over the fact that these words were published more than a century ago, only twenty-five years after the Civil War, before both world wars, before Orwell's *1984*, and the latter day world of news wires, car faxes and Internet sites. If Brandeis and Warren had only known.

Perhaps the greatest legal and cultural enigmas presented by Theodore Kaczynski – and not just by the government's use of his diaries to kill him – are those raised by Sue Halpern in her haunting 1992 essay "Migrations to Solitude: The Quest for Privacy in a Crowded World." Why do we often long for solitude but find loneliness unbearable? What happens when the walls we build around ourselves are suddenly removed – or become impenetrable? If privacy is something we count as a basic right, why are our laws, technology and lifestyle increasingly chipping away at it?

Divide and Conquer:
Senator Bob Packwood's Diary

> The question is not whether you or I must draw the blinds before we commit a crime. It is whether you and I must discipline ourselves to draw the blinds every time we enter a room, under pain of surveillance if we do not. [197]
>
> Anthony Amsterdam (1974)

On October 21, 1993, the Select Committee of Ethics of the United States Senate served a subpoena *duces tecum* to Senator Bob Packwood. The committee was investigating allegations that Senator Packwood had sexually harassed women over an extended period of time. He had threatened potential witnesses of this harassment to dissuade them from presenting evidence, and he had misused his senatorial staff to the same end. The subpoena commanded Packwood to produce entries in his personal diary from January 1, 1989, to the time of the subpoena for the ethics committee's limited inspection. Packwood had kept a daily diary of his activities since 1969. Packwood's diary "include[d] highly personal reflections and information about his private life," according to the D.C. Federal trial court. It was in light of this fact that the Ethics Committee asked to have its subpoena enforced.[198]

The federal trial court enforced the subpoena, and in so doing, treated the Fourth and Fifth Amendments as entirely separate entities. Section III of the Court's *Packwood* opinion dealt with the Fourth Amendment and Packwood's complaint that the subpoena authorized the Ethics Committee to "'rummage' through his most private thoughts and reflections, and very intimate details of his personal life."[199] The Court never denied Packwood's assertion that "numerous courts have recognized the special nature of personal papers such as diaries to which they have accorded the greatest respect, and hence the broadest of constitutional protections."[200] Because the Court recognized "the peculiarly sensitive nature of personal diaries," more than the minimum procedural requirement of probable cause would be needed. The Court balanced its interests.[201] Because the committee's subpoena proposed to conduct "a focused, temporarily limited review of a fraction of the diaries of recent origin with many passages masked to protect the most vital of Senator Packwood's interests in privacy," and because "the examination [would] occur in the presence of Senator Packwood's attorney, marked only to identify the entries perceived as relevant by the committee for Senator Packwood," the court held the subpoena "reasonable" and therefore consistent with the Fourth Amendment.[202]

Section IV of the Court's *Packwood* opinion dealt with the Fifth Amendment and *Boyd*, the case upon which Packwood was "relying principally."[203] Packwood argued that "the Supreme Court [had] *never expressly overruled the case* with respect to private papers such as diaries."[204] Citing *Fisher* and *Doe*, the Court concluded that Packwood's "act of producing" the diaries would "present . . . no risk of incrimination beyond that he has already reduced to written or recorded form."[205]

The Court recognized that "the material sought to be examined" was "extremely personal and private in nature, and merits an appropriately exalted degree of constitutional protection, [the] manner in which the Ethics Committee will review the diaries respects Senator Packwood's legitimate expectations of privacy . . . "[206] Of course, the FBI didn't ransack Packwood's home, find his journals, read every page and leak selected portions to the media. Packwood wasn't suspected of being the Unabomber.

As in Justice Brennan's opinion in *Schmerber*, the District Court's opinion in *Packwood* erected a firewall between the Fourth and Fifth Amendments. No connection was found to exist between them, much less an "intimate" one. It was simply a case of divide and conquer.

After what happened to Bob Packwood's diary, and what will probably happen to Theodore Kaczynski's, would you keep a diary? A *real* diary? An honest diary?

John Hinckley's Diary and Ronald Reagan

On March 30, 1981, the President of the United States, his Press Secretary, a Secret Service Agent, and a police officer were shot in an assassination attempt in front of the Hilton Hotel in the District of Columbia. John Hinckley was apprehended at the scene and taken into custody.[207]

On April 2, 1981, Hinckley was transferred to the Federal Correctional Institution at Butner, North Carolina to undergo psychiatric evaluation. "Formidable security measures were instituted during Hinckley's stay there: he was held in solitary confinement, kept under round-the-clock supervision . . . checked by guards every fifteen minutes, accompanied by three officers every time he left a secured area . . . access to prison personnel [was restricted], and [he was] even prohibited from receiving mail except from designated individuals."[208] Hinckley was informed that he would be frequently searched and that his mail would be read.[209] In an apparent suicide attempt, Hinckley ingested a large amount of Tylenol. The security measures were "further intensified." Searches were increased to twice daily, and he was transferred to a cell where he could be continually observed."[210]

> Under continual observation, in solitary confinement, and with knowledge that. . . his personal correspondence would be read, Hinckley's exclusive outlet for private expression was his writing. He maintained a diary and wrote notes on pads provided by the prison authorities. Some of the correctional officers assigned to guard him read these papers during the cell searches – which were conducted in Hinckley's absence – although they had not been instructed to do so by anyone at Butner..[211]

On the morning of July 23, 1981, correctional officers Meece and Stone conducted a "routine shakedown of his cell while Hinckley was taking a shower."[212] Meece searched the materials on a second bed which Hinckley used as a shelf to hold his personal effects, including writing papers and letters. The defendant kept many letters and personal papers, including attorney-client materials, in a large unmarked manila envelope. As Meece searched the contents of the envelope, item by item, his attention was drawn to certain words on a document in the defendant's handwriting. This document, written on several pages of notebook paper, was folded either in half, or in thirds and was barely legible. Meece skimmed the document and handed it to Stone who was searching other portions of the cell. At that time, Hinckley knocked on the shower room door indicating that he was ready to be let out. Officer Meece showed Stone where he had found the document and then left to accompany Hinckley from the shower room. Stone quickly read the document, replaced it in the manila envelope and reported the incident to the manager of the Mental Health Unit later [that] day.[213]

On July 24th and 27th, corrections officers seized several pages of his personal papers and a personal diary from Hinckley's cell.[214] Hinckley's counsel moved to suppress use of the seized material as evidence at trial. Although "in their motion papers counsel claimed First, Fifth and Sixth Amendment violations . . . these arguments were briefly mentioned in the papers and scarcely addressed at the hearing, the Court [would] consider only the Fourth Amendment claim."[215]

Solely on the basis of the Fourth Amendment, the *Hinckley* court found the search and seizure unreasonable:

> At the suppression hearing, testimony was offered by the manager of the Butner Mental Health Unit, the chief correctional supervisor and several correctional officers who were involved in the discovery and seizure of the materials. Because their testimony shows an indiscriminate search and reading of the defendant's papers, the Court finds that the conduct of the Butner personnel was unreasonable. The seizure of the defendant's personal notes and diary violated his Fourth Amendment rights and the government's use of the materials at trial is prohibited.[216]

. . .

Officer Meece was leafing through Hinckley's papers looking for contraband when his attention was drawn to certain words at the top of a page of Hinckley's handwritten notes. These words alone neither suggested a threat of criminal activity nor does the Court find that such a reading was justified by "special considerations peculiar to the penal system." Indeed, at this point, officer Meece should have determined instantly that the document concerned Hinckley's case. He had no basis for unfolding the document and reading it in its entirety. The reading of the document, which was illegible, required a close study that was unreasonable under the circumstances.

. . .

The seizure of Hinckley's diary, similar to the situation in Diguiseppe, was an unreasonable invasion of the defendant's privacy. No member of the psychiatric staff instructed the correctional officers that a prisoner has a reasonable expectation of privacy in his personal diary unless the diary "contained information concerning imminent danger to inmate safety or prison security . . . " The only entries in Hinckley's diary relating to his safety concern his depression, both before and after his attempted suicide. The Court does not find any legitimate government interest is served by the reading of the diary.

Like his attempted assassin, President Reagan also kept a diary. The former President's diary became an issue in the criminal trial of John Poindexter, Reagan's former national security advisor.[217]

The government charged Poindexter with conspiracy and substantive counts arising out of concealment of the National Security Counsel's Iran-Contra activities. Subpoenas *decum tecum* were filed for documents, including private diaries and notes, of the former President. In a section of the *Poindexter* opinion captioned "Lack of Specificity," the court explained:

Relying upon decisions which condemn "fishing expeditions" and which require reasonable particularity, the former President contends next that the subpoena lacks adequate specificity. Defendant responds that, not having seen President Reagan's diaries and notes, it is impossible for him to be more specific. He goes on to contend that he has furnished sufficient circumstantial evidence upon which the Court would be justified to conclude that information relating to the categories listed in his subpoena is likely to be found in the former President's diary and notes.

The Court agrees in general with that assessment. It will not place the defendant in the impossible position of having to provide exquisite specificity as a prerequisite to enforcement of the subpoena by the Court, while he is denied access to the documents in question, thus making it impossible for him to be more specific. At the same time, however, for the constitutional and privacy reasons alluded to above, the Court is not disposed to requiring President Reagan to make wholesale production of documents which ultimately may turn out to contain little or no material evidence.

The obvious answer to this dilemma, and one to which all the parties hereto have agreed as appropriate with varying degrees of enthusiasm, is an *in-camera* examination by the Court of the relevant excerpts from the former President's diaries, notes and notebooks to determine whether they contain specific evidence that should be produced.

Indeed, the legal and historical precedents indicate that in circumstances such as these a court should hold an *in-camera* review of the presidential papers at issue. Former President Reagan has already offered to submit to this Court the relevant portions of his diaries for such a review, and the Independent Counsel has urged the Court to accept the offer. Accordingly, President Reagan shall produce for the Court's *in-camera* inspection the materials sought by the subpoena, as that subpoena has been narrowed herein, by January 7, 1990.

What is here involved is a clash between two sets of rights – that of an accused in a criminal case to relevant evidence needed for his defense, and that of a former Chief Executive to be free from coercion with respect to his papers containing both personal observations and comments on matters of state. The subject is one of both delicacy and difficulty, for significant constitutional and public policy considerations underlie both sets of rights. The Court has accordingly sought to fashion a procedure that will accompany the interests of the defendant as well as those of the former President, and to minimize injury to both.[218]

Walter Leroy Moody's Diary

There is one recent diary case I have not yet discussed. Walter Leroy Moody was the man convicted for the 1989 mail bombing of my friend and mentor, Federal Appellate Judge Robert S. Vance. Moody kept a journal.[219] The federal government introduced portions of Moody's journal as evidence against him at his noncapital trial in federal court. It was not challenged by the federal appellate court. I have reserved discussion of the Moody case until now because Moody's counsel did not base his diary challenge on either the Fifth Amendment or the Fourth Amendment.

According to the reported opinion of the federal appellate court affirming Moody's federal conviction, his counsel raised several separate challenges to the legality of the government's search of his home and pickup truck. Moody's first two arguments were generalized challenges to the quantity of probable cause and the particularity of the search warrant, matters that are not germane to the subject of this chapter.

Moody's third argument was that "the government's searches violated his Fifth Amendment right against self-incrimination."[220] The appellate court, citing *Fisher* and *Andresen*, rejected Moody's Fifth Amendment argument, reasoning that the Fifth Amendment "attaches only when the government compels an individual personally to incriminate himself. Because in this case all evidence seized was obtained pursuant to a presumably valid warrant, and any statements made by Moody were voluntarily put to paper before the search, Moody cannot successfully challenge the searches under the self-incrimination clause." Given *Fisher, Andresen* and *Doe*, the court in *Moody* was correct, I believe: Walter Leroy Moody loses under the Fifth Amendment alone.

Moody's fifth argument addressed the diary issue directly, but, according to the appellate court, Moody's diary challenge was based solely on the First Amendment – not on the Fifth, Fourth or *Boyd*.[221] "Moody relies on an obscenity case, in which the defective warrant authorized executing officials to decide on their own which films were 'similar' to two films determined to be obscene by a local justice."[222] By contrast, the Court explained – again, in my view, correctly – that because Moody was suspected of sending threatening letters to Judge Vance's circuit court, and because "the government also had evidence that Moody was keeping a journal or notebook about the bombings, which gave the government the right to search for those items, Moody's First Amendment rights were in no way violated by the search."[223]

Thus, in the *Moody* case, the *Boyd* issues were not raised by counsel for Moody. Because *Boyd* was not raised, the appellate court that affirmed Moody's federal conviction had no reason to engage the issues raised in this essay. When defense counsel fails to raise *Boyd* in diary cases, judges can hardly be faulted for failing to address the issue.[224]

What has Moody to do with the Unabomber and *his* diary? The Moody *capital* case is now on appeal to the Alabama Supreme Court.[225] I now have to decide whether to send a copy of this book to Moody's appellate counsel.

My wife Deanna, who located the *Moody* opinion on *Westlaw*, laid out the dilemma: "I don't think you could make a principled distinction, that you could live with, between death row prisoners you like and those you don't like. She advised me to "give the essay to Moody's lawyers," but that I should end my involvement there, refusing "to explain how it works." She then raised an important point: The *Boyd* issue is procedurally defaulted in *Moody*, since it wasn't raised at his trials. So, even if Moody's lawyers tried to raise *Boyd* now, it would not succeed.

I thought of another dilemma. Bob Sullivan was an average young man, who had the distinction of being executed by the State of Florida for a run-of-the-mill murder. Sullivan was never my client; he was represented by the Wall Street powerhouse firm of Paul, Weiss, Rifkind, Wharton & Garrison. But as Sullivan's execution date approached, one of the capital punishment defenders I worked with in West Palm Beach came into possession of an unpublished study of capital punishment in Florida. The study, years in the making, would have been extremely useful to Sullivan's New York lawyers in their efforts to win a stay for their client. By the time the study was slated for publication, Sullivan already would have been dead for six months. The study quite literally had the power to save Bob Sullivan's life.

This was the dilemma: Should we give the unpublished study to Sullivan's New York lawyers, or would we wait until one of our *own* clients had an execution date scheduled? One of our clients had a case which provided a much better vehicle through which to raise the study in court – better than Sullivan's case. By giving the study to Sullivan's lawyers, we risked losing the issue for everyone else on Florida's death row, including our own clients' cases. Still, the study held out that possibility.

My office debated and discussed the ethical conundrum for days. My position was that we should give the study to Sullivan's lawyers. That's what we ended up doing. The lawyers tried to use the study as a basis for a stay of execution. It almost worked. In the end, however, the study bought Bob Sullivan no more than twenty-four extra hours of life. In the course of rejecting Sullivan's arguments, the courts set a precedent that was binding on all future cases: This particular study would not be enough to win a stay of execution.

A few months later, one of my own office's clients received a death warrant. In arguing for a stay, we tried to use the study. But the courts said no, based on the precedent in Bob Sullivan's case. Our client was executed on schedule.

Migrations to Solitude

[The issue is] how tightly the Fourth Amendment permits people to be driven back into the recesses of their lives by the risk of surveillance.[226]

Anthony Amsterdam (1974)

"We Americans are the tell-all type," Shari Roan wrote recently in *The L.A. Times*.[227] "No longer bound by the prudish mores of our ancestors, or even by the manners of our parents' generation, we talk and talk about the most intimate details of our lives."[228] We confess on "Sally and Ricki or Oprah," and we "write autobiographies that make readers blush and publishers wealthy."[229]

Not all of us. Not me. And not Theodore Kaczynski.

Boyd, to the extent that it remains the law of the Constitution, must compel the rule that the intersecting commands of the Fourth and Fifth Amendments forbid the Government to seize a person's writings for use as an incriminating "confession." The Supreme Court's progressive dismemberment of *Boyd* has not yet killed it completely or made this last inner sanctum totally unfit for *Boyd*'s habitation. Whether the Court would finally put *Boyd* out of its misery, or prolong this miserable remainder of it is anybody's guess even if one agrees with Brandeis in *Olmstead* that *Boyd* will be remembered as long as civil liberty lives in the United States of America: The question is whether civil liberty still does live. Certainly the question, properly preserved, is a potential candidate for *certiorari*.[230]

So far, I have focused on the possibility of an "intimate connection" between the Fourth and Fifth Amendments. I have also suggested that, in the case of a personal diary, there might as well be an intimate connection between the above two amendments and the First.[231] At the risk of allowing this argument to resemble a constitutional grab-bag opinion written by Justice Douglas, I suggest one, final intimate connection: the Eighth Amendment's guarantee against cruel and unusual punishment.

Specifically, I believe that the doctrinal formulation of the Eighth Amendment's constitutional frame of reference possesses resonance here. According to the United States Supreme Court, a government practice brings the Eighth Amendment into play if it offends the "evolving standards of decency that mark the progress of a maturing society."[232] For our government to execute Theodore Kaczynski on the basis of confessions in his diary would have been to do exactly that.

On the other hand, I'm relieved that the Kaczynski case was not the litigation vehicle that took the diary issue to the Supreme Court. "Hard cases make bad law" goes an old adage, and the Kaczynski case would offer just about the worst case scenario that I can imagine in which to present the diary issue. Kaczynski's diary was the backbone of the prosecution's case. In terms of litigation strategy, it would be better to raise the diary issue in connection with a quaint bank robber scribophile or prolix cat burglar.

On June 26, 1997, the United States Supreme Court issued its Bill of Rights for free expression on the Internet. The Court struck down, on First Amendment grounds, the Federal Communications Decency Act outlawing smut on the Information Highway. The Court's impassioned defense of First Amendment values of free expression was a fitting way in which to usher in the *fin de siècle*. The First Amendment thus would enter into laws concerning the most modern form of technologically-enhanced communication fully intact.

By contrast, the issues surrounding Kaczynski's journals harken back to the previous *fin de siècle*. When *Boyd* was decided in 1886, Americans who wanted to record their innermost fears and hopes, desires and fantasies, loves and hatreds kept diaries – touching pen to paper. The computer keyboard has, for many Americans, replaced the handwritten diary, as e-mail, fax machines and the Internet have replaced the U.S. mail (snail mail) for many Americans.

Some of us – including me – still write our diaries in longhand, in part because we fear and loathe the depersonalization that comes with computers, in part because the tactile dimensions are part of the fun in putting fountain pen to paper. And then there are reasons we can't explain, and shouldn't have to.

Regardless of whether the diary is created by Waterman ink or Microsoft Inc., the basic human impulse of an American citizen to record his or her most intimate thoughts – safe in the knowledge that their government cannot later use their words as the basis of any action – is essentially the same. The technology doesn't matter. The mysterious need to *write* – for one's self, or one's chosen intimates, or for strangers – needs to be protected. It speaks to the heart of what it means to be an American. This is as true as it was in 1886.

CHAPTER EIGHT

I wish you what I wish
myself: hard questions
and the nights to answer them,
the grace of disappointment,
and the right to seem the fool
for justice. That's enough.
Cowards might ask for more.
Heroes have died for less.[1]

Samuel Hazo

Summations

That's all I have to say about the Unabomber non-trial. As I wrote this book, another man was never far from my mind. I can't – will never – be able to think about Theodore Kaczynski without remembering Judge Robert S. Vance's fate.

His death was intensely painful for me. Judge Vance had been my first employer. But he was more than my boss; he was a wise man, mentor and a hero of the civil rights wars in Alabama. To me, he was family.

I think about him every day. I pray for his soul and his family every night. I have not found "closure" regarding his tragic demise, and I don't want it. "Closure" might lead to forgetting, and forgetting is unacceptable to me. My anger helps me remember. I miss him. I miss his presence, his advice and his wisdom. I miss his laughter.

Vance laughed with his whole body, and with his entire being. It could change the barometric pressure, up or down, in a room. His laughter sums up the way he once lived: dangerously, with brio, taking in big gulps of Alabama Democratic politics during the bad old days when George Wallace reigned supreme and the Birmingham air around Kelly Ingram Park was filled with the sound of snarling police dogs and the threat of racist bombings of churches, homes, offices. For a long time during Judge Vance's tenure, death was in the air.

But that was a good way in the past by the time 1989 rolled around. Vance survived the sixties to be appointed a federal appellate judge by President Carter in 1977. By then Judge Vance, and the South, seemed safe from the threat of bombs.

In 1989, we found out otherwise. Neither Judge Vance nor Robert Robinson, another old warrior of the racial barricades, were safe. In the wake of Oklahoma City and the World Trade Center, the Lockerbie crash, Olympic Park, all of the abortion clinics – and the Unabomber – we now know that no one is safe.

The mail-bomb that tore through Judge Vance on the afternoon of Saturday, December 16, 1989, was probably the size of a shoebox.[2] Upon returning from routine weekend errands to his home in the outskirts of Birmingham, Alabama, his wife Helen remarked that he had just received a package from a fellow federal appellate judge in Atlanta who shared his interest in horses.[3] As Judge Vance broke the package's seal, he detonated a pipe bomb packed with 80 nails. Fragments of metal and nails screamed through the kitchen at the bullet-speed of 13,000-miles-per hour. Vance was killed instantly and Helen Vance was seriously injured. A two-and-a-half inch nail had penetrated her right breast, gone through her liver and lungs, and almost exited through her back.[4]

Two days later and 400 miles away, in Savannah, Georgia, civil rights attorney Robert Robinson sat in his law office.[5] He had had an exhausting day in court, and had an hour of down-time before going to a Christmas party. So he took the opportunity to open the day's mail, including a box he doubtless took to be a gift. When he lifted the flaps of the box, the bomb exploded with such force that his hands were blown off. Three hours later, as six surgeons worked to save his life, Robbie Robinson died.[6]

Over the next few days, other mail-bombs arrived at the NAACP office in Jacksonville, Florida and at the federal courthouse in Atlanta.[7] These bombs were detected before detonating. (At the time, I had a capital case pending in the Eleventh Circuit, and I happened to be on the phone with a friend in the clerk's office when that particular bomb was discovered and the building was cleared. I'll never forget the sound of my friend's voice when he told me he had to get off the phone. After the bomb had been detected, someone inadvertently turned on the x-ray machine's conveyor belt. The bomb fell to the floor but did not explode. Later, when the bomb squad defused the thing, they learned that their protective gear would have been entirely inadequate to shield them from the explosive force of the bomb and its shrapnel.

Although they never met, the white judge and the African-American lawyer were as linked in life as they were in death. In 1963, Robbie Robinson became one of the first African-American students to enter the Savannah public high school.[8] While he was still a teenager he was arrested, along with two companions, for challenging Jim Crow laws which reserved Savannah's beaches for whites only. Mr. Robinson became the first African-American student to graduate from the University of Georgia Law School. He returned to his hometown to practice civil rights law.[9]

Meanwhile, Robert Vance, as chair of the Executive Committee of the Democratic Party of Alabama, had served with skill, courage and integrity in navigating the whitewater of racial accommodation in Birmingham – the city where the bomb, the rope and the gun had been used more eagerly to maintain segregation than anywhere else in the South.[10] When

President Jimmy Carter appointed Robert Vance to the United States Court of Appeals for the Eleventh Circuit, Vance brought his passion for racial justice with him to the bench.

It would be a crime against memory for Robert S. Vance to be remembered only – or even mostly – as the federal appeals judge who was assassinated by a mail-bomb. It would be equally criminal for Robbie Robinson to be remembered as "the other" fatal victim of the 1989 Christmas bombings, or even as the NAACP attorney who was murdered by a mail-bomb sent to his law office two days after Judge Vance was destroyed. The way they lived is far more important and interesting than the way they were annihilated.

Ray Jenkins, a masterful storyteller, has written a superb book about the 1989 crimes and the police investigations that followed and led to the conviction of Walter Leroy Moody, a man filled with a special loathing for the federal judiciary.[11] It is difficult to fully appreciate the horror and magnitude of these murders without the contextualizing biography of the victims. It would be a mistake to think that all we lost in December 1989 were a federal judge and an activist lawyer. We lost much, much more.

As with Thurgood Marshall before him, Robert S. Vance's finest moments were not when he was a federal appeals court judge, but when he was waging war with George Wallace for the soul of the Alabama Democratic Party.[12] Marshall's vehicle was the general counsel's office of the NAACP Legal Defense and Educational Fund, Inc., and his battlegrounds were the federal courts.[13] Vance's vehicle was the chairmanship of the Executive Committee of the Democratic Party of Alabama, and his battlefield was the fight for ascendancy in a party torn between George Wallace on one battlement and the National Democratic Party on the other.[14] During the Wallace days, Vance was what folks called an Alabama Democratic Party "loyalist" – meaning he was loyal to the National Democratic Party and its agenda (the 1964 Civil Rights Act; the 1965 Voting Rights Act, etc.) and its candidates.[15] In 1968, he led the first integrated delegation in the history of Alabama to the Democratic Convention.

In a lovely tribute to Judge Vance published in *The Washington Post* in early 1990, Patt Derian and Hodding Carter wrote: The South "changed because Southern blacks put their lives on the line to force change, it changed because a growing number of Southern whites decided that 'our way of life' was an affront to the teachings of their religion and the heritage of their country. Bob Vance was in the lead among them, not because he had to be there but because he loved both his state and his nation too much to live out his days in comfortable silence."[16]

Why did Vance, of all unlikely heroes, take his stand against George Wallace and the politics of race? When so many white lawyers throughout the South sought refuge in uncomfortable silence, why did Robert Vance take on Wallace, in the lion pit that was Alabama politics? Why was Robbie Robinson the one who broke the color lines at his high school and his law school?

If asked, I am certain Judge Vance – and I expect Mr. Robinson as well – would have answered as the rescuers of Jews during the Shoah answered Kristen Monroe, in her 1996 book *The Heart of Altruism*: The rescuers told Monroe that what they did was not extraordinary.[17] It was the only normal response to the events going on around them, and they acted only as people ought to behave when someone nearby is in need. One such rescuer, an ethnic German, told Moore: "One thing is important. I had no choice. I never made a moral decision to rescue Jews. I just got mad. I felt I had to do it. I came across many things that demanded my compassion."[18] I can hear Judge Vance responding, with arched brow, "I did what I did because it was the right thing to do. I got mad, and I just did it." I also hear him wondering why I was asking him the "why" question in the first place. If Vance turned the question around on me and asked why I wrote this book, I'd have the same response.

Walter Moody's death sentence for the murder of Judge Vance is somewhat ironic. In 1997, a Birmingham jury recommended to a state trial judge that Mr. Moody be put to death. Judge Vance's court spent an enormous amount of time on capital cases. As a federal judge ruling on the legality of state-imposed death sentences, Judge Vance followed the rules laid down by the Supreme Court and let most such death sentences stand. This earned him a reputation among some capital punishment abolitionists as a "hanging judge." (I always had to smile at such comments by my generational contemporaries. And I always wanted to ask: "So where the hell were *you* when Robert Vance was putting his life and livelihood on the line for racial justice in Alabama in the 1960s?" My own answer would have been: "in kindergarten, elementary school, junior high and high school.")

What my fellow abolitionists didn't know is that this particular "hanging judge" despised the death penalty. Mr. Jenkins writes that "despite the tragedy that Roy Moody's violent crime had brought to her family's life, Helen Vance still opposed the death penalty in principle, and knew that Bob Vance had died holding the same position."[19] Robert Vance Junior had expressed the same sentiments at a 1990 tribute for his father held in Birmingham.

When I worked as Judge Vance's law clerk during the early eighties, we often disagreed about his decisions in death cases. My experiences as Judge

Vance's death clerk had a lot to do with my decision to practice as a public defender for condemned prisoners in Florida.[20] As the years passed, and (I hope) as I matured, the judge's wisdom about capital punishment as a legal system made more sense to me – and I appreciated his own struggle between heartfelt personal beliefs and his duties as an Intermediate Federal Court of Appeals judge. What is more, the murder of Judge Vance forced me to reevaluate my own personal and professional convictions about capital punishment.

Before the judge was murdered, I had an intellectual understanding of how the families of murder victims felt. After the judge's murder, I had a gut-level appreciation of how the victim's family feels. Before and After. Judge Vance's assassination is the great divide for me.

Judge Vance was the only person I have loved to be murdered, and when I heard that Walter Moody's Alabama jury had recommended capital punishment, part of me silently cheered. Part of me is cheering still. But that is not my better part – the part where Judge Vance still lives.

Nothing about capital punishment is easy.

APPENDIX

The Unabomber's Victims:
Excerpts form the Government's Sentencing
Memorandum, United States v. Kaczynski
(Filed April 8, 1998)

UNITED STATES OF AMERICA, Plaintiff

v.

THEODORE JOHN KACZYNSKI, Defendant.

CR. NO. S-96-0259 GEB

GOVERNMENT'S SENTENCING MEMORANDUM

DATE:May 4, 1998

TIME:9:00 a.m.

COURT:Hon. Garland E. Burrell

INTRODUCTION

On January 22, 1998, Kaczynski pled guilty to 13 federal bombing offenses resulting in the death of three men and serious injuries to two others. During his plea colloquy Kaczynski acknowledged responsibility for a series of 16 bombings that occurred between May 25, 1978, and April 24, 1995, throughout the United States.

The plea agreement entered into by the parties calls for a sentence of life imprisonment without possibility of release and an order of restitution for the full loss caused by defendant's wrongful conduct. The offenses of conviction, as well as the applicable Sentencing Guideline provisions, require the imposition of mandatory sentences of life imprisonment.

Because this case was resolved by a plea bargain, the public and the defendant's victims continue to have a strong interest in having a full and accurate factual record in an open proceeding, so that the public may take full measure of the seriousness of the defendant's crimes and the harm they caused to the community. Therefore, notwithstanding the mandatory sentence, the United States files this memorandum to make clear that the defendant deserves the sentence that the Court is required to impose, to emphasize the harm that the defendant caused to victims and their families, and to dispel any notion that the defendant acted for any purpose other than satisfying his personal animosity. In addition, this memorandum provides a basis for the government's request that this Court make recommendations to the Bureau of Prisons regarding the terms and conditions of Kaczynski's confinement.

The seriousness of Kaczynski's crimes, his lack of remorse for his actions, and continuing threat he poses to the public, require that he be removed from society for the rest of his life. In addition, Kaczynski should be ordered to pay restitution to the survivors of his crimes in an amount commensurate with the harm he has inflicted on them, and should be ordered to disgorge any monies paid to him, or on is behalf, for writings, interviews or other information, as set forth in the plea agreement. Finally, this Court should recommend that the Bureau of Prisons incarcerate Kaczynski in a maximum security facility so that his activities can be monitored to prevent any future acts of violence or intimidation.

THE HARM WROUGHT BY KACZYNSKI

Kaczynski stands convicted of intentionally taking the lives of three men and grievously wounding two others. . . .

Gilbert Murray

Gilbert Murray was a Marine Corps veteran of the Vietnam War and a graduate of the University of California, Berkeley. A lifelong forester, he was the president of the California Forestry Association when, on April 24, 1995, he was killed at age 46 by a package bomb sent to his office by Kaczynski. The bomb so badly destroyed Gil Murray's body, that is family was allowed only to see and touch his feet and legs, below the knees, as a final farewell.

Gilbert Murray left behind a wife, two sons, a family who loved him, and many friends, colleagues, and co-workers. His wife, Connie, was introduced to Gil by her best friend, Jan Tuck, Gil's sister, when she was 16 years old. Connie and Gil began dating a few months after they met. The following year, Gil enlisted in the Marine Corps, and the two were married when Gil returned from his tour of duty in Vietnam. According to his wife, Connie, Gil "was in love with this Earth" and felt that he had been entrusted with a small patch of it to safeguard and protect. He was known as a voice of calm and reason in a highly contentious field and a man who worked hard to build bridges between differing camps. Above all, he was a dedicated father and husband, a man who "treasured" his family.

Together Connie and Gil raised two sons, Wil and Gib. Wil was 18 at the time of Gil's murder; Gib was just two weeks past his 16th birthday. Gil was always active in his sons' lives. He taught them to ski at an earlier age, watched and coached them in athletic leagues, and when they were in High School, went to their basketball, baseball and football games, even re-scheduling meetings to attend. At Gil's funeral, Wil told the congregation that his father was "the greatest man I ever met. He loved my mom, my brother and me more than life itself. He was always there for us. We always came first." For Connie Murray, her deepest regret comes from the realization that each of her sons will never know their father on an equal footing, as one adult to another.

Shortly before Gil Murray's death, his son Wil had been accepted to Cornell University where he had been recruited for the football team. There was much discussion in the family over whether they could afford to send their son to an Ivy League school which did not offer athletic scholarships. On the Sunday before Gil died, the Murray family met and decided that they would find a way to finance the education. One of the last images that Connie had of her husband was his throwing out all the catalogues for other schools that had accepted Wil. Gil was murdered the next day. Left without the family's provider, and emotionally unable to be far away from home at such a difficult time, Wil could not attend Cornell.

Thomas Mosser

Thomas Mosser was a Navy Veteran of the Vietnam war and worked for the public relations firm of Burson-Marsteller, for 25 years. He had recently been promoted to general manager of the parent company, Young and Rubicam, Inc., and had been away on a business trip. On December 9, 1994, he returned home to his family in New Jersey. Earlier that day, the postman delivered the package that had been mailed to him by Kaczynski. Thomas Mosser's wife, Susan, brought the package inside the house and placed it on a table by the front door. The package lay unopened overnight in the Mosser home only a few feet from where Thomas's daughters played with their friends.

The following day, December 10, was meant to be a special day for the Mosser household. It was the unofficial commencement of the holiday season, a time when Thomas devoted all of his time to his family, and the day when the family had planned to go out together to buy a Christmas tree. That morning, Thomas took the mail that had accumulated during his trip, including the package sent to him by Kaczynski, into the kitchen to open. His wife and 15-month-old daughter, Kelly, joined him, while another daughter, Kim, slept in her room nearby. Seconds before Thomas opened the package, Kelly scurried out of the kitchen add Susan followed her. Thomas opened the package; the ensuing blast drove shrapnel into his body, leaving a gaping hole in his head, opening up his body, and piercing is organs with nails. He died at age 50, on the floor of his own home, his wife at his side trying in vain to aid and comfort him.

Thomas Mosser left behind a wife, a son, three daughters, a family that loved him, and many friends, colleagues, and co-workers. The Christmas season is always a painful reminder of their loss. Last year, Kelly, who had only been 15 months old when her father was murdered, returned from Sunday school with a question for her mother. "Is God coming back from heaven?" she asked. When told God would indeed return, Kelly asked, "Could he bring Daddy back with him?"

Hugh Scrutton

Hugh Scrutton was a native of Sacramento and a graduate of the University of California, Davis. He had traveled the world, devoted time to art, literature, and gardening, and at age 38 was running his own computer rental business in Sacramento. Around noontime on December 11, 1985, he stepped out of his business and walked into the parking lot behind his store. There he stopped to try and pick up what looked like a wooden plank with nails protruding from it laying on the ground. In reality, the object was a bomb that Kaczynski had disguised and planted outside his store. Hugh Scrutton's simple act of courtesy, trying to remove what looked like a potential hazard to others, cost him his life. Kaczynski had rigged the concealed bomb to detonate when it was moved, and when Hugh started to lift the wood, the bomb exploded severing his right hand and driving shrapnel deep into his heart. He died at age 38, in the parking lot of the business he had only recently started, with a co-worker and a caring passerby trying desperately to save him.

Friends recall Hugh as a man who embraced life, a gentle man with a sense of humor who had traveled around the world, climbed mountains, and studied languages. He cared about politics, was "fair and kind" in business, and was remembered as "straight forward, honest, and sincere." He left behind his mother, sister, family members, a girlfriend who loved him dearly, and a circle of friends and colleagues who respected and cared for him.

The Survivors

Other individuals narrowly survived Kaczynski's attacks. Charles Epstein, a professor of pediatrics and a renowned researcher in prenatal disorders, was maimed and injured when, in the quiet of his family home, he opened the carefully disguised package bomb that Kaczynski had mailed to him. A husband and father, accomplished musician, as well as a physician who has dedicated his life to healing others, Dr. Epstein suffered permanent injuries to his hand, arm, face, and hearing. Dr. Epstein underwent weeks of emergency and reconstructive surgery, as well as medical treatment that continues to this day.

David Gelernter, a professor of computer science, was maimed and injured in his office at Yale University, when he too opened a package bomb sent to him by Kaczynski. Dr. Gelernter narrowly escaped death with the explosion, surviving only because he managed to stagger down five flights of steps and across a street to a nearby medical clinic where he was rushed to the trauma unit of a local hospital. A husband and father, as well as a noted teacher and writer, Dr. Gelernter suffered permanent injuries to his hand, arm, body, and sight. Dr. Gelernter underwent weeks of emergency and reconstructive surgery, as well as medical treatment that continues to this day.

Numerous other individuals were injured by Kaczynski's bombs. Gary Wright was injured by the bomb Kaczynski planted in the parking lot of a Salt Lake City computer store. He suffered lacerations and puncture wounds to his face, hands, arms, shoulder, and legs, and underwent surgery to remove shrapnel. Nicklaus Suino, an assistant to Professor James McConnell at the University of Michigan, was hospitalized when he opened the package bomb Kaczynski mailed to McConnell. John Hauser, then an Air Force Captain and graduate student at U.C. Berkeley, was seriously wounded by a bomb Kaczynski planted in a university computer room. John Hauser suffered permanent injuries, ending his career as an Air Force pilot and his dream of becoming an astronaut, and underwent weeks of surgery to repair the damage from the blast. Diogenes Angelakos, who died last year from cancer, was a distinguished Professor at U.C. Berkeley when he was injured by a bomb Kaczynski planted in a break room on the U.C. Berkeley campus. He was hospitalized and underwent surgery, suffering permanent injuries to his hand. Janet Smith was injured when she opened a package bomb Kaczynski mailed to the professor she worked for. She was hospitalized and underwent surgery for her injuries. Percy Wood was the President of United Airlines when he was injured in his family home by a book bomb Kaczynski mailed to him. He was hospitalized and underwent surgery for injuries to his hand, legs, and face. Eighteen passengers and crew members were treated for smoke inhalation when the flight of their passenger airliner was aborted by a fire started by one of Kaczynski's bombs in the cargo compartment. John G. Harris was a student at Northwestern University when he was injured by a disguised bomb placed in a university work room by Kaczynski. Officer Terry Marker was injured while examining the contents of a concealed bomb Kaczynski had left in a University campus parking lot.

Many people were placed directly in harm's way by Kaczynski's bombs. Only chance prevented the death and injury of many of the victims' family members and co-workers, such as the wife and daughters of Thomas Mosser and Gilbert Murray's colleagues at the California Forestry Association. Many of Kaczynski's bombs were left in heavily trafficked areas – the parking lot behind Hugh Scrutton's store, the student workrooms at Berkeley and Northwestern – and easily could have killed or injured many others.

The harm Kaczynski brought about is not limited to the physical injuries he inflicted. By his actions, Kaczynski forced family members and co-workers to witness the slaying or wounding of loved ones, friends, and colleagues. In addition, while hiding behind an alias, Kaczynski intimidated individuals and the public with letters, threatening two noted scholars for pursuing academic research, taunting one of the men he had maimed, bringing the nation's air traffic to standstill on a holiday weekend by a threat to bring down a jetliner, and coercing newspapers into publishing his turgid theories on society's shortcomings. His acts of terrorism deprived countless individuals of their sense of security in their homes, workplaces, and communities.

NOTES

CHAPTER ONE: INVENTING THE UNABOMBER (REINVENTING JOHN BROWN)

1. *See generally* RAY JENKINS, BLIND VENGEANCE (1997).

2. Theodore Kaczynski objects to my belief that he is the Unabomber. My opinion is based solely on public information, and not on our private correspondence.

3. *See*, for example, the information contained in Appendix A the Government's Sentencing Memorandum, *United States v. Kaczynski*, No. CR-S-96-259 GEB, 1998 WL 21667 (E.D. Cal. Doc. April 30, 1998).

4. Pre-Trial Discussions on Motions and Change of Plea, *United States v. Kaczynski*, No. CR-S-96-259 GEB, 1998 WL 22017 (E.D. Cal. Trans. Jan. 22, 1998).

5. *E.g.*, Richard Lacayo, *Tale of Two Brothers*, Time, April 22, 1996; William Glaberson, *Tale of Two Brothers Lends Unabom Trial a Literary Lure*, NY Times, Jan. 5, 1998.

6. *See generally* MICHAEL MELLO, DEAD WRONG (1997).

7. For a thoughtful critique of *The New York Times* coverage of Kaczynski's non-trial, *see* Peter Gardner, *'Did The New York Times Uncritically Buy Into a Diagnosis of Theodore Kaczynski as a Delusionally Paranoid Schizophrenic?'* (Unpublished paper Fall 1998) (cited with permission of the author).

8. Robert Black discusses the issue of monkey-wrenching with great force in *FIJA: Monkey-wrenching the Justice System?*, U.M.K.C.C. Rev., vol. 66, p. 11 (1997).

9. *See* Jan. 26, 1998 Statement by Theodore Kaczynski, www.lwod.com. As of January, 1999, this site is no longer online.

10. *See* Michael Mello, *The Real Capital Punishment*, Crim. L. Bull., p. 37 (Nov. 1998); Michael Mello, *Executing Rapists*, William & Mary J. Women & L., vol. 4, p. 129 (1997).

11. I believe preacher Stephen Bright appointed himself to this position.

12. William Finnegan, *Defending the Unabomber*, New Yorker, March 16, 1998, p. 54 [hereafter "Finnegan"].

13. Robert McGlone, *John Brown*, in HIS SOUL GOES MARCHING ON (1995).

14. *E.g.*, Mark Hansen, *Death's Advocate*, ABA J. Dec. 1998, p. 22 (discussing capital defense lawyer's decision to seek a death sentence for her client – at the client's request – even though prosecutors did not seek death).

15. *See generally* JOHN NOONAN, JR., PERSONS AND MASKS OF THE LAW (1976).

16. *See* Appendix A for examples of Kaczynski's explanations.

17. For the report on McVeigh's jury, *see* Nina Bernstein, *Defense's Portrait of Political Outrage May Have Backfired*, NY Times, June 14, 1997.

18. Ellen Goodman, *The Kaczynski Conundrum*, Boston Globe, Jan. 8, 1998.

19. If Kaczynski's lawyers had thought that their client might have been mentally incompetent to stand trial, then their moral and ethical duties would have been more complicated. For excellent discussions of the ethical duties of attorneys in such situations, *see* James Cohen, *The Attorney/Client Privilege, Ethical Rules and the Impaired Criminal Defendants*, U. Miami L. Rev., vol. 47, p. 539 (1993); DAVID WEXLER & BRUCE WINICK, LAW IN A THERAPEUTIC KEY (1996).

20. My narrative also was confirmed by the 1998 epilogue to Robert Graysmith's 1997 book, UNABOMBER: THE DESIRE TO KILL. I first read Graysmith's epilogue in December 1998, after my own chronology had been written.

21. DAVID GELERNTER, DRAWING LIFE: SURVIVING THE UNABOMBER (1997).

22. Finnegan, *supra.*

23. *See* Declaration of Xavier Amador, Ph.D. (Nov. 16, 1997); Declaration of David Foster, M.D. (Nov. 11, 1997); Declaration of David Foster, M.D. (Nov. 17, 1997); Declaration of Karen Froming, Ph.D. (Nov. 17, 1997).

24. *E.g.*, John Howard, AP, *Unabomber Case – Mental Defense Axed*, Dayton Daily News, Dec. 30, 1997; Bill Gannon, *Contrary Kaczynski Hampers Defense*, Newark Star-Ledger [NJ], Nov. 30, 1997.

25. AMERICAN PSYCHIATRIC ASSOCIATION, DIAGNOSTIC AND STATISTICAL MANUAL OF MENTAL DISORDERS, 285-86 (4th ed.).

26. Finnegan, *supra.* It should be noted that Kaczynski did seek psychiatric help, unsuccessfully, for depression and insomnia while resident in Montana.

27. Michael Cooper, *The Client's Always Right. Even If He's Not*, NY Times, Jan. 5, 1998.

28. Finnegan, *supra*, p. 60

29. *Ibid*, p. 61.

30. *Ibid*, (emphasis in original).

31. Michael Higgins, *A Difficult Client*, ABA Journal, March 1998.

32. Kaczynski denies this, and at least some documentary information supports Kaczynski's denial.

33. Finnegan, *supra*, p. 54. According to Robert Graysmith, defense lawyer Gary Sowards referred to Kaczynski as a "high-performing schizophrenic." *See* ROBERT GRAYSMITH, UNABOMBER, p. 410 (updated 1998 edition).

34. *Ibid*, (quoting Dr. Karen Froming).

35. *See* Steve Lopez, *So Who's Crazy, Them or Us?*, Time, Aug. 17, 1998.

36. *See* http://www.public.usit.net/ddtarr/homestea.html.

37. *Ibid.*

38. *See* http://www.homestead.org/geneorgs.html.

39. *See* http://www.countryink.com/about.html.

40. http:/members.tripod.com/~JohnClayton/stb.html (advertising John Clayton, Small Town Bound: Your Guide to Small Town Living, from Determining if Life in the Country Lane Is for You, to Choosing the Perfect Place to Set Roots, to Making Your Dream Come True (1996)).

41. *Ibid.*

42. http://www.slnet.com/cip/elgin/bvs.html (quoting Duane Elgin, Voluntary Simplicity: Toward a Way of Life That Is Outwardly Simple, Inwardly Rich (1981).

43. The Ecopsychology Institute, http://isis.csuhayward.edu/ALSS/ECO/index.html. Ecopsychology is defined as: (1) the emerging synthesis of ecology and psychology (2) the application of ecological insight to the practice of psychotherapy (3) the study of the human emotional bond with earth (4) the search for an environmentally-based standard of mental health, and (5) re-defining sanity. *See ibid. See also* http://www.igc.apc.org.html

44. http://isis.csuhayward.edu/ALSS/ECO/Final/duncan.html (quoting Garrett Duncan, The Ecopsychology Inst., The Psychological Benefits of Wilderness (1998)).

45. Virginia Postrel, *Let's Pretend: The Pageant Masquerading as Environmental Debate*, Reason, Mar. 1, 1998.

46. Finnegan, *supra.* I have not seen Kaczynski's journals in their entirety, and must trust that the diagnostician's interpretation is based in fact. The record thus far points to the fact that it is probably not.

47. Rainer Maria Rilke, Letters to a Young Poet (1908).

48. Henry David Thoreau, Walden (1959 ed.).

49. *E.g.*, Thomas Szaz, M.D., The Myth of Mental Illness (1974).

50. *See generally* Michael Foucault, Madness and Civilization: A History of Insanity in the Age of Reason (1965); Michael Foucault, The Birth of the Clinic: An Archaeology of Medical Perception (1973).

51. The Unabomber, The Unabomber Manifesto, par. 114.

52. Finnegan, *supra.*

53. AP, *Two Faces of Kaczynski Confront Jurors*, Boston Globe, Nov. 30, 1997.

54. Finnegan, *supra.*

55. Letter From William Finnegan to Theodore Kaczynski, June 1998. Finnegan, *supra.*

56. John T. Kenny, Ph.D., ABPP, Analysis of Neuropsychological Testing of Theodore J. Kaczynski, Dec. 29, 1997.

57. *See* Declaration of Phillip Resnick, M.D., *United States v. Kaczynski*, No. CR-5-96-259 GEB, 1997 WL 741193 (E.D. Cal. Doc. 1997).

58. AP, *Two Faces of Kaczynski Confront Jurors*, Boston Globe, Nov. 30, 1997.

59. *Ibid.*

60. *See* Declaration of Park Dietz, M.D., *United States v. Kaczynski*, No. CR-S-96-259 GEB, 1997 WL 741193 (E.D. Cal. Doc. 1997).

61. Finnegan, *supra.*

62. *Ibid.*

63. Forensic Evaluation of Theodore Kaczynski by Dr. Sally Johnson, Jan. 16, 1998.

64. *Ibid.*

65. *E.g.*, William Glaberson, *Lawyers For Kaczynski Agree He Is Competent to Stand Trial,* NY Times, Jan. 21, 1998; William Booth, The Washington Post, *Kaczynski Pleads in Bombings,* Valley News [VT], Jan. 23, 1998; William Glaberson, *Kaczynski Avoids A Death Sentence With Guilty Plea,* NY Times, Jan. 23, 1998; Cynthia Hubert & Denny Walsh, *Kaczynski Competent, Doctor Says,* Sacramento Bee, Jan. 21, 1998; AP, *Kaczynski Diagnosed Fit For Trial,* Jan. 21, 1998. *See also* ROBERT GRAYSMTIH, UNABOMBER: THE DESIRE TO KILL, p.425, (1998 revised and updated edition). Dr. Johnson's report was made public in Fall 1998.

66. Forensic Evaluation by Dr. Sally Johnson, *supra.*

67. Robert McFadden, *The Tortured Genius of Theodore Kaczynski,* NY Times, May 26, 1996.

68. *Ibid.*

69. *Ibid.*

70. *Ibid.*

71. *Ibid.*

72. Carey Goldberg, *Even in Vermont, the Ardor for Wood Stoves has Cooled,* NY Times, Nov. 30, 1998, p. A1.

73. David Jackson, *Man Behind the Mask,* Time, Nov. 17, 1997.

74. *Ibid.*

75. *Ibid.*

76. *Ibid.*

77. CHRIS WAITS, UNABOMBER: THE SECRET LIFE OF TED KACZYNSKI (forthcoming Jan. 1999).

78. ROBERT GRAYSMITH, UNABOMBER (1998 updated edition).

79. Telephone conversation between Michael Mello and Chris Waits, Dec. 22, 1998.

80. *Ibid.*

81. Marianne Lavalle, *Defending the Unabomber,* U.S. News and World Report, Nov. 17, 1997.

82. *Ibid.*

83. *Ibid.*

84.   Finnegan, *supra.*

85.   *E.g.*, Robert McFadden, *The Tortured Genius of Theodore Kaczynski*, NY Times, May 26, 1996. *Also see* Richard Lacayo, *A Tale of Two Brothers*, Time, April 22, 1996.

86.   Robert McFadden, *The Tortured Genius of Theodore Kaczynski*, NY Times, May 26, 1996.

87.   *Ibid.*

88.   THEODORE KACZYNSKI, TRUTH VERSUS LIES (forthcoming 1999)

89.   UNABOMBER MANIFESTO par. 115.

90.   Manual transcription, by Theodore Kaczynski, of passages redacted from forensic evaluation by Dr. Sally Johnson (from a copy of the report), Aug. 23, 1998.

91.   Forensic Evaluation of Theodore Kaczynski by Dr. Sally Johnson, M.D., Jan. 16, 1998, p. 4.

92.   *Ibid.*

93.   *Ibid.*

94.   *Ibid.*

95.   McFadden, *supra.*

96.   *Ibid.*

97.   *Ibid.*

98.   *Ibid.*

99.   Forensic evaluation of Theodore Kaczynski by Dr. Sally Johnson, Jan. 16, 1998.

100.   Telephone conversation between Michael Mello and Alston Chase, Nov. 4, 1998. For a valuable, if somewhat general, treatment of the connection between the CIA and universities, *see* ROBIN WINKS, CLOAK AND GOWN, (1987).

101.   Telephone Conversation Between Alston Chase and Michael Mello, Nov. 4, 1998.

102.   While his academic work progressed, his social life apparently did not; Kaczynski's peers reportedly found him arrogant and stand-offish.

103.   *Ibid.*

104.   The cost of the investigation was on par with Kenneth Starr's probe into the Whitewater/Sexgate incidents.

105.   Government's Sentencing Memorandum, *United States v. Kaczynski*, No. CR-S-96-259 GEB, 1998 WL 21667 (E.D. Cal. Doc. April 30, 1998).

106.   UNABOMBER MANIFESTO, par. 94.

107.   Kirkpatrick Sale, *Is There a Method to His Madness?*, The Nation, Sept. 25, 1995.

108.   Special Issue, *What Is Technology Doing To Us?*, NY Times Magazine, Sept. 28, 1997.

109.   Richard Powers, *Losing Our Souls*, NY Times, July 15, 1998.

110. For instance, in August 1998 Molly Ivins wrote:

> As Texas endures the slow, agonizing death of our entire agricultural sector by drought, a check of our media and political leaders shows we are also suffering from a bizarre silence on a topic that could be described as "the cause that dare not speak its name."
>
> Local newspapers have responded heroically to the heat wave that has now killed more than 120 Texans, unleashing community efforts to help those most in peril, keeping people informed of water shortages and conservation plans, and praising the emergency and medical workers who are saving lives. The one topic they have not addressed is: Why is this happening?
>
> Of the few articles on the subject, all are limited to the answer "El Niño," which is half right. According to climatologists, this is an El Niño drought: El Niño shifted the jet stream just enough to hold the high that normally sits over the Rockies in the summertime east over Texas, so we are not getting the clouds that normally give us some relief. But the other half of the answer, global warming has gotten little attention.
>
> A recent Dallas Morning News article gives the flavor of what little coverage global warming has gotten: "What did skies over Texas and a Washington debate about global warming share this week? An unusual amount of hot air, say experts on both meteorology and politics." Heh-heh.
>
> The media is doing so poorly on this issue that it's an embarrassment to the profession, and we are being hoisted partly on the petard of our infamous "objectivity." We continue to report global warming as though it were a "debate" among scientists. It is not.
>
> (Actually, there *is* a debate among scientists on global warming, but it is over how much and how fast it is happening, not whether it exists. The best book on the subject for serious students of meteorology is S. George Philander's "Is the Temperature Rising? The Uncertain Science of Global Warming." The best book I have found on why we are having a phony "debate" is "The Heat Is On" by Ross Gelbspan.)
>
> What we mistake for a "debate" is actually a public relations campaign by the American Petroleum Institute, which has recruited and funded a few scientists who question the entire phenomenon. They, in turn, are given equal weight by the media, as though they were precisely as objective as the 2,500 scientists who work with the United Nations' Intergovernmental Panel on Climate Change.

Molly Ivins, *In Texas, of All Places, They're Cool on Global Warming*, Boston Globe, Aug. 14, 1998.

111. RON ARNOLD, ECOTERROR: THE VIOLENT AGENDA TO SAVE NATURE (1997),

112. UNABOMBER MANIFESTO, par. 96.

113. A.P., *"Secret Life" Book Tells of Kaczynski*," Boston Globe, Dec. 14, 1998 (citing CHRIS WAITS, UNABOMBER: THE SECRET LIFE OF THEODORE KACZYNSKI (forthcoming Jan. 1999)).

114. Telephone conversation between Michael Mello and Chris Waits, Dec. 18, 1998.

115. *Ibid.*

116. Stephen Oates, To Purge This Land With Blood, p. 411 n48 (1970).

117. Robert Black, *FIJA: Monkey-wrenching the Justice System?*, p. 66, UMKCL Rev. 11, 14-15 (1997)

118. Michael Higgins, *Crazy Talk*, ABAJ Dec. 1997, p. 34 (quoting Scott Sundby).

119. See Appendix A.

120. William Glaberson, *Brother and Victim Reflect on Unabom Case's Import*, NY Times, Jan. 24, 1998.

121. Finnegan, *supra*, p. 60.

122. William Glaberson, *Rethinking a Myth*, The New York Times, Jan. 18, 1998.

123. *Ibid.*

124. *Ibid.*

125. *Ibid.*

126. Finnegan, *supra*, p. 57.

127. *Ibid.*

128. *E.g.*, David Johnston and Janny Scott, *Brother Tells of a Painful Decision*, NY Times, May 26, 1996; Robert McFadden, *The Tortured Genius of Theodore Kaczynski*, NY Times, May 26, 1996.

129. Finnegan, *supra*, p. 36.

130. Evan Thomas and Peter Annin, *A Loner's Odyssey*, Newsweek, Aug. 3, 1998.

131. Bill Dedman, *Secret Service Challenges Assassin Stereotypes*, NY Times, Aug. 9, 1998.

132. *Ibid* (quoting Secret Service, *Preventing Assassinations*).

133. Letter from Lydia Eccles to Michael Mello, Sept. 15, 1998.

134. *Ibid.*

Chapter Two: The Unabomber Non-Trial: Kafka Comes to Town

1. Faretta v. California, 422 U.S. 806 (1975).

2. *See* David Johnston & Janny Scott, *The Tortured Genius of Theodore Kaczynski: From Child of Promise to Unabom Suspect*, NY Times, May 26, 1996.
    Even before the government captured Kaczynski and accused him of being the Unabomber, the mysterious bomber made the covers of Newsweek and The Nation. *See* Tom Morganthau, *Chasing the Unabomer*, Newsweek, July 10, 1995; Kirkpatrick Sale, *Is There a Method to the Madness?*, The Nation, September 25,

1995. Both cover stories include a police artist's sketch of the face of the Unabomber during his one and only known sighting by an eyewitness who gave his description to the police. The face on the covers of Newsweek and The Nation are strikingly dissimilar to the face of Theodore Kaczynski.

Once the government had decided that Kaczynski was their man, and once Kaczynski was arrested for the bombings, the media's attention to the case, "went O.J.", as one Vermont Law School student put it. Ted the accused Unabomber instantly entered the realm of cultural mythology, a uniquely American cultural mythology: the mad math-professor genius, the recluse waging war on technology and industrialization. The title of a front page article, *Special Report: Prisoner of Rage,* in *The New York Times* says it all. The story, written by Robert McFadden (and, according to *The New York Times* story, involving the "participation" of 23 reporters and 11 others) published on Sunday, May 26, 1996, began on page one and consumed three *entire* pages inside the newspaper. And then there was the Cain and Abel dimension of the case. *see* Richard Lacayo, *A Tale of Two Brothers: No One Expected the Unabomber Saga to Encompass a Parable as Old and as Poignant as Cain and Abel,* Time Magazine, April 22, 1996, p. 44. "At least he did not go to law school." *cf.* MICHAEL MELLO, DEAD WRONG (Wisconsin 1997) (observing the media's preoccupation with the fact that suspected serial killer "Ted" Bundy had attended law school). Of course, such public fixation is not new. From Leopold and Loeb in the 1920s, through Theodore Bundy in the 1970s and 1980s, to Theodore Kaczynski today, the American media culture has had a special fascination for "geniuses" who become murderers. On Leopold and Loeb, *see* IRVING STONE, CLARENCE DARROW FOR THE DEFENSE (1941). On Bundy, *see* MICHAEL MELLO, DEAD WRONG.

3. *See* Michael Mello, Draft Initial Brief of Paul Hill, *Hill v. State* (Fla. Sup. Ct. 1995) (unfiled) (copy on file with author).

4. Michael Higgins, *Crazy Talk,* ABAJ Dec. 1997, p. 34.

5. Jan. 26, 1998 statement of Theodore Kaczynski.

6. *Ibid.*

7. Jan. 26, 1998 statement of Theodore Kaczynski.

8. Finnegan, *supra.*

9. Kaczynski's January 26, 1998 statement does not address his suicide attempt.

10. Jan. 26, 1998 Statement of Theodore Kaczynski.

11. *Ibid.*

12. *See generally* Finnegan, Describing the "profound conflict" that "had been growing between Kaczynski and his various lawyers virtually since his arrest," Finnegan appreciated, as virtually no other commentators on the case have, that "Kaczynski's quietly fierce performance raised fundamental questions about a defendant's right to participate in his own defense, the role of psychiatry in the courts, and the pathologizing of radical dissent in both the courts and the press." *Ibid,* p. 54.

Finnegan interviewed one key defense psychiatrist, and she made clear that the central facts in Kaczynski's diagnosis were his antitechnology politics and the crimes themselves. (Finnegan, *supra*, pp. 54-55.) Second, Finnegan was able to paint a portrait of the hostility Kaczynski's public defenders felt (and apparently still feel) towards J. Tony Serra, the movement lawyer willing to run Kaczynski's defense the way Kaczynski wanted; he also described the ideological defense Serra would have put on: "As Serra envisioned such a defense . . . Kaczynski would explain himself to the jury using the [Unabomber] manifesto. Eminent political scientists would be called to interpret the essay, paragraph by paragraph." (Finnegan, *supra*, p. 56. *Ibid*, pp. 55-57.) Third, Finnegan was able to describe how Kaczynski's public defenders kept him in the dark about their intentions to stake his life on a mental defect defense (*Ibid*, p. 56.) Fourth, Finnegan nailed down the marginality of the actual evidence that Kaczynski suffered (or suffers) from a bona fide mental illness that controlled his actions – unless antitechnology politics constitutes a "mental illness." (*Ibid*, pp. 60-62.) Finnegan wrote about how Kaczynski's own political ideology gave psychiatrists (and psychiatry itself) short shrift, (*Ibid*, pp. 54-55.) and described the pressures that caused Kaczynski to plead guilty, capturing the relentlessness of Kaczynski's public defenders to stake his life on a mental illness defense. (*Ibid, accord*) Michael Higgins, *A Difficult Client: Unabomber Lawyer Outlines a Strategy He Never Used*, A.B.A.J. March 1998, p. 18. He then writes of speculation that Kaczynski will attempt to "withdraw his guilty plea, arguing that it was coerced," although such efforts are characterized as "desperate." (*Ibid*, p. 63.) In addition to the Finnegan article, an excellent treatment of the chronology of events in Kaczynski's non-trial may be found in the 1998 epilogue to Robert Graysmith's book, UNABOMBER: A DESIRE TO KILL.

13. Forensic evaluation of Theodore Kaczynski by Dr. Sally Johnson, January 16, 1998, p. 31.

14. Letter from J. Tony Serra to Theodore Kaczynski, April 8, 1996.

15. Letter from J. Tony Serra to Theodore Kaczynski, Quin Denvir and Judy Clarke, Dec. 15, 1997.

16. *E.g.*, Cynthia Hubert, *Unabom Trial By Spring?*, Sacramento Bee, July 19, 1996 (characterizing Judy Clarke as a "passionate opponent of capital punishment"); *accord* Marianne Lavalle, *Defending the Unabomber*, U.S. News and World Report, Nov. 17, 1997. *See also* Order, *United States v. Kaczynski*, No. CR-S-96-259 GEB, 1997 WL 405815 (E.D. Cal. Doc. July 18, 1996).

17. *Dusky v. United States*, 362 U.S. 402, 402 (1960); *see also* 18 U.S.C. ß 4247(c)(1998).

18. David Jackson, *Man Behind the Mask*, Time, Nov. 17, 1997.

19. Forensic evaluation of Theodore Kaczynski by Dr. Sally Johnson, M.D., Jan. 16, 1998, p. 21.

20. Richard Lacayo, *A Tale of Two Brothers*, Time, April 22, 1996.

21. *Ibid*.

22. Robert McFadden, *The Tortured Genius of Theodore Kaczynski*, NY Times, May 26,

1996; David Johnson and Janny Scott, *Brother Tells of Painful Decision*, NY Times, May 26, 1996.

23. Carey Goldberg, *Diaries Disclosed in Unabom Hearing*, NY Times, Sept. 21, 1996.

24. Forensic evaluation of Theodore Kaczynski by Dr. Sally Johnson, M.D., Jan. 16, 1998, p. 21.

25. *Ibid.*

26. *Ibid.*

27. *Ibid.*

28. Orange County Register [Cal.], Sept. 21, 1996, 1996 WL 7049525 (no additional publication information available).

29. Finnegan, *supra.*

30. Tamala Edwards, *Crazy Is As Crazy Does*, Time, Feb. 2, 1998.

31. *E.g.,* Cynthia Hubert, *Unabom Trial by Spring?*, Sacramento Bee, July 19, 1996.

32. Forensic Evaluation of Theodore Kaczynski by Dr. Sally Johnson, M.D., Jan. 16, 1998, p. 22.

33. *Ibid.* Declaration of Karen Froming, Ph.D., *supra.*

34. *Ibid.*

35. Finnegan, *supra.*

36. Government's Motion for More Specific Notice under Fed. R. Crim. P. 12.2 (b) and for a Mental Examination, *United States v. Kaczynski*, No. CR-S-96-259GEB, 1997 WL 450386 (E.D. Cal. Doc. Filed July 30, 1997) (quoting Defendant's Notice and Federal Rule of Criminal Procedure 12.2(b)).

37. *Ibid,* (quoting Defendant's Notice).

38. *Ibid.*

39. *Ibid,* p. n.1.

40. *Ibid.*

41. Declarations of David Foster, M.D., *supra.*

42. Declaration of Xavier Amador, Ph.D., *supra.*

43. Finnegan, *supra.*

44. Bill Gannon, *Unabom Trial Might See Claim of Insanity*, Star-Ledger [Newark, NJ], Sept. 18, 1997.

45. *Ibid.*

46. *Ibid.*

47. *Ibid.*

48. *Ibid.*

49. *Ibid.*

50. Order, *United States v. Kaczynski*, No. CR-S-96-259 GEB, 1997 WL 609991 (E.D. Cal. Sept. 19, 1997); Notice of Appeal, *United States v. Kaczynski*, CR-S-96-259GEB, 1997 WL 610011 (E.D. Cal. Doc. Filed September 29, 1997).

51. Government's Opposition to Defendant's Motion for Reconsideration of Order Requiring More Specific Notice Under Rule 12.2(b), *United States v. Kaczynski*, CR-S-96-259GEB, 1997 WL 609996 (E.D. Cal. Doc. Filed October 3, 1997).

52. *Ibid.*

53. AP, *Two Faces of Kaczynski Confront Jurors: Unabom Suspect is Painted As Cold Killer and Mentally Ill*, Boston Globe, Nov. 30, 1997.

54. Supplement to Government's Motion to Compel Compliance with Court Order to Submit to Mental Examination, *United States v. Kaczynski*, CR-S-96-259GEB, 1997 WL 609999 (E.D. Cal. Doc. Filed October 3, 1997).

55. *Ibid.*

56. *Ibid.*

57. Cynthia Hubert, *Kaczynski Mentally Ill, Lawyers Tell Prosecution*, Sacramento Bee, Oct. 15, 1997.

58. *Ibid.*

59. John Howard, *Defense To Have Mental Health Experts Examine Kaczynski*, Associated Press, Oct. 21, 1997, 1997 WL 4889005.

60. *Ibid.*

61. Cynthia Hubert, *Court Filing Says Defense Wants to Bring Cabin to Sacramento*, Sacramento Bee, Oct. 24, 1997.

62. Government's Reply Brief in Support of its Motion to Compel Compliance with Court Order to Submit to Mental Examination, *United States v. Kaczynski*, CR-S-96-259GEB, 1997 WL 644036 (E.D. Cal. Doc. Filed October 14, 1997).

63. *Ibid.*

64. *E.g.*, Waiver of Defendant's Presence, *United States v. Kaczynski*, No. CR-S-96-259 GEB, 1997 WL 644026 (E.D. Cal. Doc. Oct. 17, 1997); Pre-Trial Transcript, Motion for Protective Order; Hearing on Scope of Mental Examination, *United States v. Kaczynski*, CR-S-96-259GEB, 1997 WL 656336 (E.D. Cal. Trans. Filed October 17, 1997) (Judy Clarke, counsel for defendant, noting: "Mr. Kaczynski's appearance has been waived".)

65. Order, *United States v. Kaczynski*, No. CR-S-96-259 GEB, 1997 WL 668395 (E.D. Cal. Doc. Oct. 22, 1997).

66. Government's Motion to Preclude Defendant from Relying on Expert Mental

Health Testimony at the Guilt Phase and to Require the Defendant to Undergo a Mental Examination Before Sentencing, *United States v. Kaczynski,* CR-S-96-259 GEB, 1997 WL 716539 (E.D. Cal. Doc. Filed November 5, 1997).

67. *Ibid.*

68. *Ibid.*

69. *Ibid.*

70. Stone, *supra,* p. 110-11 (quoting the *Richmond Enquirer,* Tues. Oct. 25, 1859).

71. Knight-Ridder Service, *Two Views of Kaczynski Emerge As Trial Looms,* Boston Globe, Nov. 9, 1997. In fact, as discussed above, the battle over Kaczynski's mental status had been going on since the summer. *e.g.,* 1997 WL 450386 (E.D. Cal. Doc. July 30, 1997); 1997 WL 556187 (E.D. Cal. Trans. Sept. 2, 1997; 1997 WL 606753 9E.D. Cal. Trans. Oct. 1, 1997); 1997 WL 606753 (E.D. Cal. Trans. Oct. 1, 1997); 1997 WL 509999 (E.D. Cal. Doc. Oct. 3, 1997); 1997 WL 644036 (E.D. Cal. Doc. Oct. 14, 1997); 1997 WL 656336 (E.D. Cal. Trans. Oct. 17, 1997); 1997 WL 716539 (E.D. Cal. Doc. Nov. 5, 1997); 1997 WL 810297 (E.D. Cal. Trans. Nov. 21, 1997).

72. AP, *Mental Illness Led to Attacks, Kaczynski's Brother Says,* San Diego Union and Tribune, Nov. 9, 1998.

73. *Ibid.*

74. Sandy Banisky, *Kaczynski Lawyers Try Risky Strategy,* Baltimore Sun, Nov. 9, 1997.

75. *Ibid.*

76. Cynthia Hubert, *Unabomber Case May Not Get to Trial,* Sacramento Bee, Nov. 9, 1997.

77   David Jackson, *Man Behind the Mask,* Time, Nov. 17, 1997, p. 52.

78. Patricia King and Daniel Klaidman, *A Hermit Goes Into the Dock,* Newsweek, Nov. 10, 1997, p. 51.

79. Linda Deutch, AP, *Kaczynski's Sparse, Remote Cabin May Spare Him, His Lawyers Hope,* Houston Chronicle, Nov. 10, 1998.

80. *Ibid.*

81. Marianne Lavelle, *Defending the Unabomber,* U.S. News and World Report, Nov. 17, 1997.

82. *Ibid.*

83. *Ibid.*

84. *Ibid.*

85. Frances McMorris, *Alleged Unabomber's Attorneys Press for "Mental Defect" Defense,* Wall St. Journal, Nov. 12, 1998.

86. *Ibid.*

87. CBS Morning News (6:30 - 7:00 am), Nov. 13, 1997.

88. *Ibid.*

89. Linda Deutsch, AP, *Jury Selection Continues As Mental Defense Wrangle Intensifies*, Houston Chronicle, Nov. 19, 1997.

90. Bill Gannon, *Contrary Kaczynski Hampers Defense*, Newark Star Ledger, Nov. 30, 1997.

91. *Ibid.*

92. Finnegan, *supra.*

93. *Ibid.*

94. *Ibid.*

95. *Ibid.*

96. Government's Brief Addressing the Timeliness of the Defendant's Assertion of His Right to Represent Himself and Judicial Estoppel, *United States v. Kaczynski*, No. CR-S-96-0259 GEB (E.D. Calif. filed January 21, 1998). *Cf.* Waiver of Defendant's presence, *United States v. Kaczynski*, No. CR-S-96-259 GEB, 1997 WL 504426 (E.D. Cal. Doc. Oct. 17, 1997); Waiver of Defendant's Presence, *United States v. Kaczynski*, No. CR-S-96-259 GEB, 1997 WL 567039 (E.D. Cal. Doc. Sept. 12, 1998); Waiver of Defendant's Presence, *United States v. Kaczynski*, No. CR-S-96-259 GEB, 1997 WL 323421 (E.D. Cal. June 13, 1997); Waiver of Defendant's Presence, *United States v. Kaczynski*, No. CR-S-96-259 GEB, 1997 WL 741242 (E.D. Cal. Doc. Nov. 25, 1997).

97. Government Status Report of Discussions Concerning Examination, Testing and Sanctions, *United States v. Kaczynski*, CR-S-96-259GEB, 1997 WL 787140 (E.D. Cal. Doc. Filed December 19, 1997).

98. *Ibid.*

99. The 12.2(b) defense is a type of mental defect defense.

100. Letter From Theodore Kaczynski to Judge Garland E. Burrell, Dec. 1, 1997.

101. Kaczynski's letters reached the judge on December 18, 1998.

102. *E.g.*, Finnegan, *supra.*

103. Finnegan, *supra.*

104. Finnegan, *supra*, p. 63. Finnegan, *supra*, p.404-407 (describing the sojourn of Kaczynski's cabin from Montana to California)

105. Finnegan, *supra*, p.404-407 (describing the sojourn of Kaczynski's cabin from Montana to California).

106. Linda Deutch, AP, *Kaczynski Cabin Arrives, Trailed by Media Caravan*, Rutland Herald [VT], Dec. 6, 1997.

107. *Ibid.*

108. *Ibid.*

109. *Ibid.*

110. Christine Craft, *Kaczynski Wants to Speak,* Sacramento News & Review, Dec. 24, 1997.

111. William Booth, The Washington Post, *The Unabomber Defense,* reprinted in Valley News [Vt.], Nov. 27, 1997.

112. William Glaberson, *Unabom Trial Yields Hint of a Big Rift,* NY Times, Dec. 20, 1997.

113. *Ibid.* According to a prosecution brief filed on December 29, 1997, "on December 18, 19 and 22, the Court held in camera hearings from which the government was excluded. Those proceedings, according to the Court, 'address[ed] Kaczynski's concerns with appointed counsel's representation.'" 1997 WL 797444 (W.D. Cal. Doc. Dec. 31, 1997).

114. Letter from J. Tony Serra to Theodore Kaczynski, Quin Denvir and Judy Clarke, Dec. 16, 1997.

115. Letter from Theodore Kaczynski to Judge Burrell, Dec. 17, 1997.

116. Reporter's Draft, Proceedings, Dec. 18, 1997.

117. *Ibid.*

118. *Ibid.*

119. *Ibid.*

120. Letter from Quin Denvir and Judy Clarke to Judge Garland E. Burrell, Jr., U.S. District Court, *United States v. Kaczynski,* CR-S-96-259GEB/GGH, 1997 WL 880692 (E.D. Cal. Doc. Filed December 19, 1997).

121. *Ibid.*

122. *Ibid.*

123. *Ibid.* "The Ninth Circuit has specifically held that the decision whether to present a diminished capacity defense, over the wishes over the defendant, is a strategic decision for counsel." *Ibid,* (citing Fritchie v. McCarthy, 664 F.2d 208, 214-15 (9th Cir. 1981) defense counsel did not render ineffective assistance of counsel by making "tactical choice" to forego a diminished capacity defense, despite the defendant's desire to have the defense presented at trial).

124. Government's Brief Addressing the Court's *In-camera, Ex Parte* Contacts with the Defendant, *United States v. Kaczynski,* CR-S-96-259GEB, 1997 WL 797444 (E.D. Cal. Doc. Filed December 29, 1997).

125. Reporter's Draft, Proceedings, Dec. 19, 1997.

126. *Ibid.*

127. Reporters Draft, *United States v. Kaczynski,* No. 96-S-2596EB (E.D. Cal. Dec. 22, 1997).

128. *Ibid.*

129. William Glaberson, *Lawyers Drop Mental Defense for Kaczynski,* NY Times, Dec. 30, 1997; *see also* Linda Deutsch, AP, *Mental State is Withdrawn As Defense,* Boston Globe, Dec. 30, 1997.

130. Lynda Gorov, *Kaczynski's Stand on His Mental State Frustrates Defense*, Boston Globe, Jan. 2, 1998.

131. Reporter's Daily Transcript (redacted), *United States v. Kaczynski*, No. CR-S-259 GEB (E.D. Cal. Dec. 24, 1997), *Sacramento Bee* web page, Sacbee home/http://www.unabombertrial.com/transcripts/122497cham.html.

132. Reporter's Draft, United States v. Kaczynski, No. CR-S-96-259 5EB (E.D. Cal. Cal. Dec. 22, 1997.

133. Reporter's Draft, *United States v. Kaczynski*, No. 96-S-259 GEB (E.D. Cal. Dec. 22, 1997), pp. 45-46.

134. Reporter's Draft, *United States v. Kaczynski*, No. 96-S-259 GEB (E. D. Cal. Dec. 22, 1995).

135. *Ibid.*

136. Reporter's Transcript, Telephonic Conference, *United States v. Kaczynski*, No. CR-S-96-259 GEB (Jan. 13, 1998), *Sacramento Bee* web page, http://www.unabombertrial.com/transcripts/122497 cham.html.

137. Richard Bonnie, *The Competence of Criminal Defendants*, 47 U. Miami L. Rev. 539, 579 (1993).

138. *Ibid*, p. 578.

139. William Glaberson, *Disrupting the Unabomber Trial, But To What End?*, NY Times Jan. 11, 1998.

140. Government's Brief Addressing the Timeliness of the Defendant's Assertion of His Right to Represent Himself and Judicial Estoppel, *United States v. Kaczynski*, No. CR-S-96-0259 GEB, 1998 extra LEXIS 7 (E.D. Calif. filed January 21, 1998).

141. Order, *United States v. Kaczynski*, No. CR-S-96-259 GEB, 1997 WL 797431 (E.D. Cal. Dec. 23, 1997).

142. *Ibid.*

143. Withdrawal of F.R. Cr. P. 12.2(b) Notice, *United States v. Kaczynski*, No. CR-S-96-259 GEB, 1997 WL 797435 (E.D. Cal. Doc. Dec. 29, 1997); Government's Motion in Limine to Preclude Defendant from Introducing Non-Expert Testimony to Show That the Defendant has a Mental Defect, *United States v. Kaczynski*, CR-S-96-259GEB, 1998 WL 15077 (E.D. Cal. Doc. Filed January 2, 1998); *see also*, William Glaberson, *Lawyers Drop Mental Defense For Kaczynski*, NY Times, Dec. 30, 1997.

144. William Glaberson, NY Times, *Unabom Defendant Offered to Plead Guilty to Spare Life*, Rutland Herald [VT], Dec. 29, 1997.

145. *Ibid.*

146. William Glaberson, *Unabom Suspect's Brother Troubled by Rejection of Plea*, NY Times, Jan. 4, 1998.

147. Pre-Trial Transcript Proceedings, *United States v. Kaczynski*, CR-S-96-259GEB, 1997 WL 811836 (E.D. Cal. Trans. December 21, 1997).

148. Pre-Trial Transcript, Dec. 21, 1997, *supra.*

149. *Ibid.*

150. *Ibid.*

151. William Glaberson, *Unabom Defense Planning Illness Strategy in 2nd stage: Formal Notice of "Mental Defect" Argument, NY Times,* Jan. 3, 1998.

152. Jan. 26, 1998 Statement of Theodore Kaczynski.

153. William Booth, The Washington Post, *Kaczynski Outburst Halts Murder Trial,* Valley News [VT], Jan. 6, 1998.

154. *Ibid.*

155. Order, *United States v. Kaczynski,* No. CR-S-96-259 GEB, 1998 WL 15049 (E.D. Cal. Doc. Jan. 9, 1998).

156. Lynda Gorov, *Kaczynski Statement Halts Unabom Trial,* Boston Globe, Jan. 6, 1998.

157. Government's Second Brief Addressing the Court's *In-camera, Ex Parte* Contacts with the Defendant, *United States v. Kaczynski,* CR-S-96-259GEB, 1998 WL 15097 (E.D. Cal. Doc. Filed January 7, 1998). Official Trial Transcript Proceedings, *United States v. Kaczynski,* CR-S-96-259GEB, 1998 WL 1930 (E.D. Cal. Trans. Filed January 5, 1998, at 8:02 am).

158. *Ibid.*

159. Glaberson, *Unabom Trial Halted.* During this in-camera meeting, Kaczynski said he wanted to communicate with Attorney J. Tony Serra. 1998 WL 10758 (E.D. Cal. Trans. Jan 5, 1998). It was also agreed that Kaczynski would meet with Attorney Kevin Clymo.

160. Pre-Trial Transcript Proceedings, *United States v. Kaczynski,* CR-S-96-259GEB, 1998 WL 10758 (E.D. Cal. Trans. Jan. 5, 1998).

161. Finnegan, *supra,* p. 55.

162. Finnegan, *supra,* p. 56.

163. *Ibid.*

164. William Booth, The Washington Post, *U.S. Judge Tells Kaczynski He Cannot Fire His Lawyers,* Valley News [VT], Jan. 8, 1998.

165. *Ibid.*

166. Pre-Trial Transcript, Jan. 5, 1998, *supra.*

167. *Ibid.*

168. *Ibid.*

169. *Ibid.*

170. *Ibid.*

171. *Ibid.*

172. *Ibid.*

173. *Ibid.*

174. *Ibid.*

175. *Ibid.*

176. *Ibid.*

177. *Ibid.*

178. *Ibid.*

179. *Ibid.*

180. *Ibid.*

181. Government's Motion in Limine to Preclude Defendant from Introducing Non-Expert Testimony to Show that the Defendant Has a Mental Defect, *United States v. Kaczynski*, No. CR-S-96-259 GEB, 1998 WL 15007 (E.D. Cal. Doc. filed January 2, 1998).

182. Order, *United States v. Kaczynski*, No. CR-S-96-259 GEB, 1998 WL 15120 (E.D. Cal. Doc. January 5, 1998).

183. Albert Camus, The Myth of Sisyphus and Other Essays (Random House 1955).

184. Pre-Trial Transcript, Discussion Motions and Change of Plea, *United States v. Kaczynski*, No. CR-S-96-259 GEB, 1998 WL 22017 (E.D. Cal. Trans. Jan. 27, 1998).

185. *Ibid.*

186. William Booth, The Washington Post, *U.S. Judge Tells Kaczynski He Cannot Fire His Lawyers*, Valley News [VT], Jan. 8, 1998.

187. Reporter's Daily Transcript, *United States v. Kaczynski*, No. CR-S-96-259 GEB (E.D. Cal. Jan. 7, 1998), *Sacramento Bee* web page, http://www.unabombertrial.com/transcripts/010798kz.html; Pre-Trial Transcript Proceedings, *United States v. Kaczynski*, No. CR-S-96-259 GEB, 1998 WL 10757 (E.D. Cal. Trans. Jan. 7, 1998 1:30 p.m.); Pre-Trial Transcript Proceedings, *United States v. Kaczynski*, No. CR-S-96-259 GEB, 1998 WL 3338 (E.D. Cal. Trans. Jan. 7, 1998 4:00 p.m.).

188. *Ibid.*

189. *Ibid*, Letter from J. Tony Serra, *United States v. Kaczynski*, No. CR-S-96-259 GEB, 1998 WL 1504 (E.D. Cal. Doc. Jan. 7, 1998). The judge later wrote:

> The Court assumes that what is referenced by "a considerable time to prepare" reflects Serra's assessment of becoming familiar with the case and integrating the case into his busy trial calendar. The Court's prior experience with Serra strongly indicates that a lengthy continuance could be required just to allow Serra to coordinate his obligations to his many clients. In one recent case that was scheduled to commence on October 22, 1996, the trial had to be continued until January 22, 1997, because Serra was representing another client who was in trial.

Subsequently, because of yet another trial conflict, that trial had to be further continued until February 11, 1997. While Serra's willingness to represent Kaczynski on a *pro bono* basis is highly commendable, since the jury has already been selected in this case, the delay likely to be engendered by his representation is not tolerable.

Order, *United States v. Kaczynski*, No. CR-S-96-259 GEB, 1998 WL 15049 (E.D. Cal. Doc. Jan. 9, 1998).

190. William Booth, *U.S. Judge Tells Kaczynski He Cannot Fire His Lawyers*, Washington Post, Jan. 8, 1998.

191. Transcript of Open-Court Proceedings, Jan. 7, 1998, *supra*.

192. *Ibid.*

193. *Ibid.*

194. Booth, *Judge Tells Kaczynski, supra*.

195. Pre-Trial Transcript, Jan. 5, 1998, *supra*.

196. Government's Brief Addressing the Timeliness of Defendant's Assertion of His Right to Represent Himself, *United States v. Kaczynski*, No. CR-S-96-0259 GEB, 1998 extra LEXIS 7 (E.D. Cal. filed Jan. 21, 1998) (citing Dean v. Superintendent, 93 F.3d 58, 61 (2nd Cir. 1996) (decision to forego insanity defense rests with client); *Foster v. Strickland,* 707 F.2d 1339, 1343-44 (11th Cir. 1983) (attorney has ethical obligation to comply with client's wishes not to pursue insanity defense); *Jeffries v. Blodgett,* 5 F.3d 1180, 1197 [9th Cir. 1993] (counsel not ineffective because he followed client's instructions at penalty phase of a capital trial not to use mitigating evidence).

194. Government's Brief Addressing the Timeliness of the Defendant's Assertion of His Right to Represent Himself and Judicial Estoppel, *United States v. Kaczynski*, No. CR-S-96-0259 GEB, 1998 extra LEXIS 7 (E.D. Calif. filed January 21, 1998).

198. Jan. 26, 1998 Statement by Theodore Kaczynski.

199. *E.g.,* Lynda Gorov, *Kaczynski As Counsel,* Boston Globe, Jan. 12, 1998.

200. Jan. 26, 1998 Statement of Theodore Kaczynski; *see also* Finnegan, *supra*.

201. Conversation Between Lydia Eccles and Michael Mello, Aug. 1998, Wilder, Vermont.

202. Michael Mello, *Kaczynski Has Right to His Defense,* Rutland Herald [VT], Jan. 15, 1998, Michael Mello, *Defense Should Assist, Not Resist,* Nat'l L. J. Jan. 26, 1998.

203. Faretta v. California, 422 U.S. 806 (1975).

204. Reporter's Daily Transcript, *United States v. Kaczynski*, No. CR-S-96-0259 GEB (E.D. Cal. Jan. 8, 1998), *Sacramento Bee* web page, Official Trial Transcript Proceedings, United States v. Kaczynski, No. CR-S-96-259 GEB, 1998 WL 4657 (E.D. Cal. Trans. Jan. 8, 1998).

205. *Ibid.*

206. Lynda Gorov, *Kaczynski Apparently Tried Suicide*, Boston Globe, Jan. 9, 1998.

207. *Ibid.*

208. Reporter's Daily Transcript, Jan. 8, 1998, *supra. See also* Order, *United States v. Kaczynski*, No. CR-S-96-259 GEB, 1998 WL 15068 (E.D. Cal. Doc. Jan. 9, 1998).

209. *Ibid.*

210. *Ibid.*

211. *Ibid.*

212. Lynda Gorov, *Kaczynski Apparently Tried Suicide*, Boston Globe, Jan. 9, 1998.

213. *Ibid.*

214. *Ibid.*

215. Finnegan, *supra.*

216. Order, *United States v. Kaczynski*, No. CR-S-96-259 GEB, 1998 WL 64767 (E.D. Cal. Doc. Jan. 9, 1998).

217. *Ibid.*

218. *Ibid.*

219. *Ibid.*

220. *Ibid.*

221. *Ibid.*

222. Letter from Lydia Eccles to Michael Mello, Sept. 15, 1998.

223. Official Trial Transcript Proceedings, *United States v. Kaczynski*, No. CR-S-96-259 GEB, 1998 WL 4767 (E.D. Cal. Jan. 9, 1998).

224. *Ibid.*

225. Order, *United States v. Kaczynski*, No. CR-S-96-259 GEB, 1998 WL 15056 (E.D. Cal. Doc. Jan. 12, 1998).

226. Official Trial Transcript Proceedings, *United States v. Kaczynski*, No. CR-S-96-259 GEB, 1998 WL 4767 (E.D. Cal. Trans. Jan. 9, 1998).

227. *Ibid.*

228. Government's Motion for a Hearing on Issues Concerning the Defendant's Representation If He Is Found Competent, *United States v. Kaczynski*, CR-S-96-259 GEB, 1998 WL 15074 (ED. Cal. Doc. filed January 15, 1998).

229. *Ibid.*

230. *Ibid.*

231. *Ibid.*

232. Glaberson, *Tortured Efforts, supra; accord* William Glaberson, *Unabom Trial: Suspect is Said to Try Suicide,* Jan. 9, 1998; William Glaberson, *Disrupting the Unabomber Trial, But to What End?,* NY Times, Jan. 11, 1998; William Glaberson, *Unabom Team Straddles a Bluff and a Hard Place,* NY Times, Jan. 20, 1998. *See also* Finnegan, *supra.*

233. William Glaberson, *Unabom Team Straddles A Bluff and a Hard Place,* NY Times, Jan. 20, 1998.

234. Unabomber Manifesto, par. 155.

235. Forensic Evaluation of Theodore Kaczynski, by Dr. Sally Johnson, M.D., Jan. 16, 1998, p. 3.

236. Reuters, *Psychiatrist Completes Evaluation of Kaczynski,* Boston Globe, Jan. 19, 1998.

237. Reuters, *Unabom Suspect Said to Cooperate,* Boston Globe, Jan. 14, 1998; Order, *United States v. Kaczynski,* No. CR-S-96-259 GEB, 1998 WL 27839 (E.D. Cal. Doc. Jan. 20, 1998).

238. *Ibid.*

239. AP, *Doctor Finishes Kaczynski Tests,* Providence Journal-Bulletin [RI], Jan. 17, 1998.

240. *Ibid.*

241. William Glaberson, *Tortured Efforts to End Spectacle of Unabom Trial,* NY Times, Jan. 12, 1998.

242. Government's Motion for a Hearing on Issues Concerning the Defendant's Representation If He Is Found Competent, *United States v. Kaczynski,* CR-S-96-259 GEB, 1998 WL 15074 (ED. Cal. Doc. filed January 15, 1998).

243. *Ibid.*

244. *Ibid.*

245. *Ibid.*

246. *Ibid.*

247. Finnegan, *supra,* p. 62.

248. Letter from Dr. Sally Johnson, *United States v. Kaczynski,* CR-S-96-259 GEB, 1998 WL 27832 (E.D. Cal. Doc. Jan. 20, 1998).

249. William Glaberson, *Lawyers For Kaczynski Agree He Is Competent To Stand Trial,* NY Times, Jan. 21, 1998.

250. William Booth, The Washington Post; *Kaczynski Pleads in Bombings,* Valley News [VT], Jan. 23, 1998.

251. Cynthia Hubert and Denny Walsh, *Kaczynski Competent, Doctor Says,* Sacramento Bee, Jan. 21, 1998.

252. AP, *Kaczynski Diagnosed Fit For Trial,* Jan. 21, 1998.

253. Forensic Evaluation of Dr. Sally Johnson, M.D., Jan. 16, 1998.

254. Forensic Evaluation of Theodore Kaczynski by Dr. Sally Johnson, M.D., Jan. 16, 1998, pp. 44-47.

255. *Ibid.*

256. William Booth, The Washington Post, *Chaotic Unabom Trial Halted*, Valley News [VT], Jan. 9, 1998. *See also* Reporter's Daily Transcript, *United States v. Kaczynski*, No. CR-S-96-0259 GEB (E.D. Cal. Jan. 20, 1998), *Sacramento Bee* web page, Pre-Trial Transcript Hearing, Re: Competency Report, *United States v. Kaczynski*, No. CR-S-96-259 GEB, 1998 WL 12393 (E.D. Cal. Trans. Jan. 20, 1998).

257. *Ibid.*

258. Barbara Novovitch, Reuters, *Kaczynski Found Fit For Unabom Trial*, Boston Globe, Jan. 21, 1998.

259. *Ibid.*

260. Finnegan, *supra*, p. 55.

261. William Glaberson, *Lawyers Say Kaczynski Can Represent Himself*, NY Times, Jan. 22, 1998.

262. Government's Brief Addressing the Timeliness of the Defendant's Assertion of His Right to Represent Himself and Judicial Estoppel, *United States v. Kaczynski*, No. CR-S-96-0259 GEB, 1998 extra LEXIS 7 (E.D. Calif. filed January 21, 1998).

263. *Ibid; see also* Government's Brief Addressing Timeliness of Defendant's Assertion of His Right to Represent Himself, *United States v. Kaczynski*, No. CR No. S-96-0259 GEB (filed Jan. 21, 1998); Defendant Kaczynski's Response, *ibid;* (filed Jan. 22, 1998).

264. Defendant Kaczynski's Response to Government's Motion for a Hearing on Issues Concerning the Defendant's Representation, *United States v. Kaczynski*, No. CR-S-96-259 GEB, 1998 extra LEXIS No. 8 (E.D. Cal. filed January 21, 1998).

265. *Ibid*, p. n. 5.

266. *Ibid.*

267. Defendant Kaczynski's Response to Government's Motion for a Hearing on Issues Concerning the Defendant's Representation, *United States v. Kaczynski*, CR-S-96-259 GEB, 1998 extra LEXIS No. 8 (E.D. Cal. filed January 21, 1998).

268. *Ibid.*

269. *Ibid.*

270. William Glaberson, *Unabom Team Straddles A Bluff and a Hard Place*, NY Times, Jan. 20, 1998.

271. Letter from Theodore Kaczynski to Judge Burrell, Jan. 21, 1998.

272. Jan. 26, 1998 Statement of Theodore Kaczynski.

273. Pre-Trial Transcript, Discussions on Motions and Change of Plea, *United States v. Kaczynski*, No. CR-S-96-259 GEB 1998 WL 22017 (E.D. Cal. Trans. Jan. 22, 1998).

274. William Booth, The Washington Post, *Kaczynski Pleads in Bombings*, Valley News [VT], Jan. 23, 1998.

275. Pre-Trial Transcript, *United States v. Kaczynski*, No. CR-S-96-259 GEB, 1998 WL 10758 (E.D. Cal. Trans. Jan. 8, 1998).

276. Pre-Trial Transcript, Discussion on Motions and Change of Plea, *supra.*

277. *Ibid.*

278. *Ibid.*

279. *Ibid.* The court's ruling that Kaczynski's request was untimely and was made for the purpose of delay was clearly erroneous. The Ninth Circuit has consistently equated the issue of timeliness with the initiation of trial proceedings. A demand for self-representation is timely "if made before meaningful trial proceedings have begun." *Schaff*, 948 F.2d at 503. Trial proceedings begin once the jury is empaneled and begins to listen to the evidence in the case. *See Fritz v. Spalding*, 682 F.2d 782, 784 (9th Cir. 1982); *see also Crawford v. Ratelle*, 5 F.3d 535 (9th Cir. 1993).

In *Fritz*, the defendant was accused of armed robbery. Thirty days before trial, Fritz moved to represent himself, claiming he and his attorney could not agree on a defense strategy. Fritz withdrew his motion to proceed *pro se* following a meeting with his attorney. On the morning of the afternoon trial, however, Fritz once again moved the court to allow him to represent himself at trial, claiming he and his attorney had honest, fundamental differences. Fritz's motion was denied by the trial court, and he was subsequently convicted. On appeal, The Washington Court of Appeals held that Fritz's request was a tactic to secure delay. The State Supreme Court denied review. Fritz filed a writ of *habeas corpus* with a federal magistrate judge, who also held that Fritz's motion on the morning of trial was untimely because it would have resulted in delay. The United States Court of Appeals for the Ninth Circuit reversed the decision. The Court held that "Fritz asserted his Faretta right on the morning of an afternoon trial, before any trial proceedings had begun. It was therefore timely as a matter of law, unless it was made for the purpose of delay." *Fritz*, 682 F.2d at 784. In holding that Fritz did not intend to secure delay, the Court reasoned that "any motion to proceed *pro se* that is made on the morning of trial is likely to cause delay; a defendant may nonetheless have bona fide reasons for not asserting his right until that time, and he may not be deprived of that right absent an affirmative showing of purpose to secure delay." *Ibid.* The court further held that a showing that a continuance would be required can be evidence of a defendant's intent to secure delay.

Eleven years later, the Ninth Circuit again addressed the issue of timeliness and delay. In *Crawford*, the defendant requested self-representation following his counsel's unsuccessful argument on a pre-trial motion made on the morning his trial was to begin. The trial court denied the motion as untimely in light of it being made on the morning of trial. The California Appellate Court affirmed, and made no finding as to whether the motion was made to secure delay. The defendant filed a *habeas* petition with the federal district court. The district court held an evidentiary hearing on the issue of delay and found that the record contained no evidence of intentional delay. The district court granted the defendant's *habeas* petition and the state appealed. The United States Court of Appeals for the Ninth Circuit held that because the defendant made his request following his dissatisfaction with counsel's pretrial motions argued on the morning of trial, he could not have been expected to make the request at an earlier time. Furthermore, the court found significant that the defendant's *Faretta* motion did not seek an additional continuance. Finally, the court held that "the mere fact that the *Faretta* motion was made on the morning of trial does not require that it be denied as untimely." *Crawford*, 5 F.3d at 535.

Like *Fritz* and *Crawford*, Kaczynski made his request to proceed *pro se* on the morning his trial was to begin. The request was made prior to the jury hearing any evidence and before any meaningful trial proceedings had begun. See *Fritz*, 682 F.2d at 784 (quoting *United States v. Chapman*, 553 F.2d 886, 895 (5th Cir. 1977)) ("a defendant must have a last clear chance to assert his constitutional right before meaningful trial proceedings have commenced." The defendant asserted his *Faretta* right on the morning of his afternoon trial and before the commencement of any trial proceedings. It was therefore timely as a matter of law.); *contra Carroll v. Gomez*, 979 F.2d 854 (9th Cir. 1992) (defendant's request to proceed *pro se* following the *completion* of the prosecutions case, held as untimely).

Further, Kaczynski communicated to the court that he was ready to proceed immediately, without a continuance. As the Ninth Circuit noted in both *Fritz* and *Crawford*, the request for a continuance is significant in determining whether a *Faretta* motion is merely a tactic to secure delay. Kaczynski's statements to the court (through Ms. Clarke) clearly established that this was not his intention. Finally, Kaczyuski could not have reasonably been expected to make his request to proceed "*pro se*" at an earlier time. Prior to trial it was Kaczynski's understanding that he and his attorneys had reached an agreement not to set forth a "mental defense" during the guilt-innocence phase of his trial. In exchange, Kaczynski had agreed to the possibility of expert psychiatric testimony during the sentencing phase, if in fact he was convicted. When Kaczynski learned that his attorneys would indirectly set forth evidence during trial (absent expert testimony) indicating "mental incapacity," he made a request to the Court to proceed *pro se*. His request was made on the morning of trial because up until the days immediately proceeding the trial, he believed his attorneys would honor their agreement. The request was made in good faith and as a final effort to avoid being portrayed as a madman. It seems *Faretta* applies to this situation.

280.   Pre-Trial Transcript, Discussion on Motions and Change of Plea, *supra*.

281.   *Ibid.*

282.   *Ibid.*

283.   *Ibid.*

284.   *Ibid.*

285.   422 U.S. 806 (1975).

286. *Ibid.*

287. *Ibid.*

288. *Ibid.*

289. *Ibid.*

290. *Ibid.*

291. *Ibid.*

292. *Ibid.*

293. *Ibid.*

294. *Ibid.*

295. Pre-Trial Transcript Discussion on Motions and Change of Plea, *supra.*

296. *Ibid.*

297. *Ibid.*

298. Lynda Gorov, *Kaczynski, in Plea Deal, Concedes He's Unabomber*, Boston Globe, Jan. 22, 1998; William Glaberson, *Kaczynski Avoids A Death Sentence With Guilty Plea*, NY Times, Jan. 23, 1998; William Booth, The Washington Post, *Kaczynski Pleads in Bombings*, Valley News [VT], Jan. 23, 1998; Lynda Gorov, *Kaczynski, in Plea Deal, Concedes He's Unabomber*, Boston Globe, Jan. 23, 1998.

299. Memorandum of Plea Agreement, *United States v. Kaczynski*, No. CR-96-259-GEB, 1998 Lexis Extra 10 (January 22, 1998).

300. Pre-Trial Discussions on Motions and Change of Plea, *United States v. Kaczynski*, No. CR-S-96-259 GEB, 1998 WL 22017 (E.D. Cal. Trans. Jan. 22, 1998).

301. Pre-Trial Transcript, Discussion on Motions and Change of Plea, *supra.*

302. Finnegan, *supra*, p. 62; *see also ibid.*

303. Lynda Gorov, *Kaczynski, in Plea Deal, Concedes He's Unabomber*, Boston Globe, Jan. 23, 1998.

304. *See* CHRIS WAITS AND DAVE SHORS, UNABOMBER: THE SECRET LIFE OF TED KACZYNSKI, p. 219, 251-56 (1999). The alleged facts set out by Waits and Shors, if accurate, demonstrate a serious and intentional violation of the rules of pretrial discovery in criminal cases.

305. Jan. 26, 1998 Statement by Theodore Kaczynski.

306. William Booth, The Washington Post, *Kaczynski Pleads in Bombings*, Valley News [VT], Jan. 23, 1998.

307. Tamala Edwards, *Crazy Is As Crazy Does*, Time, Feb. 2, 1996, p. 66.

308. William Glaberson, *Kaczynski Avoids a Death Sentence With Guilty Plea*, NY Times, Jan. 23, 1998.

309. Editorial, *Justice in the Unabomber Case*, NY Times, Jan. 23, 1998.

310. Unabomber Manifesto, par. 168.

311. DAVID GELERNTER, DRAWING LIFE: SURVIVING THE UNABOMBER (1997).

312. Official Trial Transcript, Re: Sentencing, *United States v. Kaczynski*, No. CR-S-96-259 GEB, 1998 WL 215066 (E.D. Cal. Trans. May 4, 1998).

313. *Ibid.*

314. Official Trial Transcript, Re: Sentencing, *United States v. Kaczynski*, No. CR-S-96-259 GEB, 1998 WL 215066 (E.D. Cal. Trans. May 4, 1998).

315. *Ibid; see also* David Johnson, *Judge Sentences Confessed Bomber to Four Life Terms*, NY Times, May 5, 1998; Linda Deutsch, AP, *Kaczynski Gets Four Life Sentences*, Boston Globe, May 5, 1998.

316. Letter from Lydia Eccles to Michael Mello, Sept. 8, 1998.

317. Jan. 26, 1998 Statement of Theodore Kaczynski.

318. *Ibid.*

319. *See* Appendix

320. *E.g.*, DAVID GELERNTER, DRAWING LIFE: SURVIVING THE UNABOMBER; pp. 122-23 (1997).

321. Jeff Jacoby, *The Unjust Logic of Sparing Murderers*, Boston Globe, Aug. 10, 1998 (quoting David Gelernter).

322. *Ibid.*

323. James Brooke, *Unabomber's Kin Collect Reward of $1 Million For Turning Him In*, NY Times, Aug. 21, 1998. *See also* AP, *Unabom Prosecution Cost US $1.5 Million*, Boston Globe, Aug. 20, 1998.

324. AP, *Unabom Prosecution Cost US $1.5 Million*, Boston Globe, Aug. 20, 1998.

325. Graysmith, *supra*, p. 429.

326. Finnegan, *supra*, p. 57.

327. *See generally* Roger Parloff, *When Worlds Collide*, American Lawyer, June 1995.

328. *Ibid.*

329. ABA Standard 4-5.2 (3rd ed. 1993).

330. DEBORAH RHODE, LEGAL PROFESSION pp. 380-81 (1997).

331. Unabomber Manifesto, par. 26.

332. Jan. 26, 1998 Statement of Theodore Kaczynski.

333. JOHN NOONAN, JR., PERSONS AND MASKS OF LAW (1976). I have suggested elsewhere that some capital defense lawyers have come to wear the executioner's mask. *See also* MICHAEL MELLO, DEAD WRONG (1997).

334. *E.g., Wasserstrom, Lawyers As Professionals*, Human Rights vol. 5, p.1, (1975).

335. Michael Mello, Dead Wrong (1997).

CHAPTER THREE: CONSIDERATIONS

1. Statement by Theodore Kaczynski, published by *Live Wild or Die*, Berkeley, CA (statement dated Jan. 26, 1998).

2. *See also* the 1998 epilogue to ROBERT GRAYSMITH, UNABOMBER: A DESIRE TO KILL (1998 updated edition).

3. *E.g.*, Finnegan, *supra.*

4. UNABOMBER MANIFESTO, par. 131.

5. The classic case holding that guilty pleas must be voluntary is *Brady v. United States*, 397 U.S. 742 (1970). *E.g., Moore v. Jarvis*, 885 F.2d 1565, 1570 n.9 (11th Cir. 1989); *Oppel v. Meachum*, 851 F.2d 34, 38 (2nd Cir. 1988).

It is unclear whether Kaczynski could directly appeal his guilty plea to the federal court of appeals; since the factual bases of his challenges to the plea's legality are already contained within the existing trial record, direct appeal might be appropriate, assuming Kaczynski can overcome procedural bars. Or, Kaczynski could challenge his plea by bringing a proceeding pursuant to 28 U.S.C. sec. 2255.

"That a guilty plea is a grave and solemn act to be accepted only with care and discernment has long been recognized." *Brady v. United States*, 397 U.S. 742, 748 (1970). A guilty plea must be the voluntary expression *of the defendant's own choice. Iaea v. Sunn*, 800 F.2d 861, 866 (9th Cir. 1986) (citing *Brady*, 397 U.S. at 748). "The agents of the state may not produce a plea by actual or threatened physical harm or by *mental coercion overbearing the will of the defendant." Ibid*, p. 866 (quoting *Brady*, 397 U.S. at 750). Kaczynski's case is somewhat unique in that it was not an agent of the state (i.e. the prosecutors) who coerced Kaczynski into pleading guilty, it was his own lawyers (Clarke and Denvir) as well as the trial judge.

6. In *Crandall*, a capital defendant was assigned a California public defender. Based on "minimal" factual investigation of his client's case, the public defender "concluded that Crandall did not have a triable case. [The lawyer] decided to wait out his client and the prosecutor until they both realized that a plea bargain was the best course of action. [The lawyer] was willing to wait 'as long as it took' for both Crandall and the prosecutor to 'simmer down.'" Crandall did not "simmer down." He exercised his right to self-representation in his capital trial. He was found guilty and sentenced to death.

To be sure, *Crandall* is factually distinguishable from Kaczynski's case. Crandall's lawyer did virtually no investigation; Kaczynski's lawyers conducted a massive investigation. Crandall's lawyer made little effort to establish meaningful communication with his client; Kaczynski's lawyers stayed in close communication with Kaczynski, although they apparently kept him in the dark, for as long as possible, about their plans to raise a mental defect defense.

Analytically, however, *Crandall* is germane to Kaczynski's case. In both cases, capital defendants were forced into unconstitutional choices.

7. *Ibid*, pp. 866-867; *see United States v. Moore*, 599 F.2d 310 (9th Cir. 1979) (a guilty plea that is entered because defense counsel is unprepared for trial is involuntary); *see also Peete v. Rose*, 381 F. Supp. 1167 (W.D. Tenn. 1974) (defense counsel's statement that defendant could get a "Ku Klux jury" that might give him "the chair" rendered defendant's guilty plea involuntary). The voluntariness of Kaczynski's guilty plea can be determined only by considering the totality of the circumstances. *See Brady*, 397 U.S. p. 749.

8. *See Iaea*, 800 F.2d at 866 (citing *United States v. Martinez*, 486 F.2d 15, 21 (5th Cir. 1973)) (when examining the coerciveness of a guilty plea, the concern is not solely with the defendant's subjective state of mind, but with the constitutional acceptability inducing the guilty plea).

9. *Ibid*, p. 868.

10. Theodore Kaczynski's Jan. 26, 1998 statement.

11. *See also* Crandall v. Bunnell, No. 9656644 (9th Cir. May 19, 1998).

12. Richard Bonnie, *et al.*; *Decision-Making in Criminal Defense: An Empirical Study of Insanity Pleas and the Impact of Doubted Client Competence*, J. Crim. L. & Criminology, vol. 87, p. 48 (1996).

13. The Sixth Amendment right of a guilty plea defendant – as with a defendant who goes to trial – is to the *effective* assistance of counsel. *See Hill v. Lockhart*, 474 U.S. 52 (1985). However, in the context of Kaczynski's unique sort of ineffective assistance claim – it is not clear what constitutional mode of analysis a court ought to apply. The traditional analysis of *Strickland v. Washington* doesn't seem to fit Kaczynski's type of claim. More closely akin to the facts of Kaczynski's claim – in scope and persuasiveness of effect –would be the analysis for determining whether an attorney is laboring under an unlawful conflict of interest, *e.g.*, Cuyler v. Sullivan, 446 U.S. 335 (1980), or the effective denial of counsel altogether, *e.g.*, *United States v. Cronic*, 466 U.S. 468 (1984) (companion case to *Strickland v. Washington*); *Gideon v. Wainwright*, 372 U.S. 335 (1963).

14. But *cf. Bullington v. Missouri*, 451 U.S. 430 (1980) (capital sentences are subject to double jeopardy protections); *Caspari v. Bohlem*, 114 S.Ct. 948 (1994) (*Bullington* principles limited to capital sentencing context).

15. Andrew Kopkind, *Captain Levy – Doctor's Plot*, in TRIALS OF THE RESISTANCE, p. 25 (1970). *See also* POR AMOR AL PUEBLO (1986).

16. Mirennya Navarro, *Abortion Clinic Case Revives a Legal Dilemma*, NY Times, Nov. 14, 1994.

17. "In his trial for fatally shooting a doctor and his volunteer escort outside a Pensacola abortion clinic, Paul J. Hill waged one last protest: he chose to represent himself, then refused to offer any witnesses or evidence on his own behalf. In refus-

ing to speak up, Mr. Hill made it easier for the 12 jurors hearing his case to convict him and to recommend that he die in Florida's electric chair." Mirennya Navarro, *Abortion Clinic Case Revives a Legal Dilemma*, NY Times, Nov. 14, 1994. *See generally* Roger Parloff *When Worlds Collide*, American Lawyer, June 1995. *See also* Roger Parloff *When Worlds Collide*, American Lawyer, June 1995.

18.   Jo Thomas, *McVeigh's Lawyers Cite Waco in Urging Jury to Spare His Life*, NY Times, June 7, 1997.

19.   *Ibid.*

20.   Jo Thomas, *Political Ideas of McVeigh Are Subject At Bomb Trial*, NY Times, June 11, 1997.

21.   *Ibid.*

22.   *Ibid.*

23.   Jo Thomas, *Jury Deliberates Fate of McVeigh*, NY Times, June 13, 1997.

24.   RAY JENKINS, BLIND VENGEANCE (1995).

25.   Nina Bernstein, *Defense's Portrait of Political Outrage May Have Backfired*, NY Times, June 14, 1997.

26.   Peter Amin and Tom Morgenthau, *The Verdict: Death*, Newsweek, June 23, 1997.

27.   *Ibid.*

28.   *Ibid.*

29.   *Ibid.*

30.   "*We Did The Best We Could*," National Law Journal, June 30, 1997, p. A6.

31.   *Ibid.*

32.   *Lockett v. Ohio*, 438 U.S. 387 (1978).

33.   Louis Bilionis, *Moral Appropriateness, Capital Punishment and the Lockett Doctrine*, 83 J. Crim. L. & Criminology 283, 301 (1991).

34.   *Ibid*, pp. 301-306.

35.   John Leonard, *Machine Dreams*, The Nation, May 17, 1993, p. 667 (reviewing GLYN HUGHS, THE RAPE OF THE ROSE (1993). Of the Luddite rebellion of 1811-12, Leonard writes:

> The Luddites have come down to us in our high school history texts as mindless vandals, nineteenth-century smashers of machines as the Iconoclasts were ninth-century smashers of images. From 1811 to 1812, disaffected artisans and redundants destroyed a thousand mills in the Nottingham area alone – as if, by breaking a spinning jenny, a shearing frame or a power loom, they could stop "progress" in its technological tracks. From the point of view of the Industrial Revolution, Luddites were reactionary and obstructionist. From their own point of view, the perspective of the workshop, factory floor and village green, something

had gone terribly wrong in a depressed and war-weary England of bad harvests, rising prices, redoubled population, rackrenting, food shortages, landlessness and mass unemployment. *Ibid*; For a "straight" history of the Luddite rebellion, *see* KIRKPATRICK SALE, REBELS AGAINST THE FUTURE (1995).

36.   Kirkpatrick Sale, *Is There Method in His Madness?*, The Nation, Sept. 25, 1995, p. 305.

37.   Letter from Lydia Eccles to Michael Mello, Sept. 15, 1998.

38.   *Ibid.*

39.   Robert McFadden, *The Tortured Genius of Theodore Kaczynski*, NY Times, May 26, 1996.

40.   *See generally* William Glaberson, *Tale of Two Brothers Lends Unabom Trial a Literary Lure*, NY Times, Jan. 5, 1998; Richard Layco, *A Tale of Two Brothers*, Time, April 22, 1996.

CHAPTER FOUR: JOHN BROWN'S BODY

1.   STEPHEN VINCENT BENET, JOHN BROWN'S BODY 55 (1928).

2.   For arguments that Brown was a revolutionary, *see, e.g.* HERBERT APTHEKER, ABOLITIONISM: A REVOLUTIONARY MOVEMENT pp. 123-142 (1989); TRUMAN NELSON, THE OLD MAN, (1973). Brown "studied books on guerrilla warfare and on slave revolts. [He was] fascinated by the ability of small bands to hold off larger forces in mountainous terrain." JAMES MCPHERSON, BATTLE CRY OF FREEDOM, p. 202 (1988).

RUSSELL BANKS, CLOUDSPLITTER: A NOVEL (1998). The narrator of Banks' novel is Owen Brown, John Brown's third oldest son and lieutenant (although he remained as part of the rear guard during the Harper's Ferry raid). The novel opens in 1899, forty years after the raid on Harper's Ferry. Near the end of his life, Owen is recording the final "confession" to a young academic named Oswald Garrison Villard. In real life Oswald Garrison Villard wrote a landmark book about John Brown, *See* OSWALD GARRISON VILLARD, JOHN BROWN: A BIOGRAPHY FIFTY YEARS AFTER (1910) [hereinafter "Villard"]– one of my three favorite books on John Brown. Robert Penn Warren wrote, when Villard's book was published, that it "made all other books on the subject which had appeared before 1910, seem as mere trifling with the matter." *See* ROBERT PENN WARREN, JOHN BROWN: THE MAKING OF A MARTYR, p. 442 (1929) [hereinafter "Warren"]. (Although seriously flawed on matters of interpretation, Warren did, I think, get his basic fact straight; his work has withstood the test of time, albeit not nearly as well as Villard's.) Another favorite book is Stephen Oates' definitive work TO PURGE THIS LAND WITH BLOOD (1970) [hereinafter "Oates"]. But my favorite book – about John Brown and the Civil War he ignited – also happens to be the first book I read on the subject: Stephen Vincent Benét's magnificent 1928 narrative poem JOHN BROWN'S BODY. *See* Benét, *supra*. Other books I used in this chapter as an excuse to re-read them include the primary sources reproduced in INCIDENT AT HARPER'S FERRY (E. Stone ed. 1956) [hereinafter "Stone"] and PROLOGUE TO SUMTER (P. Stern ed. 1961) along with JAMES REDPATH, THE PUBLIC LIFE OF CAPTAIN JOHN BROWN (1860) [hereinafter "Redpath"]; TRUMAN NELSON, THE OLD MAN: JOHN BROWN AT HARPER'S FERRY (1973); J.C. FURNAS, THE ROAD TO HARPER'S FERRY (1959); EDWARD RENEHAN, THE SECRET SIX (1995); BRUCE OLDS, RAISING HOLY HELL: A NOVEL (1995); DAVID POTTER, THE IMPENDING CRISIS (1976); MCPHERSON *supra.* In researching this chapter I also read RICHARD BOYER, THE LEGEND OF JOHN BROWN (1973); JOHN BROWN: THE MAKING OF A REVOLUTIONARY (Louis Ruchames ed. 1969); JOSEPH BARRY, THE STRANGE STORY OF HARPER'S FERRY (50th Anniversary Edition, 11th Printing, 1994); JOHN SCOTT AND ROBERT SCOTT, JOHN BROWN OF HARPER'S FERRY (1988); CHESTER HEARN, SIX YEARS OF HELL (1996); NATIONAL PARK SERVICE, JOHN BROWN'S RAID (no publication date given). History is not made in a vacuum, and it is not written in a vacuum; the books about John Brown provide an especially interesting case study in historiography.

3.   A member of Brown's raiding party was Dangerfield Newby, a former slave whose wife was still in bondage in Virginia; Newby was killed during the raid. Ironically, the raiders' first victim was a freed slave named Shepherd Haywood. For a description of Newby's and Haywood's deaths, *see* Benét, *supra,* p. 34-36, 37-38. Harper's Ferry is located in today's West Virginia. In 1859, Harper's Ferry was in Virginia. When Virginia seceded from the Union, what is now West Virginia seceded, in effect, from Virginia.

4.   ALLAN NEVINS, PROLOGUE TO CIVIL WAR: THE EMERGENCE OF LINCOLN, p. 98 (1950).

5.   *Ibid,* p. 100.

6.   Herman Melville, *The Portent,* in BATTLE-PIECES AND ASPECTS OF THE WAR, p.1 (1995).

7.   *e.g.,* HILL PEEBLES WILSON, JOHN BROWN: SOLDIER OF FORTUNE (1913). Edwin Cotter, Superintendent of the John Brown House and Grave in Lake Placid, New York, gave me an interesting take on Wilson's hideous book. According to Cotter, who is perhaps the wisest and most knowledgeable historian of John Brown, Wilson's book was commissioned by the widow of the former governor of Kansas; this fact came out during a lawsuit filed by Wilson for payment of money he claimed was promised to him by the governor's widow.

8.   Robert McGlone, *John Brown, Henry Wise and the Politics of Inanity,* in HIS SOUL GOES MARCHING ON: RESPONSES TO JOHN BROWN AND THE HARPER'S FERRY RAID, p. 242 (1995) [hereafter "McGlone"]. McGlone's approach in turn echoes Oates, *supra.*

9.   McGlone, *supra.*

10.   McGlone, *supra,* pp. 214-15.

11.   Oates, *supra,* pp. 331-34.

12.   *Ibid,* p. 331.

13.   Quoted in Colman McCarthy, *Murder, Inc.,* The Nation, Dec. 29, 1997, p. 32.

14.   19 Howard 393 (1857) (lower case lack of capitalization in original.)

15.   JAMES MCPHERSON, BATTLE CRY OF FREEDOM; pp. 206-213 (1988); ROBERT PENN WARREN, JOHN BROWN; PP. 395-438 (1929 & 1993); DAVID POTTER, THE IMPENDING CRISIS; pp. 371-84 (1976); TRUMAN NELSON, THE OLD MAN (1973).

16.   *E.g.*, Oates, *supra*; Villard, *supra*; Warren, *supra*.

17.   William Lloyd Garrison's *Liberator*, for example, referred to the raid as "apparently insane." Paul Finkleman, HIS SOUL GOES MARCHING ON, p. 41 (P. Finkleman, ed. 1995). Some modern historians agree. *E.g.*, Nevins, *supra*, pp. 77, 88.

18.   McGlone, *supra*, p. 213; *see also* Oates, *supra*.

19.   *Ibid.* At Kaczynski's non-trial, the calculations of prosecutors and defense attorneys were, of course, quite different from those during Brown's trial in 1859.

20.   *E.g.*, Oates, *supra*; Villard, *supra*; Warren, *supra*.

21.   Warren, *supra*, pp. 401-02.

22.   *E.g.*, Oates, *supra*; Villard, *supra*; Warren, *supra*. For a summary of the law of insanity in 1859, *see* McGlone, *supra*, p. 217

23.   Villard, *supra*, p. 508.

24.   *Ibid*, pp. 508-09.

25.   Villard, *supra*, p. 508. *See also* Oates, *supra*; Warren, *supra*.

26.   Villard, *supra*, p. 508-09. *See also* Oates, *supra*; Warren, *supra*.

27.   Villard, *supra*, p. 496. *See also* Oates, *supra*; Warren, *supra*.

28.   *E.g.*, Wilson, *supra*; ELBERT SMITH, THE DEATH OF SLAVERY; p. 37 (1967) ("John Brown was criminally insane."). *See also* Aptheker, *supra*, p. 123.

29.   Villard, *supra*, p. 509 (quoting Virginia Governor Henry Wise). Kaczynski's trial judge described Kaczynski in remarkably similar terms. Finnegan, *supra*, p. 60.

30.   Villard, *supra*, pp. 509-10.

31.   *E.g.*, Furnas, *supra*, p. 30 (arguing that Brown "restless years saw him spiral ever nearer serious mental trouble and then succumb to it periodically, with intervals of more nearly normal behavior"); Nevins, *supra*; *see also* sources cited in Oates, *supra*.

32.   McGlone, *supra*, p. 214. *See also* Roger Parloff, *When Worlds Collide*, American Lawyer, June 1995.

33.   *E.g.*, Warren, *supra*. For an interesting treatment of Brown's trial, *see* Robert Ferguson, *Story and Transcription in the Trial of John Brown*, p. 6, Yale J. Law & Humanities p. 37 (1994) *see also* McGlone, *supra*, p. 216 (discussing what McGlone aptly calls "the politics of insanity").

34.   Finnegan, *supra* (emphasis in original).

35.   *Ibid*; *see also* Higgins, *supra*.

36.   For an excellent discussion of this issue, *see* James Q. Wilson, *In Search of Madness*, NY Times, Jan. 17, 1998.

37. Stone, *supra*; Villard, *supra*; Nelson, *supra*, p. 211-12.

38. Villard, *supra*, p. 492; Stone, *supra*.

39. *Ibid.*

40. Stone, *supra*, pp. 110-11 (quoting the *Richmond Enquirer*, Tues. Oct. 25, 1859).

41. *Ibid*, pp. 114-15 (quoting *The National Intelligencer*, Oct. 29, 1859).

42. *Ibid*, p. 131 (quoting *The Baltimore Weekly Sun*, Nov. 5, 1859).

43. Stone, *supra*, p. 132 (quoting *The Baltimore Weekly Sun*, Sat. Nov. 5, 1859).

44. *Ibid.*

45. *Ibid*, pp. 132-33.

46. Villard, *supra*, p. 493; Stone, *supra*, p. 133; Oates, *supra*, pp. 324-25. Brown's judge also denied requests for a short delay to allow Brown to recover from the serious wounds he had suffered when Robert E. Lee's marines stormed the engine house at Harper's Ferry. Like Ted Kaczynski's prosecutors, Brown's prosecutors opposed delay as a defense tactic. Stone, *supra*; Redpath, *supra*. And, like Kaczynski's judge, Brown's judge justified his denial of defense motions for delay on the basis of hardship on the jury. *See* Stone, *supra*; Redpath, *supra*.

47. McGlone, *supra*, p. 218; *see also* Oates, *supra*.

48. *Ibid.*

49. *Ibid.*

50. McGlone, *supra*, p. 214; Oates, *supra* .

51. Boyer, *supra*.

52. McGlone, *supra*, p. 242.

53. Oates, *supra*.

54. *Ibid*, p. 243.

55. *Ibid*, p. 402; *see also* Stone, *supra*, pp. 141, 142, 143 (quoting Brown's lawyers' closing arguments).

56. Warren, *supra*, p. 402; Redpath, *supra*; Stone, *supra*, pp. 129-36, 403.

57. Villard, *supra*, p. 498.

58. Stone, *supra*; *accord* Redpath, *supra*; Benét, *supra* pp. 57-58; HENRY STEELE COMMAGER, DOCUMENTS OF AMERICAN HISTORY, pp. 361-2 (3rd ed. 1943).

59. Villard, *supra*, p. 498.

60. McPherson, *supra*, p. 208

61. *Ibid.* Later, Ruffin was given the honor of giving the order to fire upon Fort Sumter. Several of Brown's letters are reproduced in Redpath, *supra* .

62. In John Brown's day, the label applied was "monomania." Stone, *supra*, p. 167 (Brown was a "brave, simple-hearted and modest monomaniac") (quoting *The Boston Transcript*, reprinted in *The Liberator*, Nov. 4, 1859). *Ibid*, p. 173 ("it is fair to suppose that [Brown] had become a monomaniac") (quoting *The Buffalo Commercial Advertiser*, reprinted in *The National Intelligencer*, Nov. 1, 1859). *Ibid*, p. 185 (Brown and his allies "have become monomaniacs") (quoting Hon. Caleb Cushing, Speech in Boston, reprinted in *The National Intelligencer*, Dec. 17, 1859). *E.g.*, Villard, *supra*; Warren, *supra*. Brown was monomaniacal about slavery; Kaczynski was monomaniacal about technology. I have been called monomaniacal about capital punishment – get this boy to an asylum! I am reminded of an incident early in the history of Florida's CCR office. We were interviewing a psychologist for a job at CCR. At the end of the interviews, the job candidate said she would not work at CCR – but that she would be willing to give us a group rate for counseling.

63. Similarly, the court transcripts in Kaczynski's case alluded to "'multiple generational . . . mental illness.'" Finnegan, *supra*, p. 58.

64. McGlone, *supra*, p. 216; *see also* Villard, *supra*; Warren, *supra* .

65. *Ibid*.

66. George Hoyt, a very young Boston lawyer – the prosecutor referred to him as the "beardless boy" – asked to be appointed as Brown's assistant trial counsel. *Supra*, pp. 403-404. In fact, Hoyt was a spy – he was hired by Boston abolitionists to "go South and investigate the circumstances with an eye toward rescue." *Ibid*, p. 404.

67. Warren, *supra*, pp. 418-19.

68. Commager, *supra*, pp. 321-23. The Fugitive Slave Act transformed many Northern abolitionists – including Frederick Douglass *see* McPherson *supra*, p. 202 – from pacifists to advocates, if not practitioners, of violent resistance to the law. *See* McPherson *supra*, p. 202; Commager *supra*, pp. 224-27, 319-23, 331-32.

69. *Ibid*, pp. 420-21.

70. One of Brown's sons was killed in Kansas; two more were killed at Harper's Ferry.

71. *E.g.*, Wilson, *supra*.

72. Letter from Edwin Cotter to Michael Mello, July 1998.

73. Villard, *supra*.

74. Benét, *supra*, p. 196.

75. This is not true of Virginia's governor, whose own political ends were better served by a sane John Brown. *See* McGlone, *supra*.

76. Walter Kirn, *The Wages of Righteousness*, NY Times Book Review, Feb. 22, 1998, p. 9.

77. Oates, *supra*, p. 412 n.39. Or, as James Lowen put it: "The treatment of Brown, like the treatment of slavery and Reconstruction, has changed in American history textbooks. From 1890 to about 1970, John Brown was insane. Before 1890 and after 1970 he regained his sanity. Since Brown himself did not change after his death, his

sanity provides an inadvertent index of the level of white racism in our society." JAMES LOWEN, LIES MY TEACHER TOLD ME pp. 165-66 (1995).

78.   *Ibid*, pp. 333-34.

CHAPTER FIVE: THE POLITICS OF INSANITY

1.   JOHN SCOTT AND ROBERT SCOTT, JOHN BROWN OF HARPER'S FERRY, p. 151 (1988).

2.   Paul Finkleman, *Manufacturing Martyrdom*, in HIS SOUL GOES MARCHING ON (P. Finkleman ed. 1995); Peter Knupfer, *A Crisis in Conservatism, ibid;* Peter Wallenstein, *Incendiaries All*, in HIS SOUL GOES MARCHING ON (P. Finkleman ed. 1995), STEPHEN OATES, TO PURGE THIS LAND WITH BLOOD, p. 354 (1970); *see also* McPherson, *supra;* Oates, *supra*, pp. 354-355.

3.   *Ibid*, p. 355.

4.   *See generally*, Wallenstein, *supra. See also* McPherson, *supra.*

5.   *Ibid.*

6.   Benét, *supra*, p. 31 (from "John Brown's Prayer").

7.   *Ibid*, pp. 56-57.

8.   DANIEL BERRIGAN, THE TRIAL OF THE CATONSVILLE NINE (1970). For other fascinating treatments of political trials, see TRIALS OF THE RESISTANCE (1970); *see also, e.g.,* POR AMOR AL PUEBLO: THE TRIAL OF THE WINOOSKI, p. 44 (Ben Bradly, *et al.* eds. 1986); THE TALES OF HOFFMAN (ed. Mark Levine, *et al.* 1970); JESSICA MILFORD, THE TRIAL OF DR. SPOCK (1973).

9.   *Ibid*, p. vii-viii.

10.   STEPHEN OATES; THE FIRES OF JUBILEE: NAT TURNER'S FIERCE REBELLION (1975); ARNA BONTEMPS; BLACK THUNDER: GABRIEL'S REVOLT: VIRGINIA 1800 (1936); HERBERT APTHEKER; AMERICAN NEGRO SLAVE REVOLTS: ON NAT TURNER, DENMARK VESEY, GABRIEL & OTHERS (1943); HOWARD JONES; MUTINY ON THE AMISTAD (1987).

11.   Parloff, *supra.*

12.   *E.g.*, Michael Zuckoff, *Feds Finding Antipathy, Not Bomb Suspect, in NC*, Boston Globe, Nov. 30, 1998; Kevin Sack, *Elusive Bombing Fugitive Divides a Town*, NY Times, July 24, 1998 (discussing local public support for fugitive Eric Robert Rudolph, alleged abortion clinic bomber); on the Rudolph case generally, *see* Rick Bragg, *Bomb Kills Guard at an Alabama Abortion Clinic*, NY Times, Jan. 30, 1998; Anne Kornblut, *Clues Sought in Bombing of Alabama Abortion Clinic*, Boston Globe, Jan. 30, 1998; Rick Bragg, *Abortion Clinic Bomb Was Intended to Kill, An Official Says*, NY Times, Jan. 31, 1998; Rick Bragg, *Group Tied to 2 Bombings Says It Set Off Clinic Blast*, NY Times, Feb. 3, 1998; Rick Bragg, *Bomb Inquiry Puts Spotlight on a Man*, NY Times, Feb. 7, 1998; Kevin Sack, *North Carolina Fugitive, Sec. 1, Changed in Clinic Bombing*, NY Times, Feb. 15, 1998; Kevin Sack, *Suspect in Southern*

Bombing Is Enigma to Law Enforcement, NY Times, Feb. 28, 1998. *See also, e.g.*, Jim Yardly & David Rhode, *Abortion Doctor in Buffalo Slain; Sniper Attack Fits Violent Pattern*, NY Times, Oct. 25, 1998; Bob Hohler, *Abortion Providers Put on Alert; Killer Hunted*, Boston Globe, Oct. 27, 1998; T. Trent Gegax, *The Abortion Wars Come Home*, Newsweek, Nov. 9, 1998.

13.   For lovely descriptions of this army and its leader, *see* Benét, *supra.*

14.   DEBORAH RHODE, PROFESSIONAL RESPONSIBILITY: ETHICS BY THE PERVASIVE METHOD, p. 379 (1998) (citing Model Rule 1.2 and Ethical Consideration 7-7).

15.   *E.g.* Warren, *supra* .

16.   *Ibid.*

17.   *Ibid* (quoting Dr. Karen Froming).

18.   Wilson, *supra.*

19.   Aptheker, *supra,* p. 124.

20.   W.E.B. DUBOIS, JOHN BROWN (PREFACE) (1909).

21.   I first understood the futility of Brown's raid as executed when I visited Harper's Ferry – the topography of the land itself foreordained the raid's failure. Success demanded rapid withdrawal from the town – something Brown could have done. But instead he stayed to fight a battle he must have known he could not possibly win. *See also* Benét, *supra*; Oates, *supra*; Warren, *supra*; Villard, *supra* .

22.   Brown's study of guerrilla warfare tactics and strategy is hard to square with his so-called blunders – blunders so obvious as to allow an inference that Brown himself intended the raid to fail in its stated objectives. Brown "cut himself off from his base of supplies, failed to keep open his only avenues of retreat, dispersed his small force and bottled the bulk of them in a trap where defeat was inevitable." Bertram Wyatt-Brown, *A Volcano Beneath a Mountain of Snow*, in HIS SOUL GOES MARCHING ON, p. 25 (P. Finkleman ed. 1995) (quoting C. Vann Woodward). *But see* Karen Whitman, *Re-evaluating John Brown's Raid*, 34 West Va. History 46 (1974) (arguing that the raid was not tactically unsound). Brown carried no provisions on the raid, and he left a "mass of incriminating documents" at his base camp. Wyatt-Brown, *supra,* p. 25; and "not only did [Brown] fatally procrastinate, but he completely failed to understand why the slaves would not rise." *Ibid*, p. 26. Wyatt-Brown observes that perhaps "all these blunders might simply be attributable to Brown's confused reaction to the failure of insurrectionary slaves to materialize. Warfare is always messy, and the unforeseen often determines victory or defeat. But suppose another motive was at work: a mysterious desire not to succeed in the ordinary sense but to sow sectional discord by making the whole enterprise, and himself in particular, a human sacrifice to the cause of freedom." *Ibid*, p. 26-27.

23.   *See generally*, MCGLONE, *supra*; DAVID VON DREHLE, AMONG THE LOWEST OF THE DEAD (1995); Finnegan, *supra.*

24.   MICHAEL MELTSNER, CRUEL AND UNUSUAL (1974).

25. *See* MARTIN GOLDING; PHILOSOPHY OF LAW pp. 54-59, 60-61 (1975); JOEL FEINBERG; SOCIAL PHILOSOPHY pp. 45-52 (1973); *see generally*, PATERNALISM (R. Sartorius ed 1983); DONALD VAN DEVEER; PATERNALISTIC INTERVENTION (1986).

26. Finnegan, *supra*, p. 54.

27. Oates, *supra.*

28. CLARENCE DARROW, VERDICTS OUT OF COURT; p. 438 (A. Weinberg and L. Weinberg eds 1963).

29. *E.g.*, CLARENCE DARROW, ATTORNEY FOR THE DAMNED; pp. 89-103 (1957).

30. *Ibid*, pp. 532-41.

31. *Ibid*, pp. 174-255, 267, 490.

32. *Ibid*, pp. 16-88. For a fascinating and thoughtful discussion of how Darrow's defense of Leopold and Loeb – and of how that defense squares with the Supreme Court's modern jurisprudence of capital punishment – *see* Scott Howe, *Reassessing the Individualization Mandate in Capital Sentencing: Darrow's Defense of Leopold and Loeb*, IOWA L. REV.; vol. 79, p. 989 (1994).

33. *Ibid*, pp. 532-41.

34. Finnegan, *supra*, p. 63.

CHAPTER SIX: LIVE FREE OR DIE (YOU DECIDE)

1. Daniel Klaidman & Patricia King, *Suicide Mission*, Newsweek, Jan. 19, 1998; *see also* Lynda Gorov, *Kaczynski Apparently Tried Suicide*, Boston Globe, Jan. 9, 1998.

2. *Ibid.*

3. *Ibid.*

4. Pre-Trial Transcript, Discussions on Motions and Change of Plea, *United States v. Kaczynski*, No. CR-S-96-259 GEB, 1998 WL 22017 (E.D. Cal. Trans. Jan. 22, 1998).

5. *E.g.*, White, *Defendants Who Elect Execution,* U. PITT. L. REV. vol. 48 p. 854, (1987); Straefer, *Volunteering for Execution*, J. CRIM. L. & CRIMINOLOGY, vol. 74 p. 860, (1983); Urofsky, *The Right to Die*, J. CRIM. L. & CRIMINOLOGY, vol. 75 p. 553 (1984); Note, *The Death Row Right to Die*, S. CAL. L. REV., vol. 54 p. 575 (1981); Dieter, *Ethical Choices for Attorneys Whose Clients Elect Execution*, GEO. J. LEGAL ETHICS, vol. 3, p. 799 (1990).

6. BRAM STOKER, DRACULA, p. 371 (1897; Modern Library Edition 1996).

7. *Vacco v. Quill*, No. 95-1858, 65 U.S.L.W. 4695 (U.S. Sup. Ct. June 26, 1997); *Washington v. Glucksberg*, 65 U.S.L.W. 4669 (U.S. Sup. Ct. June 26, 1997). In *Quill* and *Glucksberg*, the Court rejected the argument that the right of a competent, terminally ill patient to choose the method and time of death does not include a Fourteenth Amendment *constitutional* right to physician assistance in carrying out

that choice. Earlier, in *Cruzan v. Mississippi Dep't of Health*, 497 U.S. 261, 281 (1990), the Court referred in *dicta* to a constitutional right to die with dignity: The Court "assume[d] that the United States Constitution would grant a competent person a constitutionally protected right to refuse lifesaving hydration and nutrition." *Cruzan*, 497 U.S. 279. The *Cruzan* Court reasoned that "[t]he choice between life and death is a deeply personal decision of obvious and overwhelming finality." *Ibid*, p. 281. All of this appears to be *dicta* because the *Cruzan* case itself upheld a Missouri statute requiring that the family or representative of a mentally incompetent person in a permanent vegetative state must establish that the patient wishes a physician actively to remove life sustaining food and hydration. *Ibid*, p. 279.

The moral and jurisprudential questions presented in *Vacco* and *Glucksberg* had already generated an extensive and excellent literature even before the cases reached the U.S. Supreme Court. *e.g.*, Kamisar, *The "Right to Die"*, Duquesne L. Rev., vol. 36 p. 481 (1996); Kamisar, *Against Assisted Suicide*, U. Det. Mercy L. Rev.; vol. 72 p. 735 (1995); O'Dowd, Crone & Balch, *Suicide: A Constitutional Right?*, Duquesne L. Rev., vol. 24, p. 1 (1985); Orenlichter, *Legalization of Physician-assisted Suicide*, B.C. L. Rev., vol. 38 p.1 (1997). The Court's decisions likely will spawn more. There is, I believe, a common cultural and jurisprudential thread linking America's ambivalence about physician-assisted suicide, capital punishment and what one astute writer has called our culture's "dysfunctional relationship with death." Boozang, *An Intimate Passing*, U. Pitt. L. Rev., vol. 58, pp. 549, 554 (1997). But that is for another book.

8.   NORMAN MAILER, THE EXECUTIONER'S SONG (1977).

9.   MICHAEL MELLO, DEAD WRONG (1997).

10.   MICHAEL MELLO, DEAD WRONG (1997); MICHAEL MELLO, "CRAZY JOE" SPAZIANO (forthcoming 2000).

11.   On the politics of capital punishment, *see generally* Uelman, *Review of Death Penalty Judgments*, Loyola-L.A. L. Rev., vol. 23 p.237 (1989); Garvy, *Politicizing Who Dies*, Yale L.J., vol. 101, p. 187 (1991); Pierce & Radelet, *The Role and Consequences of the Death Penalty in American Politics*, N.Y.C. Rev. L. & Social Change vol. 18, p. 711 (1990/91); Symposium, *Politics and the Death Penalty*, X. vol. 21 p. 239 (1994); Reidinger, *The Politics of Judging*, ABA J., April 1, 1987.

12.   112 S. Ct. 1074 (1992); Berger, *Herrera v. Collins*, William & Mary L. Rev., vol. 35, p. 943 (1994).

13.   HARVARD CLASSICS, THE APOLOGY, PHAEDO AND CRITO OF PLATO (1907 & 1980) p. 30.

14.   DOUGLAS EGERTON, GABRIEL'S REBELLION, pp. 81-82 (1993).

15.   ROBERT JOHNSON, DEATHWORK (1990).

16.   WILLIAM STYRON, DARKNESS VISIBLE (1990).

17.   *Reflections on the Guillotine*, from ALBERT CAMUS, REBELLION, RESISTANCE AND DEATH, pp. 199-200 (1962).

18.   Kafka, *The Penal Colony*, from FRANZ KAFKA, THE METAMORPHOSIS, THE PENAL COLONY AND OTHER STORIES, pp. 199-200 (1975).

19. I.F. STONE, THE TRIAL OF SOCRATES, pp. 197-214 (1988).

20. HARVARD CLASSICS, *supra*, pp. 36, 37.

21. *Ibid*, pp. 21, 23.

22. *Ibid*, pp. 16-17.

23. *Ibid*.

24. *Ibid*, p. 17.

25. *Ibid*, p. 28.

26. *Ibid*.

27. *Ibid*.

28. Stone, *supra*, p. 187.

29. *Ibid*, p. 186.

30. *Ibid*, p. 27.

31. RAINER MARIA RILKE, LETTERS TO A YOUNG POET, p. 17 (J. BURNHAM TRANS. 1992).

32. Stephen Adler, *The Cure That Kills*, American Lawyer, Sept. 1986, pp. 1, 29-33; *American Public Health Association, Policy Statement 85201: Participation of Health Professionals in Capital Punishment*, American Journal of Public Health, vol. 76, p. 339 (1986); George Annas, *Nurses and the Death Penalty*, Nursing Law and Ethics, vol. 1, p. 3 (May 1980); Paul Appelbaum, *Competence to Be Executed: Another Conundrum for Mental Health Professionals*, Hospital and Community Psychiatry, vol. 37, p. 682 (1986); Charles Ewing, *Diagnosing and Treating 'Insanity' on Death Row: Legal and Ethical Perspectives*, Behavioral Science and Law, vol. 5, p. 176 (1987); Douglas Mossman, *Assessing and Restoring Competency to Be Executed: Should Psychiatrist Participate?* Behavioral Science & Law, vol. 7, p. 397 (1987); Michael Radelet and George Barnard, *Ethics and the Psychiatric Determination of Competency to Be Executed*," American Academy of Psychiatry and Law, vol. 14, pp. 37, 197 (1988); Note, *Medical Ethics and Competency to Be Executed*, Yale L. J., vol. 96, p. 167 (1986); Barbara Ward, *Competency for Execution; Problems in Law and Psychiatry*, F.S.U.L. Rev., vol. 14, p. 36 (1986); Donald Wallace, *Incompetency for Execution*, Journal of Legal Medicine vol. 8, p. 265 (1987).

33. Used with permission of the authors.

34. Tim O'Brien, *The Vietnam In Me*, *The New York Times Magazine*, Oct. 2, 1994, pp. 150-151.

35. ENCYCLOPEDIA OF PHILOSOPHY; vol. 8, pp. 43-44.

36. WILLIAM STYRON, DARKNESS VISIBLE, pp. 35-36 (1990).

37. TIM O'BRIEN, IF I DIE IN A COMBAT ZONE, p. 137 (1969).

38. *Ibid*, p. 144.

39.   I am grateful to the poet Samuel Hazo for bringing Aristotle to my attention in this context.

40.   *Ibid*, p. 144.

41.   TRUMAN NELSON, THE OLD MAN, p. 229 (1973).

42.   Application for Stay of Execution, *Minerva v. Singletary* (U.S. Sup. Ct. filed Aug. 24, 1993).

43.   GEORGE FLETCHER, LOYALTY, p. 8 (1993).

44.   *Ibid*, p. 10.

45.   NORMAN MAILER, THE EXECUTIONER'S SONG (1977).

46.   *Spaziano v. State*, 660 So. 2d 1363, 1366-67 (Fla. 1995); MELLO, DEAD WRONG (1997).

47.   EC 7-8; Dieter; *supra*, pp. 811-12; Goodpaster, *The Trial For Life*, N.Y.U. L. Rev., vol. 58, pp. 299, 323 (1983).

48.   Dieter; *supra*, p. 812.

49.   *Ibid*, p. 813.

50.   *Ibid*, p. 813.

51.   Dieter; *supra*, p. 813.

52.   Dieter; *supra*; p. 812 (emphasis in original).

53.   Henry Schwartzschild, *The Problem of "Consensual Executions"* (unpublished 1993).

54.   *Ibid*.

55.   AP, *Inmate Executed After Sedative Overdose*, Dallas Morning News, Aug. 12, 1995; AP, *Oklahoma Killer Up for Execution Overdoses*, Dallas Morning News, Aug. 11, 1995; AP, *Murderer Is Revived, then Executed*, St. Petersburg Times, Aug. 12, 1995, p 1A.

CHAPTER SEVEN: THE MISSING LINK

1.   For an excellent discussion of the legal issues presented by Theodore Kaczynski's journal, *see* Roger Parloff, *Requiem For A Civil Liberty?*, American Lawyer, Jan. 1998. I should note at the outset that I have only seen those portions of Theodore Kaczynski's journal that have been made public. All of my knowledge of its contents comes exclusively from the sources cited in this book.

2.   The grounds for the motion [to preclude the prosecution from using Kaczynski's private journals] were brought to the attention of defense counsel by Professor Michael Mello of Vermont Law School, who has a long standing interest in the privacy of diaries, and who even gave one of his law school classes an exam question raising the Kaczynski diary issue. As noted, the issue harkens back to *Boyd v. United States*, 116 U.S. 616, an opinion issued in 1886. Private Diaries, *United States v. Kaczynski*, CR-S-96-259GEB, 1997 WL 450390 (filed July 21, 1997), p. n.4.

3. Government's Motion in Limine for Admission of Evidence Under Fed. R. Evid. 404(B) (Redacted), *United States v. Kaczynski*, CR No. S-96-0259 GEB (E.D. Calif. filed June 9, 1997), p. 4.

4. *Ibid*, p. 3.

5. *Ibid*.

6. *Ibid*, p. 4.

7. Prosecutor Robert Cleary (quoted in Transcript of Hearing, September 20, 1996) (quoted in Reply to Government's Opposition to Motion to Preclude Use of Defendant's Private Diaries, *United States v. Kaczynski*, No. CR-5-96-0259-GEB (filed July 22, 1997), p. n.5.

8. *Ibid*, p. 31.

9. *Ibid*, p. 4.

10. *Ibid*.

11. *Ibid*.

12. *Ibid*.

13. An admission is not, in legal terms, equal to a confession. It must be borne in mind that Kaczynski's admissions were not made wittingly, since he was writing them in his private journals.

14. *E.g., ibid*, p. 3.

15. *Ibid*, p. 23 n. 18.

16. *Ibid*.

17. *Ibid*, p. 33.

18. *Ibid*, p. 7.

19. *Ibid*.

20. Notice of Motion to Suppress Evidence and Memorandum of Points and Authorities in Support of Defendant's Motion to Suppress, *United States v. Kaczynski*, CR-S-96-0259 GEB (E.D. filed March 3, 1997), p. 2.

21. Memo, pp. 2-3.

22. The motion was argued on May 16, 1997. It was denied, in a 48-page order, filed on June 27, 1997. On the day before Independence Day, 1997, Kaczynski's counsel filed a suppression motion directed at the diary evidence specifically and relying on *Boyd v. United States*, 116 U.S. 616 (1886). *See* Notice of Motion and Motion to Preclude Use of Defendant's Private Diaries, *United States v. Kaczynski*, No. CR-S-96-0259-GEB (E.D. Calif. filed July 3, 1997). On July 16, 1997, the government responded to Kaczynski's diary motion based on *Boyd*. *See* Government's Brief Opposing Defendant's Motion to Preclude Use of Private Diaries, *United States v. Kaczynski*, No. S-96-259-GEB (E.D. Calif. filed July 16, 1997).

23.   The fact that the Kaczynski prosecution is *federal* implicates the federal courts' "supervisory power" over the administration of federal criminal justice. Excluding Kaczynski's journals based on this supervisory power – rather than on constitutional authority – would allow the federal judiciary to avoid the thorny constitutional issues raised by Kaczynski's journals.

  The classic definition of the federal court's supervisory power over the administration of federal criminal justice was provided by Justice Frankfurter in *McNabb v. United States*, 318 U.S. 332 (1943): While the power of this Court to undo convictions in *state* courts is limited to the enforcement of those fundamental principles of liberty and justice secured by [Fourth Amendment due process], the standards of *federal* criminal justice "are not satisfied merely by observance of those minimal historic safeguards" (emphasis added). Rather, "[i]n the exercise of its supervisory authority over the administration of criminal justice in the federal courts, [this Court has] formulated rules of evidence to be applied in federal criminal prosecutions." Thus, in *McNabb*, the Court held incriminating statements obtained during prolonged and hence unlawful detention (i.e., while the suspect was held in violation of federal statutory requirements that he be promptly taken before a committing magistrate) were inadmissible in federal courts "[q]uite apart from the Constitution."

  For a long, hard look at *McNabb* itself and the federal "supervisory power" generally, *see* Beale, *Reconsidering Supervisory Power in Criminal Cases: Constitutional and Statutory Limits on the Authority of the Federal Courts*, 84 Colum. L. Rev. 1433 (1984). Professor Beale maintains, *inter alia*, that "the supervisory power has blurred the constitutional and statutory limitations on the authority of the federal courts [and] fostered the erroneous view that the federal courts exercise general supervision over federal prosecutors and investigators"; and that "there is no statutory or constitutional source of authority broad enough to encompass all of the supervisory power decisions." *Ibid*, pp. 1434-35.

  McNabb was a signpost on the road to *Miranda v. Arizona* in 1966 and, like *Miranda* after it, *McNabb* was an unpopular decision. Hogan and Steene, *The McNabb-Mallory Rule*, Geo. L.J., vol. 47, p. 1 (1958). However, *McNabb* was resoundingly reaffirmed by the Court in *Mallory v. United States*, 354 U.S. 449 (1957). *McNabb-Mallory* remained controversial even after they had been superceded by *Miranda*. *E.g.*, Liva Baker, Miranda, p. 235 (1985) (during Abe Fortas' confirmation hearings, 'Mallory!,' Senator Strom Thurmond had thundered. 'I want that name to ring in your ears . . . Mallory, a man who raped a woman, admitted his guilt and the Supreme Court turned him loose on a techni cality . . . Can you as a justice condone such a decision as that?").

24.   116 U.S. 616 (1886).

25.   *See generally* Anthony Lewis, Gideon's Trumpet (1966).

26.   Oliver Wendell Holmes, The Common Law, p. 1 (1881).

27.   *See also* 384 U.S. 757 (1966), *Bram v. United States*, 168 U.S. 532 (1897), was decided one year after *Boyd*. Prior to *Bram*, an involuntary confession would have been

one in which torture, or some other form of physical coercion, was used to extract a confession from a suspect. *Bram* recognized other forms of coercion. Coercion might be physical or mental, anything which engendered either "hope or fear" in the mind of a suspect. The test of *Bram* is that a confession is made voluntarily if there is no inducement or compulsion of any kind. In the years following *Bram* an even higher standard was set, especially during the Warren Court era, as the high court sought to remove any element of subtle coercion in the process of questioning suspects. This led to the establishment of the *Miranda* rule.

However, the pendulum now seems to have swung back to the notion of voluntariness of the *Bram* era. *Colorado v. Connelly*, 479 U.S. 157 (1987), decided exactly one hundred years after *Bram* and a hundred and one years after *Boyd*, was a case in which a mentally ill individual confessed to murder. The Supreme Court upheld the conviction, suggesting that nothing short of actual police coercion would render a confession invalid. It is a narrow conception of voluntariness which will not aid Mr. Kaczynski's case. And it raises interesting questions. Are the journals reliable, or are they the ramblings of an unbalanced mind? And what is the nature of the evidence against Mr. Kaczynski absent the journals?

Kaczynski's case is unique. The confessions in diary form, if that is what they are, were not the product of coercion. However, neither were the diaries voluntarily given to the police. They were seized from Mr. Kaczynski's cabin, under what appears to be a valid search warrant. An argument might be made that they were compelled by reason of the seizure, but this does not comport well with existing doctrine.

In the world of *Boyd* this would have been an easy case. Now it is likely that a future Supreme Court will have to take this tough question head-on and decide whether a person's written statements may be used to incriminate him. In so doing, a Supreme Court at the dawn of the twenty-first century may find itself reaching back to the dawn of the twentieth century in search of doctrine.

28. *Schmerber v. California*, 384 U.S. 757, 761 n.5 (1967).

29. *Andresen v. Maryland*, 427 U.S. 463, 473 (1976).

30. *Fisher v. United States*, 425 U.S. 408.

31. Note, *The Rights of Criminal Defendants*, 95 Harv. L. Rev. 643, 683 (1982).

32. *Fisher*, 425 U.S. 410-13.

33. Anthony Amsterdam, *Perspectives on the Fourth Amendment*, Minn. L. Rev., vol. 58, pp. 349, 385-386 (1974): "The Fourth Amendment . . . is ordinarily treated as a monolith: wherever it restricts police activities at all, it subjects them to the same extensive restrictions that it imposes upon physical entries into dwellings. To label any police activity a "search" or "seizure" within the ambit of the Amendment is to impose those restrictions upon it. On the other hand, if it is not labeled a "search" or "seizure," it is subject to no significant restrictions of any kind. It is only "searches" or "seizures" that the Fourth Amendment requires to be reasonable: police activities of any other sort may be as unreasonable as the police please to make them."

34. 436 U.S. 547 (1978).

35.   ALLEN & KUHNS, CONSTITUTIONAL CRIMINAL PROCEDURE; 819 (2nd ed. 1991).

36.   *Ibid*, p. 818 (2nd ed. 1991).

37.   *E.g.*, Dan Billin, *Hunter "Laundering" Meeting Disputed*, Valley News, June 23, 1995; Liz
      Anderson, *Witness Credibility Key to Hunter Case*, Rutland Herald [VT], July 18, 1995;
      John Gregg, *Hunter Actions Probed by Feds*, Rutland Herald [VT], March 7, 1996,
      David Ferch, *NH Ties Suspects to a Hunter Client*, Valley News, July 20, 1995. Hunter
      attempted to respond to the government's investigation in Hunter, *My Mistake:
      Becoming Too Personally Involved With My Clients*, Valley News, March 11, 1996.
           Almost two years, to the day, after the raid, Hunter was finally indicted—but
      not for "laundering" drug money. *See* Ed Ballam, *Will Hunter is Charged With
      Fraud*, Valley News, July 9, 1997, at A1; John Gregg, *Hunter is Indicted on Fraud
      Counts*, Rutland Herald [VT], July 9, 1997, at p. 1; John Gregg, *Hunter Indictment
      Greeted With Skepticism*, Rutland Herald [VT], July 10, 1997, at p. 1. Rather, he was
      indicted on 10 counts of mail fraud and one count of bankruptcy fraud (an idea his
      prosecutors got perhaps from the Tom Cruise character in the movie *The Firm*). He
      pleaded guilty to a single count in June 1998. Your tax dollars at work. *Searching
      Lawyers*, Valley News, June 14, 1995, p. A6. *See generally* Reltz, *Clients, Lawyers and
      The Fifth Amendment*, Duke L.J., vol. 41, p. 572 (1991); Massing, *The Fifth
      Amendment, The Attorney/Client Privilege and The Prosecution of White Collar
      Crime*, Va. L. Rev., vol. 75, p. 1179 (1989).

38.   April Hensel, *A Knock on the Door, A Shocking Charge*, Rutland Herald, June 14,
      1995, p. 15

39.   *The New York Times* wrote the following article about Hunter:
           The target of the drug raid that went down here three weeks ago was not
      your usual suspect; Will Hunter is son of two ministers, graduate of Exeter,
      Yale and Harvard Law School, Rhodes scholar, former Vermont state leg-
      islator, newspaper publisher and low-paid lawyer for the down and out.
           He drives a rusty, secondhand Mazda, buys his clothes at rummage
      sales and runs his law practice out of his basement. He says he earns
      about $20,000 a year and has accepted payment in maple syrup, cheese,
      cups of coffee and the tie-dyed cummerbund he wore at his wedding
      three years ago to April Hensel, a district coordinator for the state envi-
      ronmental board.
           It was 3 a.m. on June 9, when seven agents from the Drug Enforcement
      Administration showed up at Mr. Hunter's three-bedroom frame house on
      a winding dirt road. They add a search warrant based on an affidavit that
      said he had helped a client launder drug money through a real estate firm
      Mr. Hunter had set up.
      After a three-hour search, the agents left with four computers, 200 flop-
      py discs and two crates of files.
           No charges have been filed, though there are suggestions that a
      grand jury is meeting on the matter, and people in this mountain town
      of 1,500 and in surrounding towns are standing behind Mr. Hunter their

41-year-old neighbor. The Cavendish P.T.A. sent him flowers. The local newspapers are filled with letter to the editor vowing support.

Joe Allen, the owner of the Cavendish General Store and a client of Mr. Hunter, said the other day: "He's the crusader for the little guy. Money is not his issue. I personally have faith in him."

One of Mr. Hunter's longtime friends, Peter Welch, a lawyer and former president of the Vermont Senate, said: "Will's an eccentric. He's disorganized, charming, brilliant—and he's not a crook."

See Sara Rimer, *Town Rises to Defend a Lawyer*, NY Times, July 3, 1995, p. A6. *See also* Greeta Anand, *Probe of Lawyer Leaves Some Stunned*, Boston Globe, June 18, 1995, p. 23; Sarah Strohmeyer, *The Many Trials of Will Hunter*, Valley News [Vermont], June 25, 1995, p. 1.

40.   One leading local paper editorialized:

When the government accuses a citizen of a serious crime, attention generally turns to the accused to hear what he has to say in his defense. But now that law enforcement officials have claimed that lawyer Will Hunter was involved in laundering drug money and have raided his law office to secure evidence, we're more interested in hearing what the government has to say about its behavior. It's not that money-laundering is a trivial activity. Rather, we can think of few more alarming developments than the prospect of authorities kicking down the doors of lawyers and searching files.

Last week's search of Hunter's home and office followed the arrest of Frank Sargent Jr., a Windsor resident who was indicted on four counts of cocaine distribution. Before the arrest, federal agents seized several of Sargent's properties and alleged they had been acquired or financed with profits from drug-dealing.

Hunter, a former state senator, served as Sargent's lawyer for real estate transactions. In court affidavits, federal prosecutors say that Hunter and Sargent established the Connecticut Realty Trust, Inc. and used that corporation to launder drug profits. They have not indicted Hunter. yet last Friday at 3 a.m., federal agents awakened Hunter and his wife at their Cavendish home to search for and seize records of Hunter's business relationship with Sargent.

This is frightening business, to say the least. The confidentiality of the lawyer-client relationship is sacrosanct. If the government feels free to go rummaging around the files of lawyers, how can clients feel free to fully consult with their lawyers—and how can lawyers adequately defend their constrained clients? How can we be assured that government agents won't be tempted to not only look for evidence of wrongdoing by the lawyer, but just for the heck of it, of the client, too? Such evidence might be tossed out in court, but it wouldn't necessarily have to show up. It could provide useful guidance to prosecutors looking for admissible evidence. And what about records concerning other clients? Can we be sure that government agents will resist the urge to take a peek at them, too? If enough of these raids are conducted, maybe the government will win its drug cases by default—defendants won't be able to find lawyers willing to risk such searches.

But what if a lawyer is guilty of criminal activity involving a client? Should he or she be shielded from prosecution simply out of respect for the confidential nature of client relationships?

No. But prosecutors and judges need to recognize that raids on lawyers' offices are so fraught with risk that they should be sanctioned only under the most extraordinary circumstances. Government officials might eventually make a convincing case that they had no other choice in their investigation of Hunter, but they certainly haven't made one so far. The fact that they chose to conduct their raid at 3 a.m. only raises additional questions. Did they honestly believe they wouldn't have produced the same results if the operation had been conducted at a more reasonable hour, or were they more interested in intimidating Hunter and his family and perhaps maximizing publicity?

Federal law enforcement officials could greatly reassure the public if they explained what guidelines exist to govern this type of operation. Are there certain internal tests that must be made before they launch a raid? And what sort of procedural safeguards exist to minimize abuse? Instead of appointing a federal prosecutor to oversee the search, as was done in this case, wouldn't it make more sense to allow the person being investigated to have a lawyer present?

Too much is at stake to allow policy to be established on the fly by prosecutors and judges.

See Sarah Strohmeyer, *Raid of Hunter's Law Office Unprecedented*, Valley News [Vermont], June 13, 1995, p. 1.

41.   *E.g., see* Dan Billin, *Hunter "Laundering" Meeting Disputed*, Valley News, June 23, 1995; Liz Anderson, *Witness Credibility Key to Hunter Case*, Rutland Herald [VT], July 18, 1995; John Gregg, *Hunter Actions Probed by Feds*, Rutland Herald [VT], March 7, 1996, David Ferch, *NH Ties Suspects to a Hunter Client*, Valley News, July 20, 1995. Hunter attempted to respond to the government's investigation in Hunter, *My Mistake: Becoming Too Personally Involved With My Clients*, Valley News, March 11, 1996, Ed Ballam, *Will Hunter is Charged With Fraud*, Valley News, July 9, 1997, at A1; John Gregg, *Hunter is Indicted on Fraud Counts*, Rutland Herald [VT], July 9, 1997, p. 1; John Gregg, *Hunter Indictment Greeted With Skepticism*, Rutland Herald [VT], July 10, 1997, p. 1. *Searching Lawyers*, Valley News, June 14, 1995, p. A6. *see generally* Reltz, *Clients, Lawyers and The Fifth Amendment*, 41 Duke L.J. 572 (1991); Massing, *The Fifth Amendment, The Attorney/Client Privilege and The Prosecution of White Collar Crime*, Va. L. Rev., vol. 75, p. 1179 (1989).

42.   Amsterdam, *supra.*

43.   For critiques of balancing as a constitutional methodology, *see, e.g.*, Aleinikoff, *Constitutional Law in the Age of Balancing*, Yale L.J.; vol. 96, pp. 943, 972-95 (1987);

Frantz, *Is the First Amendment Law?*, Cal L. Rev. vol. 51, pp. 729, 744-53 (1963); Frantz, *The First Amendment in the Balance,* Yale L. J. vol. 97, pp. 1424, 1440-49 (1962); Kahn, *The Court, the Community and the Judicial Balance,* Yale L.J. vol. 97, pp. 1, 47-59 (1987); Symposium, *When Is A Line as Long as a Rock is Heavy?* Hastings L.J. vol. 45, p. 707 (1994).

44. 378 U.S. 52 (1964). As discussed *infra*, the Court in *Fisher* and *Doe* has narrowed significantly any "private enclave" protected by the Fifth Amendment.

45. *Ibid. See also Ullmann v. United States,* 350 U.S. 422 (1956) (Douglas, J., dissenting).

46. 277 U.S. 438, 474 (1928).

47. LEONARD LEVY, THE FIFTH AMENDMENT; *see also Bellis v. United States,* 417 U.S. p. 87.

48. *See generally In re Grand Jury Proceedings,* 632 F.2d 1033, 1043-44 (3rd Cir. 1980), *see also Boyd,* 116 U.S. 616, 630 (1886).

49. *Ibid,* pp. 627-28.

50. 116 U.S. p. 633.

51. Prior to 1976, "an unbroken line of cases repeated the axiom that an individual's private papers were protected from compelled disclosure by the Fifth Amendment." *In re Grand Jury Proceedings,* 680 F.2d 327, 331 (3rd Cir. 1982).

52. *See generally* Margaret Radin, *Property and Personhood,* Stan. L. Rev., vol. 34, p. 957 (1982).

53. *Lochner v. New York,* 198 U.S. 45 (1905). *See generally* GERALD GUNTHER; CONSTITUTIONAL LAW, pp. 439-465 (12th ed. 1992). For example, in 1918, the Court held that Congress' power to regulate interstate commerce did not authorize it to ban the products of child labor. In 1935, the Court invalidated the centerpiece of the New Deal legislation, the Code-making process of the National Recovery Act, as an unconstitutional delegation of Congress' authority. Commentators – including Jeffrey Rosen, *The New Republic's* astute legal affairs writer – have argued cogently that the *Lochner*-era Court's substantive due process approach, as well as its corollary doctrines of dual sovereignty and states' rights, are devices deployed by activist, rather than principled conservative, courts. *E.g.,* Jeffrey Rosen, *Dual Sovereigns,* New Republic, July 28, 1997, p. 16. *See generally* FELIX FRANKFURTER; THE LABOR INJUNCTION (1930); ELIAS LEIBERMAN, GERALD EGGERT; RAILROAD UNIONS BEFORE THE BAR (1950); LABOR DISPUTES: THE BEGINNINGS OF FEDERAL STRIKE POLICY (1967); ALMONT LINDSEY; THE PULLMAN STRIKE (1942); RAY GINGER; THE BENDING CROSS: A BIOGRAPHY OF EUGENE DEBS (1949); JOSEPH RAYBACK; A HISTORY OF AMERICAN LABOR (1966); PHILLIP FONER; HISTORY OF THE AMERICAN LABOR MOVEMENT IN THE UNITED STATES (1955).

54. 387 U.S. 294 (1967), 384 U.S. 757 (1966).

55. *Katz v. United States,* 389 U.S. 347, 351 (1967). Rejecting the property-based reasoning of *Boyd,* the *Katz* Court held that the relevant Fourth Amendment inquiry is whether the police practice at issue "violated the privacy upon which [the defendant] justifiably relied." *Ibid,* p. 353. Or, as Justice Harlan explained in his famous

concurrence in *Katz*, the right Fourth Amendment question is whether the police violated a subjective "expectation of privacy" that society is prepared to recognize as 'reasonable.'" *Ibid*, p. 361 (Harlan, J., concurring).

56.   425 U.S. 391, 405-14 (1976).

57.   425 U.S. pp. 409-10.

58.   *Fisher*, 425 U.S. p. 407.

59.   425 U.S. p. 407-09.

60.   *Ibid.*

61.   *Ibid.*

62.   *Ibid*, p. 401 n.7.

63.   *Fisher v. U.S.*, 425 U.S. 391, 431 (Marshall, J., concurring).

64.   *Ibid*, pp. 432-433.

65.   *Ibid.*

66.   *Ibid*, p. 433.

67.   465 U.S. 605, 606 (1984), 425 U.S. 435, 440-45 (1976) (by implication).

68.   *Andresen v. Maryland* 427 U.S. 463, 470-77 (1976).

69.   *See In re Jeffrey Steinberg*, 837 F.2d 527, 530 (1st Cir. 1988).

70.   *See, e.g.*, Keenan, *To Act or Not?*, Touro L. Rev., vol. 13, p. 265 (1996); Scherb, *Administrative Subpoenas for Private Financial Records*, 1996 Wisc. L. Rev., p. 1075; Krent, *Of Diaries and Data Banks*, Tex. L. Rev., vol. 74, p. 49 (1995); Amar and Lettow, *Fifth Amendment First Principles*, Mich. L. Rev., vol. 93, p. 857 (1995); Worthy-Bulla, *Does the Fifth Amendment Protect the Contents of Private Papers?*, Pace L. Rev., vol. 15, p. 303 (1994); Rosenthal, *Now Its Personal*, Brook. L. Rev., vol. 60, p. 553 (1994); Amar, *Fourth Amendment First Principles*, Harv. L. Rev., vol. 107, p. 757 (1994); Demarco, *Confusion Among the Courts*, St. John's J. Leg. Comment, vol. 9, p. 219 (1993); Yeager, *Expectations of Privacy Outside the Fourth Amendment*, J. Crim. L. and Criminology, vol. 84, p. 249 (1993); Slobogin, An Empirical Look at "*Understandings Recognized and Permitted by Society*", Duke L.J., vol. 42, p. 727 (1993); Nesterlode, *Re-"Righting" the Right to Privacy in Criminal Law*, Clev. St. L. Rev., vol. 41, p. 405 (1993); Gormley, *One Hundred Years of Privacy*, Wisc. L. Rev. p. 1335 (1992); Reltz, Duke L.J., vol. 41, p. 572 (1991); Massing, *The Fifth Amendment, The Attorney/Client Privilege and The Prosecution of White Collar Crime*, Va. L. Rev., vol. 75, p. 1179 (1989); Shapiro, *From Boyd to Braswell*, Whittier L. Rev., vol. 11, p. 295 (1989); Mosteller, *Simplifying Subpoena Law: Taking the Fifth Amendment Seriously*, Va. L. Rev., vol. 73, p. 1 (1987); Rothman, *Life After Doe?*, U. Cinn. L. Rev., vol. 56, p. 387 (1987); Alito, *Documents and the Privilege Against Self-Incrimination*, U. Pitt. L. Rev., vol. 48, p. 27 (1986); Trujillo, *Are a Taxpayer's Private Papers Protected Under the Fifth Amendment?*, Temple L.Q., vol. 57, p. 467 (1986); Schnapper, *Unreasonable Searches and Seizures of Papers*, Va. L. Rev., vol. 71, p. 869

(1985); Heidt, *The Fifth Amendment Privilege and Documents*, Mo. L. Rev., vol. 49, p. 439 (1984); Berger, *Searches of Private Papers*, Fordham L. Rev., vol. 51, p. 967 (1983); Clouse, *The Constitutional Right to Withhold Private Information*, N.W. L. Rev., vol. 77, p. 655 (1982); Bradley, *Constitutional Protection of Private Papers*, Harv. CR-CL L. Rev. vol. 16, p. 461 (1981). *Ignore, e.g.*, Will, *"Dear Diary,"* B.C. L. Rev., vol. 35, p. 965 (1994).

71.   Note, *The Life and Times of* Boyd v. United States, Mich. L. Rev., vol. 76 p. 184 (1977): Thus, in light of *Andresen* and *Fisher, Boyd* is dead. No zone of privacy now exists that the government cannot enter to take an individual's property for the purpose of obtaining incriminating information. In most cases, the zone can be entered by the issuance of a subpoena; in the rest, it can be breached by a search warrant. Not all commentators have mourned the alleged death of *Boyd. E.g., Friendly, The Fifth Amendment Tomorrow*, U. Cinn. L. Rev. vol. 37, p. 671 (1968); Gerstein, *The Demise of Boyd*, UCLA L. Rev., vol. 27, p. 343 (1979).

72.   *In re Steinberg*, 837 F.2d 527, 529 (1st Cir. 1988).

73.   *Steinberg, supra*, p. 529.

74.   *Fisher* p. 414; *Doe*, p. 610 n.7; *Miller*, p. 440.

75.   *U.S. v. Lang*, 792 F.2d 1235, 1238-39 (4th Cir. 1986).

76 .   *In re Grand Jury Investigation*, 921 F.2d 1184, 1186 n.6 (11th Cir. 1991). *See also U.S. v. Mason*, 869 F.2d 414, 416 (8th Cir. 1989) ("The Masons argue that *Doe* and *Andresen* involved business records and that the Fifth Amendment continues to protect the contents of personal papers such as diaries. We need not decide this matter" because the records at issue in that case were not "personal diaries").

77.   *In re Grand Jury Subpoena*, 1 F.3d 87 (2nd Cir. 1993).

78.   *U.S. v. Wujkowski*, 929 F.2d 981, 983, 985 (4th Cir. 1991); *In re Sealed Case*, 877 F.2d 83, 84 (D.C. Cir. 1989).

79.   632 F.2d 1033, 1042 (3rd Cir. 1980), *see also Ibid*; p. 1042.

80.   Citing Gerstein, *The Demise of Boyd*, UCLA L. Rev., vol. 27, p.349 (1979); Note, *Constitutional Privacy*, Harv. L. Rev., vol. 90, p. 945 (1977), *see also* 623 F.2d p. 1044 n.23.

81.   *Ibid*, p. 1042.

82.   417 U.S. 85, 87 (1974).

83.   *I.C.C. v. Gould*, 629 F.2d 847 at 859 (3d Cir. 1980) (footnote in original).

84.   Leonard Levy, Origins of the Fifth Amendment, p. 432 (1968) (footnote in original).

85.   *See generally* L. Levy *supra* (1968) (footnote in original).

86.   19 How. St. Tr. 1029 (1765) (footnote in original).

87.   Lord Camden declared that the existence of the power of search would "open the secret cabinets and bureaus of every subject in this kingdom," and this search for private papers was prohibited because "the law obligeth no man to accuse himself;

because the necessary means of compelling self-accusation, falling upon the innocent as well as the guilty, would be both cruel and unjust." State Trials, XIX, at
pp.1029, 1038, 1041, 1063 (1765); quoted in L. Levy, *supra*, p. 393. *See* Note,
Constitutional Privacy, Harv. L. Rev. vol. 95, pp. 945, 954-55 (1977) (footnote in
original).

88.   O.J. ROGGE, THE FIRST AND THE FIFTH, p. 178 (1949) (quoting Lord Camden with
respect to the *Entick* case) (footnote in original).

89.   *Butcher v. Bailey*, 753 F2d 465, 467 (6th Cir. 1984).

90.   *Ibid.*

91.   759 F.2d 1418 (9th Cir. 1985), *see also* p. 1420

92.   647 F.2d 898 (9th Cir. 1981).

93.   *Ibid*, p. 900.

94.   *Ibid.*

95.   *Ibid* (emphasis added). The *MacKey* court quoted with apparent approval the
Pennsylvania district court's opinion in *United States v. Waltman*, 394 F.Supp. 1393,
1394 (W.D. Pa. 1972): "If this personal record (diary) was mingled with notations
of a corporate nature, the document loses the cloak of protection and privilege
guaranteed by the Fifth Amendment." As the *MacKey* court noted, Waltman was
reversed on other grounds by the Third Circuit.

96.   Whether *MacKey* survives *Terry* remains an open question in the Ninth Circuit.

97.   *E.g., People v. Miller*, 60 Cal. App. 3rd 349 (1976) (defendant's diary properly admitted); *State v. Barrett*, 401 N.E.2d 184 (Ia. 1987) (no violation of Fifth Amendment
to admit defendant's one hundred and forty-three page personal journal) 1121
(Cal. 1972) (defendant's private journals properly admitted, but Fifth Amendment
not addressed); *People v. Frank*, 700 P.2d 415 (Cal. 1985) (search warrant for defendant's diary invalid because affidavit failed to provide probable cause the diary
existed and was present at the search location). *See generally, e.g.,* 1 LAFAVE, SEARCH
AND SEIZURE (2nd ed. 1987); 8 WIGMORE, EVIDENCE secs. 2263, 2264, pp.378-86
(McNaughton rev. ed. 1961); McCORMICK, EVIDENCE secs. 125-127, pp.304-11 (3rd
ed. 1984); BURKOFF, SEARCH WARRANT LAW AND DESKBOOK sec. 18.3, pp.18-12 and
18-13. *See also Moody v. United States*, 977 F.2d 1425 (11th Cir. 1992).

98.   Chris Waits alleges that they did not have all of them.

99.   Other courts have held that *Boyd's* core "zone of privacy" for personal papers has
survived the narrowing of *Fisher* and *Doe. see In re Grand Jury Subpoena Duces
Tecum*, 741 F.Supp. 1059, 1068 (S.D.N.Y. 1990), citing *Documents and the Privilege
Against Self-Incrimination*, U. Pitt. L. Rev., vol. 48, pp. 27, 39 (1986) (*Boyd* has
endured "because its reasoning contained a kernel of truth...forcing an individual
to give up possession of these intimate writings may be psychologically comparable to prying words from his lips"); and Bradley, *Constitutional Protection for
Private Papers*, Harv. C.R.C.L. L. Rev., vol. 16, pp. 461, 480-481 (1981-1982) (the

most private papers are the "*sanctum sanctorum*" of the personality). "Indeed, such papers and statements are statements of the witness and thus among the most powerful forms of proof in the law." *Ibid*, p. 1068. As the District Court noted:

> Implicit in *Boyd* are the corollary realities that one's papers can be an extension of oneself and may exist to some extent because of the limitations of one's faculties — the ability to remember and the need or desire to write down thoughts to clearly formulate and to record them for future use. If all minds could recall perfectly . . . there would be little need to write but for the desire to share these mental processes with others or to see the satisfaction of words on paper.

741 F.Supp. at 1068. "[G]iven the limitations of the human brain, many thoughts, often fleeting and impermanent, are of little importance unless they are recorded. Just as mental input is protected in *Stanley [v. Georgia*, 394 U.S. 557 (1969)], so should mental output be protected." *Ibid*, citing Bradley, *Constitutional Protection For Private Papers*, Harv. C.R.C.L. L. Rev. vol. 16, pp. 461, 494.

"If the Fifth Amendment is to stand for our constitutional preference for an accusatorial system, it must protect the divulgence of the contents of one's mind, one's thought processes, when those testimonial divulgences – be they oral or written communications – would self-incriminate." *Ibid*, p. 1069. Among other fundamental values, the Fifth Amendment reflects "our respect for the inviolability of the human personality and of the right of each individual 'to a private enclave where he may lead a private life' ..." *Murphy v. Waterfront Comm'n*, 378 U.S. 52, 55 (1964).

Fifth Amendment considerations aside, the balance of "the interests of privacy, the desire to preserve the autonomous functioning of the individual and practical considerations outweigh the need for incriminating evidence and support the retention of the privilege for private papers." *In Re Grand Jury*, 741 F.Supp. at 1069. A combination of the First, Fourth and Fifth Amendments safeguard not only privacy and protect against self-incrimination, but also conscience, human dignity and freedom of expression of our most personal thoughts. *see Stanford v. Texas*, 379 U.S. 476, 485 (1965). Thus, even if a zone of privacy is not imputed into the Fifth Amendment, the fundamental right to privacy buttresses an exemption for personal and intimate thoughts and expressions. *In Re Grand Jury*, 741 F. Supp. at 1071, citing *Stanley v. Georgia*, 394 U.S. 557, 564 (1969) (fundamental right to privacy provided an "added dimension" for finding that First Amendment right to receive information protected rights of an individual to read "obscene matter"); Note, *Formalism*, Harv. L. Rev., vol. 90, pp. 987 & n.251 ("Unless the Fourth and Fifth Amendments can be read as putting a premium on the value of personal privacy in the face of government encroachment, it is difficult to imagine what these amendments can mean."). *Boyd*'s core zone of privacy still protects the private personal nature of our thoughts and ideas — as written in a citizen's journals, notes or diaries. It cannot be invaded by a search warrant or other process of the court.

100. *Boyd, supra*, p. 635.

101. *Ibid.*

102. *Oklahoma Press Pub. Co. v. Walling*, 327 U.S. 186 (1946) (citations omitted).

103. *State v. Andrei*, 574 A.2d 295, 298 (Me. 1990) (dicta).

104. *Moody v. United States*, 977 F.2d 1425, 1432-33 (11th Cir. 1992). Subsequent to Moody's conviction and life sentences on federal charges, the State of Alabama successfully prosecuted Moody for the capital murder of Judge Vance. At that capital trial in state court, Moody represented himself *pro se*; presumably his diaries were again introduced into evidence against him.

105. One book about the Moody case observes that the *"Moodys"* [i.e., Walter and his wife Susan] kept a handwritten journal." MARK WINNE; PRIORITY MAIL, pp. 138-39 (1995). Susan Moody was the government's star witness against her husband at the federal trial.

106. *Cf. In re Trader Roe*, 720 F.Supp. 645, 647 (N.D. Ill. 1989).

107. 574 A.2d 295 (Me. 1990).

108. *Ibid*, p. 298.

109. *Ibid*. Interestingly, the trial court appeared to focus only on the Fifth Amendment in isolation, disregarding the "intimate connection" of *Boyd* itself.

110. *Ibid*, p. 296.

111. *Ibid*, p. 298.

112. Ibid, p. 298 (citing *Bellis v. United States*, 417 U.S. 85, 87 (1974) (Fifth Amendment protects from self-incrimination through use of papers as well as through compelled oral testimony); *United States v. Calandra*, 414 U.S. 338, 346 (1974) (grand jury may not compel production of books and papers that would incriminate accused); *Schmerber v. California*, 384 U.S. 757, 763-64 (1966) (Fifth Amendment protects against "the compulsion of responses which are also communications, for example, compliance with a subpoena to produce one's papers"); *United States v. White*, 322 U.S. 694, 699 (1944) (protects from disclosure of documents to be used against accused as a witness).)

113. *Ibid*, p. 298.

114. *See* Lena Williams, *Private Thoughts, Public Revelations*, NY Times, Dec. 16, 1993 p. C1.

115. 139 Cong. Rec. S. 14, 726 (daily ed. Nov. 1, 1993) (statement of Sen Bryan).

116. *Senate Select Committee on Ethics v. Sen. Bob Packwood, Misc*, No. 93-0362 (TPJ), 1994 U.S. Dist. Lexis 472, p. #20 (D.D.C. Jan. 24, 1994), *see also ibid*, pp. 17-18.

117. RICHARD KLUGER; SIMPLE JUSTICE, vol. 2, p. 815 (1975).

118. *Olmstead v. United States*, 277 U.S. 438, 478 (1928) (Brandeis, J., dissenting), *see also* Warren and Brandeis, *The Right to Privacy*, Harv. L. Rev. vol. 4, p. 193 (1890).

119. 410 U.S. 113 (1973). *See also* 505 U.S. 833 (1992).

120. In *Griswold*, Justice Douglas argued that "specific guarantees in the Bill of Rights have penumbras formed by emanations from those guarantees that help give them life and substance." *Accord Roe* (noting that *Griswold* located right to privacy "in the penumbras of the Bill of Rights.") A penumbra is an area not in shadow and not in light; it is a hazy middle distance.

121. 381 U.S. 779 (1965). The scope of the right to privacy in *Griswold* and *Roe* are as hazy as their sources in the Constitution. One student commentator distinguished between two definitions of privacy: (1) A "right of selective disclosure," or interest in control of information; and (2) a "private autonomy" of choice about performing acts or undergoing experiences. Note, *Paris and Roe: Does Privacy Have a Principle?*, Stan. L. Rev., vol. 26, p. 1161 (1974).

   In *Griswold*, Justice Douglas denied he was *Lochner*-izing: "Overtones of some arguments suggest that [*Lochner*] should be our guide. But we decline that invitation . . . we do not sit as a super-legislature to determine the wisdom, need and propriety of laws that touch economic problems, business affairs, or social conditions. This [contraception] law, however, operates directly on an intimate relation of husband and wife . . . " *But see* Ely, *The Wages of Crying Wolf*, Yale L.J. vol. 82, p.920 (1973).

   Gunther has cited *Griswold* and *Roe*, as possible examples of a "revival of substantive due process for noneconomic rights," including privacy, autonomy, family relations and a right to die. GEROLD GUNTHER, CONSTITUTIONAL LAW, p. 491 (12th ed. 1992). Indeed, Gunther suggests, *Griswold* and *Roe* "built on a *Lochner* tradition that never really died . . . The *Lochner* era's protection of "fundamental values" was not wholly limited to economic rights: to the Court of that era, there was no sharp distinction between economic and noneconomic, 'personal' liberties: some of the *Lochner* era's decisions did protect personal rights, and the modern court has no qualms about citing those decisions." *Ibid.*

   Even the aspect of *Lochner* that curtailed economic regulation at times seems no deader than *Boyd*. Witness the Court's recent "takings" cases, for instance. *E.g., Lucas v. South Carolina Coastal Council*, 505 U.S. 1003 (1992); *Dolan v. City of Tigard*, 512 U.S. 374 (1994).

   It has been argued cogently that the liberty of contract and right to use property – the dominant rights in the *Lochner* era – possess at least as much textual and historical support as the privacy rights recognized in *Griswold* and *Roe*, and perhaps they possess more. The condemnation clause of the Fifth Amendment specifically mentions "property." So does the language of the Fourteenth Amendment. Kauper, *Penumbras, Peripheries and Emanations*, Mich. L. Rev., vol. 64, p. 235 (1965).

   A court protective of the right to property (because that right is located in the text and history of the Constitution) and skeptical of the privacy rights established by *Griswold* and *Roe* (because that right lacks support in the Constitutional text and history) ought to find the property-based reasoning of *Boyd* more recognizably legitimate than the privacy-based reasoning of *Katz*, a *Griswold*-era case.

   In fact, perhaps the time has come to give *Katz*, rather than *Boyd*, a decent burial. *See* Morgan Cloud, *The Fourth Amendment During the Lochner Era*, Stan. L. Rev., vol. 48, p. 555 (1996). Perhaps *Katz*, not *Boyd*, is dead. *E.g., Florida v. Riley*, 488 U.S. at 456 (Brennan, joined by Stevens and Marshall, dissenting) ("The opinion of the plurality of the Court reads almost as though *Katz v. United States* had never been decided"); *ibid* ("In taking this view, the plurality ignores the very essence of *Katz*"). Burying *Katz*, with its rootless question-begging, subjective standard of "expectations of privacy," and praising *Boyd*'s textually- and historically-grounded constitutional frames of reference is a tantalizing possibility. Certainly *Boyd* has seniority; it was the law of the land for a century, whereas *Katz* and its mid-1960s companions are relative newcomers. Perhaps a melding of *Boyd* and *Katz* could generate a synthesis in which the scope of one's legitimate expectation of privacy is defined, or at least animated, by the legal principles of property. *Boyd* can fairly be read as a privacy case in the first place, *In re Grand Jury Investigation*, 921 F.2d 1184, 1186 n.6 (11th Cir. 1991) (referring to "the privacy-based rationale of *Boyd*") a *Katz/Boyd* hybrid could be seen as nothing more than updating the core principles of *Boyd* with the modern rhetoric of privacy. In any event, *Boyd* and *Katz* need not require different outcomes in similar fact patterns. *Compare Hester v. United States*, 265 U.S. 57 (1924) *with Oliver v. United States*, 466 U.S. 170 (1984). But that is for another book.

122.　405 U.S. 438 (1972).

123.　Posner, *The Uncertain Protection of Privacy*, 1973 Sup. Ct. Rev., p. 173.

124.　*See, e.g., Bowers v. Hardwick*, 478 U.S. 186, 194 (1986); *Collins v. City of Harker Heights*, 503 U.S. 115, 125 (1992).

125.　*Compassion in Dying v. Washington*, 79 F.3d 790, 805 (9th Cir. 1996), *reversed*, 65 U.S.L.W. 4695 (U.S. June 26, 1997); *see also*, Loving v. Virginia, 388 U.S. 1 (1967) (holding that historical, anti-miscegenation statutes were unconstitutional); *Roe v. Wade*, 410 U.S. 113 (1973) (holding that a woman has a fundamental liberty interest to choose an abortion although not historically protected).

126.　*Planned Parenthood v. Casey*, 505 U.S. 803, 848 (1993).

127.　*See Compassion in Dying v. Washington*, 79 F.3d 790, 803 (9th Cir. 1993).

128.　*See, e.g., Romer v. Evans*, 116 S. Ct. 1620, 1631 (1996) (Scalia, J., dissenting) (dissenting opinion stating that the case most relevant to the present decision, *Bowers v. Hardwick*, was not even mentioned in the majority opinion).

129.　Laurence H. Tribe, American Constitutional Law ß 15-21 at 1420 (2d ed. 1988).

130.　*Ibid.*

131.　Minn. L. Rev., vol. 58, p. 403 (quoted in *Florida v. Riley*, 488 U.S. at 456 (Brennan, Marshall and Stevens, dissenting). Amsterdam's article has been quoted close to seven hundred times by various state and federal courts. At least six courts have quoted his statement from page 403.

　　　In 1980, Federal District Judge Douglas W. Hillman, in a suppression motion, determined that "isolated instances of aerial surveillance over 'open fields' do not offend the Constitution." *U.S. v. DeBacker*, 493 F. Supp. 1078, 1081 (1980). Judge Hillman used Amsterdam's article to determine that, in open fields cases under the Fourth Amendment, the "ultimate question . . . is not whether the surveillance . . .

occurred in 'open fields,'" but whether "the particular form of surveillance practiced by the police," if unregulated, would diminish the amount of "privacy and freedom" each citizen enjoys to a degree inconsistent with a "free and open society." *Ibid*; (citing Anthony Amsterdam, *Perspectives on the Fourth Amendment*, Minn. L. Rev., vol. 58, pp. 349, 403 (1974)).

Judge Hillman ruled that open fields are not afforded the special recognition of privacy by the courts that other areas are. *Ibid*. Additionally, he ruled that aerial surveillance from fifty feet above ground, in an area where airplanes frequently fly over the property at low altitudes, did not violate the defendant's interest in privacy. *Ibid*.

In 1985, a panel of Eleventh Circuit judges ruled in a suppression motion on appeal that the defendant did not have a reasonable expectation of privacy in his briefcase which had been stolen three days earlier and discarded near a trash dumpster. *U.S. v. O'Bryant*, 775 F. 2d 1528 (11th Cir. 1985). The court quoted from Amsterdam's article and then ruled that evidence discovered in the briefcase could not be suppressed because, although authority supported the proposition that there is a privacy interest in discarded garbage within the curtilage of one's home, that privacy interest does not exist in items that are discarded outside curtilage. *Ibid*, p. 1534.

The Supreme Court of Oregon, in 1988, upheld a circuit court decision to suppress evidence obtained by police in a burglary prosecution. *State v. Campbell*, 759 P. 2d 1040 (Or. 1988). The police had surreptitiously attached a radio transmitter to the defendant's car and traced the signal emissions, by plane, to observe the defendant entering and leaving a series of residences. The court upheld the circuit court's decision to suppress the evidence, based on the Oregon Constitution. *Ibid*. The court framed its decision with Amsterdam's article:

> In deciding whether government practices that make use of these developments are searches, we must decide whether the practice, if engaged in wholly at the discretion of the government, will significantly impair "the people's" freedom from scrutiny, for the protection of that freedom is the principle that underlies the prohibition on "unreasonable searches" set forth in Article I, section 9 [of the Oregon Constitution].

Ibid, p. 1048 (citing Anthony Amsterdam, *Perspectives on the Fourth Amendment*, Minn. L. Rev., vol. 58, pp. 349, 403 (1974)). The court then answered its question of whether the practice would impair freedom from scrutiny in the affirmative:

> Without an ongoing, meticulous examination of one's possessions, one can never be sure that one's location is not being monitored by means of a radio transmitter. Thus, individuals must more readily assume that they are the objects of government scrutiny. Professor Amsterdam and Justice Harlan, among others, have observed that freedom may be impaired as much, if not more so, by the threat of scrutiny as by the fact of scrutiny.

Ibid, (citations omitted). Since Oregon courts decide constitutional issues based on its own constitution before relying on the U.S. Constitution, the Supreme Court did not address the Fourth Amendment. *Ibid*, p. 1049.

In another Oregon case, the Court of Appeals of Oregon, in an *en banc* decision that was reversed by the Oregon Supreme Court, decided that surveillance by a helicopter, when hovering above a citizen's property for the specific purpose of determining whether he was growing marijuana, violated the Oregon Constitution. *State v. Ainsworth*, 770 P.2d 58 (Or. App. 1989) *rev'd*, 801 P. 2d 749 (Or. 1991). The court held that:

> the hovering or circling of aircraft at low elevations, when engaged in for
> the purpose of finding out what is on, or what is happening on, a per-
> son's property, would diminish the privacy and freedom of citizens to a
> point that is inconsistent with the free and open society envisioned by
> the framers of Oregon's Constitution.

Ibid, p. 61 (citing Anthony Amsterdam, *Perspectives on the Fourth Amendment*, Minn. L. Rev., vol. 58, pp. 349, 403 (1974)).

In 1990, the Supreme Court of New Jersey affirmed a superior court decision to suppress evidence of the defendants' garbage at trial. *State v. Hempele*, 576 A. 2d 793 (N.J. 1990). The court framed as its "ultimate question" as follows: "if garbage searches are 'permitted to go unregulated by constitutional restraints', the amount of privacy and freedom remaining to citizens would be diminished to a compass inconsistent with the aims of a free and open society." *Ibid*; p. 802 (citing Anthony Amsterdam, *Perspectives on the Fourth Amendment*, Minn. L. Rev., vol. 58, pp. 349, 403 (1974)).

The Court decided that, under the New Jersey Constitution, citizens do have a legitimate privacy interest in the contents of their garbage. *Ibid*; p. 805. In reference to Professor Amsterdam's article, the Court stated, "[w]e expect officers of the State to be more knowledgeable and respectful of people's privacy . . . " *Ibid*.

Finally, in 1991, the U. S. Court of Appeals for the Eighth Circuit affirmed a district court opinion denying the defendant's motion to suppress evidence of firearms that were found by police in his rented storage shed. *U.S. v. Hendrickson*, 940 F. 2d 320 (8th Cir. 1991). In reference to Professor Amsterdam's article, the appellate court framed its question of whether a storage facility manager, reporting to police officers her suspicion of the defendant's actions, violated the defendant's privacy interest. *Ibid*, p. 322. The court decided that the manager's observations did not. *Ibid*, p. 323.

132. Justice Brennan, joined in dissent by Justices Stevens and Marshall, wrote in *Florida v. Riley*, 488 U.S. 445, 463 (1983), a case involving aerial surveillance by police in a helicopter four hundred feet above the defendant's greenhouse, wrote in his eloquent dissent from the majority's holding that the aerial observation did not constitute a "search or seizure" so as to trigger the procedural requirements of the Fourth Amendment: "It is difficult to avoid the conclusion that the plurality has allowed its analysis of Riley's expectation of privacy to be colored by its distaste for the activity in which he was engaged. It is indeed easy to forget, especially in light of the current concern over drug trafficking, that the scope of the Fourth Amendment's protection does not turn on whether the activity disclosed by a search is illegal or innocuous.

We dismiss this as a 'drug case' only at the peril of our own liberties." *See also, e.g.,* David Stewart, *The Drug Exception,* ABA J., May 1990, p. 42; Salzburg, *Another Victim of the War on Drugs,* U. Pitt. L. Rev., vol. 48, p. 1 (1987); Finkleman, *The Second Casualty of War,* So. Cal. L. Rev. vol. 66, p. 1389 (1993).

133. Oral Argument, *Chandler v. Miller,* No. 96-126 1997 WL 19002; *Chandler v. Miller,* No. 96-126, 65 USLW 4243 (April 15, 1997). For various fascinating discussions on the war on drugs generally, *see The Drug War Is Lost* (Cover story), National Review, Feb. 12, 1996; Guerra, *Family Values?,* Cornell L. Rev., vol. 8, p. 343 (1996); *Pollan, Opium Made Easy,* Harpers, April 1997, p. 35; Barnett, *Bad Trip,* Yale L.J., vol. 103, p. 2593 (1994).

134. EDMUND WILSON, PATRIOTIC GORE: STUDIES IN THE LITERATURE OF THE AMERICAN CIVIL WAR 279, p. ix (1962).

135. "Diary in Fact — Diary in Form" was C. Vann Woodward's title for his introductory essay to his edited version of the classic Civil War diary of Mary Chestnut, MARY CHESTNUT'S CIVIL WAR (C. Vann Woodward ed. 1981).

136. IV OXFORD ENGLISH DICTIONARY, p. 612 (2d ed. 1989).

137. *Ibid,* (citing William Fleetwood, *Ellis Original Letter Series* I (1581)).

138. *Ibid,* (citing Benjamin Disreali, *Cur. Lit. Diaries* (1791-1823)).

139. M. H. ABRAMS, A GLOSSARY OF LITERARY TERMS, p. 15 (Holt, Rinehart & Winston 1988).

140. NELLIE PTASCHKINA, DIARY OF NELLIE PTASCHKINA, January 23, 1918 (Pauline D. Chary, trans. Jonathan Cape 1923).

141. EMILY CARR, HUNDREDS AND THOUSANDS November 23, 1930 (Clarke, Unwin & Co., Ltd. 1966).

142. KATHERINE MANSFIELD, JOURNAL OF KATHERINE MANSFIELD, 12/19/1920 (John Middleton Murray, ed. Alfred A. Knopf 1927).

143. Florida Scott-Maxwell, *The Measure of My Days* in DIARIES OF WOMEN; p. 364 (Mary Jane Moffat & Charlotte Painter eds. Vintage Books 1974).

144. MARIE BASHKIRTSEFF, MARIE BASHKIRTSEFF: THE JOURNAL OF A YOUNG ARTIST (Mary J. Serrano, trans. E.P. Dutton & Co. 1923).

145. KATHE KOLLWITZ, DIARIES AND LETTERS December 31, 1925 (Hans Kollwitz, ed. Henry Regnery Co. 1955).

146. FYODOR DOSTOYEVSKY, NOTES FROM THE UNDERGROUND (1864).

147. GEORGE BERNARD SHAW, SIXTEEN SELF-SKETCHES (1896).

148. ANNE FRANK, THE DIARY OF A YOUNG GIRL: THE CRITICAL EDITION (1989) (entry of June 12, 1942).

149. ANNE FRANK, THE DIARY OF A YOUNG GIRL; p. 8, July 1942 (Simon & Schuster 1952).

150. EMILY CARR, HUNDREDS AND THOUSANDS, November 23, 1930 (Clarke, Unwin & Co., Ltd. 1966).

151. RAINER MARIA RILKE, LETTERS TO A YOUNG POET, p. 9 (J. Burnham tr. 1992) (emphasis in original). *See also* W. KAUFMANN, EXISTENTIALISM FROM DOSTOYEVSKY TO SARTRE

152. *Ibid.*

153. *Ibid* (Emphasis added).

154. AMERICAN HERITAGE DICTIONARY OF THE ENGLISH LANGUAGE 516 (3d ed. 1992); *cf.* WEBSTER'S NINTH NEW COLLEGIATE DICTIONARY 351 (1990) ("a record of events, transactions, or observations kept daily or at frequent intervals: JOURNAL . . . a daily record of personal activities, reflections, or feelings").

155. AMERICAN HERITAGE DICTIONARY OF THE ENGLISH LANGUAGE, p. 516 (3d ed. 1992); *cf.* WEBSTER'S NINTH NEW COLLEGIATE DICTIONARY, p. 351 (1990) ("a book intended or used for a diary").

156. *Brooks Bros. v. United States,* 68 Cust. Ct. 91, 97 (1st Div. 1972) (citing *Baumgarten v. U.S.,* 49 Cust. Ct. 275 (2d Div. 1962)).

157. *Ibid.* p. 98 (citation omitted).

158. *Ibid.*

159. *Borneo Sumatra Trading Co. v. United States* 311 F. Supp. 326, 337 (1970) (quoting WEBSTER'S NEW WORLD DICTIONARY OF THE AMERICAN LANGUAGE, COLLEGE EDITION (1962)).

160. *Baumgarten v. U.S.,* 49 Cust. Ct. 275, 276 (2d Div. 1962).

161. *Sormani, et al v. U.S.* 32 Cust. Ct. 423, 424 (2d Div. 1954).

162. *Charles Scribner's Sons v. U.S.,* 574 F. Supp. 1058, 1063 (Ct. Int'l Trade 1983).

163. *Brooks Bros. v. U.S.,* 68 Cust. Ct. 91, 96-98 (1st Div. 1972).

164. Amar and Lettow, *Fifth Amendment First Principles,* Mich. L. Rev., vol. 93, pp. 857, 922 (1995).

165. STEVE THAYER, THE WEATHERMAN: A NOVEL, p. 353 (1995).

166. ANDREW HUDGINS, AFTER THE LOST WAR (1990).

167. *Ibid.*

168. A DIARY FROM DIXIE (I. Martin & M. Avery eds. 1905); A DIARY FROM DIXIE (B. Williams ed.).

169. MARY CHESTNUT'S CIVIL WAR, p. xvi (C. Vann Woodward ed. 1962).

170 . *Ibid.*

171. *Ibid.*

172. *Ibid.*

173. *Ibid.*

174. *Ibid.*

175. *Ibid,* p. xvii.

176. *Ibid.*

177. *Ibid,* p. xix.

178. *See* Government's Brief Opposing Defendant's Motion to Preclude Use of Private Diaries, *United States v. Kaczynski,* No. S-96-259-GEB (filed July 15, 1997), n.1, p. 1.

179. *E.g.,* THE DIARY OF ANNE FRANK: THE CRITICAL EDITION 248, 254, 28, 291 (1989).

180. *Ibid,* pp. 180-81.

181. *See* Gerrold van der Stroom, *The Diaries, Het Achterhius and the Translations,* in ANNE FRANK: THE CRITICAL EDITION, pp. 29-75 (1989) (prepared by the Netherlands State Institute for War Documentation). For other versions of Anne Frank's diary, *see, e.g.,* ANNE FRANK: THE DIARY OF A YOUNG GIRL (Simon & Schuster 1953); ANNE FRANK, THE DIARY OF A YOUNG GIRL: THE DEFINITIVE EDITION: A NEW TRANSLATION (Otto Frank & Mirjam Pressler eds. Doubleday 1995); ANNE FRANK'S TALES FROM THE SECRET ANNEX: THE COMPLETE VERSION – WITH NEW MATERIAL HER FATHER HAD WITHHELD FROM PUBLICATION (Doubleday & Washington Square Press (1983)). For a sampling of the literature derivative of the diary, *see, e.g.,* MEYER LEVIN, THE OBSESSION (1973); ANNE FRANK: BEYOND THE DIARY: A PHOTOGRAPHIC REMEMBRANCE (1992); CARA WILSON, LOVE, OTTO: THE LEGACY OF ANNE FRANK (1995); MEIP GIES, ANNE FRANK REMEMBERED (1987); WILLY LINDWEN, THE LAST SEVEN MONTHS OF ANNE FRANK (1991). For a poignant account of Anne Frank's death at the Bergen-Belsen concentration camp, *see* Irma Sonnenberg Menkel, *I Saw Anne Frank Die,* Newsweek, July 21, 1997, p. 16.

182. *Ibid.*

183. *Ibid.*

184. *Ibid,* p. xix.

185. *Ibid,* p. xix.

186. *Ibid,* p. xx.

187. Warren & Brandeis, *The Right to Privacy,* Harv. L. Rev., vol. 16, pp. 193, 195 n.4 (1890) (citing COOLEY ON TORTS).

188. Rilke, *supra,* pp. 17, 40, 54. Rilke defined genuine lovers as two people who serve as guardians of one another's solitude: "that love for which we must prepare painstakingly and with fervor, which will be comprised of two lonelinesses protecting one another . . . " *Ibid,* p. 72.

189. Warren and Brandeis, *The Right to Privacy,* Harvard L. Rev., vol. 5, p. 193 (1890) (Emphasis added).

190. COOLEY ON TORTS, (2nd ed.) p. 29.

191. *Ibid,* pp. 195-96.

192. *Ibid,* pp. 198-200.

193. *Ibid*, p. 205.

194. *Ibid*, pp. 206-207.

195. *Ibid*, p. 213.

196 . *Ibid*, pp. 213-214. Citations omitted. Emphasis added.

197. Minn. L. Rev., vol. 58, p. 403.

198. *Senate Select Comm. on Ethics v. Packwood*, 845 F.Supp. 17, 18 (D. D.C. 1994).

199. *Ibid*, p. 21.

200. *Ibid*, p. 22.

201. *Ibid. See also Cf. Zurcher v. Stanford Daily.*

202 . *Ibid*, p. 22.

203. *Ibid*, p. 22.

204. *Ibid.*

205. *Ibid*, p. 23.

206. *Ibid*, p. 23.

207. *United States v. Hinckley*, 672 F.2d 115, 117 (D.C. Cir. 1982).

208. *Ibid*, p. 126.

209. *Ibid.*

210. *Ibid*, p. 126.

211. *Ibid.*

212. *United States v. Hinckley*, 525 F. Supp. 1342 (D. DC 1981), *aff'd* 672 F.2d 115 (DC Cir. 1982).

213. *Ibid*, p. 1359.

214. *Ibid.* p. 1358.

215. *Ibid.*

216. *Ibid.*

217. *See* United States v. Poindexter, 727 F. Supp. 1501, 1510-11 (D.D.C. 1989).

218. *Poindexter v. United States*, 727 F.Supp. 1501, 502 (D. DC 1989).

219. The definitive book about Robert Vance and his world was published in 1997. RAY JENKINS, BLIND VENGEANCE (1997), *see also* MARK WINNE, PRIORITY MAIL, pp. 138-39, 141, 165 (1995).

220. *Moody v. United States*, 977 F.2d 1425, 1432 (11th Cir. 1992).

221. *Ibid*, p. 1432.

222. *Ibid.*

223.   *Ibid*, p. 1432.

224.   *E.g., United States v. Moody*, 977 F.2d 1425 (11th Cir 1992) (raising diary challenge based on First Amendment grounds). *See also* The divided California Court of Appeals' decision in *People v. Sanchez*, 24 Cal. App. 4th 1012, 30 Cal. Rptr. 111 (Cal. App. 2nd Dist 1994) provides a fascinating illustration of one court's difficulty when confronted with a diary issue that has not been adequately briefed by appellate counsel for the defense.

   Arthur Anthony Sanchez was tried and convicted on first degree (noncapital) murder; Sanchez was sentenced to state prison for 26 years to life. That Sanchez strangled his estranged fiancé, "Ruth Huerta, in his bedroom of his parents' house in the early afternoon of March 28, 1992, was not disputed. [Sanchez] admitted as much before and during trial. In dispute was only the degree of his culpability." *Ibid*, p. 1015, 30 Cal. Rptr. p. 113.

   Sanchez strangled his estranged fiancé in his bedroom in his parents' house. The day the body was found in Sanchez's bedroom, he surrendered to police. About a week after the crime, Sanchez's sisters decided to air out Sanchez's bedroom and look for letters. Among Sanchez's papers were writings, in his handwriting, inculpating him in Ruth Huerta's murder. *Ibid*, p. 1012, 30 Cal. Rptr. p. 114. The sisters gave the papers to an attorney, who in turn gave them to Sanchez's public defender. The public defender placed the writings in a sealed envelope and, without informing the prosecutor, delivered them – still under seal – to the clerk of the Court.

   When the prosecutor learned – from other Sanchez family members – of the writings' existence and disposition, he filed a motion with the clerk "to produce... and unseal documents in the custody of the county clerk." *Ibid*, p. 1015, 30 Cal. Rptr. p. 113., The Court granted the motion. The judge personally turned the writings over to the prosecutor, *Ibid*.

   The *Sanchez* majority then addressed the Fifth Amendment the "authority" relied upon by Sanchez's appellate attorney was *Izazagay v. Superior*, 815 P.2d 304 (Cal. 1990). *Izazagay* was a Fifth Amendment case based on *Schmerber* and *Doe* (as well as *Nobles v. United States*, 422 U.S. 225 (1975). However, the *Sanchez* majority observes, "in making this [Fifth Amendment argument, *Sanchez* appellate counsel] neither discusses the three cases cited by *Izazagay* [*Nobles, Schmerber* and *Doe*] nor any other pertinent authority." The majority of the California appellate court's panel held that neither the Fifth Amendment, nor California's reciprocal discovery statutes, were violated when Sanchez's defense attorney delivered the writings to the Court. "Although defense counsel did not explain why he delivered, under seal, the inculpatory writings to the trial court, case law suggests an explanation," the appeals court majority wrote," *Ibid*, p. 1018, 30 Cal. Rptr. p. 115, "counsel's ethical duties."

   On the crucial "obtained by compulsion" requirement of *Doe* and the other Fifth Amendment cases, the *Sanchez* majority dryly notes: Sanchez's counsel's "entire argument consists of this: 'they were obtained ... by compulsion, i.e., they were obtained against [Sanchez's] will and over his objection." The *Sanchez* majority, after discussing *Doe, Schmerber, Fisher* and the other relevant Fifth Amendment cases, concludes – quite correctly, in our view – that Sanchez's Fifth Amendment argument was "mistaken." *Ibid*.

Judge Johnson, in a dissenting opinion wrote: "from the majority's holding the defendant's diary was properly turned over to the prosecution." *Ibid*, p. 1030, 30 Cal. Rptr. p. 123. "The majority affirms the trial court's order releasing the diary to the prosecution on a ground not raised in the parties' briefs: defense counsel had [an ethical] duty to voluntarily disclose the diary anyway." *Ibid*. According to the dissent, the parties' briefs "focused exclusively on the issue of whether disclosure of the diary was permissible under the criminal discovery statute" and the Fifth Amendment. *Ibid*. The dissent agreed with the majority's Fifth Amendment argument, but disagreed that "defense counsel had an ethical duty to disclose the diary to the prosecution." *Ibid*. According to the dissent, the three cases "relied upon by the majority involved physical evidence of the crime": in one case, "the victim's wallet"; in a second, "the alleged murder weapon"; in a third, "the boots with which the defendant allegedly tried to kick the victim to death." *Ibid*, p. 1031, 30 Cal. Rptr. p. 123. And:

> . . . I, for one, would like to hear argument on whether the defendant's private thoughts committed to paper are analogous to the evidence in the above cases. I would also like to hear argument on the ramifications of a holding incriminating writings must be voluntarily turned over to the prosecution. Would an attorney defending a tax evasion or other white collar crime involving hundreds or even thousands of documents have to make a determination as to each page of each document whether it should be revealed to the prosecution? What would the ramifications of such a rule be on the defendant's right to effective assistance of counsel? If, as the majority asserts, California law clearly holds that once defense counsel accepted the diary from defendant's sister he had a duty to turn it over to the prosecutor, we should also request additional briefing on the issue of whether defendant was denied effective assistance of counsel.
>
> Although Lee involved evidence given to defense counsel by a third party, the court did not focus on the significance of that fact. I would like to hear argument on the consequences of a policy of revealing to the prosecutor information received in confidence from a third party. What effect would such a policy have on the willingness of third parties to come forward with evidence which might be helpful to the defense? What would be the effect on the defense attorney's willingness to receive such evidence? Will the mere risk that such evidence may turn out to be incriminating be sufficient to convince attorneys to adopt an attitude of calculated ignorance?
>
> Before holding defense counsel owed a duty to voluntarily turn over defendant's diary to the prosecution, a duty which the trial court merely facilitated counsel in meeting, we should hear argument on the foregoing questions and other relevant considerations the parties may choose to bring to our attention.

225. The *Moody* case and the Unabomber case share at least one additional narrative thread: the FBI crime lab. According to published newspaper accounts, in April 1997 a Justice Dept. report had "found 'serious and significant deficiencies in three units of the FBI crime lab . . . FBI experts used flawed scientific methods to analyze

bombs . . . '" Ken Foskett, *Justice Study Finds "Serious" Flaws in FBI Crime Lab Investigators*, Atlanta Journal and Constitution, April 16, 1997, p. A11. The report "found only small problems with evidence in the case of Walter Leroy Moody." *Ibid.* The FBI's crime lab was involved in the Unabomber case as well.

226. Minn. L. Rev., vol. 58 p. 402.

227. Reprinted as Roan, *Secrets and Lies*, Valley News, June 29, 1997; [VT]; p. C1.

228. *Ibid.*

229. *Ibid.*

230. As the LaFave and Israel treatise put it: "The Court [subsequent to *Doe* in 1984] has not had occasion to rule on the forced production of documents that are more likely than business records to reflect the private thoughts of the subpoenaed party. Since the act of producing such personal documents is highly likely to constitute in itself a testimonial and incriminating communication, a self-incrimination challenge ordinarily will be sustainable . . ." WAYNE LAFAVE AND GEROLD ISRAEL, CRIMINAL PROCEDURE sec. 8.12 (2nd ed. 1991).

231. A 1977 Note in the *Harvard Law Review* proposed that the "paper search" rule of *Boyd* can be seen to survive *Fisher* as a function of the *Fifth Amendment*. If that point is recognized, the author suggests, the present state of the law provides reasonable protection for the central concerns expressed in *Boyd*.

Properly read, *Fisher v. United States* stands for the proposition that no defendant may be compelled to authenticate evidence. Although this holding narrows the application of the self-incrimination clause, it adequately protects the rights of criminal defendants if the prohibitions of other amendments and evidentiary rules are properly applied. The implicit authentication doctrine of the Fifth Amendment prevents defendants from being forced to verify the case against them. The protection of the Fourth Amendment applicable to subpoenas *duces tecum* prohibits authorities from wholesale rummaging through a citizen's papers. Finally, the First Amendment can prevent the government from probing into a defendant's most personal papers. Specific amendments answer specific concerns. Drawing on all of them, courts can forge a broad constitutional protection for all citizen's rights. (Harv. L. Rev., vol. 90, p. 702.)

232. *E.g.*, *Gregg v. Georgia*, 428 U.S. 153 (1976); *Woodson v. North Carolina*, 428 U.S. 280 (1976).

CHAPTER EIGHT: SUMMATIONS

1. Samuel Hazo, *To a Commencement of Scoundrels*, in SAMUEL HAZO, THE HOLY SURPRISE OF RIGHT NOW (1995).

2. *Ibid.*

3. *Ibid.*

4.   Roy Jenkins, Blind Vengeance (1997).

5.   *Ibid.*

6.   *Ibid.*

7.   *Ibid.*

8.   *Ibid.*

9.   *Ibid.*

10.   *Ibid.*

11.   Ray Jenkins, *supra.*

12.   *Ibid.*

13.   Richard Kluger, Simple Justice (1975).

14.   Jenkins, *supra.*

15.   *Ibid.*

16.   Pat Derian and Hodding Carter, *Judge Vance's America*, Wash. Post 1990.

17.   Kristen Monroe, The Heart of Altruism (1996).

18.   *Ibid.*

19.   Jenkins, *supra.*

20.   *Ibid.*

INDEX

DATE DUE